D1207050

Ovid's Literary Loves

Influence and Innovation
in the *Amores*

Barbara Weiden Boyd

Ann Arbor

THE UNIVERSITY OF MICHIGAN PRESS

2000   1999   1998   1997   4   3   2   1

A CIP catalog record for this book is available from the British Library

Library of Congress Cataloging-in-Publication Data

Boyd, Barbara Weiden, 1952–
    Ovid's literary loves : influence and innovation in the Amores /
Barbara Weiden Boyd.
       p.   cm.
    Includes bibliographical references (p.   ) and indexes.
    ISBN 0-472-10759-3 (acid-free paper)
    1. Ovid, 43 B.C.–17 or 18 A.D. Amores. 2. Elegiac poetry, Latin—
History and criticism. 3. Love poetry, Latin—History and
criticism. 4. Influence (Literary, artistic, etc.) 5. Originality
in literature. 6. Rome—In literature.   I. Title.
PA6519.A73B69   1997
871'.01—dc21   97-24003
                                                                    CIP

Ovid's Literary Loves

for Michael and Rachel

optimis dilectissimisque

Acknowledgments

This book began its long period of labor in 1986–87, when I held a National Endowment Fellowship in the Humanities for College Teachers; it continued to mature during a subsequent sabbatical from Bowdoin College. Its progress was slowed by my return to a busy teaching life and by the birth of something greater, my precious daughter Rachel. I am grateful to the Intercollegiate Center for Classical Studies, which offered me the opportunity to teach in Rome during 1994–95: I was then at last able to bring this work to completion, and into the light of day, because of uninterrupted time to work there.

I owe a debt of gratitude to the many people who offered their wisdom and advice along the way as I wrote this book: to Stephen Hall, Peter Knox, and Richard Thomas, for reading an earlier version of parts of the manuscript and providing invaluable commentary and advice; to Nicholas Horsfall, for reading the entire manuscript closely and offering his invaluable, and inimitable, reactions to matters great and small; to many colleagues at Bowdoin, for putting up with this project, and especially to those without whose support I might not have had the opportunity to bring it to completion, Helen Cafferty, Steven Cerf, Denis Corish, A. LeRoy Greason, Barbara Kaster, David Page, Edward Pols, Gabor Brogyanyi, and Richard Chittim, the last two of whom are sorely missed but whose love of Latin poetry endures; to Barbara Held, who knows what this means although she is not a classicist; to James Franklin and Darryl Phillips, for teaching me the meaning of teamwork; to my colleagues on the Advanced Placement Latin Committee, for helping me to know Ovid better; and to Michael, for living through it.

I am also grateful to John Miller, for granting me permission to incorporate into chapter 5 excerpts from an article published earlier in *The Classical Journal;* to Mattie Kelley, Registrar of the Bowdoin College Museum of Art, for granting me permission to reproduce the Italian Renaissance drawing that appears on the jacket; to the reference librarians of Bowdoin College's Hawthorne-Longfellow Library, especially Guy Saldanha, for speedily tracking down every last one of my requests; to Nick Humez, for his thoughtful attention to detail and discerning eye; to Katie Philippon and Richard Miller, for helping me to assemble the manuscript with their usual seemingly effortless care; to the American Academy in Rome, for generously allowing me the use of its library; and to the readers and editors at the University of Michigan Press, especially Ellen Bauerle and Christina Milton, for the care and attention they have given my work. I should also point out, although it must be self-evident, that the translations of Latin poetry found in this book are my own throughout; I hope that their accuracy can compensate at least a little for their lack of elegance.

Last but not least, I extend my thanks to the great teachers and scholars who have guided my life's course, and to my students, for their willingness to learn to love Latin literature as I do.

Contents

Abbreviations and Texts   xi

Introduction: The Isolation of Ovid's *Amores*   1

Chapter 1. Reused Language: Genre and
Influence in the Interpretation of the *Amores*   19

Chapter 2. Literary Means and Ends:
Ovid's *Ludus Poeticus*   49

Chapter 3. Ovid's Visual Memory: Extended
Similes in the *Amores*   90

Chapter 4. From Authenticity to Irony: Programmatic
Poetry and Narrative Reversal in the *Amores*   132

Chapter 5. Ovid's Narrative of Poetic Immortality   165

Chapter 6. *Legisse Voluptas:* Some Thoughts
on the Future of Ovid's *Amores*   203

Bibliography   225

Index Locorum   239

General Index   245

Abbreviations and Texts

Abbreviations of the names of ancient authors and their works generally follow those used in the *Oxford Classical Dictionary,* 2d ed. (Oxford, 1970). Titles of periodicals are generally abbreviated in accordance with the guidelines published by the *American Journal of Archaeology* and/or the most recent volumes of *L'Année Philologique.* With the exception of those works listed below, works of modern scholarship are given complete citations at their first appearance in the notes; thereafter, they are cited by the author's name and an abbreviated title. Except when noted, all quotes from the *Amores* are from E.J. Kenney's second edition of the Oxford Classical Text, *P. Ovidi Nasonis Amores, Medicamina Faciei Femineae, Ars Amatoria, Remedia Amoris,* 2d ed. (Oxford, 1994).

Barsby, *Am.*	Barsby, J.A., ed. *Ovid's Amores Book One.* Oxford, 1973.
Bömer, *Met.*	Bömer, F., ed. *P. Ovidius Naso, Metamorphosen.* 7 vols. Wissenschaftliche Kommentare zu lateinischen und griechischen Schriftstellern. Heidelberg, 1969–86.
Booth	Booth, J., ed. *Ovid: The Second Book of Amores.* Warminster, 1991.
CA	Powell, J.U., ed. *Collectanea Alexandrina.* Oxford, 1925.
EV	Corte, F. della, et al., eds. *Enciclopedia Virgiliana.* 6 vols. Rome, 1984–91.
FGrHist	Jacoby, F. *Die Fragmente der griechischen Historiker.* Berlin and Leiden, 1923–.

FLP	Courtney, E., ed. *The Fragmentary Latin Poets.* Oxford, 1993.
FPL	Morel, W., ed. *Fragmenta Poetarum Latinorum.* 2d ed. Leipzig, 1927.
McKeown	McKeown, J.C., ed. *Ovid: Amores.* Vol. 1, *Text and Prolegomena.* Liverpool, 1987.
	_____. *Ovid: Amores.* Vol. 2, *A Commentary on Book One.* Leeds, 1989.
Nisbet and Hubbard	Nisbet, R.G.M., and M. Hubbard, eds. *A Commentary on Horace, Odes Book I.* Oxford, 1970.
	_____. *A Commentary on Horace, Odes Book II.* Oxford, 1978.
Norden	Norden, E., ed. *P. Vergilius Maro, Aeneis Buch VI.* 7th ed. Stuttgart, 1981.
Pfeiffer	Pfeiffer, R., ed. *Callimachus.* 2 vols. Oxford, 1949; reprinted with corrections, 1965.
RE	*Paulys Real-Encyclopädie der classischen Altertumswissenschaft.* Stuttgart, 1893–.
Servius (or Serv.)	Thilo, G., and H. Hagen, eds. *Servii Grammatici qui feruntur in Vergilii Carmina Commentarii.* 3 vols. Leipzig, 1881–1902.
SH	Lloyd-Jones, H., and P.J. Parsons, eds. *Supplementum Hellenisticum.* Berlin and New York, 1983.
Skutsch	Skutsch, O., ed. *The Annals of Quintus Ennius.* Oxford, 1985.
TLL	*Thesaurus Linguae Latinae.* Leipzig, 1900–.
Thomas, *Geo.*	Thomas, R.F., ed. *Vergil's Georgics.* 2 vols. Cambridge Greek and Latin Classics. Cambridge, 1988.

Introduction: The Isolation of Ovid's *Amores*

credulitas nunc mihi vestra nocet
Ovid *Am.* 3.12.44

Just over forty years ago, L.P. Wilkinson set out, in *Ovid Recalled,* to remedy what was then the state of affairs in Ovidian criticism: the poet had
been "out of fashion" for nearly two centuries.[1] Wilkinson proceeded to
write what amounted to a sympathetic—indeed, enthusiastic—appreciation of the Ovidian corpus, and so anticipated by three years the flurry of
activity surrounding the bimillenary of Ovid's birth. That anniversary,
1958, saw a remarkable increase of critical interest, most of it positive, in
virtually every aspect of Ovid's poetry, from the metrical refinement of his
elegiacs to the ingenuity of his narrative technique in the *Metamorphoses.*[2]
Ovid had begun to emerge from the shadow of his Augustan predecessors;
comparisons, generally invidious, between Ovid and Virgil subsided, as
scholars started to recognize the centrality of the Ovidian achievement in
the development of Roman poetry and at least tentatively to accord to
Ovid the normative status previously reserved for Virgil himself.

The Ovidian revival has taken on a distinctive and somewhat disjointed
character, however, as a result of greater patterns and trends in the study of
Latin literature and especially of Augustan poetry. Thus, pride of place has
been granted to the *Metamorphoses,* considered by moderns as by ancients
to be not only Ovid's most important and accomplished work but also his
most explicit claim to comparison with the achievement of Virgil. Masquerading as chaos, this poem is a virtuoso performance of organization
and structural cohesion, in which variety is the one unchanging, if para-

---

1. L.P. Wilkinson, *Ovid Recalled* (Cambridge, 1955), xiii.
2. See, e.g., the collections of papers in N.I. Herescu, ed., *Ovidiana: Recherches sur Ovide
publiées à l'occasion du bimillénaire de la naissance du poète* (Paris, 1958), and *Atti del convegno internazionale ovidiano,* 2 vols. (Rome, 1959).

doxical, poetic principle. Thus, it has attracted attention from an almost equally wide range of scholars, who have given us everything from new editions and commentaries to studies of the poem's place in literary history, from discussions of Ovid's style to analyses of the poem's employment of narrative techniques, and from the politics of Ovid to the feminist critiques and post-structuralist readings that his detached irony seems to invite.[3]

A second and complementary phenomenon is the renewed interest in those works left for so long to languish unread on library shelves, a class that can itself be subdivided into two distinct groups: what I would call the pre-exile "experiments in elegy," the *Heroides* and *Fasti;* and the alternately dour and desperate poetry written in exile, the *Epistulae ex Ponto* and the *Tristia.* This revisiting has been salutary in a number of ways: first, we have at least begun to move away from a reading of the post-exile poetry as purely (auto)biographical documents and toward an appreciation of their poetic merits and their relationship to the Latin elegiac tradition;[4] and second, we have started to look at the *Heroides* and *Fasti* not as indicative of the exhaustion of the genre but as part of a much larger Ovidian project to revitalize elegy by extending its boundaries, taking it into territory that, if not new, had been long untried. The *Heroides* are to be counted among Ovid's early extended experiments with narrative and narrators (a subject

---

3. The following bibliography is a representative sampling of recent (i.e., post-1975) work, primarily in English and by no means comprehensive. Texts and commentaries include W.S. Anderson, ed., *Ovidius: Metamorphoses* (Leipzig, 1977); a long-awaited Oxford Classical Text by R. Tarrant; and forthcoming Cambridge commentaries (Cambridge Greek and Latin Classics) on *Met.* 4 and *Met.* 13, by A. Keith and N. Hopkinson, respectively. On literary history and stylistic matters, see G. Rosati, *Narciso e Pigmalione: Illusione e spettacolo nelle Metamorfosi di Ovidio* (Florence, 1983); P.E. Knox, *Ovid's Metamorphoses and the Traditions of Augustan Poetry,* Cambridge Philological Society Suppl. 11 (Cambridge, 1986); S. Hinds, *The Metamorphosis of Persephone* (Cambridge, 1987); J.B. Solodow, *The World of Ovid's Metamorphoses* (Chapel Hill and London, 1988); K.S. Myers, *Ovid's Causes: Cosmology and Aetiology in the Metamorphoses* (Ann Arbor, 1994). On the politics of Ovid's poetry, see A. Barchiesi, *Il poeta e il principe: Ovidio e il discorso augusteo* (Rome and Bari, 1994), and the following works incorporating contemporary critical theory: G. Davis, *The Death of Procris: "Amor" and the Hunt in Ovid's Metamorphoses* (Rome, 1983); A.M. Keith, *The Play of Fictions: Studies in Ovid's Metamorphoses Book 2* (Ann Arbor, 1992). See also the collections of essays on Ovid in *Helios* 12 (1985), *Helios* 17 (1990), and *CJ* 90 (1995).

4. See H.B. Evans, *Publica Carmina: Ovid's Books from Exile* (Lincoln, NE, and London, 1983); B.R. Nagle, *The Poetics of Exile: Programme and Polemic in the Tristia and Epistulae ex Ponto of Ovid,* Collection Latomus 170 (Brussels, 1980); G.D. Williams, *Banished Voices: Readings in Ovid's Exile Poetry* (Cambridge, 1994); and a forthcoming Cambridge commentary (Cambridge Greek and Latin Classics) on book 1 of the *Tristia* by S. Hinds. New Teubner editions of both the *Tristia* and the *Epistulae ex Ponto* have appeared in the last decade: J.A. Richmond, ed., *P. Ovidi Nasonis Ex Ponto libri quattuor* (Leipzig, 1990), and J.B. Hall, ed., *P. Ovidi Nasonis Tristia* (Stuttgart, 1995).

to which I shall return in this book),[5] while the *Fasti* give us Ovid's transformation into a *Romanus Callimachus*, interweaving the myths, rituals, and religious lore of early Rome into a web that is ostensibly arbitrarily organized around the Roman calendar but that in fact offers us our most extended glimpse into the politics of poetry during Ovid's career.[6] These two latter works in particular have also begun to be understood as harbingers of things to come in the *Metamorphoses;* the sophisticated psychology and almost revisionist feminism of the *Heroides,* on the one hand, and the play with narrative rupture in the *Fasti,* on the other, have their obvious and more fully developed complements in Ovid's *carmen perpetuum.*[7]

The third grouping of Ovid's poetry, his earliest[8] and most genre-bound forays into amatory elegy, has a more uneven recent critical history. Taken

---

5. See H. Jacobson, *Ovid's Heroides* (Princeton, 1974); D. Kennedy, "The Epistolary Mode and the First of Ovid's *Heroides,*" *CQ* 34 (1984): 413–22; F. Verducci, *Ovid's Toyshop of the Heart: Epistulae Heroidum* (Princeton, 1985); A. Barchiesi, ed., *P. Ovidii Nasonis Epistulae Heroidum 1–3* (Florence, 1992); idem, "Future Reflexive: Two Modes of Allusion and Ovid's *Heroides,*" *HSCP* 95 (1993): 333–65; and two commentaries on selected *Heroides:* P.E. Knox, ed., *Ovid, Heroides: Select Epistles* (Cambridge, 1995) and E.J. Kenney, ed., *Ovid, Heroides: XVI–XXI* (Cambridge, 1996).

6. See J.C. McKeown, "*Fabula proposito nulla tegenda meo:* Ovid's *Fasti* and Augustan Politics," in *Poetry and Politics in the Age of Augustus,* ed. T. Woodman and D. West (Cambridge, 1984), 169–87 (237–41, nn.); A. Wallace-Hadrill, "Time for Augustus: Ovid, Augustus, and the *Fasti,*" in *Homo Viator: Classical Essays for John Bramble,* ed. M. Whitby, P. Hardie, and M. Whitby (Bristol, 1987), 221–30; J.F. Miller, *Ovid's Elegiac Festivals: Studies in the "Fasti,"* Studien zur klassischen Philologie 55 (Frankfurt am Main, 1991); the collection of articles appearing under the heading "Reconsidering Ovid's Fasti" in *Arethusa* 25 (1992), including a two-part essay by S. Hinds entitled "Arma in Ovid's *Fasti*" (81–112, 113–53); D. Feeney, "*Si licet et fas est:* Ovid's *Fasti* and the Problem of Free Speech under the Principate," in *Roman Poetry and Propaganda in the Age of Augustus,* ed. A. Powell (Bristol, 1992), 1–25; G. Herbert-Brown, *Ovid and the Fasti: A Historical Study* (Oxford, 1994); C. Newlands, "The Ending of Ovid's Fasti," in *Roman Literature and Ideology: Ramus Essays for J.P. Sullivan,* ed. A.J. Boyle (published as *Ramus* 23 [1994]), 129–43; idem, *Playing with Time: Ovid and the Fasti* (Ithaca and London, 1995). See also Barchiesi, *Il poeta e il principe,* and the forthcoming commentary (Cambridge Greek and Latin Classics) on *Fasti* 4 by E. Fantham. The *Fasti* were made more readily accessible to modern readers by the appearance of a new Teubner text in 1978: E.H. Alton, D.E.W. Wormell, and E. Courtney, eds., *Ovidius: Fasti* (Leipzig, 1978; 2d ed., 1985). On the political aspect of Ovid's poetry, see the discussion later in this introduction.

7. The fullest exploration to date of the relationship of the *Fasti* to the *Metamorphoses* is Hinds, *Metamorphosis of Persephone.*

8. The dating of the *Amores* has most recently been treated by McKeown, 1:74–89; see also R. Syme, *History in Ovid* (Oxford, 1978), 1–20. For an idiosyncratic (and not widely accepted) approach to the relationship between the *Amores, Ars,* and *Remedia,* cf. C. Murgia, "The Date of Ovid's Ars Amatoria 3," *AJP* 107 (1986): 74–94 and "Influence of Ovid's Remedia amoris on Ars Amatoria 3 and Amores 3," *CP* 81 (1986): 203–20. See also my discussion later in chap. 4, of the relationship between first and second editions.

together, the *Amores, Ars Amatoria,* and *Remedia Amoris* (along with the fragmentary *Medicamina Faciei Femineae*) have been considered Ovid's training ground, so to speak; they are the works in which he refined both his handling of meter and his sense of irony, first made the character of the narrator a prominent part of his poetry, and began what would be a life-long literary dialogue with the poets who constituted his poetic education, most especially the Augustans. Yet within this group of poems, those in which Ovid projects an explicitly pseudodidactic irony have garnered the greatest attention; Ovid's impersonation of the *praeceptor amoris* very neatly mirrors his move away from the illusion of subjective elegy.[9] A necessary consequence and implication of this interest in the didactic works is that the *Amores,* by comparison, are viewed as less successful, less accomplished, and therefore of less interest for students of Latin poetry. It is virtually inevitable that the *Amores* be looked at as in some sense an imitation and reworking of earlier amatory elegy, especially that of Propertius. And since this critical perspective offers us an Ovid who is looking back to what preceded him and is following it, rather than an Ovid who is looking ahead to an ever more daring deployment of poetic irony and narrative sophistication, the *Amores* have become a victim of biographical criticism and are most often dealt with summarily in a prologue to a fuller discussion of one of the other works, to the novelty and cleverness of which the *Amores* serve as foil.

Two issues deserve particular attention here. First is the necessary fact of comparison with his apparent models: the dominant theme in most comparative criticism is Ovid's relationship to the other elegists, especially Propertius. Thus, most studies of the *Amores,* such as they are, start from the implicit assumption that the *Amores* are in some sense responses to, even parodies of, Propertian elegy. In a recent article on the programmatic character of *Amores* 1.1, Alison Keith describes the situation perfectly when she says: "A glance at the bibliography of Ovidian scholarship . . . shows that *Am.* 1.1 has received not one article to itself; nor is there a single book assessing Ovid's literary achievement in the *Amores.* . . ."[10] She then proceeds to prove her point by presenting a reading of *Am.* 1.1 that

---

9. On the relationship of the *Amores, Ars,* and *Remedia,* see G.B. Conte, "Love without Elegy: The *Remedia amoris* and the Logic of a Genre," *Poetics Today* 10 (1989) 441–69. Cf. E. Pianezzola, ed., *L'arte di amare,* 2d ed. (Milan, 1993); A. Sharrock, *Seduction and Repetition in Ovid's Ars Amatoria II* (Oxford, 1994).

10. A.M. Keith, "*Amores* 1.1: Propertius and the Ovidian Programme," in *Studies in Latin Literature and Roman History,* vol. 6, ed. C. Deroux, Collection Latomus 217 (Brussels, 1992): 327 n. 1.

develops from its comparison with Propertius 1.1. I propose that we take a cue from what Keith has done and recognize the implications of our own inability to read the *Amores* in isolation—they are indeed important elements in the transmission of the Latin literary tradition to Ovid and so must be read in relation to the work of the poets in the generation immediately preceding him.

This in turn leads me to my second point: the *Amores* must also be read in relation to what follows—in particular, in relation to the poetry that Ovid would write during the rest of his career. My major goal in this book is to suggest that there is ample evidence in the *Amores* for a poet who is interested in doing something besides nailing down the lid of the coffin in which Roman elegy is to be interred.

The image I have just used may seem unnecessarily melodramatic; yet consider this eulogy from Lyne, who also describes the *Amores* as "posthumous" at birth: ". . . Ovid spoke for his society. It amused him for a time to write in the tradition of his predecessors, or at least to play against it. . . . We must be glad that there was a poet ingenious and irreverent enough to construct such an artifice—and *conclude a period of literary history* with such neatness" (italics mine).[11] Lyne thus imposes on the *Amores* a sort of critical closure that, I shall argue, cannot be supported by the poems themselves; in other words, he indulges (however unintentionally) in both aspects of what I would call the "progressive fallacy," that is, the critical fallacy that posits either (a) that what comes first is worst or (b) that what comes last is worst. Both modes of the progressive fallacy have been fashionable in their turn; in combination, they subject the *Amores* to an extreme sort of literary isolation.

Consider the implications of the "later means better" view. Simply put, this view assumes that poets' later work, for example, the *Bacchae* or the *Aeneid,* is in some sense better than their earlier work, for example, the *Alcestis* or the *Eclogues.* Underlying this assumption is a set of other assumptions—that, given the opportunity, poets like Euripides or Virgil will refine their technique over time, will gradually come to articulate a more mature vision than that which had inspired their earliest work, and will be more willing to innovate and take risks with their reputation later than they are when they have no reputation to risk. This version of the progressive fallacy is so dominant precisely because it is so often true, at least in general terms; and it is not my desire to be so contrary as to suggest that

---

11. R.O.A.M. Lyne, *The Latin Love Poets* (Oxford, 1980), 287 (the end of his chapter on Ovid).

the *Aeneid* is not in fact in some sense "better," more mature, and more sustained an achievement than the *Eclogues*. However, when put in these general terms, the progressive fallacy tempts us to overlook the very different characters of the two works being compared; we imply not only that there is such a thing as a single Platonic form of "perfect poem" or "perfect play" but also that every poet consciously strives to achieve this single ideal in every poem, or play, he or she writes. There are of course exceptions to this version of the progressive fallacy. Few critics find the fourth book of Horace's odes as invigorating as the three that preceded it;[12] and although critics have argued valiantly in defense of Propertius' changing vision, rare is the reader who will not confess to finding the earliest book, the Monobiblos, the best. But these exceptions are to be explained, we are told, as functions of eccentricity (e.g., Horace's increasing disengagement from politics and assumption of laureate status; Propertius' too narrowly elegiac Muse) and are not permitted to contradict a general sense of time as improvement. The implications of this version of the progressive fallacy for the *Amores* should be obvious by now: as Ovid's earliest work, they are viewed as his least satisfying, at best as a clever parody and at worst as a lifeless and parasitic imitation. Meanwhile, this version of the progressive fallacy demands that we either ignore the latest works, the *Tristia* and *Epistulae ex Ponto,* or put them in an exceptional category, sui generis because of Ovid's egregious *error.* In accordance with this version, the *Metamorphoses* is read effectively as Ovid's "last" (i.e., greatest) work.

Perhaps not coincidentally, the progressive fallacy has also tended to favor works with the highest political profile and to dismiss as jejune and enervated those works whose character is predominantly literary. This tendency will prove to be an important factor in my reading of the *Amores,* for we are dealing here with a collection that, to a degree not seen in all the other poetry books of the Augustan period, is virtually impossible to date.[13] Indeed, it is not simply a matter of dating; the collection as a whole

---

12. E. Fraenkel's reading of book 4 (*Horace* [Oxford, 1957], 400–453) is exceptionally kind, but the inference to be drawn from Suetonius' guess that Augustus forced Horace to write a fourth book (*vit. Hor.* 46) has remained popular, at least until very recently. See the recent discussions of the subject by M.C.J. Putnam, *Artifices of Eternity: Horace's Fourth Book of Odes* (Ithaca, 1986), 20–23 and by P. White, *Promised Verse: Poets in the Society of Augustan Rome* (Cambridge, MA, and London, 1993), 203. For generally balanced readings of the fourth book, see also C. Becker, *Das Spätwerk des Horaz* (Göttingen, 1963), esp. 9–13, 190–93; and S. Commager, *The Odes of Horace* (New Haven and London, 1962), 291–306.

13. Of course, this has not prevented readers from attempting to do so: see the discussions cited in n. 8 in this introduction. To note a recent example, G.B. Conte, *Latin Literature: A History,* trans. J.B. Solodow, rev. D. Fowler and G.W. Most (Baltimore and London, 1994),

only rarely glances at its sociopolitical surroundings. I do not intend to suggest that the *Amores* are free of engagement in any sort of political discourse or that Ovid is for once in his career unequivocally "pro-Augustan" in the *Amores;* yet the ideological subtext of the *Amores* is, I believe, more important for the contribution it makes to Ovid's characterization of the *amator*—on whom I shall focus in chapters 4 and 5—than for any sense of the "real world" of elegy that some critics may feel it gives. Rather, even when Ovid alludes to other poets' scenes or passages that are very much colored by their reflection of the contemporary Augustan ethos, we shall see that his interest in them is primarily literary. It is a truism that, to paraphrase Newlands, elegy is the genre of dissent:[14] prominent features of the genre are advocacy of *otium* over *negotium,* preference of the life of love over a political career, and inversion of accepted social mores and transformation of roles in an imaginary world in which free men become slaves, women rule them, and the only wars fought are the battles in bed.[15] Ovid exploits all these conventions, as required by his decision to pursue the genre and its implications; yet in the *Amores,* he rarely lingers over the political matrix in which these conventions are fixed. Rather, this matrix is taken as given, aside from the occasional opportunity for ironic levity in the face of love's onslaught. As my discussion unfolds, I shall suggest that, in writing the *Amores,* Ovid is far less interested in interrogating the anti-Augustanism of elegy per se than in exploring his own relationship, as poet, to the genre. His literary focus and its consequences provide the underpinning for this book.

The other version of the progressive fallacy tells us that "later means worse." This critical rule of thumb, responsible for generating categories

340, puts the first edition of the *Amores* at sometime around 20 B.C., just after book 1 of Horace's *Epistles.* But the evidence is slim at best: see my discussion of the two editions later, in chap. 4.

The dating of the *Heroides* is equally problematic, if not more so, given the presence of forgeries among the authentically Ovidian poems in the manuscripts as we now have them: see Jacobson, *Ovid's Heroides,* 300–318; P.E. Knox, "Ovid's *Medea* and the Authenticity of *Heroides* 12," *HSCP* 90 (1986): 207–23; idem, *Heroides: Select Epistles,* 5–12. We should probably not be surprised that the least "datable" among Ovid's works have most easily gotten forged poems added to their number; in the *Amores,* 3.[V] is the evident interloper: see E.J. Kenney, "On the *Somnium* Attributed to Ovid," *Agon* 3 (1969): 1–14.

14. The phrase is adapted from Newlands, "Ending," 130.

15. The classic formulation of the position is A. Wallace-Hadrill, "Propaganda and Dissent? Augustan Moral Legislation and the Love-Poets," *Klio* 67 (1985): 180–84; see also W. Stroh, "Ovids Liebeskunst und die Ehegesetze des Augustus," *Gymnasium* 86 (1979): 323–52, and D. Little, "Politics in Augustan Poetry," *ANRW* 2.30.1 (1982): 254–370 (esp. 316–22, on the *Amores*).

like the "golden" and "silver" ages of Latin literature, tells us that decadence from a perfect state is inevitable, whether perfection is expressed
morally or aesthetically.[16] While many a classical scholar has said, in print
and otherwise, that the movement from Greek to Latin literature is itself a
prime and extremely straightforward example of this decline, in the study
of the development of Latin literature per se this version of the progressive
fallacy takes a more circuitous route. From its earliest history we see a tension arising between, on the one hand, the Romans' perception of their
culture as heir, *epigonos,* to Greece and so in some sense doomed to a cultural inferiority complex and, on the other hand, compelling evidence to
suggest that, on the part of individual writers, this historical situation provides just the impetus necessary for a creative explosion against a traditional backdrop.[17] In this version, Virgil plays a pivotal role as a sort of
symbolic telos, the end of perfection toward which all Latin poets strive for
two hundred years; but he is the end also in another sense, the last "great"
Latin poet, by whose stature all later Latin poets are dwarfed and against
whose achievement all later Latin poetry is measured and found wanting.

At this juncture we locate Ovid, whose very proximity to Virgil makes
him all the more subject to comparison. He is hampered by both the accident of his late birth and a common perception that his poetry is flawed,
not by the roughness of a poetic expression working toward perfection (as
with, e.g., Ennius), but by the excesses of an overly refined, even decadent,
aesthetic sensibility.[18] Certainly this bias is hardly limited to Ovidian criticism; indeed, this is exactly the estimation in which Virgil himself, late-
comer and imitator, was for so long held vis-à-vis Homer.[19] Again, it is not
my purpose to argue the contrary or to suggest that we not compare Ovid
with Virgil; I shall demonstrate at length in the following pages that in
composing the *Amores* Ovid looked long and often to this predecessor,
foremost among many, and that he often wanted such comparisons to be
made. But I do want to limit severely the critical tendency to read Ovid's

---

16. See the discussion by G. Williams, *Change and Decline: Roman Literature in the Early
Empire* (Berkeley, Los Angeles, and London, 1978), 6–51, of cultural decadence as perceived
by writers in the early Roman Empire.

17. For a recent evaluation of the relationship, see E. Gruen, *Culture and National Identity in Republican Rome* (Ithaca, 1992).

18. See the valuable overview of Ovidian criticism by S. Hinds, "Generalising about
Ovid," *Ramus* 16 (1987): 4–31.

19. For a history of the dramatic shift in critical views of Virgil, see the valuable first chapter of W.R. Johnson, *Darkness Visible: A Study of Vergil's Aeneid* (Berkeley and Los Angeles,
1976).

poetry in such fatalistic terms, a tendency toward overpsychologizing, if you will. Bloom's concept of "anxiety of influence" can be useful insofar as it captures the nature of the tension alive for any poet working within a literary tradition; but it is dangerous as well, for to the extent that it is put in Freudian terms, it profoundly misrepresents, I think, the way a poet like Ovid—or Virgil or Callimachus, for that matter—sees his poetic calling and so goes about his work.[20] One purpose of this study is to bring into focus how a particular Latin poet responds and contributes to his literary history and to dispel along the way a popular view of Ovid as the superego, so to speak, of Augustan poetry, a poet with a hyper-self-consciousness, aware that his elegy stands at the conclusion to a period of literary history.

In a now-classic article, Allen demonstrated that the illusion of sincerity for which much Roman elegy is prized is just that—an illusion.[21] Unfortunately, however, while most critics have heeded Allen's words in the case of Propertius, the *Amores* have often been read as if in a vacuum. The reasons for this attitude toward the *Amores* are hard to sort out: the renewed interest in the elegists that bloomed in the sixties and resulted, over the course of the next two decades, in a number of important studies of Propertian and Tibullan elegy had only a superficial effect on how the *Amores* were read. A wide range of new books on elegy, from Luck's general overview, *Die römische Liebeselegie,* to Wimmel's specialized *Kallimachos in Rom,*[22] quickly determined that, among elegists, Propertius and Tibullus were the norm and Ovid the aberration, a Johnny-come-lately among the Augustan poets. To an age enchanted by the artifice of sincerity, Ovid's poetry appeared, if not uninspired, at the very least uninspiring. Ironically, his own cleverness, while admired by earlier generations, has worked very much to Ovid's detriment in more recent assessments of the *Amores.*

I mentioned earlier the need to remove the *Amores* from the critical isolation in which they have been left; a major factor in the promotion of this isolation has been the restrictive character of genre criticism. Conventionally, the *Amores* have been measured against the standards set by Proper-

---

20. See H. Bloom, *The Anxiety of Influence: A Theory of Poetry* (New York and London, 1973). For a helpful evaluation of the applicability of Bloom's model to the study of Latin epic, see P. Hardie, *The Epic Successors of Virgil: A Study in the Dynamics of a Tradition* (Cambridge, 1993), 116–19.

21. A.W. Allen, "'Sincerity' and the Roman Elegists," *CP* 45 (1950): 145–60; see also idem, "Sunt qui Propertium Malint," in *Critical Essays on Roman Literature: Elegy and Lyric,* ed. J.P. Sullivan (Cambridge, MA, 1962), 107–48; Conte, "Love without Elegy."

22. G. Luck, *Die römische Liebeselegie* (Heidelberg, 1959); W. Wimmel, *Kallimachos in Rom,* Hermes Einzelschrift 16 (Wiesbaden, 1960).

tius, Tibullus, and what we know of Gallus. Implicit in the comparison is an extreme version of the generic fallacy,[23] which simultaneously reinforces and is reinforced by both sides of the progressive fallacy: Ovid is the last, and so the least good, of the elegists; and as the collection is his first work, we can hardly expect it to be his best, since it is the most imitative of its predecessors.[24]

Let us look briefly at how the two fallacies I have invoked have for some time now shaped most discussions of the *Amores*. Du Quesnay, in a standard essay on the collection, suggests that the most significant aspect of the *Amores* is Ovid's obvious desire to recall Propertius books 1–3. Although he terms Ovid's techniques of imitation "creative," Propertian presence and influence are to be found everywhere, nowhere more so than in the elegiac persona assumed by Ovid. This persona is central to Du Quesnay's definition of "parody" in the *Amores*.[25] Lyne too, while enthusiastic about individual poems and special effects in the *Amores,* thinks it is clear that, at least in book 1, Ovid wants us to think of him generically, that is, as the successor to Catullus, Tibullus, and Propertius, and, like Du Quesnay, Lyne focuses on the parodic nature of the collection.[26] Otis' view is more simply put, because he uses fewer qualifications like *creative imitation:* for him, Ovid's amatory elegy is essentially "a *reductio ad absurdum* of the genre" as refined by Gallus, Tibullus, and Propertius.[27] Sullivan likewise reads the *Amores* as generic parody, and he damns them accordingly as a "debasement of the elegiac tradition."[28] Even Barsby, generally a sensitive and sympathetic Ovidian, is satisfied with a description of the collection as "basically a light-hearted reworking of the genre," although he is careful to avoid words like *parody* and *travesty.*[29] Davis, in contrast, bluntly

---

23. For the classic discussion of generic fallacy, see B. Croce, *The Aesthetic as the Science of Expression and of the Linguistic in General,* trans. C. Lyas (Cambridge, 1992), 39–43.

24. The representative character of this approach is reflected in G. Luck, "Love Elegy," in *The Cambridge History of Classical Literature,* vol. 2, *Latin Literature,* ed. E.J. Kenney and W.V. Clausen (Cambridge, 1982), 405–19. His discussion of Ovid in this chapter (esp. 416–18) repeats the approach found in his 1959 work.

25. I.M.LeM. Du Quesnay, "The *Amores,*" in *Ovid,* ed. J.W. Binns (London and Boston, 1973), 19, 35. See my discussion of persona theory later, in chap. 4.

26. Lyne, *Latin Love Poets,* 242–48.

27. B. Otis, "Ovid and the Augustans," *TAPA* 69 (1938): 197.

28. J.P. Sullivan, "Two Problems in Roman Love Elegy," *TAPA* 92 (1961): 535.

29. J.A. Barsby, *Ovid,* Greece and Rome New Surveys in the Classics 12 (Oxford, 1978), 7. Interestingly, the introduction to his commentary on book 1 is more subtle (esp. 16–18). We may sense in Barsby's work some dissatisfaction, still unresolved, with earlier efforts to pigeonhole the *Amores* as elegiac parody.

calls the collection Ovid's "travesty of Latin love elegy." Using terms like *burlesque, caricature,* and *comic reworking,* he finds Propertian imitation everywhere in the *Amores;* this critic typifies an entire group of readers in starting from the premise that Propertius takes the place of Ovid's elegiac Muse.[30] The culmination of the *Amores*-as-Propertian-parody approach is the monograph by Morgan, working on the premise that virtually all of the *Amores* contain at least a kernel of Propertian "imitation" and that, because of Ovid's apparent sense of humor, the poems can be interpreted across the board as parody.[31] Luck neatly summarizes the dominant reading of the *Amores:* in these poems, Ovid "decorates the literary heritage gracefully and dissolves its seriousness into irony and play."[32]

We can see that some of these opinions at least attempt to be positive, while others suggest that Ovid's elegy is beneath contempt; most, however, damn the *Amores* with faint praise. The illusion of sincerity is the problematic issue here; even critics who actively disavow romanticism are disappointed that Ovid expends so little effort on creating that illusion. Thus, the term *travesty,* like Sullivan's *debasement,* generally carries with it a negative connotation; *creative reworking,* however, is generally used by critics who wish to put the *Amores* in as favorable a light as possible. And *parody* stands in between, as a colorful but—at least ostensibly—also an evenhanded appraisal and so the one most likely to be used by critics who wish to appear objective in their evaluation of the *Amores.*

But is Ovid interested simply in producing a subversive revision of Propertius that is devoid of the earlier poetry's subjective illusion and indeed seeks to parody Propertius' emotional extravagance? The most

---

30. J.T. Davis, "*Risit Amor:* Aspects of Literary Burlesque in Ovid's 'Amores,' " *ANRW* 2.31.4 (1981): 2462–2506.

31. K. Morgan, *Ovid's Art of Imitation: Propertius in the Amores,* Mnemosyne Suppl. 47 (Leiden, 1977); this is a revision of her 1969 Yale University dissertation, "Propertian Imitations in Ovid's *Amores*" (written under the name K. Berman; see *DA* 30 [1970]: 3923A). See also K. Berman, "Some Propertian Imitations in Ovid's *Amores,*" *CP* 67 (1972): 170–77. She takes up where R. Neumann left off in his 1919 Göttingen dissertation, "Qua ratione Ovidius in Amoribus scribendis Properti elegiis usus sit."

32. G. Luck, *The Latin Love Elegy,* 2d ed. (London, 1969), 172 (a revised English version of *Die römische Liebeselegie*). An interesting exception to the critical rule is P. Green, *Aspects of Antiquity* (London, 1960), 118–21, who writes that the *Amores* "have been consistently under-rated by critics who . . . doubt their sincerity. . . ." (118). In the thirty-five years since he first made this comment about the *Amores,* Green has modified his approach somewhat, and in the introduction to his Penguin translation he suggests a more subtle blend of persona theory and self-portraiture for the interpretation of Ovid: see his *Ovid: The Erotic Poems* (London, 1982), 59–71. Green's approach has received little notice, however. See my discussion later, in chaps. 4 and 5.

important word here is *parody,* used with extraordinary frequency to "explain" the *Amores:* I shall propose in this book a very different interpretation, which seeks to disentangle Ovidian humor and irony from parody. To do so, it will be essential that we move beyond the generic fallacy and recognize that Ovid is not only little interested in sounding the death-knell of elegy but, if anything, eager to reinvigorate it, as well as that his way of doing so involves a comprehensive and lively grasp not only of the circumscribed world of subjective elegy but of an entire literary tradition, not bounded, but only made more interesting, by genre categories. Of course Ovid looks back to and even imitates the elegies of Propertius—and of Tibullus, Catullus, and presumably Gallus, too. My goal, however, is not to revisit this well-worn path to the exclusion of everything else; instead, I shall focus on the ways in which Ovid looks beyond elegy's limits and so invests the genre with a new sense of range and purpose.

It will be best to set the stage for my discussion by considering the generic fallacy against the general background of recent work on Augustan poetry. Genre criticism, useful as it can be in illuminating similarities between poets, is less effective in helping us to make sense of differences between poets. In the case of the *Amores,* it not only risks serious misrepresentation of Ovid's goals but also ignores what one scholar has called the "challenge of generic freedom" articulated by the Augustan poets.[33] The influence, both literal and symbolic, exerted by Callimachus establishes an important precedent for his successors in Latin poetry, a precedent recognized as more complex than simple avoidance of epic themes and style. A brief review of what remains and what we know of Callimachus' work and career reveals clearly his familiarity with stylistic propriety, genre, and canon;[34] Zetzel believes that we find in Callimachus' work a clear articulation of his studied disposition to violate "consistently and deliberately" their formal rules.[35] Recently, Alan Cameron has argued that genre per se and generic propriety are of far less importance to Callimachus than has previously been supposed; but even if we find Cameron's discussion com-

---

33. The phrase belongs to J.E.G. Zetzel, "Recreating the Canon: Augustan Poetry and the Alexandrian Past," *Critical Inquiry* 10 (1983): 101; see also Hinds, *Metamorphosis of Persephone,* 115–34. For a fundamental discussion of the concept, see W. Kroll on "Die Kreuzung der Gattungen," in *Studien zum Verständnis der römischen Literatur* (Stuttgart, 1924), 202–24.

34. Evident in any case from his groundbreaking cataloguing work in the library at Alexandria: for an overview, see R. Blum, *Kallimachos: The Alexandrian Library and the Origins of Bibliography,* trans. H. Wellisch (Madison and London, 1991) (= *Kallimachos und die Literaturverzeichnung bei den Griechen* [Frankfurt am Main, 1977]).

35. Zetzel, "Recreating the Canon," 99.

pelling, we can see that the adaptation of Callimachean techniques to Roman poetry is expressed very fully in generic and ideological terms.[36] Thus, the subject-matter and style of one genre can often be used with very conscious intent in the framework of another; and the very freedom to violate generic boundaries in fact allows a poet like Ovid to make his own ingenuity one of the central themes of his work.

When we consider the work of several other Augustan poets, we can immediately see how "generic freedom" enriches the tradition. Horace's collections of *Odes* and *Epodes* provide abundant examples not simply of experimentation with a variety of meters but of a seasoned breadth that lays claim to numerous Greek traditions simultaneously: from Archilochus to Pindar, from iambus to elegy, Horace's lyrics reveal his eagerness to give new purpose to old forms. Virgil's aims and accomplishments are even bolder: the *Eclogues,* their bucolic character tempered by both the presence of elegy and the hybridization of Callimachean style, are an auspicious opening to a career that culminates in an unambiguously Alexandrian epic.[37] Even in work on Roman elegy, the influence of other genres has been recognized to be not inconsiderable; and as Ross has demonstrated, the brief history of the elegiac tradition in Latin is best understood not in purely generic terms but as just one of a number of forms suited to express the renovation of Alexandrian poetics at Rome.[38] Ovid's *Amores,* however, are an exception to all of these generalizations: this collection tends to be seen in much narrower terms, as far more tightly controlled, and restricted, by its limited generic range.

I do not mean to suggest that a poet's choice of genre is entirely without significance and that we should avoid using such terms as *epic* and *elegy* for

36. A. Cameron, *Callimachus and His Critics* (Princeton, 1995), passim; on the Roman adaptation of Callimachean aesthetics, see especially his chap. 18; see also idem, "Genre and Style in Callimachus," *TAPA* 122 (1992): 305–12.

37. See, e.g., W. Clausen, "Callimachus and Latin Poetry," *GRBS* 5 (1964): 181–96; Z. Stewart, "The Song of Silenus," *HSCP* 64 (1959): 179–205; J.P. Elder, "*Non iniussa cano:* Virgil's Sixth Eclogue," *HSCP* 65 (1961): 109–25. See also D.O. Ross, *Backgrounds to Augustan Poetry: Gallus, Elegy, and Rome* (Cambridge, 1975), 36–38 on the "unified poetic tradition" inherited by Gallus in the sixth *Eclogue;* W. Clausen, *Virgil's Aeneid and the Tradition of Hellenistic Poetry* (Berkeley and Los Angeles, 1987); idem, ed., *Virgil: Eclogues* (Oxford, 1994), passim. The discussion of *Eclogue* 10 by G.B. Conte (*The Rhetoric of Imitation: Genre and Poetic Memory in Virgil and Other Latin Poets,* ed. C.P. Segal [Ithaca and London, 1986], 100–129) is a valuable look at generic tensions in this poem but is skewed by Conte's tendency to overlook the importance of Alexandrian self-consciousness to the Augustan poets; see my discussion later, in chap. 1.

38. Ross, *Backgrounds to Augustan Poetry,* passim.

anything more than convenience's sake. A Roman poet tells us something of great value about his aims and purpose by his choice of form; and we are right to expect in turn that the style and content of, for example, elegy will differ greatly from that of, for example, epic. As the many *recusationes* in Augustan poetry indicate, this difference has great programmatic importance and is a crucial element in identifying the Hellenistic tastes of the poets in this period. In fact, much of Roman Callimacheanism is focused precisely on this tension between generic freedom and the conscious violation of generic boundaries. Accordingly, much of the discussion that follows is concerned with how this tension is exploited by Ovid in the *Amores*. It has recently been most convincingly argued that many episodes in Ovid's *Metamorphoses* reveal a novel adaptation of primarily elegiac techniques to something that, for lack of a better term, we call epic;[39] and Farrell has made a strong case for reading at least the Polyphemus narrative of *Met.* 13 as an example of generic "polyphony," in which features of elegiac, bucolic, and epic genres are combined into something of an entirely new order.[40] I shall argue in the following chapters that the *Amores* should be understood as having a central position on the continuum of Ovid's interest in the boundaries of genre, while the inclination of many critics to read the *Amores* as a generic byway or dead-end is almost entirely the product of a parallel inclination to read through the lens of the progressive fallacy. Instead, I want to posit an Ovid who, in the process of conceiving and writing the *Amores,* and later of revising them, is deeply committed to exploring and, if possible, extending the limits of elegy by virtue of the fact that they *are* limits. The boundaries of the genre, as established through the poetry of Catullus, Propertius, and Tibullus, among others, are clear; in its very unexceptionality, the "new Gallus" has confirmed these limits.[41] Ovid, however, sees these very limits as a challenge, unhindered as he is by two thousand years of hindsight; and by finding and exploiting their weak points, he turns these boundaries into places where creative innovation can occur. In other words, I shall suggest that we read the *Amores* as forerunners of Ovid's later work in the best possible sense, rather than as forgettable juvenilia. The progressive fallacy should not prevent us from

---

39. Knox, *Ovid's Metamorphoses;* cf. Hinds, *Metamorphosis of Persephone,* 99–134.

40. J. Farrell, "Dialogue of Genres in Ovid's 'Lovesong of Polyphemus' (*Metamorphoses* 13.719–897)," *AJP* 113 (1992): 235–68.

41. See R.J. Anderson, P.J. Parsons, and R.G.M. Nisbet, "Elegiacs by Gallus from Qaṣr Ibrîm," *JRS* 69 (1979): 125–55; cf. Gallus *FLP* fr. 2 Courtney.

acknowledging that the generic range of the *Metamorphoses* is mirrored in virtually all Ovid's pre-exile poetry; and in fact it is just that territory on the generic boundaries that so consistently stimulates his imagination and his Muse. Just as the *Ars Amatoria, Remedia,* and *Medicamina* engage amatory elegy in a dialogue with (pseudo)scientific and didactic poetry, just as the *Heroides* engage elegy in a dialogue with tragedy and epic, and just as the *Metamorphoses* engage epic in an almost "stream-of-consciousness" dialogue with elegiac, bucolic, didactic, aetiological, dramatic, and scientific poetry, so the *Amores* look beyond the usual horizons of elegy to other forms. This book is devoted to an investigation of the ways in which Ovid redefines the boundaries of elegy, a redefinition that will in turn have bearing on his poetic career following the composition of the *Amores.* A better comprehension of the context in which Ovid writes can only help to dispel the isolation of the *Amores.*[42]

Two issues that have arisen in the course of the preceding pages require a bit more clarification: Ovid's very limited engagement with broader political issues in the *Amores,* and the respective roles of humor and imitation in the collection. First of all, I want to suggest that modulation is in order when we talk about the politics of literature, at least of the literature of the Augustan period.[43] The value of such modulation in any discussion of the politics of Ovid's poetry is easily made evident through brief comparison of the *Amores* with Ovid's other major elegiac poems. The similarities between the *Amores* and the *Ars Amatoria,* for example, are well known; because both are at least ostensibly amatory elegiac works, they are in fact often clustered together, in general discussions of Ovid's works, as his early amatory elegy *vel sim.* (with the *Remedia, Medicamina,* and sometimes the *Heroides* added to this cluster). Just as often, however, the *Ars* is seen as the

---

42. Ovidians will recognize that the title of this introduction is modelled on that of a well-known article by W.R. Johnson, "The Desolation of the *Fasti,*" *CJ* 74 (1978–79): 7–18. Johnson's gloomy meditation on the role of the authorial psyche in the failure of the *Fasti* otherwise differs greatly, however, from my reading of the *Amores.*

43. For an articulate statement of the alternative position, see D. Kennedy, "'Augustan' and 'Anti-Augustan': Reflections on Terms of Reference," in *Roman Poetry and Propaganda in the Age of Augustus,* ed. A. Powell (Bristol, 1992), 26–58. Kennedy is right to take on the overly simplistic polarization of this aspect of the discussion of Augustan literature; but tellingly, he nowhere makes the *Amores* central to his discussion. In this respect among others, he would appear to be following the model of his influential predecessor, P. Veyne, *Roman Erotic Elegy: Love, Poetry, and the West,* trans. D. Pellauer (Chicago, 1988) (= *L'élégie érotique romaine: L'amour, la poésie et l'Occident* [Paris, 1983]).

best of this early group and so is selected for critical emphasis and attention.[44] The basis for this work's status as *primum inter paria* is founded first
of all on its sometimes risqué scenarios of seduction and is supported by
the poem's irreverent treatment of everything in its scope—gods, heroes,
the sites and spaces of Roman power. Its explicit evocation of the seamier
details of Roman social behavior has an evident political function: Ovid
uses the normally conservative role of didactic poet to challenge and subvert the moralizing legislation characteristic of Augustus' reign. The
poem's daring humor—along with Ovid's vivid locating of episodes of
seduction in some of the most historically significant venues of Augustan
Rome[45]—has made it seem to many critics an act of defiance in the face of
social repression, and perhaps even the cause of his eventual exile.[46] Such
lines of interpretation taken together give the *Ars* a political profile—
indeed, a seriousness—that belies the humorous surface of the work; and
so its humor can be more easily tolerated, as a signal virtue rather than the
limitation it appears to be in the *Amores*.

While the *Amores* and *Ars* have much in common, however, the similarities in subject matter are very much transformed by Ovid's different
approach to the material in each case. The poet's didactic stance in the *Ars*
is precisely what gives this poem its public aspect; in speaking as a teacher
of love, Ovid invokes a narrator who is by definition both experienced and
detached, a knowing observer rather than an excited or confused participant in the love affairs he describes. In chapters 4 and 5 I shall look in some
detail at the narrator Ovid creates in the *Amores,* and I shall argue there
that the poet-lover who takes center stage in the *Amores* is a far different
sort of character from, and in some ways has a far more complicated personality than, the *praeceptor amoris* of the *Ars*. A central component of
this narrator's personality is his initial lack of knowledge regarding love
and love poetry; and the *Amores* can thus be seen as very much an exploration of what happens to this character as he discovers what elegy is in the
course of writing about love. As this subject takes on the form of elegy, it
takes on the political characteristics of the genre; but these characteristics
are hardly the sum total of the poems' meaning or purpose.

44. See, e.g., A.S. Hollis, ed., *Ovid: Ars Amatoria Book I* (Oxford, 1977), xi–xvii, and the
works cited in n. 9 in this introduction, for approaches to the *Ars*.

45. Cf. my discussion later, in chap. 6, comparing the Circus Maximus episodes in *Am.* 3.2
and *AA* 1.

46. On the possible referents of *carmen et error* (*Tr.* 2.207), see the standard survey of the
evidence in J.C. Thibeault, *The Mystery of Ovid's Exile* (Berkeley and Los Angeles, 1964); cf.
Hollis, *Ars Amatoria I,* xiii–xvii; G.P. Goold, "The Cause of Ovid's Exile," *ICS* 8 (1983):
94–107. The *carmen* of Ovid's phrase is usually identified as the *Ars*.

An even clearer example of the modulation necessary in a discussion of the political nature of poetry can be found in a comparison of the *Amores* and the *Fasti*. While it was once fashionable to read the *Fasti*—if at all—as a piece of antiquarian escapism, the poem has recently garnered renewed attention from critics who recognize its engagement with concerns central to the Augustan regime: the dates, places, and names that reenact the historical past in Ovid's present.[47] And these critics are undoubtedly right to give the political discourse of the *Fasti* their attention; a poem that offers its readers a lengthy comparison between the cruel, barely civilized, and fratricidal *parens patriae* Romulus, on the one hand, and his civilized and civilizing heir, Augustus, now proclaimed *pater patriae,* on the other (*Fasti* 2.126–44), invites us to consider explicitly and in detail how the lessons of the past are to be applied to present circumstances. Again, Ovid's subversive humor is seen to work to his advantage in this context, particularly if we choose to see him as a champion of free speech in an age of growing repression.[48] It is therefore vitally important to compare his decision to take on a topic so politically charged as the national calendar in the *Fasti* with the much more artistically introspective world of the *Amores*. Romulus, for example, exists in the *Amores,* as the referent for a few exempla (e.g., *Am.* 2.14.15–16, 3.4.39–40; cf. also 2.9.17–18); and the two explicit allusions to the *gens Iulia* are well known (*Am.* 1.2.51–52, 2.14.17–18). But Ovid does not linger over them; they are not his focus or theme but instead supply the background against which he creates his elegiac love. It is almost as if we had in the *Amores* and the *Fasti* the two "sides" of Ovid, so to speak, the one using the erotic traditions of elegy both to articulate and to ambiguate a political stance, the other working from a matrix of political and social issues and conventions to articulate an unconventional and complex poetic identity. This formulation cannot, of course, be applied with perfect precision to either the *Fasti* or the *Amores;* such tidiness would be alien to the wealth and playfulness of Ovidian creativity. I hope nonetheless that its serviceability will be demonstrated by the literary focus of this study.

In this brief overview, I have noted a pattern in most criticism of the *Amores:* while the humor of the *Ars* and the *Fasti* is felt to have political bite and so is condoned, the humor of the *Amores,* less apparently editorial or satiric in purpose, has led to its critical denigration. I intend, therefore, first to refocus attention on the alleged status of the collection as imitation and then to move toward a consideration of the intimate

---

47. See the works cited in n. 6 in this introduction, and see my discussion later, in chap. 6, of the stories of Ilia told in *Am.* 3.6 and of Rhea Silvia told at the opening of *Fasti* 3.

48. So Feeney, "*Si licet et fas est.*"

relationship between humor and imitation in the *Amores*. I propose that the humor of the *Amores* is, to a great extent, a by-product of Ovid's use of his models, as well as a result of his propensity to comment on, and so draw our attention to, what he is doing. Yet we should also understand from the outset that the very presence of humor in the *Amores,* in the face of so much earlier elegiac sincerity, is a crucial factor in the collection's mixed reception. As one scholar remarks in a discussion of burlesque in the *Metamorphoses,* "Humor alarms, dismays and paralyses the critics of Latin poetry."[49] It also, I shall argue, is too easily confused with, and so taken for, parody. Ovid's approach to humor tells us much more about his goals for his own poetry than about his view of Propertius (or any other poet, for that matter). In chapters 4 and 5, therefore, I shall return to the role of Ovid's humor in shaping his originality, and vice versa.

I believe Ovid conceived the *Amores* to be not simply the replica of a tradition but rather a contribution to that tradition. Ovid's desire to take the genre of elegy beyond its usual limits has generally been read instead as a trial-and-error experiment. In the current state of isolation in which the *Amores* are read, even McKeown's superb new edition with commentary, filled as it is to overflowing with a valuable collection of data about usage, meter, topoi, allusions, rhetorical figures, and so forth, refrains from assigning any real originality to Ovid. Instead, McKeown presents as the collection's virtue a resolution of the paradox of earlier, mainly Propertian, elegy, in which trivial themes are treated seriously: Ovid simply trivializes what is already inherently trivial. McKeown sees in the *Amores* a light genre handled with "unrelenting lightness"[50]—the end result of which is not to expand but to contract the genre. From this perspective, imitation tends to be seen as a natural part of the process of contraction, a demonstration of Ovidian virtuosity at the expense of the vitality of the genre. This inclination to undercut the importance of the whole by reading Ovid's humorous irony as the sum total of his poetic intent hampers our ability to appreciate the originality of the *Amores*. With this proposition, I turn first to the nature and purpose of imitation in the *Amores*.

---

49. N.M. Horsfall, "Epic and Burlesque in Ovid, *Met.* viii.260 ff.," *CJ* 74 (1979): 319. Horsfall's demonstration of how Ovid uses identifiably "epic" diction and style to heighten the incongruity of his Calydonian boar-hunt illustrates clearly the difference between burlesque and parody and so anticipates some of the issues I take up in chap. 1.

50. The first two volumes of McKeown's projected four-volume edition have appeared. This verdict appears at 1:14. One might well compare McKeown's view with the opinion expressed by Luck in *Die römische Liebeselegie,* several decades ago: see n. 32 in this introduction.

Chapter 1

Reused Language: Genre and Influence in the Interpretation of the *Amores*

condicio optima est ultimi: parata verba invenit,
quae aliter instructa novam faciem habent
Seneca *Epist.* 79.6

The perplexity of modern scholars trying to capture the essence of what they see as Ovidian imitative technique is reflected in the chaos that characterizes their descriptions of the phenomenon. Their language is both fluent and incoherent: it includes the terms *imitation, allusion, reference; echo, reminiscence, reworking; copy, emulation, parody, burlesque; model, inspiration, influence, source;* and even the all-embracing *intertextuality.* Clearly, all of these terms are not interchangeable; yet as we look at the recent history of Ovidian criticism, we find few scholars even implicitly agreeing on a consistent terminology, and even fewer are bothering to make distinctions. But these and other modes of appraisal are abundantly imprecise and more often reflect trends in literary criticism than achieve a precise description of the relationship between multiple texts (and their authors). One thing, however, is clear: the use of each of these terms involves a judgment about a given combination of humor and imitation in Ovid. More often than not, the application of such terms is guided far less by any inherent meaning than by the degree of approbation or disapprobation in which a given reader holds the *Amores.*

In this chapter, I hope both to simplify and to clarify a method for reading imitation in the *Amores,* incorporating into my discussion the implications both of generic boundaries and of the critical dissonance that results from Ovid's sometimes unsettling and almost always ironic sense of humor. Do we call Virgil's imitation of Homer, for example, "creative" because it is generally serious (and vice versa)? Likewise, do we call Ovid's

19

imitation of Propertius "parodic" and "derivative" because it is humorous (and vice versa)? Again, while Virgil's imitations of Homer are recognized as a point of departure for the engagement of a vast literary tradition, are Ovid's imitations in the *Amores* truly genre-bound and in fact all but limited to Propertius? It should be clear by now that I want to challenge these and similar assumptions and propose in their place a more open-ended reading of the *Amores* and a better appreciation of Ovid's poetic vision as manifested in this work. It will be useful to begin by looking at a well-known but not well-understood example of Ovidian imitation. I shall then look at the current status of the study of poetic imitation and propose what I consider to be the most helpful terminology for describing Ovid's imitativeness. Finally, I shall return to the text of the *Amores* in pursuit of clarification and refinement of some important differences in Ovid's use of the literary past.[1]

We begin with Ovid's treatment of a well-known amatory subject, the propemptikon, in *Am.* 2.11:

> Prima malas docuit mirantibus aequoris undis
>   Peliaco pinus vertice caesa vias,
> quae concurrentes inter temeraria cautes
>   conspicuam fulvo vellere vexit ovem.
> o utinam, ne quis remo freta longa moveret,   5
>   Argo funestas pressa bibisset aquas!
> ecce fugit notumque torum sociosque Penates
>   fallacesque vias ire Corinna parat.
> quam tibi, me miserum, Zephyros Eurosque timebo
>   et gelidum Borean egelidumque Notum!   10
> non illic urbes, non tu mirabere silvas:
>   una est iniusti caerula forma maris.
> nec medius tenues conchas pictosque lapillos
>   pontus habet: bibuli litoris illa mora est.
> litora marmoreis pedibus signate, puellae   15

---

1. On imitation, see in particular the following classic studies of Alexandrian intertextuality: G. Pasquali, "Arte allusiva," *Italia che scrive* 25 (1942): 185–87 (= *Stravaganze quarte e supreme* [Venice, 1951], 11–20); Clausen, "Callimachus and Latin Poetry"; G. Giangrande, " 'Arte Allusiva' and Alexandrian Epic Poetry," *CQ* 17 (1967): 85–97. See also R.F. Thomas, "Virgil's *Georgics* and the Art of Reference," *HSCP* 90 (1986): 171–98, and the important discussions of imitation and Callimachean poetics mentioned in my introduction n. 37.

(hactenus est tutum, cetera caeca via est),
et vobis alii ventorum proelia narrent,
    quas Scylla infestet quasve Charybdis aquas,
et quibus emineant violenta Ceraunia saxis,
    quo lateant Syrtes magna minorque sinu.   20
haec alii referant; at vos, quod quisque loquetur,
    credite: credenti nulla procella nocet.
sero respicitur tellus, ubi fune soluto
    currit in inmensum panda carina salum,
navita sollicitus cum ventos horret iniquos   25
    et prope tam letum quam prope cernit aquam.
quod si concussas Triton exasperet undas,
    quam tibi sit toto nullus in ore color!
tum generosa voces fecundae sidera Ledae
    et 'felix' dicas 'quem sua terra tenet!'   30
tutius est fovisse torum, legisse libellos,
    Threiciam digitis increpuisse lyram.
at si vana ferunt volucres mea dicta procellae,
    aequa tamen puppi sit Galatea tuae:
vestrum crimen erit talis iactura puellae,   35
    Nereidesque deae Nereidumque pater.
vade memor nostri vento reditura secundo;
    impleat illa tuos fortior aura sinus.
tum mare in haec magnus proclinet litora Nereus,
    huc venti spirent, huc agat aestus aquas.   40
ipsa roges, Zephyri veniant in lintea soli,
    ipsa tua moveas turgida vela manu.
primus ego aspiciam notam de litore puppim
    et dicam 'nostros advehit illa deos!'
excipiamque umeris et multa sine ordine carpam   45
    oscula; pro reditu victima vota cadet,
inque tori formam molles sternentur harenae
    et cumulus mensae quilibet esse potest.
illic apposito narrabis multa Lyaeo,
    paene sit ut mediis obruta navis aquis,   50
dumque ad me properas, neque iniquae tempora noctis
    nec te praecipites extimuisse Notos.
omnia pro veris credam, sint ficta licebit:
    cur ego non votis blandiar ipse meis?

haec mihi quam primum caelo nitidissimus alto 55
 Lucifer admisso tempora portet equo.

[[1] The pine tree cut on the peak of Mt. Pelion was the first to teach evil ways as the waves of the sea marveled; reckless, between the clashing rocks it carried off the sheep remarkable for its golden fleece. Oh, if only the Argo, overcome in a storm, had drunk the deadly waters, so that no one could disturb the wide seas with an oar! Look—Corinna flees her familiar bed and shared household gods and prepares to travel on treacherous paths. Oh, woe is me!—how I shall fear on your behalf the western breezes and southeast winds and chill Boreas and less-chill Notus! You will not marvel at cities there or at forests; alone [to be seen] is the sky-blue shape of the unfair sea. Nor does the middle of the sea have delicate shells and colorful pebbles: that is the delay of the thirsty shore.

[15] Girls, press on the shores with your marble-white feet (so far it is safe; the rest of the journey is unknown), and let others tell you of the battles of the winds, of the waters that Scylla and those that Charybdis disturb, and with what rocks the fearsome Ceraunian promontories project forth, and in what bay the great and the lesser Syrtes hide. Let others tell of these things; you, meanwhile, believe what each one says— no squall does harm to the credulous. [23] The land is looked back on too late, when once the line is loosened and the curved keel runs on the measureless salt sea, when the troubled sailor shudders at the cruel winds and sees death as close as the water itself. But if Triton should strike and provoke the waves, how completely would the color drain from your face! Then would you call on the well-born stars of fertile Leda and say, "Happy is he whom his own land holds!" It is safer to keep to your bed, to read books of poetry, and to make the Thracian lyre resound with your fingers.

[33] But if the swift squalls carry off my words spoken in vain, may Galatea be kind nevertheless to your ship; the loss of such a girl will be a source of reproach for you, divine Nereids and Nereids' father. Travel mindful of me, and plan to return with a favorable wind; let that later breeze fill your sails more strongly. Then let great Nereus incline the sea to these shores; let the winds blow hither; hither let the wave drive its waters. You yourself could ask the western breezes alone to come into your sails; you yourself could move the sluggish sails with your hands. I shall be the first to discern your familiar ship from the shore and to say,

"That ship is carrying my gods!"; and I shall take you up on my shoulders and snatch many kisses in no order; the victim I have vowed in exchange for your safe return will fall at the altar, and the easily molded sands will be leveled into the shape of a bed, and whatever little mound you please can serve as a table.

[49] When [a cup of] Lyaeus has been set by you there, you will tell of many things: how the ship was almost overcome in the middle of the sea, and that while you were hurrying to me you feared neither the hours of cruel night nor the headstrong south winds. I shall believe everything as true, although it may be contrived: why should I not be deluded by my own desires? Let the morning star shining most brightly high in the heavens give its horse free rein and bring this time to me as quickly as possible.]

A standard way to determine what Ovid is doing in this poem is to look for Ovid's model. Of course, there is an implicit assumption about imitation in this method, that says that the meaning of Ovidian elegy is dependent, perhaps overly so, on its source(s) of inspiration; the consequences of this assumption will become evident in this chapter. One elegiac predecessor is repeatedly invoked by readers of *Am.* 2.11: Propertius 1.8a, in which the poet fears Cynthia's imminent departure and so wishes that bad weather may delay it—and her—indefinitely.[2] If we look at Propertius' propemptikon closely, we see that many of the motifs are similar, in particular the preoccupation with weather (cf. especially Prop. 1.8a.2–20 and Ovid *Am.* 2.11.9–42). And one phrase used by both poets stands out, the half-pentameter *sit Galatea tuae*, at Propertius 1.8a.18 and *Am.* 2.11.34. Each poet uses the phrase at a turning point of sorts, when, after having imagined the horrors that await his beloved, he wishes that the *puella*'s trip, however undesirable it may be, will be safe.

sed quocumque modo de me, periura, mereris,
> **sit Galatea tuae** non aliena viae.

> (Prop. 1.8a.17–18)

[Yet however you behave toward me, oh faithless woman, may Galatea be favorable to your journey.]

---

2. Neumann, "Qua ratione Ovidius," 93–102; Morgan, *Ovid's Art of Imitation,* 75–77, following W. Görler, "Ovids Propemptikon (*Amores* 2.11)," *Hermes* 93 (1965): 338–47.

at si vana ferunt volucres mea dicta procellae,
aequa tamen puppi **sit Galatea tuae.**

(*Am.* 2.11.33–34)

[But if the swift squalls carry off my words spoken in vain, may Galatea
be kind nevertheless to your ship.]

Is this repetition, along with the propemptikon context, sufficient to support an interpretation of Ovid's poem as an imitation of the Propertian
elegy? I shall return to the mention of Galatea shortly to argue that indeed
it is not; but first I want to complicate things a bit, by pointing out a few
other imitative details in the poem. First, I quote the succinct list given by
Diggle: " . . . The poem is modelled on Propertius 1.8. The opening echoes
the opening of Catullus 64 and of Euripides' *Medea* (and Ennius' translation) and possibly the *Argonautica* of Varro of Atax. The ending echoes
the ending of Tibullus 1.3. . . ."[3] Diggle then proceeds to demonstrate the
likelihood of yet another "mark of literary indebtedness," the allusion to
Dido's bridal bed at *Aen.* 4.648–49 (*notumque cubile*), as well as to the
Penates carried by Aeneas (*sociique Penates, Aen.* 3.15), in the odd phras-
ing of *Am.* 2.11.7, *notumque torum sociosque Penates.*[4]

Indeed, once we start looking at *Am.* 2.11 from the broader perspective
opened up by Diggle, we can add still further to his list. Consider, for
example, the appearance at 2.11.10 of the rare word *egelidus,* preceded in
Latin poetry only twice elsewhere; the first instance is in the opening line of
Catullus 46, *iam ver egelidos refert tepores,* and the second is at *Aen.* 8.610.[5]
Diggle has already noted the allusion to Catullus 64, Euripides' and
Ennius' *Medeas,* and Varro's *Argonautica:* we can be more precise and note
that Ovid's opening allusion (*Am.* 2.11.1–6) to the beginning of Catullus
64 incorporates Catullus' allusions to the imprecations against sailing
famous from various prior literary treatments of the voyage of the Argo.[6]
Taking my and Diggle's suggestions together, then, we seem to have just as
much reason to look to both Catullus and Virgil as models for Ovid as we
do to look to Propertius.

---

3. J. Diggle, "Corinna's Bed (*Amores* 2.11.7)," *PCPhS* 209 (1983): 21.

4. Diggle, "Corinna's Bed," 22. The latter phrase appears nowhere else besides the *Aeneid*
and *Amores* passages referred to here.

5. *TLL* 5.2, col. 230.50–84: see Servius, on Virg. *Aen.* 8.610, and C.J. Fordyce, ed., *Catullus* (Oxford, 1961) on Cat. 46.1.

6. See Booth, ad loc., and R.F. Thomas, "Catullus and the Polemics of Poetic Reference
(Poem 64.1–18)," *AJP* 103 (1982): 162–63.

Again, we have a concluding parallel with Tibullus 1.3.89–94, as mentioned by Diggle. In a sort of reverse propemptikon, Tibullus had imagined his reunion with Delia: he hopes to appear suddenly, as if descended from heaven, and concludes with a prayer that dawn will see the fulfillment of his wishes. Ovid too (*Am.* 2.11.43–56) imagines a happy reunion, with Corinna, and concludes with the hope that dawn will come as soon as possible to bring him what he wishes for. How important a model, or influence, should we consider this poem? I would add as well the fact that the Propertian propemptikon itself has important models, as we see from its similarity to Virgil's tenth *Eclogue:* we may well suspect that a Gallan predecessor serves as a hyparchetype for both.[7] In other words, if Ovid is looking to any of these models (as he probably is), it is very likely that he looks to *all* of them; he is not singling one out for particular imitation or parody but rather seeks to embrace an entire tradition in his treatment of the topos.

Finally, I would add to our list of "imitations" a conspicuous reminiscence of the descriptions of the famous storms of *Aen.* 1.81–147 and of its Homeric model, *Od.* 5.291–332: in *Am.* 2.11.9–30, Ovid graphically catalogues the terrors that await a sailor (*navita sollicitus,* 25) caught in a storm at sea; the list includes the conflicting winds (*Zephyros Eurosque . . . / . . . gelidum Borean egelidumque Notum,* 9–10), the dangerous Syrtes (20; cf. *Aen.* 1.111), and even Triton (27; cf. *Aen.* 1.144). Ovid ends the terrifying scene by putting on Corinna's lips an exclamation (*Felix . . . quem sua terra tenet!* 30) that recalls Aeneas' first speech in the *Aeneid* (*O terque quaterque beati, / quis ante ora patrum Troiae sub moenibus altis / contigit oppetere!* . . . , 1.94–96) and Odysseus' earlier outburst (τρίς μάκαρες Δαναοὶ καὶ τετράκις οἳ τότ' ὄλοντο, *Od.* 5.306); while her words may at first seem less despairing than Aeneas' or Odysseus', the double entendre captured by *tenet* confirms Corinna's familiarity with an epic hero's fate. Finally, Ovid reaffirms his dependence on the two epic storms by quoting Homer's description of the struggling winds even more precisely than had Virgil himself: Ovid's opening couplet, *quam tibi, me miserum, Zephyros Eurosque timebo / et gelidum Borean egelidumque Notum!* (9–10), includes in two verses the same catalogue of winds Homer had mentioned at *Od.* 5.295–96, σὺν δ' Εὖρός τε Νότος τ' ἔπεσον, Ζέφυρός τε δυσαής, / καὶ Βορέης αἰθρηγενέτης, μέγα κῦμα κυλίνδων. Virgil, in contrast, lists Homer's first two winds but replaces the second pair with Africus and uses

---

7. See Ross, *Backgrounds to Augustan Poetry,* 85–86.

Homer's last three words describing Boreas to describe not Boreas but the other three winds: *una Eurusque Notusque ruunt creberque procellis / Africus, et vastos volvunt ad litora fluctus* (1.85–86).[8]

Several of Ovid's other references to dangers at sea (Scylla, Charybdis, and Ceraunia, 18–19)[9] evoke in a more general way the risks faced by epic heroes and so reinforce the implied comparison of Corinna to her epic predecessors. In fact, Ovid himself tells his reader that there are epic models for this scene: *et vobis alii ventorum proelia narrent* (17). His use of the *recusatio* here ("This is not really my sort of topic . . .") is meant to remind us that storms at sea are really subject matter fit for epic, not elegiac territory. Yet from the beginning of the poem, with its allusion to the voyage of the Argo and all the literary treatments surrounding that fatal trip, with its reminiscences of other propemptika, Ovid has been incorporating nonelegiac as well as elegiac topoi and subjects into his description of Corinna's threatened trip. Thus, her threat to leave him and so take away his hard-won elegiac subject matter also becomes an opportunity for Ovid to move beyond the boundaries of elegy and look to a wide range of models for his inspiration.

But let us return to his mention of Galatea and its apparent echo of a line in a Propertian propemptikon. In support of her contention that Ovid's elegy is an imitation of Propertius 1.8, Morgan comments, "Such an appeal to Galatea is found in no other Latin propemptikon."[10] It is equally true, however, that reference to Galatea in such a poem would hardly be unusual, given both the marine and amatory associations of her name; furthermore, in Ovid's poem, mention of Galatea is part of a longer passage containing several references to the Nereids and their father (33–40). Galatea is as common a name for a Nereid in, for example, Virgil as it is in Propertius.[11] At the same time, we may well imagine that, in com-

---

8. What Virgil has done here is structurally reminiscent of what Thomas, "Art of Reference," 193–95, calls "conflation," although the choice of Africus in particular to replace Boreas and Zephyrus may serve primarily to foreshadow Aeneas' imminent encounter with Dido in Carthage, rather than to balance a specific reference to Homer with one to a Hellenistic poet: cf. F. della Corte, *La mappa dell' Eneide* (Florence, 1972), 82. On Ovid's combination of Virgilian and Homeric models here, see also Thomas, "Art of Reference," on "window reference": see my discussion in chap. 2.

9. On the interest of the Augustan poets in particular in (Acro-)Ceraunia, see J. O'Hara, "Etymological Wordplay in Apollonius of Rhodes, *Aeneid* 3, and *Georgics* 1," *Phoenix* 44 (1990): 375–76.

10. Morgan, *Ovid's Art of Imitation,* 75 n. 11.

11. The name is applied to a Nereid at Virg. *Ecl.* 7.37, 9.39, and *Aen.* 9.103; cf. also Prop. 3.2.7. Philoxenus of Cythera wrote a dithyramb, entitled either Κύκλωψ or Γαλάτεια, in which Galatea, mistress of Dionysius of Syracuse, is said to have been portrayed as a sea nymph. See

posing *Am.* 2.11, Ovid did look to other propemptika and so was inspired by Propertius, among others, to include a reference to Galatea in his own poem.[12] But under these circumstances, should we really call what results "imitation"?[13] We should also note that *Galatea* is not the easiest of words to fit into this meter; that *sit Galatea tuae* is in and of itself an almost meaningless cluster of three words; and that only the complete pentameter in both poems yields meaning. Three questions, then, arise: How likely is Ovid to borrow, or "imitate," wording of little meaning? Would Ovid expect such a borrowing to be recognized by his readers? And what implications does so brief a borrowing, if it is one, have for an interpretation of the poem?

Conte has recently proposed an answer to the first and second of these questions by his description of what Peter Knox[14] has dubbed "the memorability test."

Before the allusion can have the desired effect on the reader, it must first exert that effect on the poet. The more easily the original can be recognized—the more "quotable" (because memorable) it is—the more intense and immediate its effect will be. The reader's collaboration is indispensable to the poet if the active phase of allusion is to take effect. Thus allusion will occur as a literary act if a sympathetic vibration can be set up between the poet's and the reader's memories when these are directed to a source already stored in both. Reference should be made to a poetic *setting* rather than to individual *lines*. A single word in the new poem will often be enough to condense a whole poetic situation and to revive its mood. . . . On the other hand, a lengthy periphrastic expansion may be needed to sound the resonances contained in a single word or phrase in the original—resonances the new poet wishes to make explicit.[15]

N. Hopkinson, ed., *A Hellenistic Anthology* (Cambridge, 1988), 148–49, and Clausen, *Eclogues,* on *Ecl.* 1.30. Cf. also Call. frr. 378–79 Pf., attributed to a hexameter poem Γαλάτεια on the contents of which Pfeiffer speculates, ad loc. A.S.F. Gow, ed., *Theocritus,* 2d ed. (Cambridge, 1952), 2:118 (introduction to *Id.* 6), reports what is known of a cult of the sea nymph Galatea. Of course, Galatea begins her career as a Nereid in the Nereid catalogues at Hom. *Il.* 18.45 and Hes. *Th.* 250.

12. Hor. *Odes* 3.27, an ironic propemptikon containing the myth of Europa, is addressed to a Galatea: see F. Cairns, *Generic Composition in Greek and Roman Poetry* (Edinburgh, 1972), 191–92. See also K. Quinn, *Latin Explorations* (London, 1963), 248, 270–71.

13. Booth does, on *Am.* 2.11.34: ". . . Ovid names her here in direct imitation of Prop. i. 8A.18."

14. *Per litteras.*

15. Conte, *Rhetoric of Imitation,* 35–36 (italics his).

I shall return presently to consider more fully the nature of imitation and allusion as described by Conte; first, let us apply "the memorability test" to the case at hand. One other important principle should be added to Conte's definition: we need to be able to determine that the alleged borrowing by Ovid reflects a feature of diction or style that is characteristically, even uniquely, Propertian. Aside from Galatea's name itself, however, nothing in these words provides a "link"; and as I have already noted, this name is not exclusive to Propertius and Ovid. Are we looking at a coincidence truly memorable for both the poet and his readers? It seems scarcely reasonable—or useful—to me to give Propertius pride of place among Ovid's models and to call *Am.* 2.11, therefore, an imitation of Propertius on the basis of a shared half-line, particularly when we can see so many other influences playing an active role in Ovid's literary imagination.

An alternative approach to this similarity may well prove more productive: if we insist on the statistical unlikeliness of finding the same three words repeated in the same sequence from one poem of a given type to another of the same type without the intervention of memory, we may well see this echo only as a most casual sort of borrowing, of little or no importance to the interpretation of *Am.* 2.11 as a whole, but reflecting instead Ovid's grounding in and mastery of the Augustan literary tradition.[16] It is a token of Ovid's education and training, much as we may construe any number of other discrete items of data drawn from elsewhere in the same poem. To put it another way, the poetry of the past, particularly that poetry that, beginning with Catullus, displays the neoteric *doctrina* of which Ovid himself is a master, has become an active part of Ovid's poetic vocabulary. It is thus not enough simply to identify words, phrases, and other repetitions and label them evidence of imitation; far greater attention needs to be paid to the contexts in which such "evidence" occurs, and a far greater understanding of the meaning of imitation needs to be developed.

Before we abandon *sit Galatea tuae* entirely, however, one other related point about this phrase is worth making: it is also a convenient metrical

---

16. Of course, one alternative explanation has gone unmentioned, for lack of evidence: a no longer extant common archetype for both Propertius and Ovid. Idle speculation is useless; but such an explanation would change any current view of the relationship between the two poems. Perhaps relevant here is the suggestion by Nisbet and Hubbard, on *Odes* 1.3, that conventional elements in the propemptikon may go back to Cinna or even Callimachus; cf. O'Hara, "Etymological Wordplay," 375–76.

tag. In an article on primarily textual matters, Goold observed Ovid's tendency to compose using what Goold calls "formulae." His remarks are relevant here.

> Just as Homer's versification is characterized by an elaborate art of impromptu composition, so too the fluent versification of Ovid relies upon a similar, even if less easily analyzed, technique: the poet has instinctively evolved a large repertoire of formulaic epithets and tags, together with numerous devices to admit them, which enables him to versify rapidly.[17]

Though they have received little attention from later critics, these comments offer a provocative alternative to what Latinists have recently begun to call "intertextuality."[18] Of particular interest is Goold's sense of the "instinctive" nature of much Ovidian versification; as we shall presently see, this sense broadly but succinctly anticipates what Conte calls "poetic memory." Conte's critical method focuses on the dynamics of poetic language. In his words, "poetic language is reused language"; whether its reuse is conscious or not is of relatively minor importance to Conte and the intertextualists.[19] Rather than calling *Am.* 2.11 an "imitation" of a Propertian propemptikon, then, we—and Ovid—are better served by supposing that such elements as prayer to the Nereid Galatea "belong" to propemptika in the learned style; thus, we have a case not of one poet imitating another in any strict sense but of one poem assuming features that allow it

---

17. G.P. Goold, *"Amatoria Critica,"* *HSCP* 69 (1965): 24; see also B.R. Nagle, "Ovid, 'Facile' or 'Formulaic'? A Metrical Mannerism and Its Implications," *QUCC* 54 (1987): 73–90. See E. Bednara, "De sermone dactylicorum Latinorum quaestiones," *ALL* 14 (1906): 317–60 and 532–604, for a catalogue of devices developed by Latin poets, especially Catullus and Ovid, to adapt the dactylic hexameter to the Latin language. See W. Kroll, "La lingua poetica latina," in *La lingua poetica latina,* ed. A. Lunelli, 2d ed. (Bologna, 1980), esp. 24–56 (= *Studien zum Verständnis der römischen Literatur* [Stuttgart, 1924], 257–74), for a discussion of the development of formulaic poetic language in Latin poetry from Ennius to Ovid in particular.

18. For a clear illustration of its operation and interpretation, see R.O.A.M. Lyne, "Vergil's *Aeneid:* Subversion by Intertextuality, Catullus 66.39–40 and Other Examples," *G&R* 41 (1994): 187–204.

19. Conte, *Rhetoric of Imitation,* 43. Conte's critique of what he describes as Pasquali's "privileging of the moment of *intentionality* in the 'poetic memory'" (26; italics his) is fundamental to his approach. However, even though Conte wishes to deemphasize the role of competitive *aemulatio* in ancient poetry, Conte's audience will find him not in practice entirely dismissive of intentionality; see also Lyne, "Subversion by Intertextuality," 200 (app. 2).

to participate in a literary tradition. In Ovid's case, the formulaic vocabulary is so broad and accomplished that to speak of "imitation" of Propertius is not only simplistic but also misleading. Of course Ovid is using Propertius; of course, too, he does so instinctively. Most important, he does so in a context in which he both takes advantage of the signals of a given genre and transcends them.

By the term *instinctive,* however, I do not mean "unconscious" or "unintentional." I wish to temper Conte's approach, for, unlike him, I believe that the imitative process is fundamentally intentional in Ovid's case. With the example we have just considered, I want simply to suggest that Ovid cares relatively little about the specifics of the Propertian propemptikon; its importance lies in the poetic tradition that its language transmits. Meanwhile, I hope it is beginning to become apparent that intentionality in technique does not always translate into a simple or quantifiable intentionality in meaning and vice versa; Goold's formulaic approach permits us to recognize Ovid's use of his models without necessarily ascribing to that use an excessive amount of significance, except as an index of Ovid's training and tradition.[20] In one sense, the *Amores* are testimony to the "poetic memory" of Ovid, if we think of poetic memory as something that its possessor can activate and exploit. Ovid never simply imitates; rather, he knows how to reuse poetic language to make it his own.

In the course of this brief discussion of *Am.* 2.11, I have attempted to demonstrate that what we call imitation can include a wide variety of literary phenomena and can have an equally wide range of meanings in the process of interpretation. It is time now to establish a working definition of several terms that I have already used. We need to attempt effectively to differentiate between *parallels, formulae,* and truly active *references* to source texts. I have already illustrated that a *parallel* does not necessarily indicate an imitation but can simply be a common topos; a *formula* can be a very precise mark of a poetic tradition, yet virtually devoid of referen-

---

20. I recognize that here I may appear to be indulging in the sort of subjective assessment of authorial intention to which Lyne objects in "Subversion by Intertextuality," esp. 197–98. At least some subjectivity, it seems to me, is inescapable (as his article too demonstrates despite itself); I hope in the remainder of my discussion to demonstrate persuasively the virtue of not assuming that all intertextual relationships are created equal. I also hope to be as explicit as possible regarding what Lyne calls "the Fallacy of Audience Limitation" (197). When I suggest that Ovid's use of poetic language is not meant to evoke strongly a particular context, it is not my intent to let the audience off the hook, as it were, or to suggest that we need not look for a "deeper meaning" in what Ovid writes; rather, my point is to emphasize both the complexity of the creative process and the implications that this complexity has in Ovid's case for our grasp of other poetic effects, like tone and humor.

tiality; and an authentic *reference* may transcend in its complexity a supposed correspondence to a single source and is likely instead to engage in a complex relationship with literary tradition as a whole. Critics are right to assert that Ovid did not write the *Amores* in a vacuum; neither did any other Augustan poet work in isolation. It therefore surpasses literary logic to infer that Propertius is *fons et origo* for all we find in the *Amores* and that Ovid would not quite naturally have looked for inspiration to all the poets who shaped his literary consciousness. Ovid is a poet whose work is imbued with tradition; we therefore must avoid at all costs the temptation to count Propertian imitations as if they were created in isolation and easily quantified as such. If taken to its logical extreme, the generic fallacy, with support from the progressive fallacy, would have us read the *Amores* as little more than a Propertian cento.

The idea I wish to pursue in this chapter is that any single model for understanding Ovid's art of imitation, and, more broadly, of poetic creativity, cannot stand by itself, without nuance or modulation; Ovid is always inviting his reader to wonder just how far he or she should take this similarity, or allusion, or reference, or . . . ? It should also be clear that, even where Ovid cites a model verbatim (and he does so rarely), it is one thing to establish the source or sources of influence, another to understand and interpret the meaning of this influence. Let us turn now to look more carefully at the relationship between imitation and interpretation.

I have already suggested that we read the *Amores* not simply as a flat response to or parody of Propertius but rather as a work that operates on a number of levels, or in several dimensions, at once. For Ovid there are no artificial divisions or invisible lines separating genres, demarcating what he may and what he may not make his own in his poetry.[21] Instead, his work is the intentional and natural outcome of the tradition that engendered it. The *Amores* may well be a beginner's project, as Ovid's narrative of their genesis would suggest;[22] but neither should we dismiss this collection as a beginner's mistake, a juvenile effort that the poet will later try to live down. It is important to remember that from the perspective of his exile Ovid looked back on the *Amores* not with embarrassment, not as a profoundly immature, if polished, work of purely derivative character, not even as

---

21. See Hinds, *Metamorphosis of Persephone;* cf. also my earlier discussion in my introduction. This does not mean, of course, that he does not recognize the differences among genres; of course he does. But as we shall see, if anything, these differences appeal to Ovid precisely because they present him with new possibilities.

22. See chap. 4.

flawed by youthful excess, but, as he indicates at *Tr.* 4.10.53–60, as the basis for his claim to equal standing with Gallus, Tibullus, and Propertius. Recent speculation on the publication history of the *Amores* suggests that Ovid returned to the collection more than once, and over a long period of time, to improve it;[23] it is much to be doubted that he would have done so had he wanted to disown it. I shall make a case in the following pages for reading the *Amores* not as the entombment of elegy but as Ovid's earliest foray beyond the boundaries of genre.

As a consequence of our better understanding of Ovid's use of literary tradition, a linear or point-to-point approach to imitation becomes inadequate; it can only limit us to a "compare-and-contrast," "then-and-now" reading of the *Amores.* Instead, I want to propose a more highly articulated approach that takes into account a wide range of factors. Imitation is not one thing but many different phenomena. It serves a number of purposes and can be recognized in a number of ways. In exploring this variety, we can arrive at a much fuller sense of Ovid's aims, and his accomplishment, in the *Amores.*

Let us look first at how we recognize an imitation. Form and theme are two major components in the process of recognition. I begin with an obvious example: the *Aeneid* has the form of an epic, in meter and in grandness; and it embraces a theme of epic proportion, the struggles of a hero driven by the gods. Thus, it quite inevitably sends us back to Homer, to the prototypes of epic form and theme. Precisely these features, form and theme, make Ovid's connection to Propertius so apparent: the *Amores* take on elegiac form and develop elegiac themes. In other words, they are identifiable as products of a particular genre and can therefore be expected to imitate their antecedents—much as children carry the traits of their parents, individualized but recognizable. Imitation of form and theme is the kind of imitation that we most often and most easily identify, as we have seen with, for example, the propemptikon *Am.* 2.11; and this sort of parallelism, supported as it is by the generic fallacy, leads us to overlook other, more subtle types of imitation, including the *oppositio in imitando* so well known from Callimachus and his heirs.[24] Conversely, when an elegy involves imitation of a form or theme not traditionally associated with elegy, modern critics tend not to discern it, although such imitation can often be the basis for innovation and experimentation on the part of the poet. Indeed, this sort of imitation is crucial to Alexandrian poetics; and

---

23. See my introduction n. 8 and my discussion in chap. 4.
24. See Giangrande, " 'Arte Allusiva.' "

Virgil, for example, provides not one but numerous examples of it in the *Georgics,* a poem that is predominantly Hesiodic in form but that is indebted as well to ethnographers, writers of agricultural tracts, and elegists (including Gallus), among many others, for its content, and perhaps also to the *Aetia* of Callimachus for its overall structure and design in four books.[25]

Virgil again provides us with a helpful starting point, for in recent Virgilian studies a typology of sorts for the differentiation and analysis of types of imitation has begun to be developed. A useful description of this development, beginning with Knauer's virtually exhaustive study of Homeric influence on the *Aeneid,* appears as the first chapter of Farrell's recent book on the *Georgics.*[26] As Farrell shows, the most recent studies of Virgilian imitation have resulted in two dominant strains, represented, on the one hand, by the highly self-conscious, Alexandrian, and referential poetics articulated by Thomas and, on the other, by the intertextual poetics of Conte, who distinguishes between the "Exemplary Model" and the "Code Model" as the bases of stylistic and generic imitation, respectively. The Exemplary Model, "the single word to be precisely imitated," is the one that philological precision is best able to detect and interpret; the Code Model, meanwhile, is the system of generic rules familiar beforehand to both a poet and his or her audience.[27] However at odds with each other the approaches of Thomas and Conte may seem (and the differences are, I would suggest, not insurmountable), they have brought Virgilian studies to a new threshhold that transcends the generic fallacy and allows for, even demands, a multilayered reading of Virgil's poetry.[28]

Imitation of form and theme, including but not restricted to the intentional overstepping of generic bounds, occurs on a grand scale; that is, we associate this type of imitation with entire poems or with substantial portions of a work (i.e., with Conte's Code Model). Such imitation is primarily helpful to a poet in establishing a background or context for the poet's

25. See R.F. Thomas, "Callimachus, the *Victoria Berenices,* and Roman Poetry," *CQ* 33 (1983): 92–101.

26. J. Farrell, *Vergil's Georgics and the Traditions of Ancient Epic: The Art of Allusion in Literary History* (New York, 1991).

27. See Conte, *Rhetoric of Imitation,* 30–31.

28. Farrell, *Vergil's Georgics and the Traditions of Ancient Epic,* 25, the most recent contributor to the discussion, suggests that a comprehensive typology of allusion is not feasible. His survey of instances and types of allusion in the *Georgics* nonetheless offers an elaborate and valuable classification of Virgilian examples: see his index, s.v. "Allusion, type," with seventeen entries.

creativity, and it essentially functions as a type of parallelism. Imitation in content, however—and here I include precise features, such as style, diction, and metrical character—is a much more flexible and subtle technique, adopted by a poet when the poet wishes, as the poet wishes, and to the extent that the poet wishes. This sort of imitation is even more likely than that of form and theme to be playful, or allusive, or learned, or a mixture of all three. As such, it becomes in itself a stylistic device, part of a poem's character and a means of establishing that poem's place in a tradition that challenges generic boundaries. For Alexandrian poets, this latter sort of imitation is as important as the former, since through it each poet in turn can engage in the literary dialogue that constructs the poet's literary identity. Through such imitation, a poet like Callimachus can refer to Homer, Herodotus, Pindar, and Hesiod in quick succession, achieving simultaneously any number of effects: the poet may do so for the sake of paying homage to multiple literary ancestors, engaging in polemic, displaying learning or playfulness, or establishing his or her own credentials. One-upsmanship goes hand in hand with the poet's desire to make an original contribution.[29] Thomas has recently suggested that we call these emulative phenomena not "imitations" but "references," since it is their purpose to "send back" the reader to a source text.[30] His terminological observations should also remind us that the term *reference* implies a more active (and less straightforwardly hierarchical) engagement of one text with another than does the term *imitation,* and may therefore help us to differentiate among various types of imitation, as well as their differing interpretations. For Thomas, a reference is a challenge to both the source text and the reader to involve themselves in the work currently under consideration. The goal is to invite comparison and so to establish a new set of relationships between model and descendant.

But comparison itself is a concept not without its limitations: in comparing two poems, or episodes, or styles, should we emphasize the differences or the similarities? We should emphasize both, of course; but do the similarities and differences exist purely for the sake of comparison? Comparison is at the heart of *aemulatio,* a basic feature of Hellenistic and Alexandrian poetry; but, as Conte shows, not all imitation is *aemulatio,* nor does it exist solely for the purpose of comparison. The polemical function of *aemulatio* in particular is, I believe, far less pronounced in Ovid than in, for example, Catullus or Virgil. Thomas' categories of reference will therefore prove useful in the following pages; but as we shall see in

29. See Giangrande, " 'Arte Allusiva.' "
30. Thomas, "Art of Reference," 172 n. 8.

looking at the *Amores,* not all imitations are referential, at least not in the sense Thomas describes in his study of Virgil. Sometimes, of course, context is uppermost in Ovid's mind and he includes in his poetry a reference that demands our active recollection of a particular source or multiple sources. But just as frequently, as we have already seen, Ovid's imitations are not emphatically referential; that is, they are far more indicative of the poet's means than of his end. In Goold's terms, they are formulaic; in Conte's terms, they are indicative of the poetry's participation in poetic memory. If we insist on seeing these imitations as strongly referential, we give their sources more weight than they can bear in the process of interpretation; meanwhile, we may well be insensitive to the effect of the imitation itself in situ.

I do not intend to imply here that Ovid's imitations are necessarily less meaningful or profound than those we find in Virgil; but it is important to recognize that imitations can serve different purposes in different places. Ross' discussion of the imitativeness of Propertius 1.3 provides valuable guidance here: in that poem, the appearance of Catullan diction and style is not intended to evoke the reminiscence of a particular poem or poems but rather demonstrates, to the delight of Propertius' well-read audience, that here is a new practitioner of the neoteric aesthetic, a poet who has so immersed himself in the work of his predecessor Catullus that he can bring that work to life again in a new guise. Style is everything; content matters little by comparison.[31] This maxim is never more true than it is of Ovid, for whom the work of his predecessors is a constant resource to be exploited to his own ends. In imitating them, Ovid is often motivated primarily by the desire to evoke a literary tradition; close reference to a particular poem, scene, or passage is frequently not indicated.

Conversely, we shall see that some of the most telling imitations in the *Amores* are not based on verbal repetition but represent new readings of landmark texts, Conte's Code Models, in the Alexandrian tradition. Here we enter on a type of criticism that, to those who find evidence in word counts and statistics alone, may seem hopelessly impressionistic; yet I think it is possible, using criteria that are far from entirely subjective, to show that the influence that Virgil, Propertius, and many others had on Ovid is not entirely measurable in terms of diction but can be seen as well in Ovid's reflection on and reinterpretation of distinctively neoteric materials and Augustan themes.

As we proceed, it will be useful to attempt to reconstruct an image of

---

31. See Ross, *Backgrounds to Augustan Poetry,* 54–57.

exactly how Ovid trained himself and honed his poetic skill, immersing himself in the works of the great (and not so great) poets who preceded him. I believe that Ovid also either had a fine memory or made a point of studying the technical features of verse he read—or both. This material would have served as the basis for his poetic memory. Certainly his decision to write erotic elegy is, in Conte's terms, evidence enough of poetry's innately imitative nature. The borrowings and imitations we find in the *Amores* are intended neither to deceive nor to diminish; rather, they represent appropriation in the truest sense of that word. Finally, the wide range of contexts in which Ovid's poetic memory is operative—from the broad allusion to and translation of Catullan literary polemic we saw in the opening of *Am.* 2.11, to the generously comprehensive grasp not only of the conventions of the propemptikon but to all the other conceivable episodes in the literary tradition that might have lent themselves to treatment as propemptika—indicates that the way in which Ovid imitates is not always the same, in style or in significance. Often, Ovid avoids straightforward imitation even as he is profoundly allusive; conversely, many instances of obvious verbal repetition will not bear the burden of overinterpretation. I also want to emphasize here the importance of multiple reference in Ovid, a process that invites generous (but not infinite) flexibility in our reading of Ovidian imitation: since it is always changing, our expectations cannot always remain the same. We can rely only on Ovid's changeability.

I turn now to a consideration of several other examples of so-called imitation in the *Amores*. In each case, I shall look at a relatively brief passage or scene for which the inspiration has generally been identified as Propertius; and in each case, I shall submit the alleged imitation to the "memorability test" and see what happens when we look more broadly for Ovid's models and attempt to evaluate his interest in them. I have tried to choose examples that illustrate the different types of problems we encounter when we talk about imitation; after discussing them, I shall draw some general conclusions and suggest how we might go about creating an alternative way of reading Ovid's *Amores*.

I begin with two examples of presumed "imitation" that involve small and precise details. Though they do so in very different ways, both examples challenge us to think carefully about the process of composing poetry and demonstrate that Ovid's poetic memory gives him a rich vocabulary that both embraces the tradition and sweeps it aside. Consider *Am.* 1.6.51–54:

fallimur: impulsa est animoso ianua vento.
    ei mihi, quam longe spem tulit aura meam!
si satis es raptae, Borea, memor **Orithyiae,**
    huc ades et surdas flamine tunde foris.

[I am deceived: the door was struck by a lively wind. Alas, how far off the breeze has taken my hope! If you are mindful enough, Boreas, of Orithyia whom you stole, be present here and pound the deaf door with your blast.]

The context is a paraclausithyron; Ovid asks Boreas, notorious as the rapist of Orithyia, to help him break down the door that separates him from his beloved. The appearance here of the name *Orithyia* in the context of an allusion to her rape by Boreas leads Morgan to argue that this passage is an Ovidian parody of Propertius' serious tone in an epicedion lamenting the death of the young Paetus (3.7.11–14):[32]

sed tua nunc volucres astant super ossa marinae,
    nunc tibi pro tumulo Carpathium omne mare est.
infelix Aquilo, raptae timor **Orithyiae,**
    quae spolia ex illo tanta fuere tibi?

[But marine birds now stand atop your bones; now the entire Carpathian sea serves as your burial mound. Unlucky North Wind, souce of fear for Orithyia whom you stole, what great spoils did you receive from him?]

It is clear that in both cases the mythological allusion is meant to enhance the lofty tone of the passage and that the pathos of Propertius' apostrophe to Aquilo[33] is in stark contrast to the humorous effect of Ovid's appeal to

---

32. Morgan, *Ovid's Art of Imitation,* 42–43.

33. Propertius' naming of Aquilo follows immediately on his reference to the *Carpathium mare,* the two of which are also linked at Prop. 2.5.11, *non ita Carpathiae variant aquilonibus undae.* M. Rothstein, ed., *Die Elegien de Sextus Propertius* (Berlin, 1920–24; reprint, New York, 1979), vol. 1, comments on Prop. 2.5.11: " . . . die augusteischen Dichter gebrauchen den Namen oft in umfassenderer Bedeutung oder auch, wie hier, typisch, zur Bezeichnung des sturmbewegten Meeres. Es hat seinen Namen von der zwischen Kreta und Rhodus gelegenen kleinen Insel Karpathos, die mit diesen beiden Inseln zusammen das ägäische Meer nach Süden hin abschliesst und schon in den homerischen Hymnus auf Apollo V. 43 das Beiwort ἠνεμόεσσα führt."

Boreas. But does the appearance in both poems of the spondaic hexameter-ending *Orithyiae* justify our seeing one as an imitation—indeed, parody—of the other?[34] *Orithyiae* in the same position also occurs at Propertius 1.20.31 to designate the lineage of Zetes and Calais, Orithyia's children by Boreas (*iam Pandioniae cessit genus Orithyiae*), in a setting ornate with highly mannered diction and considered by Ross to be suggestive of Gallus in both substance and style.[35] Indeed, given its appearance in both Virgil's *laudes Galli* (*Geo.* 4.463) and Propertius' homage to Gallus in 1.20, there may be cause to suspect that this particular spondaic hexameter-ending was brought into Latin by Gallus. Meanwhile, once we learn that mention of Orithyia at hexameter-end appears elsewhere in Latin poetry, the case for specific parody of Propertius 3.7 in particular is no longer so clear; instead, Ovid appears to offer us a broadly witty adaptation, in a suitable context, of a notoriously Alexandrian metrical device, the spondaic hexameter. To specify a single source for Ovid's spondaic hexameter is to interpret narrowly and specifically what is far more likely to be yet another index of Ovid's long steeping in a broad poetic tradition. The spondaic line-end adds a suitably weighty tone to Ovid's prayer for superhuman strength to help him break down his lover's door, and its elegance is in stark contrast with the violence at which he hints through the reference to Boreas. *Orithyiae* alone does not, however, pass "the memorability test": its appearance is formulaic, in Goold's sense—a token again of the poetic memory that provides the underpinning for the *Amores*.[36]

My second example also has a metrical resonance, but unlike the case of *Orithyiae,* it has not, to my knowledge, received much comment.[37] Consider the highly stylized word order of the couplet with which *Am.* 2.10 opens (1–2):

---

34. Curiously, Morgan does not point to the presence of the epithet *raptae* in both lines or to the fact that the north wind is addressed in both; the two points together might have strengthened her argument.

35. Ross, *Backgrounds to Augustan Poetry,* 80. Apollonius uses the name at *Argon.* 1.212, in a passage describing Orithyia's rape and subsequent motherhood. Besides the instances mentioned in the text, *Orithyia* at hexameter-end also occurs in Latin at Virg. *Aen.* 12.83 and Ov. *Met.* 6.683.

36. There is really no place else in the hexameter for the quadrisyllable *Orithyiae* to go—another reason to emphasize its formulaic character.

37. For a general discussion of the poem (and its Propertian affinities, especially to 2.22), see J. Booth and A.C.F. Verity, "Critical Appreciations, IV: Ovid, *Amores* 2.10," *G&R* 25 (1978): 125–40. They note Ovid's "conscious verbal artistry" (128) in the first couplet but do not mention the Gallan pentameter.

Tu mihi, tu certe, memini, Graecine, negabas
uno posse aliquem tempore amare duas.

[You, Graecinus, I recall, you certainly are the one who used to tell me
that no-one could love two girls at one time.]

Until the recent discovery at Qaṣr Ibrîm,[38] only one pentameter verse sur-
vived from all of Gallus' poetry: *uno tellures dividit amne duas* (*FPL* 99
Morel). The line describes the river Hypanis, separating Asia and Europe,
and is as elegant as it is learned: a central verb separates two nouns and
their epithets, distributed so as to create the interlocking effect of a golden
line (*aB verb Ab*) and to emphasize through placement the distinction
between *uno* and *duas*. Ovid's placement of *uno* and *duas* at the beginning
and the end of his pentameter repeats the Gallan design; and although the
patterning of the rest of Ovid's line differs from Gallus', we can see in it the
same careful attention to balance and interlocking design: *a verb B A verb
b*. Ovid has no interest in reminding us of the Hypanis; but, struck by the
elegance of the Gallan verse, he re-creates its most remarkable feature in
an elegant pentameter alleging the impossibility of loving two women at
one time. Ovid does not evoke the model's content or context (as far as we
know), only its style; but in translating into an entirely new setting a stylistic feature made memorable by Gallus, Ovid appropriates the literary tradition in which he is writing. Even his use of the parenthetical *memini* in
line 1 is provocative: it is almost as if Ovid is signaling the fact that the
statement that he here ascribes to his addressee Graecinus is a recollection
of something seen in earlier verse, rather than his own words.[39] I suggest
that in this case we really are dealing with a reference to Gallus and that
this wording passes "the memorability test"; yet there is very little about
the Gallan verse that Ovid wants to evoke other than its elegant design.
What kind of imitation, then, is this? Is Thomas' category of "casual reference," that is, "the use of language which recalls a specific antecedent,
but only in a general sense, where the existence of that antecedent is only
minimally important to the new context,"[40] satisfactory for explaining the

---

38. See Anderson, Parsons, and Nisbet, "Elegiacs by Gallus." See also P.E. Knox, "The
Old Gallus," *Hermes* 113 (1985): 497, on another Ovidian adaptation of Gallus at *Her.* 19.42.

39. On *memini* and the like as footnoting devices, see J.F. Miller, "Ovidian Allusion and
the Vocabulary of Memory," *MD* 30 (1993): 153–64; see also my discussion in chap. 3. The
addressee of the poem, Graecinus, is probably the same as the addressee of *ex Ponto* 1.6, 2.6,
and 4.9; of his identity nothing else is known.

40. Thomas, "Art of Reference," 175.

Gallan word pattern here? And what would such a reference mean?[41] Since we cannot be certain about the context in which the Gallan verse originally appeared, we should refrain from any conclusive assertion regarding the relationship between Ovid and Gallus here; we can only note that, while there is strong reason to believe that we have an Ovidian reference to Gallus, there is virtually no reason to see this reference as particularly meaningful.

Let us turn now to a longer passage. Our reading of *Am.* 2.11 has already shown how important the larger context can be for understanding individual imitations. It has also demonstrated that a reading adhering entirely to generic considerations can give us incomplete results at best. In the following instance, generic interpretation is further vitiated by any attempt to isolate a single source text for Ovid's "imitation."

---

41. We can complicate matters even further if we look at another example with evident similarities to this one. At *Am.* 2.9.17–18, Ovid writes:

> Roma, nisi immensum vires promosset in orbem,
>
> stramineis esset nunc quoque tecta casis.

Ovid beseeches Cupid to leave him alone, since he has already been conquered by love, and he refers to the triumph that can be had by this god over so many other people. Rome, he suggests, would still be a simple rustic place had it not energetically pursued military success; Cupid should get going! The noun-epithet combination *stramineis . . . casis* that encloses the pentameter resembles that of Prop. 2.16.19–20:

> atque utinam Romae nemo esset dives, et ipse
>
> straminea posset dux habitare casa!

Propertius is describing the avarice that sends Cynthia off in pursuit of a lover who, unlike Propertius, can give her many gifts; the poet wishes that it were possible to return to that simple time before wealth was a motive in people's actions. The likelihood that Ovid is borrowing Propertius' language here is good, given both the identical placement of the two words in the line and the probability that *stramineus* is a Propertian coinage. But does this make Ovid's poem a parody of the Propertius elegy? Does his use of Propertian language in a non-Propertian way show Ovid's intent to undermine the serious Augustanism of Propertius' poem? (See Morgan, *Ovid's Art of Imitation,* 30–31). The borrowing of a noun and its epithet is hardly enough on which to build a case for the parody of an entire poem. Until we consider the poem as a whole, there is no way to know whether Ovid's wording is virtually formulaic, reflective of his "poetic memory," or, alternatively, so memorable to his audience as to be part of a large-scale assault on the ethos of the Propertian elegy. Meanwhile, there is substantial evidence to suggest that, in sentiment, Ovid's poem exploits a rich vein of late republican and early Augustan moralizing sentiment about the moral superiority of early Rome as typified by edifices like the *casa Romuli;* see White, *Promised Verse,* 182–90. It seems far more likely that Ovid and Propertius share a common inspiration, contemporary reflection on the good old days. R.M. Ogilvie, *A Commentary on Livy Books 1–5* (Oxford, 1965), on Livy 5.53.8, cites numerous instances in which the *casa Romuli* has the ethical value of Lincoln's log cabin: see, e.g., Virg. *Aen.* 8.654; Cic. *de Rep.* 2.2–4; D.H. 1.79. Cf. also S.B. Platner and T. Ashby, *A Topographical Dictionary of Ancient Rome* (Oxford, 1929), s.v. *Casa Romuli.* In the Livy passage, Camillus mentions the *casa Romuli* in his pious and patriotic speech offering reasons not to abandon Rome.

Ovid begins *Am.* 3.3 with his own variation on a conventional topos, the worthlessness of a lover's oath (1–14):

> Esse deos, i, crede: fidem iurata fefellit,
>   et facies illi quae fuit ante manet.
> quam longos habuit nondum periura capillos,
>   tam longos, postquam numina laesit, habet.
> candida, candorem roseo suffusa rubore,   5
>   ante fuit: niveo lucet in ore rubor.
> pes erat exiguus: pedis est artissima forma.
>   longa decensque fuit: longa decensque manet.
> argutos habuit: radiant ut sidus ocelli,
>   per quos mentita est perfida saepe mihi.   10
> scilicet aeterni falsum iurare puellis
>   di quoque concedunt, formaque numen habet.
> perque suos illam nuper iurasse recordor
>   perque meos oculos: et doluere mei.

[That there are gods—go on, believe: though bound by an oath, she violated my trust, and the appearance that she had before remains hers. After offending the gods, she has hair as long as she did when she had not yet broken her oath. She was shining white before, her complexion suffused with a rosy blush: her blush shines forth still on her snow-white face. Her foot was slight: very slender still is the shape of her foot. She was tall and beautiful: tall and beautiful she remains. She had bright eyes: the eyes with which the treacherous woman often lied to me still shine like a star. Clearly even the immortal gods allow girls to swear falsely, and beauty has divine power. I recall that recently she swore by her eyes and by mine; and mine felt pain.]

This topos appears in poetry as early as Hesiod (fr. 124) and is well known from Plato's mention of the ἀφροδίσιος ὅρκος (*Symp.* 183b). It becomes subject matter for the neoteric Catullus (in, e.g., poems 70, 72, and 76), thanks to the intervention of Callimachus *Epigr.* 25 Pf.:

> Ὤμοσε Καλλίγνωτος Ἰωνίδι μήποτ᾽ ἐκείνης
>   ἕξειν μήτε φίλον κρέσσονα μήτε φίλην.
> ὤμοσεν· ἀλλὰ λέγουσιν ἀληθέα τοὺς ἐν ἔρωτι
>   ὅρκους μὴ δύνειν οὔατ᾽ ἐς ἀθανάτων.

νῦν δ' ὁ μὲν ἀρσενικῷ θέρεται πυρί, τῆς δὲ ταλαίνης   5
νύμφης ὡς Μεγαρέων οὐ λόγος οὐδ' ἀριθμός.

[Callignotus swore to Ionis that he would never have anyone more dear to him, neither boy nor girl. So he swore; but truly they say that oaths sworn in love do not enter the ears of the gods. Now he burns with desire for a boy, but of the poor girl, as of the Megarians, there is neither word nor reckoning.]

It then turns up, with logical frequency, in all the writers of so-called personal love poetry of the Augustan period, from Horace, to Propertius, to Tibullus, to Lygdamus, to Ovid.[42] A parallel passage in Propertius, however, has received the most attention (1.15.33–38):[43]

tam tibi ne viles isti videantur ocelli,
    per quos saepe mihi credita perfidia est!
hos tu iurabas, si quid mentita fuisses,   35
    ut tibi suppositis exciderent manibus:
et contra magnum potes hos attollere Solem,
    nec tremis admissae conscia nequitiae?

[Don't let seem so cheap to you these eyes because of which your treachery was often believed by me! You swore on these that, if you had lied at all, you would put your hands to them and they would fall [from your head]. And are you able to raise them to face great Sol, and do you not tremble, conscious as you are of the wickedness you have committed?]

There are indeed several parallels between this Propertian scene and the second half of the *Amores* passage quoted earlier: the words *per quos* and *saepe mihi* appear in both; the adjective *perfida* echoes the noun *perfidia;* and Propertius' verb *credita est* has its parallel in Ovid's verb *mentita est.* But how distinctive are any of these similarities—that is, how rare are they otherwise? And is the last of these, an apparent syntactical similarity, any-

---

42. For collections of some of the major parallels, see R.G. Bury, ed., *The Symposium of Plato* (Cambridge, 1932); L. Coco, ed., *Callimaco: Epigrammi* (Manduria, Bari, and Rome, 1988), 110–13; Nisbet and Hubbard, 2:122–23 (on *Odes* 2.8); K.F. Smith, ed., *The Elegies of Albius Tibullus* (New York and Cincinnati, 1913), on Tib. 1.4.21–26.

43. See Morgan, *Ovid's Art of Imitation,* 33–34; Berman [Morgan], "Some Propertian Imitations," 171–72.

thing more than coincidental? Although one critic has argued that Ovid's use of *ocellus* rather than *oculus* in line 9, when the latter of these is otherwise more frequent in *Amores* 3, is compelling evidence of Ovid's dependence on the Propertian passage, "the memorability test" presents a serious challenge here, too. Can we really base much, if any, argument on *ocellus* versus *oculus* when the first is the standard and unexceptionable form in elegy and here manages also to carry just the right note of pathos in its context?[44] Finally, and most important of all, are we really to believe that Ovid expected his audience, on the basis of these parallels, to find here a specific reference by Ovid to Propertius 1.15 and so to find special point in the change of tone from the earlier to the later poem? Even if we grant that Ovid's couplets may intentionally echo Propertius', we need not conclude that anything in this "imitation" alone has particularly far-reaching implications for the tone of Ovid's poem. In fact, further consideration of all the evidence suggests that Ovid is far less interested in the ostensible sources for his image than in doing something new with material that is virtually formulaic, in Goold's sense of the term.[45]

Support for this alternative approach comes from another Ovidian

---

44. See Morgan, *Ovid's Art of Imitation*, 34 n. 21; but H. Tränkle, *Die Sprachkunst des Properz und die Tradition der lateinischen Dichtersprache*, Hermes Einzelschrift 15 (Wiesbaden, 1960), 28, calls *ocellus* "ein Kennwort der Liebeselegie"; cf. also P. Watson, "Axelson Revisited: The Selection of Vocabulary in Latin Poetry," *CQ* 35 (1985): 445–47. See also my chap. 6 n. 1.

45. Cf. the situation at *Am.* 1.14.25–26, when Ovid writes: *quam se praebuerant ferro patienter et igni, / ut fieret torto nexilis orbe sinus!* Ovid's use of the expression *ferro et igni* to describe the torment that Corinna's hair had regularly to endure has obviously mock-heroic intent: the expression is more normally used of the means used to sack a city (Barsby, *Am.*, ad loc.; *TLL* 6.1, col. 586.6–12). At 1.1.25–28, Propertius uses a similar image in an important programmatic context, as he describes the hopeless love that drives him to write poetry. If possible, he would like his love to be surgically removed and the wound cauterized (see D.R. Shackleton Bailey, *Propertiana* [Cambridge, 1956], and P. Fedeli, ed., *Sexti Properti Elegiarum Libri IV* [Stuttgart, 1984], ad loc.): *et vos, qui sero lapsum revocatis, amici, / quaerite non sani pectoris auxilia. / fortiter et ferrum saevos patiemur et ignis, / sit modo libertas quae velit ira loqui.* From the apparent similarity of the two passages, Morgan, *Ovid's Art of Imitation*, 42, concludes that Ovid is mocking "the Propertian stance of heroic endurance." In fact, however, the parallelism between the two cannot in this case be explained by an appeal to borrowing or imitation. Rather, both poets use formulaic language, one for serious effect and the other humorously. It seems highly unlikely that the Propertian passage has even a fleeting significance for Ovid. In particular, we may note that the metaphor's medical associations as developed by Propertius are not especially prominent in the Ovidian elegy, where the poet's concern is rather with the means of siege and assault. Cf. Ovid's allusion to *ferrum* and *ignis* at *Am.* 1.6.57–58 (*aut ego iam ferroque igneque paratior ipse, / quem face sustineo, tecta superba petam*) in a context much closer to, but still not imitative of, Prop. 1.1.27–28.

source: *Am.* 2.16. In this poem, Ovid reminds Corinna, and us, that she swore solemnly to stay with him (43–46):

> at mihi te comitem iuraras usque futuram
> per me perque oculos, sidera nostra, tuos:
> verba puellarum, foliis leviora caducis,   45
> irrita, qua visum est, ventus et unda ferunt.

[But you swore that you would be my companion always, by me and by your eyes, my stars; but the words of girls, lighter than falling leaves, wind and wave carry off unfulfilled, just as is their wont.]

A comparison of the two Ovidian passages indicates that they are closely related. The wording *iuraras . . . / per me perque oculos . . . tuos* in 2.16.44 closely parallels *perque suos illam . . . iurasse . . . / perque meos oculos* in 3.3.13–14, and in both poems Corinna's eyes are compared to stars: compare *oculos, sidera nostra, tuos* in 2.16.14 and *radiant ut sidus ocelli* in 3.3.9. But these two Ovidian comparisons do not recall the context of Propertius 1.15. In fact, a far closer parallel is provided by another poem, Propertius 2.3, in which the poet compares Cynthia's eyes to stars: *oculi, geminae, sidera nostra, faces* (14). The comparison of eyes to stars is a striking image, reinforced in Ovid *Am.* 2.16 as in Propertius 2.3 by the unusual effect of so-called neoteric apposition.[46] Meanwhile, we can also see that, in the passage from *Am.* 2.16, there are elements that are not seen in either the *Am.* 3.3 passage or the two Propertian passages but that are elsewhere integral to the *amoris perfidia* topos: the ease with which a lover's promises can be swept away by wind and water recalls not only Catullus 70 (. . . *mulier cupido quod dicit amanti, / in vento et rapida scribere oportet aqua,* 3–4) but also its transformation into the description of Ariadne's abandonment at 64.58–59 (*immemor at iuvenis fugiens pellit vada remis, / irrita ventosae linquens promissa procellae*).[47]

If we return to the opening of *Am.* 3.3 for a final assessment of its relationship to a Propertian model, we can also more clearly see now that Ovid's preoccupation with Corinna's lovely eyes and with the oath she

---

46. On the construction, see O. Skutsch, "Zu Vergils Eklogen," *RhM* 99 (1956): 193–201; cf. H.E. Pillinger, "Some Callimachean Influences on Propertius, Book 4," *HSCP* 73 (1969): 184, and J.B. Solodow, "*Raucae, tua cura, palumbes:* Study of a Poetic Word Order," *HSCP* 90 (1986): 129–53 (esp. 142). Cf. also Ov. *Her.* 19(20).55–56.

47. Cf. also Cat. 30.10, 64.142, 65.17.

swore by them becomes his focal point only at line 9. What is the focus of the four preceding couplets? In fact, the mention of Corinna's eyes comes as the culmination of a catalogue, as Ovid lists ironically the many ways in which her beauty (*facies,* 2) has remained unchanged despite her treachery: she has not lost her hair (3–4), her pink-and-white complexion still glows (5–6), and she has not suddenly developed elephantiasis of the foot (7–8). The conceit that the body part by which one takes an oath will feel the consequences of the oath's betrayal is vividly evoked by Horace, whose treacherous Barine not only is not harmed by her perjury but seems to become more beautiful on account of it (*Odes* 2.8.1–8):

> Ulla si iuris tibi peierati
> poena, Barine, nocuisset umquam,
> dente si nigro fieres vel uno
> > turpior ungui,
>
> crederem: sed tu simul obligasti   5
> perfidum votis caput, enitescis
> pulchrior multo, iuvenumque prodis
> > publica cura.

[If any penalty for a perjured oath had ever harmed you, Barine, if you were to become uglier by so much as a blackened tooth or a single fingernail, I would believe you. But as soon as you bind your lying head with oaths, you begin to shine forth more beautiful by far, and you turn out to be the beloved of all our youth.]

We have by now moved far from an interpretation of *Am.* 3.3.1–14 (previously cited) as a direct imitation of and response to Propertius 1.15. Instead, we now see Ovid's synthesis of several themes—the physical consequences of *perfidia,* swearing by the eyes, and the eyes as stars—articulated in diction that recalls not only several scenes in Propertius but also the opening of a Horatian ode (it is no coincidence that Ovid echoes the vividness of Horace's opening by giving his elegy the same starting point), a pithy anaphora introduced by Callimachus and adapted by Catullus, and even a prior episode in the *Amores.* All are models, at least superficially; that is, all are encoded in the poetic memory tapped by Ovid. Yet none of them does what Ovid does with the material—he links all of the thematic threads together in the imagery he uses to describe Corinna's *perfidia* and then proceeds to make this imagery central to the poem as a whole. Corinna has sworn, we learn in line 12, not only by her eyes but also by those of her lover; and apparently what he has seen has revealed her treachery.

Ovid then proceeds to question the point of oath taking, blasphemously implying that perhaps the real problem is that the gods do not exist at all: *Aut sine re nomen deus est frustraque timetur* / *et stulta populos credulitate movet* (23–24). Alternatively, if they do in fact exist, the problem is rather that the gods themselves are easily controlled by *puellae: aut, si quis deus est, teneras amat ille puellas—* / *nimirum solas omnia posse iubet* (25–26). In fact, Ovid begins ironically to think that if he were a god he would probably do the same! He would even perjure himself to swear that the oaths of deceitful *puellae* were reliable (43–46).

In the midst of this sophistry, the motif of causing pain to another's eyes appears again twice: Ovid arrives at the idea of thinking of himself as a god when he realizes that, just like him, the gods have eyes too; their possession of this attribute is the reason they are so vulnerable to feminine wiles (*di quoque habent oculos, di quoque pectus habent,* 42). Having thus come to realize the ineluctability of pain through betrayal, Ovid resigns himself to his fate; he asks only that his *puella* refrain in the future from causing pain to his eyes (*tu tamen illorum* [i. e., *divorum*] *moderatius utere dono,* / *aut oculis certe parce, puella, meis,* 47–48).

Ovid has taken a commonplace theme, then, and has given it new life, first of all by giving it the novel twist that becomes the hinge for an entire poem. The effect is so clever that we almost forget one important thing: we never even learn in this poem what Ovid has seen. His emphasis on eyes and sight is in brilliant counterpoint to the fact that, through it all, we are left in the dark. Ovid demonstrates here the ability to take the momentary and make it the occasion for an entire elegy, something we shall see him do again.[48] It is evident now that this poem is not an "imitation" of Propertius: rather, many different influences, from Callimachus to Catullus, Propertius, and Horace, have played a role in shaping Ovid's literary imagination. Ovid uses the poetry of the past *without* imitating it thanks primarily to his reliance on poetic memory. He has read widely—as, he presumes, have his readers. His professional's eye for the clever—and useful—turn of phrase and his almost preternatural talent at versification separate him from his audience even as he uses the language of poetry to engage that audience in a widening of the horizons of elegy.

---

48. See especially my discussion later, in chap. 3, on similes.

In the course of this discussion, we also have seen one other important phenomenon, Ovid's predilection for clever self-reference or self-imitation, which deserves special comment here but will also be a topic worthy of continuing notice in this book. Ovid's inclination toward internal reference has been long recognized, and its implications have recently come to be valued elsewhere in his poetry, especially in the *Metamorphoses;*[49] but it is important here to observe Ovid's use of self-reference in his earliest work, since it demonstrates yet another way in which the *Amores* are anything but an aberration in Ovid's career. It will be useful as well to observe here that self-imitation really indicates two different, though related, phenomena: (1) "internal reference" proper, that is, reference, as in *Am.* 3.3, to a scene in an earlier poem in the same collection, 2.16 (by using the word *earlier* here, I mean to indicate both that 2.16 comes first in the narrative of the *Amores*[50] and that it comes first in the experience of reading); and (2) self-imitation, that is, reference across works, from, for example, the *Metamorphoses* to something memorable in another, earlier poem or collection, for example, the *Amores.* A straightforward instance that incorporates both kinds of self-reference is Ovid's reuse of the eyes-as-stars simile from *Am.* 2.16.44 and 3.3.9 twice in the *Metamorphoses,* at 1.498–99 and 3.420;[51] in the concluding chapter of this book, I shall examine several examples of self-imitation on a grander scale. Meanwhile, the instance we have just looked at offers us two operating premises that will be helpful in the consideration of other examples: (1) self-reference in Ovid tends not to involve precise quotation or exact repetition of all details but rather plays on the balance between repetition and variation; and (2) self-reference in Ovid tends to be combined with other, "external" allusions—that is, allusions to poets other than Ovid himself—the end result being multiple and layered reference. As a result of this second tendency in particular, Ovid can complicate allusion by collapsing many models into his own invention. Any attempt, then, to locate in a particular Propertian poem or passage the predominant model for a single elegy by Ovid is unlikely to lead to satisfactory results; indeed, it is unlikely that any single poet or poem will furnish Ovid with all the inspiration he needs for any one poem. We shall see repeatedly in the corpus of the *Amores*—filled as it is with many such inter-

---

49. It is the premise of, e.g., Hinds' book *Metamorphosis of Persephone;* see my further discussion later, in chap. 6.

50. See my discussion later, in chap. 4, on the *Amores* as narrative.

51. The former occurs in the quintessentially "elegiac" narrative of Daphne and Apollo (see Knox, *Ovid's Metamorphoses,* 14–18), and the latter instance includes an example of neoteric apposition; see Bömer, *Met.,* ad locc.

nal references that in turn look back to Propertius and many other models, often simultaneously—that Ovid not only imitates but also invigorates and expands the vocabulary and the vision of elegiac poetry precisely by avoiding imitation of a simple sort. Ovid is not intent on rewriting the past; his references to the poetic tradition that has preceded him show that, having mastered it, he is intent on transforming it to serve his own poetic vision and aims.

Kenney has described the *Amores* as a "tour de force," a "feat of literary originality" in which Ovid imparted "to a well-established form with the inherent limitations of love elegy [a] new semblance of vitality."[52] In the following chapters, I shall examine features of the collection that have been overlooked or poorly understood, features that remove the *Amores* from isolation and point us to a new understanding of the collection as vital participant in an uninterrupted tradition of poetic experimentation and innovation. Both Ovid's brilliant comprehension of the interrelationship between style and genre and the skill he demonstrates to everyone's satisfaction later in his career—that is, the ability to exploit and transform the very poetic memory that empowers him—will be seen to have their origins in the *Amores*.

---

52. Kenney, "Ovid," in *The Cambridge History of Classical Literature,* vol. 2, *Latin Literature,* ed. E.J. Kenney and W.V. Clausen (Cambridge, 1982), 420–21.

Chapter 2

Literary Means and Ends:
Ovid's *Ludus Poeticus*

scribens versiculos uterque nostrum
ludebat numero modo hoc modo illoc,
reddens mutua per iocum atque vinum.
Catullus 50.4–6

The *Amores* is a poetry collection both more and less than traditional, if by
reference to "tradition" we mean the genre of elegy. Poetic memory, while
alert to generic convention, is not limited by it; and the formulaic style
invites transformations of poetic language without being dominated by its
models. In the present chapter, therefore, I want to consider in greater
detail both the breadth of Ovid's embrace of the tradition he has inherited
and the means by which he places his own signature on the reused language
of Latin poetry. The evidence for Ovid's formulaic style is ubiquitous and
tells us much about his reading habits. In some cases, furthermore, he does
indeed "refer" us, in Thomas' sense of the word, to the work of his predecessors; and in others, we shall see Conte's concept of "poetic memory" at
work, offering as it does a model of interpretation that engages Ovid's
poetry in a dialogue about literary tradition.[1]

But can we tell precisely when we are dealing with reference as opposed
to poetic memory or when the activation of poetic memory amounts to
anything more than a parallel? The answer to these questions is, I think,
sometimes yes and sometimes no, both tantalizing and frustrating. At least
to some extent, the boundaries we establish between these phenomena are
artificial; the poems I shall look at in this chapter demonstrate that, at least
for Ovid, they can be and are used together, as parts in a seamless whole.

---

1. See my discussions earlier, in chap. 1, of Thomas' typology of reference and Conte's
"poetic memory."

Any attempt to answer these questions is further complicated by an issue that stems from Ovid's distinctive approach to his models: the meaning of his uses of tradition. Particular difficulty arises when Ovid uses language or images that are highly charged in tone in their original context but are freed from their social or ethical particularity when reused by Ovid. This difference can make Ovid's reuse of such materials seem facile, even parodic; but I propose that we see it instead as his attempt to revitalize and renew Augustan poetry by substituting for its particularities and moral and political urgency a focus on his personal relationship to a literary tradition. By looking at several scenes and entire poems in the *Amores,* I believe it will be possible at least to begin to clarify both the ways in which Ovid views the literary past and the meaning, or lack thereof, that Ovid's sources have for his use of them. I have chosen the following examples because they help us to move beyond equating Ovid's inspiration and purpose with Propertius and parody, respectively; but I want also to make it clear that the sum of Ovid's elegies is greater than their imitative or formulaic parts. In the *Amores,* Ovid pushes elegy to broaden its sights without betraying its fundamentally Hellenistic origins; and at least in their support of this purpose the *Amores* are themselves to be adjudged models for the elegiac interests that will subsequently consume so much of Ovid's literary career.

A further goal of this chapter is to begin to make sense of Ovid's relationship to and use of Virgil in the *Amores.* It has been usual to assert—and I shall hardly disagree—that in the *Metamorphoses* Ovid looks constantly back to his greatest model, Virgil, and that even in revising Virgil's worldview, "Ovid hat Vergil immer vor Augen."[2] Bömer's exhaustive commentaries on both the *Fasti* and the *Metamorphoses* are filled with Virgilian precedents; and he has also written more generally on the profound influence of Virgil on the next generation of poets, not just in matters of language and style but in subject matter, approach, and even attitude.[3] Both in theory and in practice, however, the omnipresence of Virgil has been, if not utterly ignored, reduced to a source for one of two extremes, either crude parody or incidental effect, by those who focus on the *Amores.*

---

2. F. Bömer, "Der Kampf der Stiere: Interpretationen zu einem poetischen Gleichnis bei Ovid (am. II 12,25f. met. IX 46ff.) und zur Frage der 'Erlebnisdichtung' der augusteischen Zeit," *Gymnasium* 81 (1974): 511; Bömer, *Met.,* on 2.277, 3.305, 4.128, 7.812. Cf. Bömer, "Ovid und die Sprache Vergils," *Gymnasium* 66 (1959): 285 (= *Ovid,* ed. M. von Albrecht and E. Zinn, Wege der Forschung 92 [Darmstadt, 1968], 198): "Vergil ist auch dem Ovid allgegenwärtig." Cf. also R. Lamacchia, "Ovidio interprete di Virgilio," *Maia* 12 (1960): 310–30.

3. See Bömer, "Ovid und die Sprache Vergils."

Witness the critical perspective of S. Döpp, who, in a monograph on Virgil's influence on Ovid, comments, "Zwischen den Werken Virgils und den kecken 'Amores' Ovids kann es nur wenige Berührungen geben."[4] He then proceeds to catalogue the few Virgilian elements he does detect in the *Amores:* most are limited to two or three words borrowed from Virgil and to references to characters in Virgil's poetry;[5] and I would characterize virtually all of them as formulaic. Thus, while they show us, unsurprisingly, that Ovid knew the Virgilian poems well, they tell us little about Ovid himself or about the *Amores.*

In fact, Döpp locates only one real reference to Virgil in the *Amores,* at 3.13.31–34 on Juno's Faliscan festival:

Argiva est pompae facies: Agamemnone caeso
　et scelus et patrias fugit Halaesus opes
iamque pererratis profugus terraque fretoque
　moenia felici condidit alta manu.

[The appearance of the procession is Argive: when Agamemnon was killed, Halaesus fled both the crime and his patrimony, and after having wandered over land and sea in exile, with auspicious hand he founded lofty city walls.]

Döpp notes that, in reporting the Argive origins of the cult, Ovid describes Halaesus' wanderings in language clearly intended to recall the description of Aeneas' wanderings at the opening of the *Aeneid (Italiam fato profugus Laviniaque venit / litora, multum ille et terris iactatus et alto / . . . / multa quoque et bello passus, dum conderet urbem,* 1.2–5).[6] Döpp also thinks that Ovid's notice of Halaesus' flight after the death of Agamemnon is an allusion to *Aen.* 7.723–24, *hinc Agamemnonius, Troiani nominis hostis, / curru iungit Halaesus equos.* But what sort of imitation is this? What does it

---

4. S. Döpp, *Virgilischer Einfluss im Werk Ovids* (Munich, 1969), 13; see also the superficial treatment by A. Salvatore, "Virgilio e Ovidio elegiaco," in *Virgilio e gli Augustei,* ed. M. Gigante (Naples, 1990), esp. 182–88. Bömer, "Ovid und die Sprache Vergils," shows a more thoughtful grasp of the subject and is less constrained by generic limitations; but even he is prone to the progressive fallacy and so looks at the *Amores* only as occasional harbingers of things to come.

5. E.g., *pulcher Iule* at *Am.* 3.9.14; cf. *Aen.* 5.570, 7.107, 9.293 and 310; see Döpp, *Vergilischer Einfluss,* 15.

6. Döpp, *Vergilischer Einfluss,* 15–16. See also Du Quesnay, "The *Amores,*" 28; Miller, *Ovid's Elegiac Festivals,* 55–56. Cf. L. Cahoon, "Juno's Chaste Festival and Ovid's Wanton Loves: *Amores* 3.13," *CA* 2 (1983): 6–7.

mean? Does it pass "the memorability test"? And how important is the model to the new context? Only through an attempt to answer these questions can we begin to see both how and why Ovid is using Virgil here.

Ovid's vivid evocation of the opening lines of the *Aeneid* would seem in and of itself enough to allow these lines to pass "the memorability test." Yet Ovid does something entirely un-Virgilian with the material: by using Virgilian language in an unfamiliar context (*profugus; et terris iactatus et alto; conderet urbem, Aen.* 1.3–5 ≈ *pererratis profugus terraque fretoque; moenia . . . condidit alta, Am.* 3.13.33–34), by replacing the Trojan Aeneas as subject with his natural enemy, a Greek, Halaesus, and by suppressing Virgil's identification of Halaesus as *Troiani nominis hostis* (*Aen.* 7.723), Ovid performs the sort of "correction" so dear to Alexandrian poets. Moreover, by embedding this reference into a poem on the worship of Juno, Ovid recalls the important and hostile role played by Juno in the earlier poem, as the implacable enemy of another exiled wanderer. This reference gives the conclusion of the elegy an ironic piety, as Ovid prays that Juno may remain always friendly: *sint mihi, sint populo semper amica suo* (36). We may wish to see in this an example of Thomas' category of "apparent reference," more generally identified as *oppositio in imitando.*[7]

Döpp makes very little of this imitation, because he expects to find little meaning or purpose in it; indeed, he is inclined to write it off as nothing more than Ovid's glib and meaningless appropriation of Virgilian diction, typical of the formulaic character of Ovidian composition I have already described. Thus, it is crucial that we recognize the importance of context here. Even as Ovid invokes Juno's continuing benevolence toward her elegiac worshipers, he recalls her unceasing hatred for the epic hero. Much as we saw in our discussion of *Am.* 2.11 in the previous chapter, then, Ovid uses the difference between elegy and epic as a means to include epic in the elegiac repertoire. This is no *recusatio;* the generic paradox iself becomes a part of Ovid's narrative. Notice also how, in this brief but precise reference to Virgil, Ovid repeatedly subverts and depoliticizes his model, as he transforms the stuff of Roman national epic into a parenthetical and obscuran-

---

7. Thomas, "Art of Reference," 172, 185; cf. Giangrande, " 'Arte Allusiva,' " 85–97. I suspect that we would have greater appreciation of Ovid's use of Virgil in this poem if we were in possession of the *Origines,* in which Cato apparently reported the Argive origins of the Falisci; Cato may well have provided also the basic details of the ritual described by Ovid in *Am.* 3.13. See Pliny *NH* 3.51; the description of the ritual at D.H. 1.21 may be based on Cato as well. On the connection between Cato and Virgil, see also N.M. Horsfall, *EV* 3: 495, s.v. *Messapo,* on Virgil's treatment of the stories of Messapus and Halaesus. Ovid probably wished to indicate his indebtedness both to Virgil and to Virgil's antiquarian source(s).

tist allusion suited to aetiological elegy. We shall see repeatedly Ovid's ability to both evoke a model and make something new out of its most basic paradigm: it is no coincidence that here Ovid alludes to the very opening of the *Aeneid,* for he can count on the likelihood that his readers will remember this scene and its implications vividly.[8] At the same time, he embeds this reference in a larger, non-Virgilian whole; Virgil is thus a starting point rather than a goal.

I shall return at the close of this chapter to consider more fully the nature of Ovid's poetic relationship to Virgil; but it will be helpful first to work through several extended examples of Ovid's use of the traditions of Latin poetry, in the course of which his continuing interest in Virgilian poetics and Virgilian imagery will become apparent. I turn now to a reading of two poems, each of which helps greatly toward an understanding of not only the techniques but also the aims that characterize the *Amores.* Strictly speaking, neither elegy is an imitation, at least not in the most precise and limited sense of that word; yet each typifies Ovid's distinctive combination of formulaic composition, poetic memory, and reference. In an exemplary fashion, the two poems embody the breadth of Ovid's engagement with a living literary tradition and invite us to look at the *Amores* generally in a new light. The two poems I have chosen have received little extended critical discussion, because the association of each with a Propertian model is tenuous and so neither can easily be read as parody. Taken together, however, both illustrate how wide-ranging in theme and style the *Amores,* and Ovid, can be.

On occasion, Ovid wears his reading on his sleeve; often, however, his indebtedness to his tradition reveals itself to be both more subtle and more profound than we might at first expect. A case in point is *Am.* 2.16, a poem generally read as a combination of autobiography (because of the extensive description of Sulmo) and conventional exploration of a common elegiac theme, the consequences of separation from one's beloved. In fact, aside from several studies of the play here on the two word-pairs *ignis/ardor* and *abest/adest* in 11–12, this poem has generally escaped consideration as an imaginative creation.[9] A closer examination both of

---

8. On the signature quality of poetic openings, see Conte, *Rhetoric of Imitation,* 76–87.

9. A notable exception is the sensitive and valuable discussion by V. Pöschl, "Ovid und Horaz," *RCCM* 1 (1959): 15–25. Although my discussion of *Am.* 2.16 is quite different from his, I am indebted to his emphasis on landscape. On the "epigram," see, e.g., L. Alfonsi, "Amores II,16,11–12," *Latomus* 18 (1959): 800–802. Cf. also F.W. Lenz, "Io ed il paese di Sulmona (Amores ii,16)," in *Atti del convegno internazionale ovidiano* (Rome, 1959), 2:59–68;

specific details in Ovid's landscape and of the way in which this landscape reflects the broader themes of the elegy, however, indicates that Ovid is concerned far less with geographical or topographical accuracy than with locating his Sulmo among the literary landscapes of Augustan poetry. Sulmo's landscape is not just reported but created by Ovid, and the implications of this creation concern us here. It will be useful to begin our discussion by reviewing some details of the poem.

In the first ten lines Ovid provides a bit of apparent autobiography in describing his home, Sulmo, in the territory of the Paeligni (1–10):

> Pars me Sulmo tenet Paeligni tertia ruris,
>   parva, sed irriguis ora salubris aquis.
> sol licet admoto tellurem sidere findat
>   et micet Icarii stella proterva canis,
> arva pererrantur Paeligna liquentibus undis,   5
>   et viret in tenero fertilis herba solo.
> terra ferax Cereris multoque feracior uvis,
>   dat quoque baciferam Pallada rarus ager,
> perque resurgentes rivis labentibus herbas
>   gramineus madidam caespes obumbrat humum.   10

[Sulmo, a third part of the Paelignian countryside, holds me—a small place, but with the waters irrigating it, it is a healthful territory. When its star moves near, the sun may split the earth, and the oppressive star of the Icarian dog may flash: but watery waves wander through the Paelignian fields, and the green grass flourishes in the tender soil. The land is productive of Ceres and even more fruitful in grapes; an occasional field also gives olive-bearing Pallas. And throughout the meadows shooting up from flowing streams, the grassy turf shades the moist soil.]

It is a fertile spot, thriving even in the hottest summer sun; cool streams edged by shade keep the climate in balance. One thing is missing, however: the woman Ovid loves. In her absence, he still burns with the fire of love (*at meus ignis abest—verbo peccavimus uno: / quae movet ardores, est procul;*

---

idem, "Noch einmal 'Io ed il paese di Sulmona,' " *RCCM* 4 (1962): 150–53 (almost entirely concerned with numerical symmetry and proportion in 2.16); B.E. Stirrup, "Structure and Separation: A Comparative Analysis of Ovid, Amores II.11 and II.16," *Eranos* 74 (1976): 32–52.

ardor adest, 11–12), and he goes so far as to reject immortality if it means being separated from her (13–14). Ovid proceeds to curse those who invented and first cut roads, since roads are responsible for the separation of lovers; he then modifies the curse by wishing that, for as long as roads must exist, there be a rule that *puellae* be accompanied on their travels by the young men who love them (15–18). Were this the current state of affairs, Ovid would gladly go anywhere in the world with his *domina;* he would risk the harshest climates and sea monsters and would be on hand to save his *puella* should a shipwreck occur (19–32). Without her, however, even his lovely Sulmo is not to be endured; he might as well be at the ends of the earth, among savages (33–40):

> at sine te, quamvis operosi vitibus agri
> > me teneant, quamvis amnibus arva natent
> et vocet in rivos currentem rusticus undam,   35
> > frigidaque arboreas mulceat aura comas,
> non ego Paelignos videor celebrare salubres,
> > non ego natalem, rura paterna, locum,
> sed Scythiam Cilicasque feros viridesque Britannos
> > quaeque Prometheo saxa cruore rubent.   40

[But without you—although the fields busy with vines may keep me, although the plowland may swim with streams, and a countryman may call the running water into channels, and a cool breeze may stroke the tresses of the trees—I seem to frequent not the healthful Paelignian territory, not my birthplace and paternal farm, but rather [the lands of] Scythia and the fierce Cilices and the green Britanni and the rocks that are reddened with Prometheus' blood.]

It is only natural that they be together; so why are they apart? Because she has not kept her faith with him (41–46). He closes with the wish that she may race home as quickly as possible and that the landscape will conspire with him to speed her on her course (47–52).

The general scenario is familiar in elegy; we might compare, for example, Tibullus 1.3, in which the poet fantasizes a death far from home and without Delia. He wants nothing more than to be at home and laments the passing of the Saturnian age, when roads did not yet exist. Even closer are several elegies in the Monobiblos: the propemptikon 1.8a, in which Propertius begs Cynthia not to sail off with another lover; and the pair 1.17 and

18, in which Propertius finds himself in two harsh landscapes, a storm at sea and a deserted forest, separated from Cynthia.[10] A number of features nonetheless make Ovid's elegy stand out in this group and suggest that several other components in the literary tradition are equally important, if not more so, to Ovid in the composition of 2.16. Two factors attract particular attention: the care and precision expended by Ovid in detailing the landscape of his beloved Sulmo; and the corresponding thematic importance of the relationship between love and landscape. Earlier I used the word *balance* in characterizing Ovid's description of the Paelignian landscape; as we shall see, the interplay of love and landscape here corresponds to the balance—and imbalance—between physical and emotional states described in this poem. It is my intention to demonstrate here that the relationship between climactic and emotional balance in *Am.* 2.16 is indebted as much to Gallus, Virgil, and Horace as to Propertius and Tibullus. This poem may best be read as a creation resulting from Ovid's careful reminiscence of several Augustan models in the area of literary landscape, rather than simply as Ovid's "version" of a particular type of elegy. As Booth comments in her discussion of this poem, "The rich fabric of familiar themes, inverted, varied and interwoven is something new."[11]

Landscape has long been recognized as a theme of great interest to the Augustan poets. Only recently, however, have two scholars focused our attention on the significant differences between various landscapes in the poetry of Virgil and Horace: Richard Thomas has traced the application of ancient ethnographical theory in Latin poetry, and David Ross has demonstrated how the conventions of ethnographical literature are exploited as metaphors in the *Georgics.*[12] While both Ross and Thomas focus on the literary aspects of the landscapes envisioned by the Augustan poets, their readings are also informed by the fundamental presupposition that poetic landscapes can offer alternatives to or reflect the harsh realities of contemporary Realpolitik; thus, they are metaphors not just for alter-

---

10. See Booth, 78–81 and ad loc.; cf. Ross' discussion of 1.18 in *Backgrounds to Augustan Poetry,* 71–74, and cf. E.W. Leach, "Propertius 1.17: The Experimental Voyage," *YCS* 19 (1966): 209–32. Morgan, *Ovid's Art of Imitation,* detects no similarities between these poems and Ovid's and makes no mention of them. Davis, "*Risit Amor,*" reads *Am.* 2.16 as a burlesque, i.e., a comic reworking and trivialization, of Prop. 1.17.

11. Booth, 78–79 (unfortunately, however, Booth nonetheless subscribes to the traditional idea of a "relationship" between Propertius and Ovid in this poem).

12. R.F. Thomas, *Lands and Peoples in Roman Poetry: The Ethnographical Tradition,* Cambridge Philological Society Suppl. 7 (Cambridge, 1982); D.O. Ross, *Virgil's Elements: Physics and Poetry in the Georgics* (Princeton, 1987).

native genres but also for the consequences of moral and social upheaval as
manifested in the lives of individuals. We shall see in Ovid's treatment of
landscape that the latter of these metaphorical functions is of only incidental concern to the *poeta;* rather, his focus is on the literary character of
Sulmo and on its role in defining both his poetry and himself as poet.

Thomas begins his discussion of the Augustan uses of ethnography
with consideration of a poem-opening remarkably similar to the beginning
of *Am.* 2.16, that is, Horace *Epist.* 1.16.1–16:[13]

> Ne perconteris, fundus meus, optime Quincti,
> arvo pascat erum an bacis opulentet olivae,
> pomisne an pratis an amicta vitibus ulmo,
> scribetur tibi forma loquaciter et situs agri.
> Continui montes, ni dissocientur opaca   5
> valle, sed ut veniens dextrum latus adspiciat Sol,
> laevum discedens curru fugiente vaporet.
> temperiem laudes. quid si rubicunda benigni
> corna vepres et pruna ferant, si quercus et ilex
> multa fruge pecus, multa dominum iuvet umbra?   10
> dicas adductum propius frondere Tarentum.
> fons etiam rivo dare nomen idoneus, ut nec
> frigidior Thracam nec purior ambiat Hebrus,
> infirmo capiti fluit utilis, utilis alvo.
> hae latebrae dulces et, iam si credis, amoenae   15
> incolumem tibi me praestant Septembribus horis.

[Lest you inquire, my dear Quinctius, whether my farm feeds its master
from the plowed field or enriches him with berries of olive, or with fruits
or meadows or the elm embraced by vines, I shall write you at length a
description of the nature and location of the farmland. The ridge of
mountains is continuous, were they not interrupted by a shady valley,
but so that the sun as it rises looks toward the right flank of the ridge
and heats the left when it departs in its fleeing chariot. You would praise
its moderate climate. What if the fruitful bramble bushes were to bear
ruddy cornel cherries and plums, if the Italian oak and the holm oak
were to sustain a herd with their abundant fruit, if an abundance of

---

13. Here I follow the Latin text preferred by R. Mayer, ed., *Horace: Epistles I* (Cambridge,
1994); Mayer describes his text as "founded upon the Oxford edition of Wickham-Garrod
and the Teubner edition of D.R. Shackleton Bailey" (52).

shade were to delight its owner? You would say that Tarentum has been brought near and is in leaf. A spring that deserves to give its name even to a river flows here, [its water] useful for light-headedness and the digestion; the Hebrus winding through Thrace is neither colder nor purer. This sweet and, if you believe me by now, pleasant retreat offers me to you safe and sound in the season of September.]

Horace here employs traditional ethnographical categories[14] to describe his home, the Sabine farm, and so provides a model for Ovid's opening. He focuses on three features: the physical geography of the area (5–8); the climate (*temperies,* 8; 15–16); and the farm's agricultural produce (8–10). Furthermore, although the inhabitants of the place are not mentioned specifically, the effect this environment has on them is implied (*utilis,* 14); Horace thus manages to allude to yet another ethnographical category, the character of the inhabitants, in his opening. The whole effect of the passage is to suggest that this setting is ideal: as Thomas comments, "the farm's balanced climate, the unusual productivity, and the coolness and clarity of its health-giving spring are all to be seen as ethnographical *thaumasia.*"[15] The value of Horace's use of the ethnographical model lies in the fact that it enables us to see this landscape not simply as a bit of autobiography but as a poetic creation with metaphoric relevance to the major themes of the poem. Horace's Sabine farm is not simply a place on the map: it is a literary landscape, far removed from the uncertainty and political upheaval of Roman life.

The parallels between this description and that of Ovid's Sulmo should be clear, particularly when we look again at the opening of *Am.* 2.16. Ovid's treatment of Sulmo is less technical than is that of the corresponding landscape in Horace's epistle;[16] nonetheless, Ovid's familiarity with ethnographical method is obvious and shows the extent to which the ethnographical tradition has been absorbed by his poetry. Like Horace, he begins with reference to the physical geography of Sulmo: it is a small region and one of three divisions of the Paelignian territory (1–2; cf. Pliny *NH* 3.106). Next, we hear of its climate: it is apparently subject to the

---

14. See K. Trüdinger, *Studien zur Geschichte der griechisch-römischen Ethnographie* (Basel, 1918); A. Schroeder, "De ethnographiae antiquae locis quibusdam communibus observationes" (Diss. Halle, 1921); Thomas, *Lands and Peoples,* 1–7 (Thomas' discussion of Horace's sixteenth epistle follows his more general discussion, pp. 8–17).

15. Thomas, *Lands and Peoples,* 17.

16. See Thomas, *Lands and Peoples,* 9–17, on Horace's use of technical vocabulary.

harshest heat of midsummer (3–4), but remains nonetheless well watered and green (5–6). And the fertility of the place is little short of astounding: it produces grain, the vine, and the olive (7–8), and we may infer from the mention of *resurgentes . . . herbas* and *gramineus . . . caespes* (9–10) that it provides pasture for flocks and herds as well. As in Horace's poem, so here the character of the inhabitants is not a prominent detail; but the emphasis on the healthfulness of the water (*inriguis ora salubris aquis,* 2) points indirectly to them and to their good fortune in environment.[17]

Sulmo seems perfect, and several elements in Ovid's description of it recall the idealization of landscape seen in Horace: the climate of Sulmo is well balanced, even at the hottest time of the year (3–6); the water supply there is both abundant and beneficial (2, 5, 9–10); and the productivity of the land there is extraordinary (7–10). It is a geographical commonplace familiar from both ethnographical literature and agricultural treatises that no one type of soil is equally well suited to all types of produce; thus, different areas are renowned for different crops. Ross draws our attention to how Virgil develops this theme at length in the second *Georgic: nec vero terrae ferre omnes omnia possunt* (109).[18] According to Virgil, fields have varying characters (*arvorum ingenia, Geo.* 2.177); the four major categories, or *ingenia,* are distinguished by the produce they best support—the olive (179–83), the vine (184–94), herds and flocks (195–202), and grain (203–11). Each type of soil is very distinctive and calls for a very different type of labor.[19] Yet Ovid's home, Sulmo, has examples of all these varieties and thus proves the exception to Virgil's rule.[20] Ovid's encomium of Sulmo

17. Also comparable, though less precisely so, is the picture of Tarentum offered in Hor. *Odes* 2.6.10–22; cf. Nisbet and Hubbard, on 2.6, esp. pp. 95–96.

18. See Varro *RR* 1.5–9 and Ross, *Virgil's Elements,* 110–11; cf. 43.

19. See Ross, *Virgil's Elements,* 130–34; Thomas, *Geo.,* on 2.117–205; and K.D. White, *Roman Farming* (Ithaca, 1970), 86–109.

20. Cf. Nisbet and Hubbard, who comment in their introduction to *Odes* 2.6 that "instead of saying that different areas produce different things . . . , Horace applies to Tarentum what Varro had said of Italy, that it produces everything best (*rust.* 1.2.6, Prop. 3.22.18 *natura hic posuit quidque ubique fuit,* Dion. Hal. *ant. Rom.* 1.36.3)." In fact, at only one point in the second *Georgic* does Virgil suggest that one country can support all four major categories of produce. The *laudes Italiae* (2.136–76) begins with a description of what this land can and cannot produce (140–44): *haec loca non tauri spirantes naribus ignem / invertere satis immanis dentibus hydri, / nec galeis densisque virum seges horruit hastis; / sed gravidae **fruges** et Bacchi Massicus **umor** / implevere; tenent **oleae armentaque** laeta.* Virgil's list here is identical with that Ovid will later provide in *Am.* 2.16; thus, Virgil's idealized Italy and Ovid's Sulmo are essentially identical agricultural landscapes. The implications and ironies of Virgil's idealization of Italy have been fully explored in Thomas, *Lands and Peoples,* 35–40 (cf. Thomas, *Geo.,* on 2.136–76), and Ross, *Virgil's Elements,* 115–19; it is important here that we recognize that

reflects the reality of the place even as it ignores the political ironies of Virgilian ethnography. Ovid evokes the Latin poetic tradition but suppresses its moral implications; his Sulmo effortlessly embodies the perfection inaccessible to the endlessly laboring farmers of the *Georgics.*

Ovid then moves on to describe the one flaw in this landscape: *at meus ignis abest* (11). In this couplet, noted for its epigrammatic brevity, Ovid captures the imbalance within himself: although his surroundings are ideal, no physical environment, however temperate, can fully satisfy him as long as his beloved is absent. Creating a contrast between *ignis abest* and *ardor adest,* Ovid also underlines the contradiction inherent in his predicament: the heat of love can persist even when its source is gone, while the absence of one's love can make even the warmest summer's heat ineffective. Thus, for all its balance, the ideal environment of Sulmo is useless—and pointless.

Conversely, Ovid imagines that even the harshest, most cruel and unbalanced environments would become tolerable in the company of his mistress. He would gladly travel to both the coldest and the warmest ends of the earth—typified by the northernmost Alps and the southernmost Libyan Syrtes—as long as he was with her (19–22). The mention of the Syrtes induces Ovid to catalogue the other famous threats at sea he is prepared to face: Scylla and Charybdis, as well as the promontory of Malea. Ovid is ready even for shipwreck: he will carry his beloved across the seas, if need be. Leander's nightly swim to Hero was a similar show of devotion (27–32). The progression of ideas here is noteworthy, particularly when we compare the threatening seas in the world beyond Sulmo to the healthful and nourishing streams that make Ovid's home so delightful. The reference to Hero and Leander, a story first found in Hellenistic poetry,[21] is equally functional: it reminds us of the universality of human experience (*amor omnibus idem,* Virgil *Geo.* 3.244). Virgil had used the same myth to illustrate just this point in the third *Georgic* (258–63); given the importance of

---

Ovid's Sulmo, like Horace's Sabine farm and Tarentum, is described in intentionally and recognizably idealizing terms. Ovid does not just report but creates Sulmo's landscape; and he creates it in response to a tradition whose literary possibilities are first fully realized in Augustan poetry by Virgil and Horace.

21. As we now know from *SH* 951; cf. *SH* 901A. Cf. Thomas, *Geo.,* and R.A.B. Mynors, ed., *Virgil: Georgics* (Oxford, 1990), on 3.258–63, and Booth, on *Am.* 2.16.32; C. Perkell, *The Poet's Truth* (Berkeley, 1989), 181–82; G. Miles, *Virgil's Georgics: A New Interpretation* (Berkeley, Los Angeles, and London, 1980), 198 n. 19; and Cameron, *Callimachus and His Critics,* 49.

Virgil's poetry elsewhere in this elegy, it may not be wholly coincidental that we find this particular myth so used by Ovid here.[22]

The company of his *domina,* then, would transform even the most brutal environment into one Ovid is willing to endure; her absence, however, makes lovely Sulmo seem a wasteland (33–40). The *sine te* of this section balances the *cum domina* of the previous scenes; and again Ovid's point is the contradictoriness of it all, as he sees distant and desolate Scythia, the Caucasus, the Cilices, and the Britons in place of the fertility and well-watered coolness that surround him. An enforced emotional solitude cuts him off from the world around him. He uses an agricultural analogy familiar from erotic poetry[23] to capture the essence of his predicament and to emphasize the imbalance between love and landscape in this poem (41–42):

ulmus amat vitem, vitis non deserit ulmum:
    separor a domina cur ego saepe mea?

[The elm loves the vine; the vine does not leave the elm: why am I often separated from my mistress?]

The movement of this poem and its contrasts between harsh and temperate, love and separation, and balance and imbalance as physical and emotional conditions, show the care with which Ovid develops the literary potential of his landscape. The balanced structure of this poem underscores the contrasts detailed throughout. In the emphasis on these contrasts, too, we can see the articulation of Ovid's literary indebtedness. He has by no means limited himself to the models we have already considered, however; rather, Ovid also looks here to the landscapes of the *Eclogues.* Two poems in Virgil's collection provide particular inspiration for Ovid's

---

22. Virgil's reference to the story of Hero and Leander is the first such allusion extant in ancient literature, aside from the apparent Hellenistic source mentioned in n. 21 in this chapter; cf. also *AA* 2.249–50 and Hor. *Epist.* 1.3.3–5. Virgil and Ovid use some of the same language to evoke this myth. For both, Leander is simply *iuvenis.* And both emphasize the darkness in which Leander swims: *nocte natat caeca* (Virg. *Geo.* 3.260); *via caeca fuit* (Ovid *Am.* 2.16.32). It is highly probable, therefore, that Ovid knew the *Georgics* passage as one, if not the only, anterior allusion to the tale. Nonetheless, the way in which both Virgil and Horace allude to this myth—neither character is mentioned by name—suggests that the story was well known: see Thomas, *Geo.,* ad loc., and idem, "Prose into Poetry: Tradition and Meaning in Virgil's *Georgics,*" *HSCP* 91 (1987): 250–51. Ovid need not, therefore, be dependent solely upon his two Augustan predecessors for this touch.

23. See Booth, ad loc.; Nisbet and Hubbard, on *Odes* 2.15.4; and Thomas, *Geo.,* on 1.2.

lament, the second and tenth *Eclogues.* Significantly, these two poems are
also, at least in part, laments for departed or lost lovers—Corydon for
Alexis and Gallus for Lycoris. And in each, environment is an important
means of expressing the desolation and desperation of the deserted lovers.
Here we move to a metaphorical function of landscape that is far more
congenial to the poetic concerns of Ovid than is the political connotation
of landscape in the *Georgics.*

Let us look at the second *Eclogue* first. Using the same cliché exploited
by Ovid in his play on *ignis* and *ardor,* Virgil begins by describing Corydon
as on fire (*Corydon ardebat,* 1). The flame of desire sends the shepherd to
seek out shade (*inter densas, umbrosa cacumina, fagos,* 3), where he pours
out his solitary lament (*ibi haec incondita solus / montibus et silvis studio
iactabat inani,* 4–5). Like Ovid in *Am.* 2.16, Corydon is not in sympathy
with his landscape. Whereas all the creatures surrounding him naturally
seek coolness and shade from the midday sun, he continues to burn (8–13):

> 'nunc etiam pecudes umbras et frigora captant,
> nunc viridis etiam occultant spineta lacertos,
> Thestylis et rapido fessis messoribus aestu   10
> alia serpyllumque herbas contundit olentis.
> at mecum raucis, tua dum vestigia lustro,
> sole sub ardenti resonant arbusta cicadis. . . .'

["Now even the flocks seek shade and cool, now the thorn-hedges hide
the green lizards, and Thestylis pounds the garlic and wild thyme, fragrant plants, for the harvesters wearied by the fierce heat. But for me,
while I follow your footsteps in search of you, the bushes resound with
the noisy cicada under the blazing sun . . . ."]

But the heat Corydon feels is primarily emotional, not physical, and so
signifies the emotional imbalance between him and his landscape. As he
notes near the close of his lament, he continues to burn although the sun is
setting and the shadows are growing (67–68):

> 'et sol crescentis decedens duplicat umbras;
> me tamen urit amor: quis enim modus adsit amori? . . .'

["And the sun as it departs doubles the growing shadows. Love burns me
nonetheless: for what limit can there be to love? . . . ."]

The imbalance caused by Alexis' absence contravenes all of Corydon's experience of nature; and the repetition of his wish for togetherness (*libeat mecum* . . . / . . . *mecum* . . . *imitabere,* 27–31) only emphasizes Corydon's very real isolation.[24]

Gallus' predicament in the tenth *Eclogue* parallels that of Corydon, though it is even more desperate; this desperation is reflected in the extreme changes of scenery the poet-lover imagines. Although he is in Arcadia, and although the landscape itself joins him in his lament (13–15), this place cannot, much as he wants it to, sustain him in the absence of Lycoris (42–43):

'hic gelidi fontes, hic mollia prata, Lycori,
hic nemus; hic ipso tecum consumerer aevo . . .'

["Here are cool springs, here soft meadows, Lycoris, here a grove; here with you I would be destroyed by time alone . . ."]

Like Ovid, Gallus places only one condition on experience: he wants to be together with his beloved (*tecum*). This condition is beyond his control, however, and so he will travel instead to a deserted forest, home only to wild beasts, in the hope that the loneliness of the place will complement his own loneliness and thus provide an appropriate *medicina furoris* (52–57):

'certum est in silvis inter spelaea ferarum
malle pati tenerisque meos incidere amores
arboribus: crescent illae, crescetis, amores.
interea mixtis lustrabo Maenala Nymphis   55
aut acris venabor apros. non me ulla vetabunt
frigora Parthenios canibus circumdare saltus. . . .'

["I have decided that it is preferable to endure in the woods among the dens of the wild beasts and to carve my love into the tender trees; as they grow, so will you grow, my love. Meanwhile, I shall wander Mt. Maenalus in the company of Nymphs or shall hunt fierce boar. No chills will prevent me from surrounding the Parthenian glens with hunting-dogs. . . ."]

---

24. See M.C.J. Putnam, *Virgil's Pastoral Art* (Princeton, 1970), 100–101.

But as Gallus himself eventually acknowledges, no change of scenery can remedy his situation. He thus carries to its logical conclusion the reverse side of Ovid's belief that any environment will be endurable in the company of his beloved. Neither in Thrace nor in Ethiopia, the northernmost and southernmost extremes of the world, can Gallus escape the *furor* of his love (64–69):

> 'non illum nostri possunt mutare labores,
> nec si frigoribus mediis Hebrumque bibamus   65
> Sithoniasque nives hiemis subeamus aquosae,
> nec si, cum moriens alta liber aret in ulmo,
> Aethiopum versemus ovis sub sidere Cancri.
> omnia vincit Amor: et nos cedamus Amori.'

["Our struggles cannot change that god [Love], not if we should drink from the Hebrus in the middle of the cold, not if we should endure the Sithonian snows of a watery winter, not if, when the dying bark grows dry on the lofty elm, we should pasture the sheep herds of the Ethiopians under the constellation of Cancer. Love conquers all things: let us too yield to love."]

For both Ovid and Gallus, love and love alone shapes one's perception and experience of environment.[25]

We may well see in Gallus' comprehension of his predicament, or Virgil's portrayal of it, a despair wholly absent from Ovid's poem: Ovid displays an unrealistic optimism more like that of Corydon. But the terms in which the two think about the relationship and the sympathy between emotional state and physical environment are identical: for both, experience is transformed by love, and love is expressed through the language of landscape. Thus, when Ovid recalls the treachery of his *puella* in leaving him, he chooses to describe her faithlessness in terms that, while commonplaces, aptly reflect his sensitivity to nature and his environment (*Am.* 2.16.43–46):[26]

---

25. On the landscape of *Ecl.* 10, see Clausen, *Eclogues,* 288–90.

26. See A. Otto, *Die Sprichwörter und sprichwörtlichen Redensarten der Römer,* 2d ed. (Leipzig, 1890; reprint, Hildesheim and New York, 1971), s.vv. *ventus* 2, *folium* 1. For the schema Cornelianum *oculos, sidera nostra, tuos,* see my chap. 1 n. 46. I suspect that we may well have here an example of the device as it actually appeared in Gallus.

at mihi te comitem iuraras usque futuram
    per me perque oculos, **sidera** nostra, tuos:
verba puellarum, **foliis** leviora caducis,   45
    irrita, qua visum est, **ventus et unda** ferunt.

[But you swore that you would be my companion always, by me and by your eyes, my stars; but the words of girls, lighter than falling leaves, wind and wave carry off unfulfilled, just as is their wont.]

And calling on the power of his own love, Ovid asks that no natural obstacle prevent his *puella* from reaching him in Sulmo as quickly as possible (51–52):

at vos, qua veniet, **tumidi** subsidite **montes,**
    et **faciles curvis vallibus** este **viae.**

[As for you, swollen mountains, subside wherever she will come; and roads, be easy in your sloping valleys.]

Even the perfect landscape, it seems, can (paradoxically) be made more perfect under the power and influence of love: *omnia vincit Amor.*

Our reading of the tenth *Eclogue* is necessarily complicated by the overwhelming likelihood that much of it is in fact Gallan, transformed though it is by its placement in a Virgilian context that is partly response and partly homage to Gallus. Ross has argued compellingly for a reading of this poem that finds it a reprise of Gallan poetics, as well as the dramatic development by Virgil of his own belief in the power—and limitations—of poetry.[27] For our purposes, the landscapes of this poem are of particular interest: Gallus and Virgil with him explore here the sympathy of landscape and love in ways that offer significant points of contact between this poem and Ovid's. But how much of this landscape is Virgil's, and how much Gallus'? Ross has shown that the landscapes of Gallan elegy exerted an important influence on Propertius as well as on Virgil; we may therefore infer that landscape was of special interest to Gallus and was an especially notable feature of his work. I suspect that if we try to go further, however, and attempt to assign one detail to Gallus, a second to Virgil, and so on, we will have begun a task that is both futile and of little interest to and for our

---

27. Ross, *Backgrounds to Augustan Poetry,* 85–106; cf. the review by J.E.G. Zetzel, "Gallus, Elegy, and Ross," *CP* 72 (1977): 249–60.

reading of Ovid. Unlike us, Ovid probably had access to Gallus' *Amores;* and we can have little doubt that he knew this work well, even to the point of being indebted to it for his title.[28] But it is certain as well that he knew Virgil's Gallus and so shaped the landscape of *Am.* 2.16 as part of a continuum, neither strictly Virgilian nor strictly Gallan, but encompassing instead a living tradition. The tenth *Eclogue* is therefore a doubly valuable poem, preserving as it does both for Ovid and for us not one but two layers of that tradition.

In *Am.* 2.16, then, we have little that can be labeled purely and simply imitative or referential; instead, this poem is best seen as Ovid's visit to a poetic landscape rich in elegiac potential and filled with poetic memories. To read this poem simply as modeled on Horace or, to a greater extent, on Virgil, however, would be drastically to skew both the aims and the accomplishments of Ovid, to whom the political implications of landscape are of only secondary concern as he describes Sulmo. By lovingly envisioning the landscape around Sulmo, Ovid personalizes the literary tradition he has inherited; and it is clear that the literary connotations of this landscape are of far greater interest to him than are its associations with the political or moral metaphors of Horace and Virgil. In adding Sulmo to the Roman literary map, Ovid makes himself not only heir to but a creative participant in the transformative power of Augustan poetics. By personalizing the map of elegy, he makes room for himself within its expanding bounds.

Two features of Ovidian poetics as seen in the preceding discussion deserve repetition as we turn to our next poem. First of all, I have talked of Ovid's desire to personalize the literary tradition, to put his stamp on it, so to speak, when he uses it. Thus, the poetry that inspires him serves as a means, but not as an end in itself: Ovid does not simply regurgitate the poetry he has read but uses it to create a place for himself among Latin poets. An important, if implicit, aspect of this personalization is Ovid's relative lack of engagement with what had been the burning political and social concerns of the Augustan poets working a few years before him. The result is a collection that is almost literally timeless in its lack of concern for extraliterary discourse.[29] A second noteworthy point is the seamlessness

---

28. I have already discussed an example of Ovid's awareness of Gallan style in chap. 1.

29. Aside from the two datable references recognized by Syme, *History in Ovid,* 3–8; see also White, *Promised Verse,* 87–91, on the reality of the generic social situations that poetry like the *Amores* reflects. Cf. the more general issue of dating the *Amores,* which I discuss later, in chap. 4.

with which Ovid puts together materials from a wide range of sources. There is nothing in the design of 2.16 that we can call specifically referential, in Thomas' sense; yet the entire poem looks to recognizable, and potent, sources of influence. At the same time, no one model dominates. Ovid's facile poetic memory provides the key to an aspect of his style that is far too little recognized and understood: multiple allusion. In the remainder of this chapter and in much of the next, we shall see examples of Ovid's repeated interest in novel combinations of source materials, combinations whose primary purpose appears to be to create pleasure in the reader who recognizes what Ovid is reading and how he writes. Through the *Amores* Ovid tells us what kind of a poet he is; his multiple allusions not only demonstrate his technical virtuosity but affirm the self-consciously Hellenistic character of the collection. Again, it is tempting to seek the purpose of an allusion or allusions and to use the results to define the poet's purpose or theme; but more often than not in Ovid's case, the allusion *is* the purpose of the allusion. The striking results that can arise from the combination of multiple allusions tend to exist for their own sake and have little to say about the sources that these allusions reflect.

Am. 3.10 vividly illustrates this feature of Ovidian poetics. In this elegy on Corinna's worship of Ceres, we find a vivid combination of Ovidian originality, on the one hand, and learning, on the other. Like *Am.* 2.16, this poem too has received little critical attention—perhaps because, unlike Propertius 2.33, on Cynthia's Isis worship,[30] Ovid's poem does not make much of a contribution to the narrative about his relationship with Corinna. Ostensibly, this elegy presents Ovid's brief against the *secubitus* practiced by his *puella* as an important part of the annual ritual in honor of Ceres; in fact, Ovid uses the occasion as the pretense for a narrative elegy describing Ceres' dalliance with Iasius on Crete and its consequences. This narrative in turn serves as a sort of reverse aetiology for the ritual purity of Ceres' worshipers. Throughout, Ovid displays a marvelous ability to draw from disparate sources, to merge them in previously unknown ways, and so to create a poem totally his own. His accomplishment here prefigures what he will later do with Ceres and Proserpina in the *Fasti* and the *Metamorphoses.*[31]

Formally, *Am.* 3.10 combines features from the literary hymn and the

---

30. Ovid's poem is treated as an imitation of Propertius' by Neumann, "Qua ratione Ovidius," 89–93; in fact, he puts this "imitation" in the category of Ovidian elegies "quae omnino et inventione et compositione a Propertio pendere videntur" (41).

31. See Hinds, *Metamorphosis of Persephone,* 51–98.

aetiological elegy, both quintessentially Callimachean endeavors; as we shall see, these elements of the poem's form are reflected in its substance as well. The narrative is framed by two passages, each three couplets in length, in which Ovid addresses his complaint to Ceres: the period of her annual ritual does him harm, since he is then deprived of his bedmate. Ovid then asks the question that introduces an aetiological motif to the elegy: why does Ceres begrudge her worshipers what she herself enjoyed? She is otherwise a gracious and generous goddess (1–6, 43–48):

> **Annua** venerunt Cerealis **tempora** sacri:
>   **secubat** in vacuo sola puella toro.
> **flava** Ceres, tenues spicis redimita capillos,
>   cur inhibes **sacris** commoda nostra **tuis**?
> te, **dea, munificam** gentes, ubi quaeque, loquuntur,   5
>   nec minus humanis invidet ulla bonis.
>
> . . . .
>
> qui tibi **secubitus** tristes, **dea flava,** fuissent,
>   hos cogor **sacris** nunc ego ferre **tuis.**
> cur ego sim tristis, cum sit tibi nata reperta   45
>   regnaque quam Iuno sorte minora regnat?
> **festa dies** Veneremque vocat cantusque merumque:
>   haec decet ad dominos **munera** ferre deos.

[The annual period for the ritual in honor of Ceres has come; my girl lies alone in an empty bed. Blonde Ceres, your fine hair crowned with ears of grain, why do you restrain us with your rites from what is satisfying? You, goddess, people everywhere call generous, and no goddess begrudges human happiness less. . . .

[43] The joyless bed that was yours, blonde goddess, I am now forced to endure because of your rites. Why should I be disconsolate, when your daughter was found and now rules a kingdom just smaller by chance than the one over which Juno reigns? A festival day calls for Venus and song and wine: it is fitting to bring these as gifts to the gods our lords.]

Ovid starts out with what seems to be a distinct recollection of Propertius' Isis poem (*Tristia iam redeunt iterum sollemnia nobis: / Cynthia iam noctes est operata decem,* Prop. 2.33.1–2); but that his elegy has an integrity of its own and will take a very different direction is evident from the way in which Ovid weaves this reference into the structure of his own poem. Propertius' elegy is not hymnic; Ovid's is. The hymnic framing device of careful balance between the opening and closing sections, a feature familiar from the Callimachean hymns, is marked in *Am.* 3.10: the diction of the first passage is reflected in the second, as Ovid invokes Ceres' generally fertile beneficence.[32]

The hymnic structure of the elegy makes its contents all the more surprising. The narrative centers on a traditional theme, Ceres' function as fertility goddess; but this traditional theme is put to an unusual, and appropriately elegiac, use. Though profoundly associated with agriculture and the country, Ceres is by no means unsophisticated or uninterested in the erotic side of life; thus, in describing Ceres, Ovid recalls both the literal meaning of *rusticus* and its erotic connotation (*nec tamen est, quamvis agros amet illa feraces, / **rustica** nec viduum pectus amoris habet,* 17–18).[33] In fact, Ovid continues, she herself experienced love and so caused a temporary imbalance in agricultural fertility, forgetting all lands except the place of her erotic encounter, Crete; here, the earth was productive without limit. And so Ovid returns to his starting point: why should a goddess who is herself not chaste expect chastity of her worshipers? The solemn framework of the poem emphasizes by contrast the humorousness of Ovid's plaintive self-interest.

Callimachean as well is Ovid's interest in developing at length a remarkably obscure myth concerning Ceres. The story of Ceres' love for Iasion is told as early as Homer, who mentions both the love affair itself and the vengeance of Zeus that follows (ὡς δ' ὁπότ' Ἰασίωνι ἐϋπλόκαμος Δημήτηρ / ᾧ θυμῷ εἴξασα μίγη φιλότητι καὶ εὐνῇ / νειῷ ἔνι τριπόλῳ· οὐδὲ δὴν ἦεν ἄπυστος / Ζεύς, ὅς μιν κατέπεφνε βαλὼν ἀργῆτι κεραυνῷ, *Od.* 5.125–28). Hesiod, calling Ceres' consort by the variant name *Iasios,* is the first to locate their union on Crete (Δημήτηρ μὲν Πλοῦτον ἐγείνατο, δῖα θεάων, / Ἰασίῳ ἥρωι μιγεῖσ' ἐρατῇ φιλότητι / νειῷ ἔνι τριπόλῳ, Κρήτης ἐν πίονι δήμῳ, *Theog.* 969–71). But both of these early notices are brief, and they provide only the raw material for Ovid's tale; and no other extended narrative on the topic is extant or clearly known from testimonia

---

32. For the symmetrical frame in Callimachean hymns, see N. Hopkinson, ed., *Callimachus: Hymn to Demeter* (Cambridge, 1984), 3, 10–11. F.W. Lenz, "Ceresfest: Eine Studie zu Ovid Amores 3,10," *SIFC* 10 (1933): 306, notes the similarity in the diction of the two sections.

33. R. Pichon, *De sermone amatorio apud Latinos elegiarum scriptores* (Paris, 1902), 256, writes: "*rustici* praecipue vocantur qui artis amatoriae non sunt periti, sed sese praebent rudes et quasi impeditos." All the examples given by Pichon for this meaning are from Ovid.

to have existed.[34] In choosing this theme, Ovid emulates the Hellenistic predilection for using the Homeric poems, as well as others of their vintage, "as primary source-material for essentially non-epic treatment."[35]

Of course, other narratives connected with Ceres exist. Two are in the form of literary hymns: the *Homeric Hymn to Demeter* and Callimachus' sixth hymn. The first of these, however, is directly and at length concerned with Ceres' loss of her daughter, a story to which Ovid alludes only briefly at the close of his poem (45–46);[36] and in the second, Callimachus uses the well-known narrative of the Homeric hymn as foil to the central story of Erysichthon. Furthermore, neither of the Greek hymns mentions Iasion/Iasios, and only in the Homeric hymn is Ceres associated, very briefly and in a very different context, with Crete: she herself claims to

---

34. See Ovid's brief notice of the same story at *Met.* 9.422–23, and Bömer, *Met.*, ad loc. It is tempting to look to Philetas' *Demeter* as Ovid's source, but we can infer very little about this poem from the scanty fragments we have: see Pfeiffer, on Call. *Aet.* fr. 1.9–12 and 2:47; *CA* 90–91; *SH* 673–75; and P.E. Knox, "The Poetry of Philetas," *PLLS* 7 (1993): 61–83, who reviews all the evidence. Knox (69–73) thinks it very likely that Philetas' *Demeter* presented the same tale (i.e., the rape of Persephone and its aftermath) that we know from several other sources, and that it influenced Ovid's several treatments of the myth. A.W. Bulloch, however, takes the severe (and, to my mind, less compelling) position that most, if not all, of Philetas' poetry disappeared within two hundred years of being written, so that to the Roman poets he was little more than a name: see his chapter on "Hellenistic Poetry," in *The Cambridge History of Classical Literature,* vol. 1: *Greek Literature,* ed. P.E. Easterling and B.M.W. Knox (Cambridge, 1985), 545. E.L. Bowie, in "Theocritus' Seventh *Idyll,* Philetas, and Longus," *CQ* 35 (1985): 80–84, argues on the basis of slender but suggestive evidence that both Virgil and Propertius, and perhaps others, had direct access to at least some of the poetry of Philetas; for further discussion on Philetas' influence on Virgil, see I.M.LeM. Du Quesnay, "Vergil's First *Eclogue,*" *PLLS* 3 (1981): 39–40, and R.F. Thomas, "The Old Man Revisited: Memory, Reference, and Genre in Virg., Georg. 4,116–48," *MD* 29 (1992): 35–70. We also know of a *Ceres* by Calvus, a poem generally identified as an epithalamium (*FPL* 85 Morel = Calvus *FLP* fr. 6 Courtney). Two lines from this poem, as preserved by the Veronese scholia on *Aen.* 4.58, tantalizingly associate Ceres with marriage: *et leges sanctas docuit et cara iugavit / corpora conubiis et magnas condidit urbes.* H. LeBonniec, *Le Culte de Cérès à Rome* (Paris, 1958), 77–88 argues that Virgil follows Calvus in suggesting, at *Aen.* 4.57–59, that Ceres is a goddess of marriage. It is therefore possible, but not ascertainable, that Ovid knew this motif from Calvus. Cf. A.S. Pease, ed., *Virgil: Aeneid Book IV* (Cambridge, MA, 1935), on 4.58; H. Bardon, *La littérature latine inconnue, I: L'époque republicaine* (Paris, 1952), 342–43. More generally on the sacred marriage of Demeter and Iasion, see Diod. Sic. 5.49, and cf. R.F. Willetts, *Cretan Cults and Festivals* (London, 1962), 148–52.

35. Bulloch, "Hellenistic Poetry," 546.

36. Lenz, "Ceresfest," 306–9, discusses and rejects the hypothesis put forth by Ehwald that these lines are interpolated. Hinds, *Metamorphosis of Persephone,* 51–98, makes a compelling case for Ovid's intimate familiarity with the Homeric hymn elsewhere in his poetry; Knox, "The Poetry of Philetas," 69–73 would make Ovid's indebtedness to tradition more wide-ranging, with the inclusion of Philetas and his *Demeter* in the genealogy of Ovid's Ceres narratives.

have come to Greece from Crete, an allegation that, as one recent com-
mentator notes, is "suitable to a false tale."[37] In the Homeric hymn, Ceres
uses the "Cretan lie" to conceal her real identity. In Ovid's poem, however,
deception plays no role. Instead, Ovid expressly alludes to the tradition
that all Cretans are liars so that he can deny it (19–20):

> Cretes erunt testes; nec fingunt omnia Cretes:
>   Crete nutrito terra superba Iove.

[The Cretans will be my witnesses—and the Cretans do not feign everything: the land of Crete is proud in having nurtured Jupiter.]

Callimachus had made a special point of telling us that he would not tell
the story of Demeter's search for Persephone (μὴ μὴ ταῦτα λέγωμες ἃ
δάκρυον ἄγαγε Δηοῖ, h. 6.17); Ovid's avoidance of the story is therefore
very much in keeping with the spirit of Callimachus' hymn, if not with its
substance. In fact, even as Ovid disassociates his from other literary versions of the Ceres myth, he displays his familiarity with Callimachus'
poetry, in particular the hymns. This allusion to the lying character of Cretans refers directly back to the Callimachean hymn to Zeus,[38] which opens
with an inquiry into the varying traditions surrounding Zeus' birth (h.
1.4–9):

πῶς καί νιν, Δικταῖον ἀείσομεν ἠὲ Λυκαῖον;
ἐν δοιῇ μάλα θυμός, ἐπεὶ γένος ἀμφήριστον.   5
Ζεῦ, σὲ μὲν Ἰδαίοισιν ἐν οὔρεσί φασι γενέσθαι,
Ζεῦ, σὲ δ' ἐν Ἀρκαδίῃ· πότεροι, πάτερ, ἐψεύσαντο;
'Κρῆτες ἀεὶ ψεῦσται'· καὶ γὰρ τάφον, ὦ ἄνα, σεῖο
Κρῆτες ἐτεκτήναντο· σὺ δ' οὐ θάνες, ἐσσὶ γὰρ αἰεί.

[How shall we hymn him—as Dictaean or Lycaean? I am of two minds,
since his birth is disputed. Zeus, some say that you were born on the
heights of Ida, others, in Arcadia. Which of these, father, has lied? "Cre-

---

37. N.J. Richardson, ed., *The Homeric Hymn to Demeter* (Oxford, 1974), on *h. Cer.* 123; in
so claiming, the goddess appears to be inspired by Odysseus' famous lies as narrated by
Homer.
   38. See G.R. McLennan, ed., *Callimachus: Hymn to Zeus* (Rome, 1977). See also S.J. Heyworth, "Deceitful Crete: *Aeneid* 3.84 [*sic*] and the *Hymns* of Callimachus," *CQ* 43 (1993):
255–57.

tans are always liars"; and indeed, o lord, the Cretans have erected a tomb for you. But you did not die, for you are always.]

Callimachus here uses the famous saying attributed to Epimenides[39] to justify his intention to follow the alternative Arcadian tradition regarding the locale of Zeus' birth. Ovid, however, pointedly refers to the context in which Callimachus had used the proverb but manages simultaneously to contradict, or correct, him: *Crete nutrito terra superba Iove.*

An Alexandrian interest in the variation and conflation of myths also reveals itself in Ovid's description of Iasius as a hunter (*viderat Iasium Cretaea diva sub Ida / figentem certa terga ferina manu,* 25–26). This description is very different from the early identification of Iasius as a farmer,[40] and indicates that Ovid has conflated two characters of the same name, one from Crete and one from Arcadia. Again Ovid looks to Callimachus, in whose hymn for Artemis, Iasius is an Arcadian (*h.* 3.216). Callimachus' Iasius is the father of the huntress Atalanta and so is by implication associated with hunting;[41] the Cretan, in contrast, is never so described except by Ovid.[42] The intentional conflation we see here recalls in yet another way the opening of Callimachus' hymn to Zeus: just as Callimachus had given us an Arcadian origin for Zeus, instead of the better-known Cretan tradition, Ovid offers us an Arcadian Iasius instead of the Cretan Iasion/Iasios found in Hesiod. I shall return shortly to consider the implications of this

---

39. See Pfeiffer ad loc., McLennan, *Hymn to Zeus,* ad loc.

40. Schol. on Hom. *Od.* 5.125: γεωργὸς ἦν. The mention of Iasion at Theocr. *Id.* 3.50 does not specify his occupation, but includes him among mortals who loved goddesses; several others in this group (Melampus and Adonis) are characterized by Theocritus as shepherds, probably in accordance with the larger bucolic setting of the poem. On Iasion/Iasios, see Gundel, *RE* 17:752–58, s.v. *Iasion,* and R. Rocca, *EV* 2:886, s.v. *Iasio.* At *Aen.* 3.168, *Iasius pater* is mentioned as, along with Dardanus, one of the ancestors of the Trojans, who had originally come to Troy from Italy. He and Dardanus therefore advised the Trojans to return to Italy, rather than going to Crete. See also Hellanicus, *FGrHist* 4 F 23, for the story that Dardanus and his followers settled in Italy, Iasius and his in Samothrace. It is possible that this Iasius and Iasion/Iasios consort of Demeter are one and the same, but the rather spare testimonia (collected by Gundel, loc. cit.), invite only speculation.

41. See also Theognis 1288 West. Apollodorus 3.9.2 calls him Ἴασος; cf. Prop. 1.1.10, *saevitiam durae . . . Iasidos.* For the possibility that the name invites etymological play, see also K. Dowden, *Death and the Maiden: Girls' Initiation Rites in Greek Mythology* (London and New York, 1989), 122, and N.M. Horsfall, "Virgil, Parthenius and the Art of Mythological Reference," *Vergilius* 37 (1991): 34.

42. Ovid's Cretan version of Iasius may also owe something to another Callimachean character mentioned in the same hymn to Artemis, that is, Minos, described by Callimachus as wandering distractedly through the hills of Crete seeking his beloved Britomartis: ἧς ποτε Μίνως / πτοιηθεὶς ὑπ' ἔρωτι κατέδραμεν οὔρεα Κρήτης (*h.* 3.190–91).

conflation for the poem; it is sufficient now to observe how Ovid provides striking evidence of his desire both to align himself with Callimachean poetic traditions and to declare his intent to innovate, not imitate. Indeed, this is one of the strongest echoes we have heard in the *Amores* of Callimachean competitive polemic, and it easily passes "the memorability test." It is most appropriate that we hear this echo in a setting that simultaneously approximates and avoids Callimachean reminiscence.

Callimachus is not the only inspirational presence behind *Am.* 3.10. Ovid's predilection for multiple allusion appears again in his praise of Ceres' abundant gifts to humanity, where Virgil provides an important antecedent. Ovid writes (3.10.7–14):

> **ante** nec hirsuti torrebant farra **coloni,**
>   nec notum terris area nomen erat,
> sed **glandem quercus, oracula prima,** ferebant;
>   haec erat et teneri caespitis herba cibus.   10
> **prima Ceres docuit** turgescere semen in agris,
>   falce coloratas subsecuitque comas;
> **prima** iugis tauros supponere colla **coegit**
>   **et veterem curvo dente revellit humum.**

[Previously, unshorn farmers did not toast their spelt, nor was *threshing-floor* a term known on earth. Rather, oaks, the first source of oracles, bore the acorn; this and the green blades of tender turf were food. Ceres was the first to teach the seed to swell in the fields, and with her sickle she trimmed her flaxen tresses; she was the first to compel bulls to submit their necks to the yoke and to tear up the ancient soil with the curved tooth of a plow.]

In abbreviated form Ovid here recalls the passage on the origins of agriculture in the first *Georgic* (125–49); the beginning and ending in particular are worth quoting (125–28, 147–49):

> **ante** Iovem nulli subigebant arva **coloni:**
> ne signare quidem aut partiri limite campum
> fas erat; in medium quaerebant, ipsaque tellus
> omnia liberius nullo poscente ferebat.
>
> . . . .
>
> **prima Ceres ferro mortalis vertere terram**

instituit, cum iam **glandes** atque arbuta **sacrae**
deficerent **silvae** et victum **Dodona** negaret.

[Before Jupiter, no farmers subdued the plowland: it was not permitted
to divide the field with a boundary or even to mark it out; people sought
for the common good, and earth herself bore all things the more generously for having no one ask. . . .
   [147] Ceres was the first to instruct mortals how to turn the soil with
iron, when once the acorns and the wild strawberries of the sacred forest were failing and Dodona was refusing food.]

Ovid's mention of the acorn as the first food is a conventional, indeed, formulaic, feature in descriptions of preagricultural humanity; but Ovid
points specifically to Virgil by the way in which he associates these acorns
so closely with the oracle of Jupiter at Dodona and its oaks. This association is very important to Virgil in the opening invocation of the *Georgics:*
the acorns that Ceres' grain supersedes (*Liber et alma Ceres, vestro si
munere tellus / Chaoniam pingui glandem mutavit arista,* 1.7–8) are Chaon-
ian, that is, Dodonan.[43] As if to underline the Virgilian provenance of his
description, Ovid draws our attention to the association between acorn
and oracle by using a highly stylized neoteric device, the appositional construction *quercus, oracula prima;* and his equation of acorn with oracle
confirms Virgil's mention, elsewhere in the *Georgics,* of the oracular reputation of the Dodonan oaks (*habitae Grais oracula quercus,* 2.16).[44] The
overall—and intentional—effect is that of a traditional description of
Ceres as πρῶτος εὑρέτης, developed before the poet moves on to an
untraditional narrative.[45] Ironically, Ovid draws attention to the novelty of

---

43. See also *Geo.* 2.67, *Chaoniique patris glandes;* and cf. Ross, *Virgil's Elements,* 34, 100,
172.
   44. On the *Georgics* passage, see Thomas, *Geo.,* ad loc. On Ovid's appositional construction, see Skutsch, "Zu Vergils Eklogen." Solodow, "*Raucae, tua cura, palumbes,*" 133, does
not note this example of the construction because it does not fit his definition of "inserted
apposition." The author of the *Culex* appears to have noticed Ovid's recollection of Virgil
and combines references to both poets in his description of the *quercus* and its acorns: *quam
[scil. Phyllida] comitabantur, fatalia carmina, quercus, / quercus ante datae Cereris quam sem-
ina vitae / (illas Triptolemi mutavit sulcus aristis)* (134–36).
   45. On the πρῶτος εὑρέτης, see Hopkinson, *Hymn to Demeter,* on *h.* 6.19 (the topos is a
standard element in hymns), and R.L. Hunter, ed., *Eubulus: The Fragments* (Cambridge,
1983), on fr. 72.1; the latter makes reference to F. Leo, *Plautinische Forschungen,* 2d ed.
(Berlin, 1912), 151–54, and to Nisbet and Hubbard, on *Odes* 1.3.12. Ceres is similarly
described by Lucretius, albeit skeptically, at 5.14–15, *namque Ceres fertur fruges Liberque*

his tale by calling the story *crimina nota* (24),[46] since it is attested by none other than the land of liars, Crete.

In this carefully structured poem, then, the entire first half serves as prologue to the story itself. We have been prepared for a tale that is intended at least in part to glorify Ceres' munificence in traditional terms; yet Ovid's bold locating of the story in Crete, home of liars, and his even bolder challenge to Callimachus raise the question of how much Ovid in fact relies on tradition for this tale. As the second half of the poem begins, Ovid portrays a Ceres whose erotic sensibility and responses are those not of a goddess but of an all too vulnerable mortal woman (25–28):

> viderat Iasium Cretaea diva sub Ida
> >figentem certa terga ferina manu;
> vidit et, ut tenerae flammam rapuere medullae,
> >hinc pudor, ex illa parte trahebat amor.

[The goddess had seen Iasius beneath Cretan Ida as he pierced the hides of wild beasts with a sure hand; she saw him and, as her tender marrow caught the flame, shame pulled her in one direction, love in the other.]

I have already noted that, in depicting Iasius as a hunter here rather than as a farmer, Ovid displays his erudition by conflating two characters with the same name. But what narrative purpose does Iasius' hunting serve? The answer is not, I think, hard to find, if only we look to several other hunter-lovers in Augustan poetry. We have already seen the importance of Virgil's Gallus to Ovid; in the tenth *Eclogue,* this Gallus proposes to himself to turn to hunting to assuage the *furor* of his love (55–61):

---

liquoris / vitigeni laticem mortalibus instituisse. Lenz, "Ceresfest," 301–2, has argued that Tibullus' influence lies behind Ovid's poem as well; see also Du Quesnay, "The *Amores,*" 24–25. But the similarities of prayer form to which Lenz points are formulaic. Cf., e.g., the repetition of *prima* in Ovid's prayer to Aurora, *Am.* 1.13.15–16. And the postponed -*que,* which Lenz identifies as conclusively Tibullan, is common in the Ovidian pentameter and is not by itself clearly an index of Tibullan influence: see M. Platnauer, *Latin Elegiac Verse* (Cambridge, 1951; reprint, Hamden, CT, 1971), 91–92. It has also been suggested that the analogy between blond hair and ripe grain (Ov. *Am.* 1.13.12, 36) is a Tibullan innovation: see G. Williams, *Tradition and Originality in Roman Poetry* (Oxford, 1968), 504. But the goddess' blondness goes back to Homer (*Il.* 5.500; cf. *h. Cer.* 302 and Richardson, *Homeric Hymn to Demeter,* ad loc.), and Serv., on *Geo.* 1.96, recognizes the symbolism of the color for Virgil: **flava** *dicitur propter aristarum colorem in maturitate.*

46. F. Munari, ed., *P. Ovidi Nasonis Amores,* 4th ed. (Florence, 1964), reads *nostra* here; but *nota* is preferable because of its evocation of the Callimachean claim to testimony (cf. n. 53 in this chapter).

'interea mixtis lustrabo Maenala Nymphis   55
aut acris venabor apros. non me ulla vetabunt
frigora Parthenios canibus circumdare saltus.
iam mihi per rupes videor lucosque sonantis
ire, libet Partho torquere Cydonia cornu
spicula—tamquam haec sit nostri medicina furoris,   60
aut deus ille malis hominum mitescere discat.'

["Meanwhile, I shall wander Mt. Maenalus in the company of Nymphs
or shall hunt fierce boar. No chills will prevent me from surrounding the
Parthenian glens with hunting-dogs. Even now I seem to be going along
the cliffs and through sounding groves, and it pleases me to shoot
Cydonian arrows from the Parthian bow—as if this should be a cure for
my lovesickness, or that notorious god should learn to be moved by the
troubles of humans."]

As Ross has argued, in so portraying Gallus, Virgil is most probably adapting a scene from Gallus' poetry; and an important programmatic passage
in Propertius indicates that this scene originally depicted Milanion, who
was able to win Atalanta's love through his *obsequium* (1.1.9–16):[47]

Milanion nullos fugiendo, Tulle, labores
    saevitiam durae contudit Iasidos.   10
nam modo Partheniis amens errabat in antris,
    ibat et hirsutas ille videre feras;
ille etiam Hylaei percussus vulnere rami
    saucius Arcadiis rupibus ingemuit.
ergo velocem potuit domuisse puellam: 15
    tantum in amore preces et bene facta valent.

[By avoiding no hardship, Tullus, Milanion subdued the cruelty of the
harsh daughter of Iasus. For now he would wander distractedly in
Parthenian groves, and he would go to look on the shaggy wild beasts;
and struck and wounded by the Hylaean club, he lamented in pain on
the Arcadian cliffs. Thus he was able to tame the swift girl: so powerful
are prayers and good deeds in love.]

---

47. Ross, *Backgrounds to Augustan Poetry,* 61–65, 89–91; see also R. Rosen and J. Farrell,
"Acontius, Milanion, and Gallus: Vergil, *Ecl.* 10.52–61," *TAPA* 116 (1986): 241–54.

Ovid's description of Iasius is by contrast brief and unelaborated, and it focuses most of our attention on Ceres; nonetheless, in giving us the Arcadian Iasius as hunter and lover, Ovid conveys a poetic memory of the love of Milanion and Atalanta as a paradigm for Ceres and her Cretan consort.

Ovid's scene also carries the poetic memory of Virgil's description of Dido as she falls in love. With the fire of love in her bones, she is like a wounded deer (*Aen.* 4.66–73):

> est mollis flamma medullas[48]
> interea et tacitum vivit sub pectore vulnus.
> uritur infelix Dido totaque vagatur
> urbe furens, qualis coniecta cerva sagitta,
> quam procul incautam nemora inter Cresia fixit   70
> pastor agens telis liquitque volatile ferrum
> nescius: illa fuga silvas saltusque peragrat
> Dictaeos; haeret lateri letalis harundo.

[A flame eats away, meanwhile, at her tender marrow, and a silent wound lives beneath her breast. Unhappy Dido burns, and she wanders raging throughout the city, like a doe when an arrow has been shot; a shepherd, pursuing her among the Cretan groves while she was off her guard, has pierced her from afar with his arrows, all unknowing, and has left the winged iron [in her]. She roams the woods and Dictaean glens in flight, as the deadly shaft clings to her flank.]

Dido's obsession makes her inattentive to her duties as a queen; just as nothing will grow when the world beyond Crete is neglected by Ceres, so at Carthage all activity and progress cease (*Aen.* 4.86–89). By mentioning the Cretan locale twice in his simile, Virgil increases the vividness of Dido's tragedy; these references, along with the implicit analogy of Aeneas to a hunting shepherd, in turn recall *Aen.* 4.143–50, in which Aeneas, equipped for the hunt, is compared to Apollo, whom the Cretans worship.[49] Ovid's Ceres follows in Dido's footsteps, becoming another victim of the wound of love while in Crete. The outcomes of these two loves are of course quite

---

48. Cf. Virgil's *mollis medullas* and Ovid's *tenerae medullae* (*Am.* 3.10.27). Cf. also Cat. 35.15, 64.92–93; Pease, *Aeneid IV,* on 4.66.

49. See G. Duclos, *"Nemora inter Cresia,"* *CJ* 66 (1971): 193–95. For the association of Apollo with Crete, see also F. Williams, "A Theophany in Theocritus," *CQ* 21 (1971): 139–40, and Heyworth, "Deceitful Crete."

different, for Dido is human and Ceres divine; but in dwelling on how Ceres' love for Iasius begins, Ovid humanizes Ceres and so places her in a long line of vulnerable erotic heroines.[50] Her love thus becomes an appropriate subject for elegiac treatment, unlikely though this idea may be at first; and so *Am.* 3.10 makes a reality of the *adynaton* expressed by Ovid at *Am.* 1.1.9, when he has yet to write amatory elegy: *quis probet in silvis Cererem regnare iugosis . . .* ?[51]

The all but universal famine caused by Ceres' amatory distraction and withdrawal is a more familiar feature of narratives concerning this goddess.[52] Ovid's description of what happens—the seed that is sown does not sprout in the dry furrows, although the soil has been well worked by both mattock and plow (29–34)—is much the same as that given in the Homeric hymn depicting the famine that Demeter causes in her anger (*h. Cer.* 305–9). But Ovid's Ceres is motivated by love, whereas her predecessor is moved to wrathful grief by the loss of a child. Perhaps to emphasize the very different character he has given the goddess, Ovid does not mention that Ceres becomes a mother by Iasius, too; her maternal character, so prominent in both the Homeric hymn and in the notice of this story given by Hesiod, is irrelevant to Ovid's romance.

Every step of the way, then, Ovid uses literary traditions about Ceres only to reject them. In typically Alexandrian fashion, he is at pains to display his mastery of what has gone before and to live up to Callimachus' claim to knowledge of the arcane and obscure (ἀμάρτυρον οὐδὲν ἀείδω, fr. 612 Pf.). He calls his story here a narrative of *crimina nota* (24); but this "Alexandrian footnote,"[53] while suggesting that the story of Ceres and Iasius is attested elsewhere, in fact draws attention to the poem's novelty. This story never has been told before; it is Ovid's innovation.

The vitality of Ovid's dialogue with literary tradition makes *Am.* 3.10 a match in technique for any of the narrative elegies of Propertius 4.[54] Yet we

---

50. See Cat. 64.86–93 and W. Kroll, ed., *C. Valerius Catullus,* 6th ed. (Stuttgart, 1980), ad loc., for the humanizing of Ariadne; cf. also Clausen, *Virgil's Aeneid,* 44, and the possible neoteric treatment of Ceres as patronness of marriage noted in n. 34 in this chapter.

51. I discuss *Am.* 1.1 further in chapter 4.

52. See Richardson, *Homeric Hymn to Demeter,* on *h. Cer.* 305–33.

53. So named by Ross, *Backgrounds to Augustan Poetry,* 78; see also Hinds, *Metamorphosis of Persephone,* 40, 58 n. 22. N.M. Horsfall, "Camilla, o i limiti dell' invenzione," *Athenaeum* 66 (1988): 31–51, argues convincingly that the claim to authority invoked so frequently in Alexandrian poetry may sometimes be used to legitimize stories without actual authority; see also idem, *Virgilio: L'epopea in alambicco* (Naples, 1991), 117–33 (a revised version of "Virgil and the Illusory Footnote," *PLLS* 6 [1990]: 49–63).

54. The best discussion of Propertius' Callimacheanism in book 4 is by Pillinger, "Callimachean Influences on Propertius."

should note an important difference, too, between, for example, the Tarpeia elegy, Propertius 4.4, and Ovid's eroticization of the Ceres myth. The topics that Propertius chooses for aetiological treatment in book 4 are by and large reflective of a compromise between the private and erotic world of Roman elegy and the challenge presented to private poetry by the triumph of Augustan values; thus, Propertius can exploit the tension between, on the one hand, the aetiological possibilities of the Tarpeia myth and, on the other, the conflict between public and private values inherent in her love and its consequences.[55] Ovid's treatment of Ceres' love, however, appears to have no similarly Augustan (or anti-Augustan) dimension. Rather, its points of contact and interest are other poems and other literary depictions of women in love. Even the patent similarities between Dido and Ceres do not exploit the tensions between public and private in Virgil's portrayal of the Carthaginian queen. Ovid is responding not to contemporary politics but to a poetic tradition.

Its aetiological dimension, meanwhile, often causes this poem to be read less as one of the *Amores* than as a precursor of the *Fasti*. Yet Ovid's linking of aetiology to the Roman festival calendar in the latter poem gives the *Fasti* precisely the political dimension lacking in the *Amores*. It is essential, furthermore, that we treat *Am.* 3.10 as an organic part of its collection; after all, Ovid did not edit it out of the second edition.[56] This erotic narrative of literary innovation, for which his own erotic—and literary— predicament acts as backdrop, properly belongs in a collection of poems on love and poetry. At the same time, it serves as a precursor of poetic change, as Ovid increasingly separates himself from the Corinna narrative in book 3 of the *Amores* and looks ahead to other projects. In the determined literariness of *Am.* 3.10, we see in one poet a master of "memorability" and a student of poetic memory.

Earlier in this chapter I commented on Ovid's predilection for Virgil, and I have since discussed several occasions on which Virgil has played an important role in mediating between the poetry of the past and Ovid's imagination. It should be evident by now that neither the restrictive and shallow sort of search for Virgilian "influences" on the *Amores* undertaken by Döpp nor even the more generous admission of Virgilian presence in Ovid as seen by Bömer is adequate; Ovid reads Virgil neither simply to imi-

---

55. See B. Weiden Boyd, "Tarpeia's Tomb: A Note on Propertius 4.4," *AJP* 105 (1984): 85–86.

56. See my discussion later, in chapter 4, on the two editions of the *Amores*.

tate him nor to trivialize him. We have also seen in the course of this chapter substantial evidence for the wide range of Ovid's literary vision: Virgil is a focal point, but he does not thereby obscure Ovid's view of or access to other poets and their poetry. James O'Hara has recently characterized Ovid as "Vergil's best reader."[57] I want to take this characterization a bit further and suggest, in fact, that we find in the *Amores* evidence that Virgil is in some sense Ovid's teacher; that is, he leads Ovid to read what he has read, to get inside his poetry and see its inner workings, to learn how to be an Augustan poet. A visual metaphor may help to capture the relationship between the two poets and their poetry: again and again, Virgil is the lens through which Ovid gains access to the literary past. At once microscope and telescope, the lens Virgil provides can help us, too, to open up the *Amores* and to see how Ovid has made these poems, in the setting of the almost infinite universe of learned Alexandrian tradition. Thomas has introduced another metaphor that can be helpful, too, that of the window: Ovid's revision of Virgil often serves as window onto a multilayered complex of allusion, looking far beyond Virgil himself, to the texts that had a formative influence on the earlier poet.

I hope it is evident by now how far we have moved from the generic and progressive fallacies with which this book began. Again, I have no desire to invoke a simplistic model of "anxiety of influence"; when Ovid looks to Virgil, he looks to (and through) the poet who, like no other, has determined the very essence of Augustan poetry, broadening it beyond generic horizons to a scope not conceived of so thoroughly by any other poet since Callimachus himself. Ovid's respect for the Virgilian achievement, in the *Eclogues,* the *Georgics,* and the *Aeneid,* is patent throughout the *Amores;* but this respect is complemented by an intimacy and ease that make Ovid's use of Virgil appear more like the *ludus poeticus* between Catullus and Calvus described in Catullus 50 than homage at a respectful—or jealous or trivializing—distance. Ovid uses Virgil not to define Virgil's contribution to the tradition but, as he uses his other sources of inspiration, to establish his own individuality. The imitativeness of the *Amores* in one sense documents Ovid's growth into the role of poet, a role he has learned through careful study of Virgil and the other poets who have contributed to the traditions of Latin poetry.

I have already noted that Ovid's imitations of Virgil are rarely exact; indeed, at least on occasion he appears to go out of his way to use Virgil in

---

57. J. O'Hara, "Vergil's Best Reader? Ovidian Commentary on Vergilian Etymological Wordplay," *CJ* 91 (1996): 255–76; cf. Hinds, *Metamorphosis of Persephone,* 16.

the creation of a particularly non-Virgilian scene, as in the description of the Argive Halaesus in *Am.* 3.13. "Und damit können wir bei Ovid fast mit Sicherheit rechnen: wenn er ein Motiv oder eine Wendung Vergils auf-nimmt, dann tut er es nach Möglichkeit *nicht* unter den gleichen Vorausset-zungen," comments Bömer.[58] Ovid's fondness for variation does not mean, however, that Ovid's aim is to undermine Virgil, to make fun of or other-wise to diminish the Virgilian achievement. It does mean, however, that all too often we overlook the presence of Virgil in the *Amores;* what we do see, furthermore, tends, as with the parallels noted by Döpp, to be superficial and little indicative of Ovid's engagement with the poetry of Virgil.

A superb example of how Virgil's poetry serves as the stimulus for mul-tiple allusion in an entirely non-Virgilian context occurs in *Am.* 2.12, which develops two favorite Ovidian themes, *militia amoris* and the triumph of love. Ovid draws an explicit comparison between himself and a triumphant general; he is returning in proud possession of his captive prize, Corinna (1–4):

> Ite triumphales circum mea tempora laurus:
>   vicimus; in nostro est ecce Corinna sinu,
> quam vir, quam custos, quam ianua firma (tot hostes!)
>   servabant, ne qua posset ab arte capi.

> [Go, triumphal laurel, around my brow; we have won. Look—Corinna is now in my embrace, the woman whom a husband, a doorkeeper, and a strong door (so many opponents!) protected, so that she might not be won by any means.]

To magnify his accomplishment, Ovid first declares that, unlike the Atri-dae, for example, he need not share the rewards of his victory with any fel-low fighters: *me duce ad hanc voti finem, me milite veni; / ipse eques, ipse pedes, signifer ipse fui* (13–14). He then moves on to a list of generalities intended to illustrate that women (and men's desire for them) have been the causes of the greatest battles in Greek and Roman history (17–26):

> nec belli est nova causa mei: nisi rapta fuisset
>   Tyndaris, Europae pax Asiaeque foret.
> femina silvestres Lapithas populumque biformem

---

58. Bömer, "Ovid und die Sprache Vergils," 276 (italics his).

turpiter apposito vertit in arma mero;   20
femina Troianos iterum nova bella movere
    impulit in regno, iuste Latine, tuo;
femina Romanis etiamnunc Vrbe recenti
    immisit soceros armaque saeva dedit.
vidi ego pro nivea pugnantes coniuge tauros: 25
    spectatrix animos ipsa iuvenca dabat.

[Nor is the cause of my war new: had Tyndareus' daughter not been stolen, there would be peace between Europe and Asia. Woman disgracefully drove the wild Lapiths and the race of two shapes to take up arms, after wine had been served; woman drove the Trojans to stir up new wars again, fair-minded Latinus, in your kingdom; giving them fierce weapons, woman brought fathers-in-law against their new Roman sons-in-law when the city was still young. I have seen bulls fighting over a snow-white mate; as she watched, the heifer herself spurred them on.]

This catalogue of exempla starts out predictably enough, with Helen; Ovid's second example, also Greek, is Hippodamia, for whose sake the Lapiths and Centaurs were moved to a brawl. Ovid then provides two corresponding Roman examples, Lavinia and the Sabine women. To this point, the list is rather conventional; in fact, aside from the reference to Lavinia, it follows exactly the list of exempla at Propertius 2.6.15–22 (Trojan war, Lapiths and Centaurs, Romulus and the Sabine women).[59] In this setting, the concluding exemplum, a heifer watching two bulls fight for her, comes as something of a surprise: it disregards the symmetries not simply of nationality but even of humanity.

The mention of Lavinia and Latinus in the central couplet here is enough for Döpp to find in these lines a reference to the *Aeneid*;[60] but aside from the fact that Ovid's *iuste Latine* echoes in a most general way one of Virgil's first mentions of Latinus (*rex arva Latinus et urbes / iam senior longa placidas in pace regebat, Aen.* 7.45–46), there is nothing in Ovid's description to prevent us from seeing in Ennius, Naevius, Cato, or Livy— or, indeed, in all of them taken together—an equally probable source or

---

59. See Booth, 65.
60. Döpp, *Vergilischer Einfluss,* 13; cf. Booth, ad loc., and G.K. Galinsky, *Ovid's Metamorphoses: An Introduction to the Basic Aspects* (Berkeley, 1975), 26–31.

point of reference;[61] the Virgilian echo here is formulaic. Virgil's presence and influence are indeed of real importance to Ovid's catalogue, but not where Döpp finds them; rather, the model provided by Virgil comes to the fore in the final and climactic example in Ovid's list, the description of the heifer and her jealous bulls. We should recall here two Virgilian models, a scene from the third book of the *Georgics* and a simile in the *Aeneid* imitating the earlier *Georgics* episode.[62] In the third *Georgic,* Virgil develops at some length the description of a heifer that arouses amatory *furor* in competing bulls and compels them to do battle out of their desire (215–23):

carpit enim viris paulatim uritque videndo   215
femina, nec nemorum patitur meminisse nec herbae
dulcibus illa quidem inlecebris, et saepe superbos
cornibus inter se subigit decernere amantis.
pascitur in magna Sila formosa **iuvenca:**
illi alternantes multa vi proelia miscent   220
vulneribus crebris; lavit ater corpora sanguis,
versaque in obnixos urgentur cornua vasto
cum gemitu; reboant silvaeque et longus Olympus.

[For the female wears away at their strength bit by bit and makes them
burn at the sight of her, and with her sweet charms she does not permit
them to recall grove or pasture; often, she compels her proud lovers to
use their horns to decide the contest between themselves. The lovely
heifer grazes on great Mt. Sila; her suitors join in battle, raining wounds

---

61. For that matter, there is no reason not to see a Virgilian model for all of Ovid's exempla here: Helen is mentioned at *Aen.* 1.650 and 7.363–64 (in addition to her appearance, as *Tyndaris,* in the Helen episode); Hippodamia is mentioned at *Geo.* 3.7; the Lapiths are mentioned at *Geo.* 2.455–57 and 3.115, and at *Aen.* 6.601 and 7.305, 307; and the Sabine women are mentioned at *Aen.* 8.635. Of course, the Propertian list in 2.6 is formally most apposite. On the historical and poetic traditions of the Lavinia episode, see Ogilvie, *Livy Books 1–5,* introduction, esp. pp. 32–35.

62. P. Brandt, ed., *P. Ovidi Nasonis Amorum libri tres* (Leipzig, 1911), ad loc., notes the *Georgics* passage. Typically, however, the *Eclogues* and the *Georgics* are rarely seen as sources for Ovid: cf. Döpp, *Vergilischer Einfluss,* 14, who comments, "Wie die nämentlichen Erwähnungen Virgils zeigen, war Virgil für Ovid vor allem der Dichter der Aeneis. Immer wenn Ovid auf den Aeneas-mythos Bezug nimmt, wird er auf Virgils Epos anspielen." E.J. Kenney, "Nequitiae Poeta," in *Ovidiana: Recherches sur Ovide publiées à l'occasion du bimillénaire de la naissance du poète,* ed. N.I. Herescu (Paris, 1958), 201–9, shows by contrast that Ovid was indeed familiar with the *Georgics* and that he exploited it frequently in the *Ars;* but even Kenney restricts himself to the generic paradigm (a didactic model for a pseudodidactic poem).

down on each other with great force. The dark blood bathes their bodies; their horns turned, they are driven upon their opponent with a great bellowing; the forests and the expanse of Olympus resound.]

Virgil later recalls this scene in *Aen.* 12, when he uses the image of two fighting bulls in a simile describing the confrontation of Turnus and Aeneas (715–23):

ac velut ingenti Sila summove Taburno	715
cum duo conversis **inimica in proelia tauri**	
frontibus incurrunt, pavidi cessere magistri,	
stat pecus omne metu mutum, mussantque **iuvencae**	
quis nemori imperitet, quem tota armenta sequantur;	
illi inter sese multa vi vulnera miscent	720
cornuaque obnixi infigunt et sanguine largo	
colla armosque lavant, gemitu nemus omne remugit:	
non aliter Tros Aeneas et Daunius heros . . .	

[And it was just as when, on great Sila or highest Taburnus, two bulls rush on each other, horns opposed, in hostile battle. After their timid herdsmen withdraw, the whole herd stands dumb with fear, and the heifers expect in silence the one who will rule the glen, whom all the herds will follow. The bulls exchange wounds among themselves with great force, and bearing down they drive their horns deep, bathing necks and shoulders in streams of blood. The whole grove bellows with their groans. Not otherwise the Trojan Aeneas and the Daunian hero [met in battle] . . .]

It has been observed that, in transforming an episode that is not a simile in the *Georgics* into a simile in the *Aeneid,* Virgil recalls an earlier setting of the image, in Apollonius. At *Argon.* 2.88–89, Apollonius employs a brief simile comparing the boxing match between Amycus and Polydeuces to the struggle of opposing bulls over a heifer: ἂψ δ᾽ αὖτις συνόρουσαν ἐναντίοι, ἠΰτε ταύρω / φορβάδος ἀμφὶ βοὸς κεκοτηότε δηριάασθον. Commentators on the *Georgics* generally note this simile but have little to say about its role in the formation of Virgil's scene;[63] the brevity and lack of specificity in Apollonius' simile make it seem to some critics to be of little

---

63. See Thomas, *Geo.,* on 3.217–18; cf. also Mynors, *Georgics,* on 3.215–41. See also R. Hunter, "Bulls and Boxers in Apollonius and Vergil," *CQ* 39 (1989): 557–61.

interest to Virgil.[64] Yet the anonymity of Ovid's exemplum is an exact replica of that in Apollonius' simile: here, therefore, we have a clear example of "window" reference, as Ovid makes multiple reference to both Virgilian scenes and simultaneously looks past, or behind, them, to Apollonius.

Virgil must have looked as well to Sophocles *Tr.* 497–530, the first stasimon of the play, in which the battle of Heracles and Achelous for Deianeira is described: Achelous is described as having the appearance of a bull (ὑψίκερω τετραόρου φάσμα ταύρου, 507–9); the contest of the two heroes involves the "confusion of bulls' horns"[65] (ἦν δὲ τόξων πάταγος, ταυρείων τ' ἀνάμιγδα κεράτων, 517–19; cf. *conversis . . . frontibus* and *cornuaque obnixi infigunt, Aen.* 12.716–17, 721); and Deianeira herself sits apart on a hill and watches them, ὥστε πόρτις ἐρήμα (530).[66] As is typical of Virgil, this Sophoclean model has other than descriptive implica-

---

64. Ross, *Virgil's Elements,* 160, mentions it briefly in his discussion of the relationship between the *Geo.* 3 episode and the *Aen.* 12 simile, only to dismiss it: "The simile [of *Aen.* 12] has no dignifying Homeric precedent (Apollonius has a one-and-a-half-line version, too brief to have 'influenced' Virgil, *Argon.* 2.88–89). . . ." Yet it is unthinkable that Virgil did not know Apollonius' simile: the very fact that he elevates the battle of the bulls to the subject matter of an extended simile in the *Aeneid* tells us that it is very likely that he does look to Apollonius, if only for the formal precedent. Hunter, "Bulls and Boxers," has recently shown, furthermore, that the parallel between a bulls' fight and a boxing match as described by Virgil at *Geo.* 3.233–34 reflects back on the diction of fighting in 220–27 and thus does indeed acknowledge the specific context in which Apollonius' simile occurs; Virgil has simply reversed the relationship between image and reality: "Whereas Vergil presents his bulls warring over a mate as boxers, Apollonius' boxers are like bulls warring over a mate" (558).

65. The translation is that of M. Jameson, *Sophocles: The Women of Trachis,* in *Sophocles II,* ed. D. Grene and R. Lattimore (Chicago, 1957), 91.

66. For the comparison of a lovely girl to a calf, see also the descriptions of Polyxena at Eur. *Hec.* 205–6, and of Iphigeneia at Eur. *IT* 359 and perhaps *IA* 1080–83 (though the text is unreliable in both the *Hec.* and *IA* passages), and see J. Mossman, *Wild Justice: A Study of Euripides' Hecuba* (Oxford, 1995), 147–49 and n. 20. At *h. Cer.* 174, young girls running are compared to frolicking heifers, but the comparison is made on account of the girls' speed, not on account of their beauty or desirability per se.

The scholiast on Soph. *Tr.* 521 observes the problem posed by the plural ταυρείων . . . κεράτων, and he comments, μετώπων· τοῦτο ἐπὶ Ἀχελώου; but in her commentary on the play (*Sophocles: Trachiniae* [Cambridge, 1982], ad loc.), P.E. Easterling notes that Sophocles makes no effort to distinguish between Heracles and the bull-like appearance of Achelous. See also M. Davies, ed., *Sophocles: Trachiniae* (Oxford, 1991), ad loc., and Hardie, *The Epic Successors of Virgil,* 23. That Ovid knew the Sophoclean passage and had it in mind is shown clearly by his reuse of it at *Met.* 9.46–49, in the description of the battle of Achelous and Heracles: *non aliter vidi fortes concurrere tauros, / cum pretium pugnae toto nitidissima saltu / expetitur coniunx: spectant armenta paventque / nescia, quem maneat tanti victoria regni.* See Bömer, *Met.,* ad loc.; Booth, ad loc.; Bömer, "Der Kampf der Stiere," 510. See also A.Y. Campbell, "Sophocles' *Trachiniae:* Discussions of Some Textual Problems," *CQ* 8 (1958): 21–23.

tions: it also supports a theme that is of great importance elsewhere in the *Aeneid,* the character of and myths surrounding Hercules as a model for Aeneas.[67]

In all of these similes, the context for the comparison is the human sphere: warriors are like bulls fighting over a heifer. The grandeur and heroic distance provided by the simile framework for these comparisons are lacking, however, in the *Georgics* episode; the corresponding blurring of boundaries between the human and bovine worlds can be either grotesque or strangely suggestive, depending on how it is handled. Ovid senses this dangerous ambiguity, and in his catalogue of exempla, he exploits it.[68]

Let us return to the two Virgilian passages again briefly. In his study of the *Georgics,* Ross looks at both of them closely and makes several observations helpful to our discussion.

> . . . The [*Georgics*] passage is a remarkable achievement: Virgil has managed somehow to stay just this side of the comic. Beginning right off with the *formosa iuvenca,* there are phrases and turns that are of almost Ovidian wit; in fact, anyone reading the passage with an eye or ear ready for its comic possibilities must wonder whether Virgil has managed to keep this side of the comic. Burlesque is the obvious danger, the mock-heroic attitude that puts great themes in incongruously small and unheroic settings; another danger is the superficiality of the anthropomorphic, amusing but insignificant. How does Virgil manage to avoid these dangers?
>
> . . . Again [i.e., in the *Aeneid*], the comic is dangerously close to the surface. . . . The simile has no dignifying Homeric precedent . . . : as the direct similarities of language show clearly enough, the precedent is Virgil's own version in the *Georgics,* with all its own inherent dangers.[69]

---

67. See, e.g., J. Henry, *Aeneidea,* vol. 1 (London and Dublin, 1873), 187–95; V. Buchheit, *Vergil über die Sendung Roms,* Gymnasium Beiheft 3 (Heidelberg, 1973), 116–33; G. Binder, *Aeneas und Augustus* (Meisenheim, 1971); G.K. Galinsky, "The Hercules-Cacus Episode in *Aeneid* VIII," *AJP* 87 (1966): 18–51; idem, *The Herakles Theme: The Adaptations of the Hero in Literature from Homer to the Twentieth Century* (Oxford, 1972), esp. 141–46; K.W. Gransden, ed., *Virgil: Aeneid Book VIII* (Cambridge, 1976), 17–20 and his introduction to 8.190–305.

68. The following chapter will consider at some length the relationship between Ovidian exempla and similes. See also n. 73 in this chapter, on Ovid's use of *vidi ego* to introduce the heifer-and-bulls exemplum here.

69. Ross, *Virgil's Elements,* 159–60.

Ross concludes that Virgil manages to avoid these dangers thanks to the richness of the literary tradition on which he draws and to which he draws our attention: according to Ross, Aeschylus, Apollonius, and Calvus all contribute to these passages (he does not mention the Sophoclean precedent, the existence of which simply strengthens his case).[70] There is no reductio ad absurdum in Virgil; instead, he endows these strange scenes with a heroic monumentality that is authentic and moving.[71]

Ovid's purpose, however, is quite different from Virgil's, and he exploits the incongruity overcome by both Virgil and the models behind Virgil's two scenes. Ovid chooses not to recall explicitly either the intricate literary associations or the attendant tragic pathos of the Virgilian passages and their predecessors. Instead, he gives us the scene in its baldest terms. Ovid thus subverts precisely the theme of the Virgilian scenes, the ravages of *furor*. Ross finds the most dangerous aspect of Virgil's treatment of heifer and bulls to be the "strange anthropomorphism" that permeates both passages; and I think it is exactly this aspect that Ovid remarked and wished to emphasize—and so make grotesque—in *Am.* 2.12. The placement of the *iuvenca* exemplum at the climactic close of Ovid's list is intended to heighten our expectations, after four other exempla drawn from the heroic past; yet the specific equation of a cow with human women, introduced as abruptly as it is, can only shock, since Ovid simultaneously suppresses any indication that we are to think of a heroic analogy.[72] As the words *vidi ego* (25) announce, this is explicitly *not* a simile, although we may well be skeptical about the likelihood that this exemplum is any more immediate to Ovid's experience than are the mythological instances in the preceding couplets. In fact, the didactic *vidi ego* is not autobiographical but an emphatic reminder of Virgil's use of the same expression in the *Georgics*.[73]

Whereas a sort of emotional anthropomorphism heightens the pathos

---

70. Ross, *Virgil's Elements,* 162–63. See also R.F. Thomas, "Gadflies (Virg. *Geo.* 3.146–148)," *HSCP* 86 (1982): 83–85.

71. It is no coincidence that, in the *Aeneid* simile, the single cow of the *Georgics* has become plural (*mussantque iuvencae,* 718); likewise, the erotic context for the bulls' strife is suppressed. Virgil knows exactly how far he can take such imagery and how much he can accomplish through a combination of suggestiveness and self-reference.

72. Note how Virgil does the exact opposite, and with remarkably different results, with the Hero-and-Leander exemplum at *Geo.* 3.258–63, an almost palpable example of what Ross calls the "strange anthropomorphism" of Virgil. I thank Richard Thomas for this observation. See also my discussion of Virgil's Hero and Leander earlier in this chapter.

73. See Bömer, "Der Kampf der Stiere," 503–13; Thomas, *Geo.,* on 1.193, 1.316–18. For further clarification of Ovid's use of *vidi ego* here and similar phrases elsewhere, see my discussion later in chap. 3.

of Virgil's heifer and her bulls, Ovid suggests its inverse, husbandry free of *furor,* as mortal passions are put on the same level with animal lust. Virgil enhances the anthropomorphic pathos of the *Georgics* scene by introducing the *iuvenca* with the word *femina* (216); only three lines later, and then not until the very end of the line, does he reveal her true identity. As Thomas notes, the placement of *femina* is itself emphatic; and the word occurs only here in the *Georgics.* Before Virgil, the application of *femina* to animals occurs virtually only in adjectival usages or scientific contexts. Thomas' comment is worth quoting: "The effect of the word in the present line is unmistakable: if only momentarily, the boundary between man and animal is once again broken."[74] Ovid likewise plays with his readers' expectations, but he pushes them far beyond the limits observed by Virgil. First of all, he pointedly avoids Virgil's novel use of *femina* and in doing so breaks away from the anaphora of *femina* with which his three earlier exempla begin. Instead, he introduces this heifer ambiguously, as *nivea coniuge.* While the adjective *niveus* has associations with the neoteric tradition, it is also commonly used of animals;[75] only at the end of the hexameter, with the word *tauros,* do we know for certain the direction this exemplum is taking. Correspondingly, the word *iuvenca* is placed as close to the end of the couplet as it can be, given the demands of the pentameter. With the couplet complete, we may well suspect that Ovid chose *coniunx* both to increase the shock value of the exemplum and to play on the etymology of the word; certainly its placement, in the line preceding *iuvenca* but following the anaphora, is intended to mislead.[76] We can be sure that Ovid expected his reader to recognize the double reference to Virgil here and to recall the import of those earlier texts for the new poem. The recollection of Turnus and Aeneas' struggle, as of Heracles and Achelous' before it, is stripped of epic grandeur, however, by the disappearance of the simile; most important, the *furor* of the *Georgics* scene is gone. We are left with

---

74. Thomas, *Geo.,* on 3.215–16. Thomas refers to earlier material in the same book, throughout which animals are likened to humans; cf., in particular, Virgil's use of *maritus* to describe a bull at *Geo.* 3.125.

75. See D.O. Ross, *Style and Tradition in Catullus* (Cambridge, MA, 1969), 61–62; Clausen, *Virgil's Aeneid,* 103–4. Cf. Bömer, *Met.,* on 1.610.

76. This is the first instance in extant Latin literature of *coniunx* used of animals: see *TLL* 4, col. 343.56, and Bömer, *Met.,* on 9.48. The pseudo-Ovidian author of *Am.* 3.[5] (see Kenney, "On the *Somnium* Attributed to Ovid") uses *maritus* and *coniunx* of bull and cow at 3.5.15–16. Isid. *Orig.* 9.7.9 gives the standard etymology: *coniuges appellati propter iugum, quod imponitur matrimonio coniungendis.* On the epic propriety of *coniunx,* see B. Axelson, *Unpoetische Wörter* (Lund, 1945), 57–58.

Ovid's abrupt and ironic restatement of the principle Virgil intended to illustrate in the third *Georgic: amor omnibus idem* (244). *Me quoque . . .* (27), concludes Ovid.

This irony is underlined by a final difference. In the *Georgics* and *Aeneid* passages we have considered, the wounds are physical and the blood flows freely (*lavit ater corpora sanguis, Geo.* 3.221; *sanguine largo / colla armosque lavant, Aen.* 12.721–22); Ovid, meanwhile, assures us that, in his case, the battle has been bloodless (*victoria . . . / in qua, quaecumque est, sanguine praeda caret,* 5–6; *sine caede,* 27). It might be argued by some that we are dangerously close to parody here; but as Ovid demonstrates, the exempla are essentially self-referential.[77] His translation of this imagery to an elegiac setting is calculated both to give the world of erotic poetry new breadth and to define its essential difference, even as it looks to its past beyond the boundaries of elegy.

The purpose of the preceding discussion has been to show just how quickly and how far Ovid's *Amores* can stray beyond Propertian models and the boundaries of genre. The term *multiple allusion* aptly describes the way in which Ovid draws on not one model but many in creating his elegiac world; the exempla of *Am.* 2.12 illustrate this effect perfectly. The issue of intent, however, has led to a surprising conclusion: though he displays an obvious literary debt to his predecessors, and most especially to Virgil, Ovid has no desire to invest his own poetry with the worldview of his models. At best, they serve as foils; most often, they provide only a momentary point of contact, from which Ovid then spins off to do something unexpected with the material. Again, we can see that Ovid's poetry is virtually never free from parallels, poetic memories, formulaic modes of expression, even specific references; yet at these very points of contact with literary tradition, Ovid breaks free from our expectation. Ovid writes always conscious of his past, the language of which becomes his means of shaping a very different present. The multiple allusiveness of Ovidian style is not primarily a commentary on Virgil, or Propertius, or any other supposed influence; rather, it defines Ovid himself.

---

77. R. Whitaker, *Myth and Personal Experience in Roman Love-Elegy: A Study in Poetic Technique,* Hypomnemata 76 (Göttingen, 1983), 137–38, overlooks the effect achieved by Ovid in designing this series of exempla. For a more general explanation of Ovid's use of exempla, see my discussion later, in chap. 3.

Chapter 3

Ovid's Visual Memory:
Extended Similes in the *Amores*

omnibus historiis se meus aptat amor
Ovid *Am.* 2.4.44

nimium amator ingenii sui
Quintilian *Inst.* 10.1.88

Among the many features of Ovid's style in the *Amores* that have been sin-
gled out for censure, his extended similes take pride of place.[1] Critics have
found them vulnerable for three reasons: they seem generically inappropriate, since they "belong" to epic; they serve only to heighten the self-consciousness of the *Amores,* rather than to enhance the ruse of sincerity
expected of elegy; and they are by and large blatantly imitative. Thus, the
charge of bad taste (not to mention derivativeness) has echoed particularly
loud and long in discussions of Ovidian similes; however distracting it may
be, it therefore needs to be addressed. In this chapter, I concern myself with
two of the perceived problems with Ovid's extended similes, propriety and
imitation, since they are closely connected. The issue of sincerity is a larger
one, already addressed briefly in my opening pages,[2] and I shall return to it
more directly in chapter 4.

I want to begin by suggesting the general direction I wish to take and by
establishing some of the subsidiary routes by which we may reach our des-
tination. The question of taste—in this case, bad taste—is, it seems to me,
a red herring. At the very least, before we decide whether or not Ovid has
succeeded in achieving his poetic goals, we must be confident that we
understand what those goals are; and I shall indicate more fully in the next

---

1. On the term *extended simile* and related nomenclature, see my discussion later in this
chapter.

2. See my introduction.

chapter why the critical assumption of bad taste as a goal in itself says more about the prejudices of modern readers than it does about the realities of Ovid's literary aspirations.

Rather than address the question of taste, then, I begin by asking why Ovid might have been attracted to extended similes in the first place. The parodic possibilities are of course obvious; and yet, as the similes themselves will show, Ovid has little interest in mocking or belittling his sources. Instead, we see again that Ovid approaches this device, virtually synonymous with epic, as a means both to transcend the boundaries of genre and to engage in dialogue with the tradition. The effect, too, is noteworthy. In part because they are so unexpected in elegy, and in part because they provide concentrated focus on a very detailed image or set of images, Ovid's extended similes create a new emphasis on the visual and concrete in a genre seemingly overgrown with convention. Their vividness competes constantly with their imitativeness: how can something so clearly a product of the poetic memory be so precisely suited to its new setting and even so realistic?

I shall return to these matters later in this chapter; but I turn now to the issue of generic propriety and to the distinctively "epic" character of extended similes. I have already described extended similes as virtually synonymous with epic; and any reader of post-Homeric poetry, especially epic, already knows that such similes often serve as the focal point of allusion and reference to the epic tradition. Extended similes of this sort are therefore frequently called "epic" similes. Yet there is nothing about extended similes besides usage that is inherently characteristic of epic; and usage is itself not an inherent condition, after all. In fact, from Homer onward it is the recurring burden of the extended simile to introduce into epic poetry subject matter drawn not only from outside the plot but in fact almost entirely from outside the sphere of the heroic world. The homely, domestic, and natural focus of Homeric similes is well known; as Edwards comments, "The purpose of a simile is to encourage the listener's imagination by likening something in the narrative of the heroic past to something which is directly within his own experience: and so the majority of Homeric similes are drawn from everyday life."[3] Thus, to paraphrase a familiar phrase, we can think of the similes in epic as representing "l'anti-épopée chez l'épopée."[4]

---

3. M.W. Edwards, *The Iliad: A Commentary*, vol. 5, *Books 17–20* (Cambridge, 1991), 35.

4. Cf. H. Foley, " 'Reverse Similes' and Sex Roles in the *Odyssey*," in *Women in the Ancient World: The Arethusa Papers*, ed. J. Peradotto and J.P. Sullivan (Albany, NY, 1984), 59–78. The most valuable brief introduction to the character and habits of the Homeric simile is by Edwards, *Iliad 17–20*.

Another factor in this attempt at generic definition provides only negative results but is of at least practical usefulness nonetheless: I refer to the virtual impossibility of achieving a precise count for such similes in a given author. Many such counts have been attempted; yet the varying results they produce reveal the arbitrariness of the criteria generally used by scholars in defining and categorizing similes.[5] An apt demonstration of the problem is provided by Williams, who, in a discussion of Propertius' similarity to Callimachus, counts as similes only those instances introduced by *ac veluti;* he finds three examples, one of which, he proceeds to note, can be discounted because it is closer to analogy than to simile (2.3.47–50). There remain only two "real" examples in Propertius (at 2.15.51–54 and 3.15.31–34), according to Williams;[6] and each of these is limited to one couplet and so delays the narrative proper for only two lines. Williams' point is to show that, while Propertius is fond of exempla, "[t]he figure of the extended simile was too heavy and ornate, too distracting, to be used in love poetry that purported to be personal statement."[7]

Williams' restrictive definition, or set of requirements, for the epic simile betrays a basic methodological flaw typical of many such studies: it presupposes that exempla and similes are radical alternatives, mutually uncongenial, rather than complements occupying different locations on the continuum of analogy. This continuum allows for variation in style and tone. Thus, because of its prominent role in epic, the extended simile carries epic associations even when used in nonepic settings, associations generally not possessed by the exemplum. That the extended simile carries epic associations does not mean, however, that the simile cannot be used else-

---

5. See the brief summary for Homer in Edwards, *Iliad 17–20,* 24. For collections of Ovid's similes, see J.A. Washietl, "De similitudinibus imaginibusque Ovidianis" (Diss. Vienna, 1883); S.G. Owen, "Ovid's Use of the Simile," *CR* 45 (1931): 97–106; E.G. Wilkins, "A Classification of the Similes of Ovid," *CW* 25 (1932): 73–78, 81–86; and T.F. Brunner, "The Function of the Simile in Ovid's *Metamorphoses,*" *CJ* 61 (1965–66): 354–63. A comparison of these surveys (as provided recently by R. Tabacco, "Le similitudini in Ovidio: Rassegna degli studi e prospettive di ricerca," *BStudLat* 25 [1995]: 129–71) shows how many variables can enter into the categorization and classification of similes.

6. Williams, *Tradition and Originality,* 776–77; cf. idem, *Figures of Thought in Roman Poetry* (New Haven and London, 1980), 62–63. Studies like that of G. Mader, "The Apollo Similes at Propertius 4.6.31–36," *Hermes* 118 (1990): 325–34, disregard Williams' strictures.

7. Williams, *Figures of Thought,* 62. Not surprisingly, Williams simply omits Ovid from consideration in his discussion. On exempla in elegy, see Whitaker, *Myth and Personal Experience in Roman Love-Elegy,* and the works cited in nn. 14 and 18 in this chapter. On Propertius' use of exempla, see also J.H. Gaisser, "Mythological *Exempla* in Propertius 1.2 and 1.15," *AJP* 98 (1977): 381–91, and F.M. Dunn, "The Lover Reflected in the *Exemplum:* A Study of Propertius 1.3 and 2.6," *ICS* 10 (1985): 233–59.

where; rather, it can be used for illustrative purposes much as an exemplum is, but it carries with it as well the memory of its epic associations. We have already seen an instance in which Ovid assumes our familiarity with the epic associations of similes, by drawing attention to the fact that similes and exempla can be almost identical in content but radically dissimilar in tone: I refer to the catalogue of exempla in *Am.* 2.12 that I discussed at the close of chapter 2. The analogies drawn by Ovid between his winning of Corinna and the triumph of love in the stories of Helen, Lavinia, and others culminate in an exemplum depicting bulls competing for a heifer, an exemplum that has roots in the similes of Sophocles, Apollonius, and Virgil. As I suggested earlier, Ovid exploits the less than lofty imagery of the exemplum by depriving it of its earlier simile setting; and he draws our attention to this operation with his claim to autopsy, *vidi ego* . . . . (*Am.* 2.12.25). Bömer has demonstrated that this claim can hardly be a literal truth and that it instead draws on a literary topos;[8] I propose that we take this a step further and suggest that Ovid's claim to autopsy is an allusion not to what he has seen in the Italian countryside but to what he has read—in this case, he has read the earlier similes.[9] Ovid thus emphasizes that the difference between exemplum and simile is not one of kind but one of degree, and that the continuum of analogy, as I have called it, allows him both to associate such devices with each other and to remove them from their respective moorings.[10] The strictures of generic propriety, therefore, are misapplied to the extended simile: its background in epic settings invites Ovid to use it in his poetry, as an important means of moving beyond the usual boundaries of elegy. For this reason, of course, I prefer to call the device "extended" rather than "epic," giving preference to an essential characteristic, not a circumstantial one.

The close connection between exemplum and simile has generally been overlooked precisely because of the simile's circumstantial history. In other words, while the exemplum has generally been treated as rhetorical, that is, prosaic and didactic, the simile has been characterized as epic and so poetic. Thus, the rhetorical exempla of Ovid have received restrained, if

---

8. Bömer, "Der Kampf der Stiere"; cf. my fuller discussion earlier, in chap. 2, and see n. 20 in this chapter.

9. Cf. Thomas, "The Old Man Revisited," 44–51; Miller, "Ovidian Allusion."

10. For a complementary discussion of the continuum of analogy as exploited by Catullus in poem 68b, see D. Feeney, " 'Shall I compare thee . . . ?': Catullus 68b and the Limits of Analogy," in *Author and Audience in Latin Literature,* ed. T. Woodman and J. Powell (Cambridge, 1992), 33–44. See also Whitaker, *Myth and Personal Experience in Roman Love-Elegy,* and the references cited in nn. 14 and 17 in this chapter.

begrudging, treatment, as somehow appropriate (if tedious) in erotodidac-
tic elegy, while the high-flown "poetic" pretensions of his extended similes
have seemed generally ill suited to his subject matter. As we shall soon see,
however, Ovid sometimes builds his extended similes out of just the sort of
material we would normally expect to find in an exemplum. Again, the difference between the two types of analogy is one of degree, and Ovid
exploits this difference to give his elegy qualities that transcend our "horizon of expectations."[11]

Homer himself offers an instructive example of the close relationship
between exemplum and simile; this illustration demonstrates that, because
the two figures serve similar rhetorical functions, we should not be surprised to see them used in parallel ways. A striking example of an extended
simile consisting of three comparanda and functioning much like a series
of exempla appears in *Il.* 14, as Homer describes the sound made by warriors marching into battle (394–401):

οὔτε θαλάσσης κῦμα τόσον βοάᾳ ποτὶ χέρσον,
ποντόθεν ὀρνύμενον πνοιῇ Βορέω ἀλεγεινῇ·   395
οὔτε πυρὸς τόσσος γε ποτὶ βρόμος αἰθομένοιο
οὔρεος ἐν βήσσης, ὅτε τ᾽ ὤρετο καιέμεν ὕλην·
οὔτ᾽ ἄνεμος τόσσον γε περὶ δρυσὶν ὑψικόμοισι
ἠπύει, ὅς τε μάλιστα μέγα βρέμεται χαλεπαίνων,
ὅσση ἄρα Τρώων καὶ Ἀχαιῶν ἔπλετο φωνὴ   400
δεινὸν ἀϋσάντων, ὅτ᾽ ἐπ᾽ ἀλλήλοισιν ὄρουσαν.

[Not so loudly bellows the wave of the sea on the shore, driven from the
sea by a fierce blast of Boreas; nor so great is the roar of burning fire in
a mountain glen, when it leaps up to burn wood; nor does the wind
sound so loudly around the lofty tresses of the oaks, and roar very
greatly and groan, as great as was the sound of the Trojans and the
Greeks shouting fearsomely, when they rose up against each other.]

Three elemental forces, water, fire, and wind, are described over the course
of six lines, easily divisible into three pairs. Each pair of verses is self-
standing; thus, this simile is extended not by detailed elaboration on one
comparandum over several verses but by the multiplication of parallel
comparanda, each allotted only two verses. If anything, the separateness

---

11. This term originates with H.R. Jauss: see, e.g., *Toward an Aesthetic of Reception,* trans.
T. Bahti (Minneapolis, 1982), 88–89.

of each comparandum from the others is emphasized by the structure of the lines: each couplet begins with οὔτε; the next word specifies the element to which each couplet is devoted (θαλάσσης κῦμα, πυρός, ἄνεμος); and in third position is the comparative τόσον/τόσσος/τόσσον.[12] As we shall soon see, Ovid follows this or a similar pattern very closely; as with exempla, so with similes he generally allows the metrical structure of the poetry to shape the material. In fact, this Homeric simile indicates that even Ovid's "elegizing" of the extended simile does not violate generic principles; rather, the Homeric precedent validates the Ovidian innovation.

It has also not been customary to treat similes and exempla as originating from the same desire to enhance the visual effectiveness of the passages in which they occur.[13] An examination of this shared function will therefore prove useful. The exemplum, generally based on subject matter drawn from mythology, history, or nature, is a rhetorical device recognized from antiquity for its ability to illustrate and amplify. Because the exemplum usually embodies a general principle, it presumes to illustrate what is both concrete and true; and its illustrative function is reinforced by its appeal to analogy.[14] As the anonymous author of the *ad Herennium* observes, exemplum and simile serve comparable functions: *exemplum est alicuius facti aut dicti praeteriti cum certi auctoris nomine propositio. id sumitur isdem de*

---

12. Interestingly, Virgil simultaneously imitates and corrects this simile at *Geo.* 4.260–63: *tum sonus auditur gravior, tractimque susurrant, / frigidus ut quondam silvis immurmurat Auster, / ut mare sollicitum stridit refluentibus undis, / aestuat ut clausis rapidus fornacibus ignis.* The imitation (noted by Servius, ad loc.) consists not only in its triple form but in Virgil's punning replacement of οὔτε with *ut* (see Farrell, *Vergil's Georgics and the Traditions of Ancient Epic,* 248–49); at the same time, Virgil improves on Homer, compressing six lines into three and avoiding the exactly parallel structure of the Homeric lines.

13. On visual effects, see G. Zanker, *Realism in Alexandrian Poetry* (London and Sydney, 1987), who considers only poetry of the Hellenistic period, but whose study has interesting implications for Augustan poetry; see my further discussion later, in chap. 4, on Ovidian realism. See also Johnson's emphasis on the "negative image" effect of Virgil's similes (*Darkness Visible,* 49–134) and my discussion of this effect later in this chapter. I note in passing that the movement of Ovid's similes in the *Amores* whets the appetite for the sort of visual effects that are so striking in the *Metamorphoses,* when simile becomes reality: see the episode from *Metamorphoses* discussed later, in chap. 6.

Of course, the visual effectiveness of similes is nothing new in Hellenistic or Roman verse: the Alexandrian critics appreciated the contributions of σαφήνεια and ἐνάργεια made to Homer's poetry by similes. See, e.g., A. Clausing, "Kritik und Exegese der homerischen Gleichnisse im Altertum" (Diss. Freiburg, 1913), esp. 55–56; and N.J. Richardson, "Literary Criticism in the Exegetical Scholia to the *Iliad:* A Sketch," *CQ* 30 (1980): 276–77, 279–80.

14. See H.V. Canter, "The Mythological Paradigm in Greek and Latin Poetry," *AJP* 33 (1954): 201–24; Williams, *Figures of Thought,* 62–94. Cf. Whitaker, *Myth and Personal Experience in Roman Love-Elegy.*

causis quibus similitudo (4.49.62).[15] The writer continues with a description of the four effects of an exemplum: the object it is used to illustrate is made more brilliant (*ornatior*), clearer (*apertior*), and more plausible (*probabilior*), and becomes so vivid that it seems visible (*ante oculos*). In other words, a major benefit of the exemplum, as of the simile, is its ability to effect vividness (*exprimit omnia perspicue ut res prope dicam manu temptari possit*, 4.49.62). Unlike the simile, however, the exemplum generally focuses on particular individuals familiar from history or myth or on the sort of natural and scientific lore commonly found in didactic treatises. Indeed, the didactic function of the exemplum is paramount: historical exempla, especially when used in rhetoric and historiography, tend to serve a moralizing purpose, while both mythological and "natural" exempla draw on truisms that they in turn reaffirm, often rather simplistically. Similes, however, rely on contrast to effect comparisons. Earlier I quoted Edwards' classic definition of the Homeric simile as illustrating the unfamiliar through the everyday; Lyne, meanwhile, reformulates the relationship between simile and setting, observing that Homer and Virgil both use the unfamiliar to illustrate the familiar.[16] From either vantage-point, therefore, the effect of the simile, while still visual, can often be far less precise and far more suggestive than is that of the exemplum; in fact, the visual effectiveness of similes can be very deceptive.

I shall return to this effect later in this chapter. First, let us look more closely at Ovid's exempla. Ovid's fondness for this device, sometimes in lengthy catalogues, is well known; and this feature of his verse has not been immune to criticism.[17] Because exempla serve, however superficially, as

---

15. Cf. Cic. *de Orat.* 3.205, *tum duo illa quae maxime movent, similitudo et exemplum;* and see A.D. Leeman, *Orationis Ratio* (Amsterdam, 1963), 40. In *Ancient Rhetorical Theories of Simile and Comparison* (Cambridge, MA, 1969), M. McCall documents the lack of clarity in ancient rhetorical writings regarding similes and argues that the simile as we know it is essentially a modern category; the ancient rhetoricians did not differentiate, at least not consistently, between it and a number of other types of comparison. It will become clear in what follows that, while I agree with McCall that the theoretical categories of comparison are not resolved in ancient rhetoric, there appears to have been a practical understanding of at least the extended simile as distinctively "epic" from as early as the Hellenistic period: see also K. Snipes, "Literary Interpretation in the Homeric Scholia: The Similes of the *Iliad,*" *AJP* 109 (1988): 205–8, who observes that a distinction between similes based on length is perhaps to be dated as early as Alexandrian scholars working on Homer.

16. R.O.A.M. Lyne, *Words and the Poet: Characteristic Techniques of Style in Vergil's Aeneid* (Oxford, 1989), 65–66.

17. On Ovidian exempla, see, inter alios, Washietl, "De similitudinibus"; H. Renz, *Mythologische Beispiele in Ovids erotischer Elegie* (Würzburg, 1935); J.T. Davis, "*Exempla* and Anti-*exempla* in the *Amores* of Ovid," *Latomus* 39 (1980): 412–17; P. Watson, "Mytho-

types of proof, they bear the added burden of being reminiscent of rhetoric and thus of Ovid's rhetorical training.[18] Two sets of examples chosen from early on in the *Amores,* the exempla from *Am.* 1.1 and 1.2, illustrate the type. In the opening poem of the collection, Ovid responds to Cupid's theft of a foot from his verse by protesting that poetry is, after all, no business of this god (1.1.1–6). According to the poet, the realms of love and of poetry are so mutually exclusive that any mingling of them would be, so he alleges, a reversal of the natural order of things. Ovid uses three couplets of oxymoronic exempla to make the point (7–12):

'quid si praeripiat flavae Venus arma Minervae,
    ventilet accensas flava Minerva faces?
quis probet in silvis Cererem regnare iugosis,
    lege pharetratae virginis arva coli?   10
crinibus insignem quis acuta cuspide Phoebum
    instruat, Aoniam Marte movente lyram? . . .'

["What if Venus were to take up the weapons of blonde Minerva, and blonde Minerva in turn were to fan the kindled flames of love? Who would allow Ceres to reign in the mountain forests, and the fields to be cultivated in accordance with the principles of the quivered virgin? Who would equip Phoebus, distinguished for his tresses, with a sharp spear, while Mars commenced the Aonian lyre? . . ."]

logical Exempla in Ovid's *Ars Amatoria,*" *CP* 78 (1983): 117–26. Williams, *Tradition and Originality,* 512, in a discussion of *Am.* 1.5, is strongly critical of what he calls "exhaustive enumeration" in the *Amores,* and he is troubled by Ovid's "extremely orderly, even rigidly logical, process of exposition," which leaves no room for surprise and suggestiveness. See now the elegant rebuttal of Hinds, "Generalising about Ovid," 11: "Williams is certainly right to see an interest in catalogues as an Ovidian trait. But what my analysis of *Am.* 1.5.3–6 perhaps shows is that increased enumeration does not necessarily imply increased explicitness. Catalogues are not inherently 'counter-poetic,' and in this case Ovid's accumulation of light-effects serves to generate, not to disperse, an atmosphere of poetic suggestiveness and mystery." Hinds' observation will be found to have more general application in what follows.

18. A typical example of the appeal to Ovid's rhetorical training as the all-purpose explanation for his style is found in McKeown 1:68–71 and *passim* on individual poems; see esp. vol. 2, on 1.10.25–28, an animal exemplum introduced to illustrate human sexuality. For the rhetorical use of exempla, see K. Alewell, "Über das rhetorische ΠΑΡΑΔΕΙΓΜΑ" (Diss. Leipzig, 1913), who focuses on historical exempla, and McCall, *Ancient Rhetorical Theories.* See also H. Kornhardt, *Exemplum: Eine bedeutungsgeschichtliche Studie* (Göttingen, 1936) and B. Price, "Παράδειγμα and *Exemplum* in Ancient Rhetorical Theory" (Ph.D. diss., University of California, Berkeley, 1975).

The exemplary nature of these mythological references is grounded in their familiarity: who in the world could not answer these incredulous rhetorical questions? The effectiveness of the exempla is reinforced by the structure of the lines: each pair of contrasted gods is given one couplet, and within each couplet one verse is given to each divinity. Thus, Venus and Minerva are set opposite each other in 7–8; Ceres and Diana, the *pharetrata virgo,* in 9–10; and Apollo and Mars in 11–12. Details provide variety: the balance of the three questions is offset by the change from *quid si* in 7 to *quis* in 9 and the subsequent postposition of *quis* in 11; the first couplet is structured as two *si*-clauses, the second as two indirect statements following *probet,* the third as a deliberative question followed by an ablative absolute, and so on. The guiding principle is obvious: the elegiac couplet is exploited for maximum potential and becomes a vehicle for meaning in its structure as well as in its content.

In *Am.* 1.2, Ovid uses exempla drawn from nature to demonstrate that resistance to love is pointless (11–16):

> vidi ego iactatas mota face crescere flammas
>   et rursus nullo concutiente mori.
> verbera plura ferunt quam quos iuvat usus aratri,
>   detractant prensi dum iuga prima, boves.
> asper equus duris contunditur ora lupatis: 15
>   frena minus sentit, quisquis ad arma facit.

[I have seen that, when a torch is shaken, the flames thrown forth grow, then die back down when no one stirs them. When cattle that have been checked reject the yoke at first, they endure more lashes than do those whom the work of the plow pleases. The untamed horse endures bruises on the mouth from a cruel curb; any horse that makes ready for riding equipment feels the reins less.]

Again we see a combination of pattern and variation holding the three exempla together. As in the previous instance, here too Ovid uses material so familiar it is virtually a cliché; by opening these lines with the words *vidi ego,* however, Ovid insists that these exempla be taken seriously.[19] In other

---

19. I have printed the text as it appears in McKeown's edition. Kenney (both editions) prefers to read *vidi* with the MSS instead of the *rursus* found in Porcius Latro *apud* Sen. *Contr.* 2.2.8 (on which, see my next note): see McKeown, ad loc., and Goold's discussion of the alternatives, "*Amatoria Critica,*" 18–19.

words, even as he uses a patently rhetorical device familiar from didactic poetry, Ovid asserts a connection between exemplum and personal experience.[20] Of course, the almost formulaic style of these exempla suggests that they are anything but sincere; and to modern tastes at least, they seem little more than rhetorical filler. Of far more interest here than Ovid's supposed educational background, however, are the effects these exempla have on his poems: they both heighten the visual effectiveness of his elegy and call into question this poetry's spontaneity and sincerity.

The potential of the extended simile for multidimensional allusion and reference requires clarification, too. To provide this clarification, I shall make an extended comparison of my own and look at the critical history of one of the best-known—and indeed, prototypical—extended similes in Latin poetry. I begin with what is probably the most famous piece of simile criticism from antiquity, Aulus Gellius *NA* 9.9.12–14:

Et quoniam de transferendis sententiis loquor, memini audisse me ex Valeri Probi discipulis, docti hominis et in legendis pensitandisque veteribus scriptis bene callidi, solitum eum dicere nihil quicquam tam inprospere Vergilium ex Homero vertisse quam versus hos amoenissimos, quos de Nausicaa Homerus fecit:

Οἵη δ᾽ Ἄρτεμις εἶσι κατ᾽ οὔρεος ἰοχέαιρα,
ἣ κατὰ Τηΰγετον περιμήκετον ἢ Ἐρύμανθον,
τερπομένη κάπροισι καὶ ὠκείῃς ἐλάφοισιν·
τῇ δέ θ᾽ ἅμα νύμφαι, κοῦραι Διὸς αἰγιόχοιο,
ἀγρονόμοι παίζουσι· γέγηθε δέ τε φρένα Λητώ·
πασάων δ᾽ ὕπερ ἥ γε κάρη ἔχει ἠδὲ μέτωπα,
ῥεῖα δ᾽ ἀριγνώτη πέλεται, καλαὶ δέ τε πᾶσαι,—

qualis in Eurotae ripis aut per iuga Cynthi
exercet Diana choros, quam mille secutae
hinc atque hinc glomerantur Oriades. illa pharetram
fert humero gradiensque deas supereminet omnis.
Latonae tacitum pertemptant gaudia pectus.

---

20. Ovid's appeal to sincerity here occurs even as he draws on a textbook declamation by Porcius Latro: see McKeown, ad loc. and 1:68–69, quoting Sen. *Contr.* 2.2.8. Thus, we have another example of literary reference masquerading as autopsy. On *vidi* (*ego*) and the like in didactic poetry, see Thomas, *Geo.*, on 1.193–97, 1.316–18; cf. also *Geo.* 1.472, 2.32. *Vidi ego* also draws attention to the visual dimension of the exempla: they are didactically effective precisely because they are so vivid.

Primum omnium id visum esse dicebant Probo, quod aput Homerum quidem virgo Nausicaa ludibunda inter familiares puellas in locis solis recte atque commode confertur cum Diana venante in iugis montium inter agrestes deas, nequaquam autem conveniens Vergilium fecisse, quoniam Dido in urbe media ingrediens inter Tyrios principes cultu atque incessu serio, 'instans operi', sicut ipse ait, 'regnisque futuris', nihil eius similitudinis capere possit, quae lusibus atque venatibus Dianae congruat; . . .

[And since I am speaking of the translation of ideas, I recall that I heard from the students of Valerius Probus, a learned man very skillful in reading and thinking about ancient texts, that he was accustomed to say that Virgil had translated nothing from Homer so unsuccessfully as those delightful verses that Homer composed about Nausicaa:

Just as Artemis goes, flinging arrows, down the mountain ridge, over lofty Taugetus or Erymanthus, delighting in the boars and the swift deer: Nymphs in their country haunts, the daughters of aegis-bearing Zeus, frolic in her company; and Leto rejoices in her heart; above them all she stands, her head and face above, and easily stands out among them as she goes—though they are all fair;

Just as on the banks of the Eurotas or along the ridges of Cynthus Diana trains her dancing company; following her, a thousand mountain nymphs assemble from this place and that; she carries a quiver on her shoulder and, as she advances, towers over all the goddesses. Joy stirs Leto's silent heart deep within her . . .

They said that it seemed to Probus first of all that whereas in Homer the maiden Nausicaa, playing with her serving maids in a lonely place, is compared rightly and appropriately with Diana hunting on the mountain-ridges among the woodland goddesses, Virgil did this not at all appropriately, since Dido comes in to the middle of the city among the Tyrian chiefs with solemn dress and step, "urging on the work," Virgil says, "and the future kingdom," and can take on none of that similarity that harmonizes with the games and hunting of Diana; . . .]

Aulus Gellius reports that Valerius Probus, the noted grammarian of the first century A.D., felt that the results of Virgil's "translation" of Homer

Od. 6.102–8 were particularly unsuccessful in the simile at *Aen.* 1.498–502 comparing Dido to Diana among her attendants. Probus adduces the Homeric model, in which Nausicaa is compared to Artemis with her nymphs; but whereas he finds the Homeric verses delightful (*amoenissimos*), Virgil's imitation is unsuitable (*nequaquam conveniens*), since there seem to be no similarities between Dido and Diana. As Clausen has recently noted, this anecdote tells us far more about the woeful state of affairs in the Roman classroom than it does about Virgil;[21] but Probus' discussion remains of exceptional interest, for it establishes a precedent for the juxta-position of Virgilian with Homeric similes and reflects an implicit judgment that his imitation is simply borrowing or translation and that it is borrow-ing of an inferior sort at that. We see here an early instance of the progres-sive fallacy in operation; this time Virgil is its victim, as he has been so often—but not so often as Ovid—in the history of classical scholarship.[22]

Because of its striking similarity to more modern criticisms of Ovid, I want to look at Probus' method and his results carefully. His juxtaposition of Virgilian simile and Homeric model is accurate insofar as we can be sure that Virgil has Homer in mind; but Probus' analysis is also incomplete, in that he ignores or is unaware of the intermediary role played by Apollonius between these two similes. I refer again to Clausen, who has shown that Apollonius' adaptation of the Homeric simile at *Argon.* 3.876–86[23] is also very much in Virgil's mind in his depiction of Dido. But here I am not con-cerned so much with the specifics of Virgil's borrowings as with the more general premise to be derived from what Virgil has done: unlike Probus, who was mistaken in assuming that Virgil's simile participates in a one-to-one relationship with a Homeric model, we can see that Virgil's frame of

---

21. Clausen, *Virgil's Aeneid,* 132 n. 13. Cf. also H.D. Jocelyn, "The Annotations of M. Valerius Probus," *CQ* 34 (1984): 464–65, and idem, "The Annotations of M. Valerius Probus, III: Some Virgilian Scholia," *CQ* 35 (1985): 474: ". . . dimly perceptible [is] the activity of a scholar who thought well of his own powers of judgement and who impressed posterity. Unfortunately a large emphasis has to be placed on the adverb 'dimly.'"

22. After surveying the continuing history of the progressive fallacy in discussions of this simile, V. Pöschl, *Die Dichtkunst Vergils: Bild und Symbol in der Äneis,* 3d ed. (New York and Berlin, 1977), 84–93, offers a more sympathetic reading of his own. See also R. Rieks, "Die Gleichnisse Vergils," *ANRW* 2.31.2 (1981): 1034–38.

23. οἵη δὲ λιαροῖσιν ἐφ' ὕδασι Παρθενίοιο, / ἠὲ καὶ Ἀμνισοῖο λοεσσαμένη ποταμοῖο, / χρυσείοις Λητὼις ἐφ' ἅρμασιν ἑστηυῖα / ὠκείαις κεμάδεσσι διεξελάσῃσι κολώνας, / τηλόθεν ἀντιόωσα πολυκνίσου ἑκατόμβης· / τῇ δ' ἅμα νύμφαι ἕπονται ἀμορβάδες, αἱ μὲν ἐπ' αὐτῆς / ἀγρόμεναι πηγῆς Ἀμνισίδος, αἱ δὲ λιποῦσαι / ἄλσεα καὶ σκοπιὰς πολυπίδακας· ἀμφὶ δὲ θῆρες / κνυζηθμῷ σαίνουσιν ὑποτρομέοντες ἰοῦσαν· / ὣς αἵ γ' ἐσσεύοντο δι' ἄστεος, ἀμφὶ δὲ λαοὶ / εἶκον ἀλευάμενοι βασιληΐδος ὄμματα κούρης. See Clausen, *Virgil's Aeneid,* 18–21; see also C. Conrardy, "De Vergilio Apollonii Rhodii imitatore" (Diss. Fribourg, 1904), 29–31.

reference is not simply a single Homeric source. I will call the sort of imitation that Probus hypothesizes here "one-dimensional"; this term denotes a type of composition that really is inferior borrowing, since the poet responsible for the imitation uses virtually no independent judgment in his translation and does not intervene in any creative way between the source of the imitation and its new context. As recent interpretations have shown, Virgil's imitations are never inert or one-dimensional in any sense: instead, he frequently weaves a dense web of memories and associations through his grasp on the poetic memory and habit of multiple reference and so enriches the coloration of his primary narrative. We know well by now that imitation in Virgil repays our attention by sounding the depths of ambiguity and inviting the very multiplicity of meanings that Probus ignores, and that Virgil's similes in particular, by virtue of their character, invite comparison with earlier models.

Yet Virgil's fate is not Ovid's; and so the charge of uninspired borrowing has dogged Ovid's poetry, nowhere more so than in the *Amores*. Ovid is the consummate *heteros heuretes:* in the two preceding chapters, I have demonstrated how almost any raw material, from the smallest metrical tag to an erudite Alexandrianism or a distinctive literary topos, can serve as his entry into a dialogue with the inherited past. In this he hardly differs from his Augustan predecessors, except in the degree to which he is inclined to use such material; but unlike his predecessors, Ovid is considered the master of the one-dimensional imitation. My primary goal in the last chapter was to shatter this truism; and the examples considered there offer ample indication of Ovid's breadth of literary reach. *Am.* 2.16 and 3.10 also suggest in their vitality how alive the *ludus poeticus* is for Ovid, that his elegy is not simply the cul-de-sac at the end of a one-way street of derivativeness but rather really engages the tradition firsthand and anticipates its response. All told, these poems illustrate that Ovid too weaves a dense web, handling with ease a supply of the most variegated materials of which a living poetic tradition is composed.

This leads in turn to a second truism: Ovid's imitations say nothing about both the new and the source contexts, and they function primarily to provide the newer work with a respectable pedigree. Ovid's extended similes in particular have been the focus of harsh criticism on this point, probably because they are so evidently the result of rhetorical self-indulgence. Quintilian's famous comment about Ovid's style, cited at the opening of this chapter, is broadly based and seems to pertain to many aspects of

Ovid's poetry;[24] and the similes are clearly, by any measure, excessive. At the same time, I believe it is more useful to ask why his similes self-consciously draw attention to themselves than to be troubled by and thus dismissive of them. I want to focus, therefore, on the settings in which Ovid includes these similes and on their more general effect on the narrative of the *Amores*. I believe that Ovid wants both to exploit and to subvert the epic background of the simile, using this device for visual emphasis even as he draws subject matter reminiscent of the heroic past into an elegiac environment; thus, excess is necessary (as well as being congenial in any case to Ovid's writing style). When Odysseus cries like a bereaved woman (*Od.* 8.523–31), for example, Homer uses the image not to exploit its incongruity but to create sympathy for our character, remind us of his wife, and generally reflect on the universality of Odysseus' plight; when Ovid brings epic imagery to bear on the world of his elegy, however, its status as poetic memory both transforms the elegiac present and reminds us how long ago the heroic past is.[25] We saw a different aspect of this process in Ovid's use of the Halaesus myth in *Am.* 3.13;[26] Ovid takes advantage of the contrast between the two genres both to expand the horizons of elegy and to illustrate the unbridgeable gap between two literary worlds.

I turn now to the extended similes of the *Amores*. Edwards provides a useful distinction between short and extended (or what he simply calls "long") similes: short similes have no finite verb, while long similes consist of at least one entire clause.[27] Given Ovid's usage of extended similes in the *Amores,* however, it seems practical to modify this definition somewhat and to designate as extended similes (or simile clusters, in cases like the example from Hom. *Il.* 14 quoted earlier in this chapter) those that extend

---

24. Cf. *Inst.* 10.1.98; Sen. *Contr.* 2.10.12 and 4.28.17.

25. Ovid also takes special advantage of similes to experiment with other distinctive stylistic devices. We see several instances of high style, features like artificial and elaborate word order and enjambment, that are special effects particularly appropriate to an epicizing simile; other features, like newly coined words, complement the very visual character of Ovidian similes. I shall comment on these features more fully in the following discussion. On Ovid's style generally, see E.J. Kenney, "The Style of the *Metamorphoses*," in *Ovid,* ed. J.W. Binns (London and Boston, 1973), 116–53; Knox, *Ovid's Metamorphoses,* 27–47; Bömer, "Ovid und die Sprache Vergils"; and J. Booth, "Aspects of Ovid's Language," *ANRW* 2.31.4 (1981): 2686–2700.

26. See my discussion in chap. 2.

27. Edwards, *Iliad 17–20,* 24; see also M. Coffey, "The Function of the Homeric Simile," *AJP* 78 (1957): 113–32.

beyond a single couplet; as we shall see, the longer similes lend themselves most naturally to multiple allusion and extensive experimentation.[28] The apparent disproportion of similes more than a couplet in length has attracted the disapprobation of critics; but I shall show that the lengthiness of some of Ovid's similes is not simply a by-product of his desire to indulge in generic impropriety but tells us something about his new perspective on elegy. The introduction of the extended simile to elegy widens the scope of the genre's embrace. The extended simile is therefore not optional, nor is its function simply ornamental; rather, it presents Ovid with a crucial means of bringing the poetry of the past within the boundaries of his new elegiac project. The images embedded in Ovid's similes mirror his renovating vision of elegy.

The first Ovidian simile to which we shall turn is perhaps the best-known simile in the *Amores,* the opening of 1.10. Its familiarity is primarily a result of critics' inclination to see in it a straightforward example of Ovid's imitation of Propertius; this view will therefore provide us with a good starting point.

Ovid begins his poem with a series of three couplets, each of which describes a mythological heroine whose beauty has earned her love—and rape: Helen, Leda, and Amymone (1–7):

Qualis ab Eurota Phrygiis avecta carinis
    coniugibus belli causa duobus erat,
qualis erat Lede, quam plumis abditus albis
    callidus in falsa lusit adulter ave,
qualis Amymone siccis erravit in Argis,   5
    cum premeret summi verticis urna comas,
talis eras: . . .

[Just like the one who was carried off by Phrygian ships from Eurotas and was the cause of war for her two mates; just like Leda, who was tricked by the clever wife-cheater in the false guise of a bird, hidden in white feathers; just like Amymone, who wandered in dry Argos, with a water jar weighing down the hair on her head: so did you appear. . . .]

---

28. See Snipes, "Literary Interpretation in the Homeric Scholia." Feeney's discussion of the analogies of Cat. 68b, "Limits of Analogy," shows by demonstration that the relative affectiveness of the analogies in that poem depends on their length.

The *qualis* with which each couplet opens is balanced by *talis* in line 7, at which point Ovid goes on to explain that in Corinna's case, appearances have been betrayed by reality: she has tarted herself up and is now no better than a common prostitute. Attention is demanded also by the structure of the simile itself: each of the three couplets contains its own comparandum, so that, while extended over six verses, this simile might just as easily be said to consist of three separate similes strung together by anaphora and asyndeton. Thus, they formally resemble nothing so much as the exempla of didactic elegy; as we shall see, however, their incorporation into an extended simile has more than formal implications.

The critics are virtually unanimous in seeing this opening as a one-dimensional adaptation of the beginning of Propertius 1.3, which contains one of the few extended similes in the entire Propertian corpus:[29]

Qualis Thesea iacuit cedente carina
 languida desertis Cnosia litoribus;
qualis et accubuit primo Cepheia somno
 libera iam duris cotibus Andromede;
nec minus assiduis Edonis fessa choreis   5
 qualis in herboso concidit Apidano:
talis visa mihi mollem spirare quietem
 Cynthia non certis nixa caput manibus. . . .

[Just like the Cnosian girl, who lay languid on the deserted shore as Theseus' ship departed; just like Cepheus' daughter, Andromeda, who lay in first sleep, now freed from the sharp rocks; and just like the Edonian girl, who fell into sleep on the grassy bank of Apidanus, exhausted by continual dancing—like these Cynthia seemed to me to breathe gentle sleep, resting her head on her unsteady hands. . . .]

The structural parallels between the two similes are evident, and it is not my aim to deny them: both imitation of structure and imitation of position

---

29. For comparison of the two similes, see L.C. Curran, "Ovid *Amores* 1.10," *Phoenix* 18 (1964): 314–19; A.G. Lee, "Tenerorum Lusor Amorum," in *Critical Essays on Roman Literature: Elegy and Lyric,* ed. J.P. Sullivan (Cambridge, MA, 1962), 155; Barsby, *Am.,* 117; Morgan, *Ovid's Art of Imitation,* 70–71. I note also that this does not fit Williams' criteria for an extended simile in Propertius, cited in n. 6 in this chapter.

are familiar characteristics of Alexandrian poetry.[30] In this instance, furthermore, Ovid appears to be following Propertius' lead in elevating otherwise straightforward mythological exempla to the "epic" stature of the extended simile. I want to make a case, however, for a broadening of perspective as we consider Ovid's simile. First of all, Ovid uses none of the specific exempla used by Propertius in the ostensible model. In fact, only the first of the couplets has an apparent Propertian antecedent, and that is in Propertius 1.2 (*nec Phrygium falso traxit candore maritum / avecta externis Hippodamia rotis,* 19–20), not 1.3. The context is another Propertian list of heroines, brought in as exempla to support Propertius' recommendation that Cynthia avoid the use of artificial *cultus* to enhance her looks. The relevance of Propertius' theme in 1.2 to Ovid's is obvious, and another reminiscence of the same poem is suggested later in this elegy, when Ovid develops a description of *nudus Amor:* compare Ovid's *et puer est et nudus Amor, sine sordibus annos / et nullas vestes, ut sit apertus, habet (Am.* 1.10.15–16) and Propertius' *crede mihi, non ulla tuae est medicina figurae: / nudus Amor formae non amat artificem* (1.2.7–8).

But let us return to Ovid's opening couplet and its ostensible Propertian model. How "memorable" is this reference, after all? As we realize at the end of the Propertian exemplum from 1.2, the lovers in question are Pelops and Hippodamia; but much of the language used earlier in the Propertian couplet, especially **Phrygium** . . . *maritum and* **avecta externis** . . . *rotis,* leads us to expect Helen rather than Hippodamia. At least the epithets *Phrygium* and *avecta externis,* if not the nouns *maritum* and *rotis,* lead us to anticipate a reference to the most famous rape of all. Were Hippodamia not mentioned by name, we might therefore be expected to misconstrue the allusion. When Ovid begins his simile, he satisfies this expectation, restoring Helen and Paris to the scene while managing to mention neither by name. Instead, he juxtaposes geographical allusions to Sparta (Eurotas) and Troy (Phrygia), before revealing all in the pentameter with the words *belli causa.* Ovid thus alludes to Propertius while avoiding imitation of him.

We have now expanded our perspective somewhat on Ovid's look back at the tradition, and we have seen one dimension yield to two. Before I move on to my next example, however, two observations remain to be made. When critics call what we have just seen "imitation," they are not just guilty of terminological inaccuracy but also run the risk of misunderstanding Ovid's frame of reference. What we really have here is an exploita-

---

30. See chap. 1.

tion of our expectations, as Ovid manages to evoke and yet avoid imitation through antithesis; in doing so, he offers a superb example of Alexandrian *oppositio in imitando*.[31] Another detail, at once subtle and suggestive, has to my knowledge not been noted elsewhere: the first half of the first line, *qualis ab Eurota,* gives this simile a long and interesting pedigree, associating it first and foremost with a passage I discussed earlier in this chapter, Virgil's extended simile describing Dido's entrance in *Aen.* 1. Even Ovid's *talis eras* (7) echoes the words which Virgil closes his simile, *talis erat Dido* (*Aen.* 1.503). But we can take this point a step further: the fact that a number of other Latin poets begin similes with a form of *qualis* and a mention of the Eurotas (e.g., Catullus at 64.89, *quales Eurotae progignunt flumina myrtus,* and Propertius at 3.14.17, *qualis et Eurotae Pollux et Castor harenis*) should lead us to suspect a Hellenistic model. And there is just such a simile-opening in Callimachus' fifth hymn, in what is itself an allusive context: ἁ δὲ δὶς ἑξήκοντα διαθρέξασα διαύλως, / οἷα παρ' Εὐρώτᾳ τοὶ Λακεδαιμόνιοι / ἀστέρες, ἐμπεράμως ἐνετρίψατο λιτὰ λαβοῖσα / χρίματα, τᾶς ἰδίας ἔκγονα φυταλιᾶς (*h.* 5.23–26).[32] The recurrence of this wording in the works of several poets suggests both that a continuing tradition of simile imitation exists, and that the openings of similes have an especially strong hold on the poetic memory.[33]

Finally, it is worthwhile to step back from the details of this simile for a

---

31. See Giangrande, " 'Arte Allusiva.' "

32. For Propertius' pointed use of the Callimachean simile, see B. Weiden Boyd, "Propertius on the Banks of the Eurotas (A Note on 3.14.17–20)," *CQ* 37 (1987): 527–28.

33. McKeown, ad loc., lists the parallels but finds no particular significance in them.
Before moving on to the next Ovidian simile, I offer a further conjectural suggestion. In the context in which this simile-opening first appears, that is, in the fifth hymn, Callimachus is interested in glorifying Athena's beauty and showing her superiority to all would-be competitors. First, Callimachus oddly uses a description of the judgment of Paris to make this point—this use is odd, of course, because even the least Callimachean of readers would know that, after all, Athena did not win. Bulloch argues in his commentary on this hymn, however, that Callimachus' rather eccentric and convoluted means of focusing on Athena's beauty works in part because it relies on a recognizable imitation of Theocritus' eighteenth Idyll, an epithalamium to Helen, in which Helen's attendants extol her beauty as compared with their own (see A.W. Bulloch, ed., *Callimachus: The Fifth Hymn* [Cambridge, 1985], on *h.* 5.23–28). The similarity to which Callimachus wishes to draw our attention by his reminiscence of Theocritus is that the subject of both passages is a woman outstanding in beauty among her companions. In this, we see an obvious similarity to the subject and context of the Homeric, Apollonian, and Virgilian similes I have already mentioned; and we might also observe that Helen reappears in Ovid's recollection of his most direct model, Virgil. Again, I want to emphasize that the connection here is admittedly rather tenuous; nonetheless, I think it at least possible that Ovid, while building a simile that appears structurally Propertian but starts with an opening reminiscent of a memorable Virgilian simile, wants to show also that he is aware of the ultimate source for this simile-opening in Callimachus and Theocritus.

moment and look at its overall effect. As we have seen, the simile serves to emphasize the deceptiveness of Corinna's appearance; it heightens the contrast between illusion and reality. This contrast is important to Ovid and may well help to explain why he is so fond of similes generally. As a vehicle for imagery, the simile can be both visually realistic and intellectually deceptive: the extended simile, by virtue of its ability to bring every detail into painstaking focus while offering a multiplicity of alternative visions, is a means to both emphasize and undermine visual realism. The simile we have just considered, for example, while suggesting a visual effect, is in fact not directly visual at all. Ovid *seems* to want to compare the beauty of three mythological heroines to that of his beloved; but the terms of his comparison emphasize not physical appearances but the circumstances of rape. In other cases, as we shall see, the visual impact of a simile is not illusory but real; but in these cases, Ovid's realism is itself often deceptive. Zanker has observed that one of the main impulses behind visual realism in poetry is "the desire to confront the past and interpret it for the present";[34] when this function of realism is set against Ovid's densely allusive similes, the end result is a striking combination of literary homage and self-reflective literary criticism. This impression is reinforced when we observe that, in opening his elegy with the words *qualis ab Eurota,* Ovid is exploiting the poetic memory so powerfully aroused by the opening of a poem.[35] On the one hand, Ovid recalls the first appearance of Dido, entering as she does in a passage that belies her impending doom; on the other, he hints at Propertius' Cynthia, whose awakening and speech in the course of 1.3 serve to dismantle the image of her suggested in the opening of the poem. And last but not least, I note that, later in the same poem, Ovid fully abandons the allusiveness of the opening, replacing the playfulness of the extended simile with a series of crude exempla on the relative greediness and sexual behavior of prostitutes and animals (1.10.21–28).[36] Thus, even as Ovid calls into question the conventions of elegiac love, he uses the literary traditions that make its expression possible.

It may at first seem self-contradictory to suggest that an extended simile can at least temporarily blur[37] our view of what is presented; yet such blur-

---

34. Zanker, *Realism in Alexandrian Poetry,* 28.

35. On the role played by the incipit in poetic memory and allusion, see Conte, *Rhetoric of Imitation,* 70–73.

36. See McKeown, ad loc.

37. In my diction I am indebted to Johnson, *Darkness Visible,* 49–99, where that author describes the effect of blurred and negative images in Virgil's similes.

ring does indeed occur, in a variety of ways. On the simplest level, the comparanda contained in a simile may actually be negative images, that is, verbal pictures that depict the opposite of what is happening in the narrative. Similes introduced by *non sic* and the like explicitly direct our attention to the opposition; others, such as the Ovidian example and its models we have just considered, are revealed to be negative images only as the narrative proceeds. In some cases, the extended simile need not be explicitly negative to have a blurring effect; rather, the accumulation of comparanda causes confusion. In the simile from *Am.* 1.10 just considered, Corinna is compared to three different heroines. The catalogue effectively removes us from the narrative proper (in fact, in 1.10 it preempts the narrative entirely), and it establishes an intellectual distance: instead of thinking about Corinna, we wonder what the comparanda have in common and which is most apt. Precision may appear to be the primary goal; yet the sort of "overprecision" achieved can itself be confusing, intellectualizing rather than focusing the comparison. In his discussion of alternatives in Homeric similes, Fränkel aptly describes the result as "Unbestimmtheit."[38]

A brief Virgilian example will illustrate the blurring effect of some similes (*Aen.* 9.433–37):

volvitur Euryalus leto, pulchrosque per artus
it cruor inque umeros cervix conlapsa recumbit:
purpureus veluti cum flos succisus aratro   435
languescit moriens, lassove papavera collo
demisere caput pluvia cum forte gravantur.

[Euryalus rolls in death, and the blood flows down along his fair limbs, and his neck gives way and falls back on his shoulders—just as when a purple flower cut by the plow droops in death, or like poppies that let their heads sink on their weakened necks when by chance they are weighed down by rain.]

In five lines, Virgil moves from a vivid and precise description of Euryalus' death—virtually every word in verses 433–34 contributes to the picture— to a comparison of Euryalus' lolling head to a dying purple flower, cut by

---

38. H. Fränkel, *Die homerischen Gleichnisse* (Göttingen, 1921), 109: "Solche Unbestimmtheit gibt dem Gleichnisvorgang eine gewisse Blässe und Unwirklichkeit, die es nicht vergessen lässt dass hier nur ein Zwischenspiel von geringerer Wichtigkeit den Hauptvorgang unterbricht."

a plow, or to poppies weighed down by rain. Why does Virgil extend the comparison to two terms? Precision only appears to be primary; in fact, the choice of comparisons both extends the emotional intensity of the narrative and intellectualizes it, leaving us to decide which of the two types of flowers described is more apt. Virgil shifts our attention from the immediacy of Euryalus' death (*leto*), first to the dying *purpureus flos* (*moriens*), then to the poppies, whose death is circumvented by Virgil's description—instead of dying, their heads droop (*demisere caput*) on tired necks (*lasso collo*), and they are weighed down (*gravantur*).[39] A significant effect of Virgil's multiple simile is, then, to distance us from the Nisus and Euryalus episode even as we pause to appreciate its imagery. The flowers take on human features, to be sure; simultaneously, human suffering is replaced by agricultural necessity (*succisus aratro*) or simply by the forces of nature (*pluvia cum forte gravantur*). There is also a purely literary dimension to Virgil's equivocation: in pausing to suggest two alternative comparisons, Virgil also invites us to think about his sources for these comparisons.[40] Again, the immediacy of the scene itself is compromised by its literary self-consciousness.

Already inclined by elegy's structure to explore alternative visions in extended similes, Ovid finds the intellectual appeal of the multiple simile to be especially well suited to his intellectualized love.[41] The next simile we shall look at demonstrates both the suggestiveness of overprecision and the deceptive seductiveness of the blurred vision that results. In *Am.* 2.5, Ovid describes his distress and outrage at seeing his *puella* with another lover. On learning that she has been caught in the act, the *puella* blushes (33–42):

> haec ego, quaeque dolor linguae dictavit; at illi
>   conscia purpureus venit in ora pudor,
> quale coloratum Tithoni coniuge caelum   35

---

39. See Johnson, *Darkness Visible,* 59–66, on the "dissolving pathos" of this episode.

40. See Stesichorus fr. S15.ii.14–17 in D. Page, ed., *Supplementum Lyricis Graecis* (Oxford, 1974); for Stesichorus' debt to Homer, see D.L. Page, "Stesichorus: *The Geryoneis,*" *JHS* 93 (1973): 153, and C. Segal, "Archaic Choral Lyric," in *The Cambridge History of Classical Literature,* vol. 1, *Greek Literature,* ed. P.E. Easterling and B.M.W. Knox (Cambridge, 1985), 190. On the range of Virgilian allusion here, see Johnson, *Darkness Visible,* 62–65; R.D. Griffith, "Literary Allusion in Vergil, *Aeneid* 9.435ff," *Vergilius* 31 (1985): 40–44; and D. Fowler, "Virgil on Killing Virgins," in *Homo Viator: Classical Essays for John Bramble,* ed. M. Whitby, P. Hardie, and M. Whitby (Bristol, 1987), 188–90.

41. See further chap. 4.

subrubet, aut sponso visa puella novo;
quale rosae fulgent inter sua lilia mixtae
    aut ubi cantatis Luna laborat equis
aut quod, ne longis flavescere possit ab annis,
    Maeonis Assyrium femina tinxit ebur.   40
his erat aut alicui color ille simillimus horum,
    et numquam casu pulchrior illa fuit.

[I said these things, and everything that grief brought to my tongue; but
a rosy blush came into her knowing face, like the sky that reddens
upward when it is colored by the mate of Tithonus, or a girl [blushing]
when she is seen by her newly betrothed; like roses that gleam mixed
among lilies, or the moon when she labors under an eclipse, her horses
charmed, or Assyrian ivory that a Maeonian girl has dyed lest it grow
yellow with age. Her complexion was like these—or at least like one of
these—and she was never fairer by chance.]

It has long been recognized that this elaborate simile is indebted at least in
part to Virgil's description of Lavinia's blush at *Aen.* 12.64–69:

accepit vocem lacrimis Lavinia matris
flagrantis perfusa genas, cui plurimus ignem   65
subiecit rubor et calefacta per ora cucurrit.
Indum sanguineo veluti violaverit ostro
si quis ebur, aut mixta rubent ubi lilia multa
alba rosa, talis virgo dabat ore colores.

[Lavinia listened with tears to the voice of her mother, and her burning
cheeks were suffused with color: a great blush brought fire with it and
raced through her flushed face. Just as when someone has dyed Indian
ivory with bloody purple, or when white lilies take on a blush when
mixed with many a rose: such hues did the maiden show on her face.]

While Virgil's simile receives the sort of attention we would expect, however, Ovid's has in modern times been the subject of little discussion other
than the negative sort.[42] Even Guy Lee, generally a sympathetic Ovidian,

---

42. See A. Zingerle, *Ovidius und sein Verhältnis zu den Vorgängern und gleichzeitigen römischen Dichtern* (Innsbruck, 1869), 1:114 n. 2; followed by Washietl, "De similitudinibus,"
37–38, 118–20. See also G. Némethy, ed., *P. Ovidii Nasonis Amores* (Budapest, 1907), and

condemns this simile as a weak specimen of artistic expansion: "Though each couplet is well made, the effect of their combination is diminishing and it would have been better to cut, even though the decision was painful. . . . One could wish that Ovid had carried further the process of excision that reduced the first edition of the *Amores* from five books to the three we now have."[43] Lee does not wonder whether there might not be another way to approach what appears to him to be generic impropriety. I suggest it is more productive to question whether Ovid has a motive for looking to Virgil here—and how such a reference may be influenced by the surrounding non-Virgilian material in the simile.

The Ovidian blush is described through five *comparanda:* (1) the reddening of the sky when Aurora rises (*coloratum . . . caelum*); (2) a girl seen by her betrothed (*sponso visa puella novo*); (3) roses mixed with lilies (*rosae . . . inter sua lilia mixtae*); (4) the moon in eclipse;[44] (5) ivory that has been dyed (*Assyrium . . . ebur*). It is far longer, and more involved, than is the *Aeneid* simile; but let us begin with Ovid's indebtedness to Virgil. Ovid has incorporated (in reverse order) both parts of the Virgilian simile. Virgil and Ovid are the two earliest Latin poets to describe the combination of lilies and roses,[45] while the dyeing of ivory is described elsewhere only in the

Booth, ad loc. J.-M. Frécaut, *L'esprit et l'humour chez Ovide* (Grenoble, 1972), 66, notices the Virgilian parallel but treats Ovid's simile as a parody. A recent school text also notes the parallel, but its discussion of the two similes is limited to a brief note: see R. Maltby, ed., *Latin Love Elegy* (Bristol and Chicago, 1980), 139. On a more positive note, McKeown, 1:38, discusses both the Virgilian and the Homeric models, seeing this as a good example of Ovid's sophistication. McKeown has little interest in Ovid's narrative purpose, however (vol. 3, with commentary on the poems in book 2, has not yet appeared).

Although he does not discuss the Ovidian simile, Lyne's discussion of the Virgilian episode is valuable: see "Lavinia's Blush: Vergil, *Aeneid* 12.64–70," *G&R* 30 (1983): 55–64. Lyne's main concern is to argue that, by means of this description, Virgil characterizes Lavinia as inflamed with love for Turnus. Lyne also suggests that the Homeric model for the first half of the simile (see my discussion) is not simply picturesque: while Homer uses the simile of dyed ivory to describe the wound Menelaus receives in battle, the Virgilian adaptation depicts the *vulnus amoris* from which Lavinia suffers. Lyne then refers the second half of Virgil's simile to Apollonius' description of Medea's blush at *Argon.* 3.297–98 (again, see my discussion here), but he finds no exact parallel for the simile in earlier literature. Instead, he discusses in general the erotic connotations of color-and-flower imagery in Virgil and several other Latin poets, and he concludes that in each passage this imagery has epithalamial associations. See also my n. 45 in this chapter.

43. Lee, "Tenerorum Lusor Amorum," 175.

44. For *luna laborans* as a technical term for eclipse, see *TLL* 7.2, col. 807.38–50 (s.v. *laboro*); W. Richter, "Lunae labores," *WS,* n.s., 11 (1977): 96–105.

45. See Stat. *Silv.* 1.2.22 (not coincidentally, an epithalamium) and Calp. *Ecl.* 3.78; cf. also Nemes. *Ecl.* 2.24. Pliny *NH* 21.24 comments on how lovely the two flowers look when grown together. The combination of white and red (or purple) is an erotic commonplace: see, e.g.,

Homeric simile recognized by Servius as Virgil's model (ὡς δ' ὅτε τίς τ' ἐλέφαντα γυνὴ φοίνικι μιήνῃ / Μῃονὶς ἠὲ Κάειρα, παρήιον ἔμμεναι ἵππων, *Il.* 4.141–42).[46] The way in which Ovid expands on the Virgilian material, however, indicates his interest in doing more than simply reproducing one model.

Let us look more closely at the organization of Ovid's simile. That the two terms of comparison in Virgil's simile have been combined with three others in the Ovidian passage suggests that the recognition of Virgil's presence here is intended to be gradual. Other features in Ovid's simile lead to the same conclusion: he begins rather unsurprisingly with a variation on an epic formula, the rising of Aurora. The visual pun of the sky's blushing at Aurora's arrival is a self-reference to an earlier poem in the *Amores,* 1.13, in which Ovid had asked Aurora to slow her course and lengthen the night. In that poem, Ovid had addressed Aurora more as a lover would address his *puella* than as a human would address a god; she responded to his forwardness by blushing—that is, by rising—and so presented herself as a rosy-cheeked, rather than a rosy-fingered, dawn (*iurgia finieram. scires audisse: rubebat, / nec tamen adsueto tardius orta dies,* 1.13.47–48). In 2.5, Ovid recalls the goddess last seen blushing by using a tried and true Alexandrian device, identifying her not by her name but by the periphrasis *Tithoni coniuge.*[47] The placement of *subrubet* in enjambment at the opening of the pentameter,[48] together with the enclosing arrangement of *coloratum . . . caelum* in the hexameter,[49] strengthens the coloring of the blush. After this very decorative but conventional opening, Ovid moves from the divine sphere to the human (*sponso, puella*), suggesting similar scenarios in both passages, the first between husband and wife, the second between a young girl and her betrothed. Two images, blushing and marriage, give the two parts of the couplet an internal unity and balance. Ovid begins to describe the blush of his *puella* as if she were a bride. Simultane-

---

Hinds, *Metamorphosis of Persephone,* 78–79; Bömer, *Met.,* on 5.392; and the examples cited by P.J. Enk, ed., *Sex. Propertii Elegiarum Liber Secundus* (Leiden, 1962), vol. 2, on Prop. 2.3.11–12. For the two colors used to describe a blush, see Enn. *Ann.* 362 Skutsch; Bömer, *Met.,* on 3.423 and 6.46–47.

46. On the dyeing of ivory, see Blümner, *RE* 10:2364, s.v. *Elfenbein.*

47. See Ross, *Backgrounds to Augustan Poetry,* 62.

48. The verb *subrubeo* appears to be an Ovidian import into poetry, used by him elsewhere in its more common technical sense, that is, of ripening grapes (*AA* 2.316).

49. Cf. the use of *coloro* by Propertius at 3.13.15–16, *felix Eois lex funeris una maritis, / quos Aurora suis rubra colorat equis!* For other colorful descriptions of Aurora, see Virg. *Aen.* 6.535 and 7.26 and their Homeric models; Tib. 1.3.93–94. Cf. also Ov. *Met.* 2.113, 3.150, etc.

ously, he anticipates specific allusion to Lavinia and the more general context of the Virgilian simile, although this anticipation becomes apparent
only on a second reading.

In the next couplet, the emphasis shifts from the blush itself to its color.
In both halves, the contrast between light and dark is paramount—in the
contrast of *rosae* among *lilia,* and in the obscuring of the moon's *candor*
through eclipse. While alluding casually to a Propertian pentameter,[50]
Ovid puts us in mind of yet another virginal, and Virgilian, blush, that of
Phoebe at *Geo.* 1.430–31: *at si virgineum suffuderit ore ruborem, / ventus
erit: vento semper rubet aurea Phoebe.*[51] The description of Luna also
serves as a chiastic complement to the earlier reference to Aurora; and as
we have already seen, Virgil provides the model for the roses-and-lilies
comparison. Finally, Ovid introduces this specific allusion to Lavinia's
blush immediately after the erotic imagery of the preceding couplet. He
thus hints at a movement from general to particular, from all betrothed
girls to that most innocent of *virgines* in the *Aeneid,* Lavinia. This sharp-
ening of focus will heighten the contrast of our return from simile to reality a few lines later.

The Virgilian associations of the roses-and-lilies simile are confirmed in
Ovid's next couplet, with an adaptation of Virgil's description of the dyeing of ivory. The specificity of subject matter and certain stylistic similarities (the use of proper adjectives [*Indum* in Virgil, *Maeonis* and *Assyrium* in
Ovid]; the delaying of the word *ebur* to the very end of each clause) show
Ovid's debt to Virgil; again, however, Ovid avoids straight imitation.
Instead of Virgil's unusual *violaverit,* Ovid uses the comparatively bland
tinxit; and whereas Virgil had emphasized the color of the dye (*sanguineo
. . . ostro*), Ovid makes no mention of color at all, providing instead a
"double negative" description of the discoloration to be avoided by dyeing

---

50. Morgan, *Ovid's Art of Imitation,* 32–33, identifies only one "imitation" in the Ovidian
simile: the words *Luna laborat equis* (38) apparently echo the same pentameter ending at Prop.
2.34.52 (*Luna laboret equis*). While the Propertian line may be recalled by Ovid, however,
there is no reason, given the two very different contexts in which the line-end appears, as well
as the fact that the ablative construction in each is different, to see the reference as anything
more than casual, or as one of Goold's formulae; cf. my earlier discussion of *sit Galatea tuae,*
in chap. 1. On the interpretation of the difficult Propertian line, see A. Allen, "The Moon's
Horses," *CQ* 25 (1975): 153–55. Cf. also the similar line-end at Prop. 3.13.16, cited in n. 49 in
this chapter.

51. I am indebted for this observation to Richard Thomas. Thomas, *Geo.,* notes ad loc.
that these lines are embedded in Virgil's reference to Aratus' acrostic (*Phaen.* 783–87), in a
larger section on the moon's signs; shortly thereafter (*Phaen.* 803), Aratus calls the moon
"blushing" (ἐρευθομένη). Ovid may well have recognized in the blushing but virginal
Phoebe/Luna another predecessor for Lavinia—and thus, for his own *puella.*

ivory (*ne longis flavescere possit ab annis*).[52] Again, while Virgil identifies the ivory as Indian, Ovid avoids the conventional epithet *Indum* and uses instead the unparalleled *Assyrium*.[53] Finally, Virgil alludes only vaguely (*si quis*) to the ivory-worker; Ovid, conversely, is specific about both nationality and gender (*Maeonis . . . femina*).

In drawing our attention to the artisan, Ovid indicates that he has not simply looked to Virgil but has returned to Homer himself: Ovid's *Maeonis femina* reintroduces to the simile the γυνὴ Μηονίς described by Homer but omitted by Virgil.[54] Nonetheless, we should note at the same time that whereas Homer had identified the artisan as a Maeonian *or* Carian woman, Ovid uses only the first of these epithets, as if to confirm the specifically Homeric provenance of this detail while avoiding simple imitation of Homer. Elsewhere in his poetry Ovid regularly uses epithets having to do with Maeonia in specific reference to Homer.[55] Homeric epic is likely to be the immediate source of inspiration as well for Ovid's erudite allusion to the discoloration of ivory with age. Homer several times describes ivory as "newly sawn" (πριστός/νεόπριστος, *Od.* 8.404, 18.196, 19.564) to indicate its whiteness when fresh, the implication being that ivory changes color with time. Of most immediate interest for our discussion is the description, at *Od.* 18.196, of Penelope's complexion as whiter than ivory (λευκοτέρην δ' ἄρα μιν θῆκε πριστοῦ ἐλέφαντος); the relevance of this comparison to a description of his *puella*'s reddening cheeks will not have been lost on Ovid.[56]

The allusive variety of the three couplets we have examined illustrates

---

52. In doing so, he uses *flavesco* in an unparalleled sense: see *TLL* 6.1, col. 887.20. Originally applied to the color of grain, *flavesco* was gradually extended to grain's blooming and maturation and then transferred to other growing things. Ovid also uses it to describe the color of sand (*Met.* 9.36).

53. On the traditional provenance of ivory, see Cat. 64.48 (*Indo . . . dente*); Virg. *Geo.* 1.57 (*India mittit ebur*); Hor. *Odes* 1.31.6 (*ebur Indicum*); Ov. *Medic.* 10 (*sectile deliciis India praebet ebur*); and *TLL* 5.2, col. 19.40–45 and col. 21.80–82. Ovid here provides us with the sole reference to Assyrian ivory (and, as P. Knox has commented, makes one wonder from what animal this ivory comes); curiously, Virgil once uses the epithet to describe a type of dye: *alba neque Assyrio fucatur lana veneno* (*Geo.* 2.465; Servius glosses *veneno* with *colore*). He is imitated in turn by the authors of the *Culex* (*Assyrio . . . colore*, 62) and the *Ciris* (*Assyrio . . . ostro*, 440).

54. This is a good example of what Thomas, "Art of Reference," 188, describes as a window reference: see my relevant discussion earlier, in chap. 2.

55. See, e.g., *Am.* 1.15.9, 3.9.25; *AA* 2.4; *Rem.* 373. Cf. Hor. *Odes* 4.9.5. The adjective *Maeonis* is used in Latin poetry only by Ovid.

56. Blümner, *RE* 10:2363, comments that νεόπριστος describes ivory that is white, "im Gegensatz zu alterem, bereits gelb gewordenem." The yellowing of ivory alluded to at Prop. 4.7.82 seems to reflect an entirely different, and purely Italian, tradition: see *RE* 10:2365–66.

the complexity of which Ovid is capable in the *Amores:* he brings together disparate but complementary imagery and recasts it in such a way that, while recalling a specific model, it takes on new meaning in a new context. Ovid makes a place for this blush in a long literary tradition by developing this elaborate series of similes to describe the *purpureus pudor* (34) of his *puella.* He thus evokes an image straight out of Hellenistic poetry and locates it in an entirely new setting. Her surprise at being caught and her abashed reaction (*spectabat terram: terram spectare decebat; / maesta erat in vultu: maesta decenter erat,* 43–44) evoke not only Apollonius' description of Medea's blush (ἀπαλὰς δὲ μετετρωπᾶτο παρειὰς / ἐς χλόον, ἄλλοτ᾽ ἔρευθος, ἀκηδείῃσι νόοιο, 3.297–98),[57] but the blushes of several other Alexandrian heroines as well, such as Apollonius' Hypsipyle and Callimachus' Pieria.[58] Unlike these erotic heroines, however, and unlike Virgil's Lavinia, Ovid's *puella* is not in the flush of first love; her downcast eyes are a product not of her modesty but of her shame at being found out. It is surely no coincidence that one element in Virgil's simile, the erotic *furor* that is emphasized by the words *flagrantis genas, ignem subiecit rubor,* and *calefacta per ora,* is entirely absent from Ovid's poem.[59] Much as this *puella* may remind us of her predecessors, she lacks their emotional involvement. She is not in love—at least not with Ovid. At last Ovid realizes that, despite appearances, his *puella*'s blush is nothing like the literary blushes of the past. She is, after all, not an innocent maiden but all too experienced in the arts of love. The simile describing her, drawing abundantly on poetic memory, uses the negative image technique to create a deliberately misleading character analysis of the *puella.* It is typical of the realist Ovid to use his own literary experience to deprive his *puella* of her innocence. In this case, her innocence is simply a literary illusion.[60]

---

57. Cited by Lyne, "Lavinia's Blush," 59–60 as a model for Lavinia's blush.

58. See A.R. *Argon.* 1.790–91, ἡ δ᾽ ἐγκλιδὸν ὄσσε βαλοῦσα / παρθενικὰς ἐρύθηνε παρήιδας; Call. *Aet.* 3, fr. 80.10–11 Pf., αἰδοῖ δ᾽ ὡς φοί[νικι] τεὰς ἐρύθουσα παρειὰς / ἔννεπες ὀφ[θαλμο]ῖς . . . (cf. Pfeiffer, ad loc). See also the last line of Cat. 65, describing a young maiden's blush when her lover's gift falls from her lap (*huic manat tristi conscius ore rubor,* 24); and Musae. 160–61, παρθενικὴ δ᾽ ἄφθογγος ἐπὶ χθόνα πῆξεν ὀπωπὴν /αἰδοῖ ἐρευθιόωσαν ὑποκλέπτουσα παρειήν.

59. See Lyne, "Lavinia's Blush," 57, on this imagery: "It seems a tremendous amount of heat to attribute to a blush." I have already noted *furor*'s thematic importance to Virgil in another context, as well as its elegiac subversion by Ovid: see my discussion of *Geo.* 3.215–23 in chap. 2.

60. At the close of the extended simile, Ovid comments almost offhandedly that his *puella* had never appeared more beautiful than when she blushed (*et numquam casu pulchrior illa fuit,* 42). The meaning of *casu* here has never been adequately explained, and Housman

The similes just adduced from *Am.* 1.10 and 2.5 illustrate how Ovid goes about incorporating past tradition into his modern elegy: we see in both instances that Ovid starts with something known and actually exploits the fact that the known opening can lead unexpectedly to the unknown. One is reminded of a composer who introduces a theme with a sequence of notes reminiscent of or identical to the opening of a famous and influential earlier work. Even as we hear the echo, we are made conscious of the new arrangement; thus, the provocation of musical memory goes hand in hand with its complement, the sensation of something entirely new. As befits the device, however, Ovid does not always achieve this effect in quite the same way; and the illusion of reference takes precedence over actual allusion. The result is an extended simile that, for all its evocative familiarity, has no one major model or source of inspiration yet explicitly declares its debt to our memory of such similes. Let us now turn to another brilliant example of this effect, from the opening of *Am.* 1.14.

In *Am.* 1.14, Ovid chooses a situation with exceptional visual potential. The scenario is simply ridiculous: against Ovid's wishes, Corinna has dyed her hair, and she has had disastrous results—it has all fallen out. After announcing this disaster, Ovid breaks into an extended simile eulogizing Corinna's lost glory (1–12):

Dicebam 'medicare tuos desiste capillos';
    tingere quam possis, iam tibi nulla coma est.
at si passa fores, quid erat spatiosius illis?
    contigerant imum qua patet usque latus.
quid, quod erant tenues et quos ornare timeres,   5
    vela colorati qualia Seres habent,
vel pede quod gracili deducit aranea filum,
    cum leve deserta sub trabe nectit opus?
nec tamen ater erat neque erat tamen aureus ille
    sed, quamvis neuter, mixtus uterque color,   10
qualem clivosae madidis in vallibus Idae
    ardua derepto cortice cedrus habet.

---

wished to emend it to *visu;* he was rightly disturbed by the difficulty of the MS reading. But it is at least possible to interpret the line containing *casu* as meaning "she was never more lovely by accident," i.e., that the loveliness of her blush is a result not of chance or accident but of *ars.* On the antithesis of *casu/ars,* see Rosati, *Narciso e Pigmalione,* 80.

[I used to say "Stop tinting your hair"; now you have no hair that you can tint. But if you had allowed it to be, what was more luxuriant? It touched the lowest part of your side, all the way to its furthest extent. What of the fact that your hair was fine, so that you hesitated to adorn it, like the fabrics that the dark-skinned Seres have or the thread that a spider spins with its nimble foot when it weaves its delicate web beneath a deserted beam? It was neither black nor that gold color but both colors mixed together without being either, like the color of the lofty cedar in the dewy valleys of steep Ida when its bark has been stripped away.]

In answer to his own question (*quid, quod erant tenues . . .* ?, 5), Ovid tells us that her hair was fine, needed no decoration, and was like silk or the slender thread that the spider spins, working away in some forgotten corner up in the rafters. What exactly is Ovid describing? The emphasis seems to be on the texture of her hair, although comparison with a cobweb seems at first sight not especially felicitous. Ovid then moves to color, telling us what the hair was not: it was neither black nor golden but a combination of the two, like the color of an Idaean cedar when its bark has been stripped off. The cumulative effect of the three similes is suggestive, rather than precise, and yet the very fact that Ovid is using similes contributes to the visual effectiveness of the description. Of course, the visual emphasis here is misleading; after all, what Ovid describes no longer exists. The *puella* is bald and so has no hair left for Ovid to describe. This reality makes the ironic delicacy of Ovid's simile here all the more emphatic; emphasis on the ephemeral beauty of her hair is also effected by the use of prosaic rhetorical formulae (*quid, quod . . .* ?, 5; *adde quod,* 13) to support Ovid's argument.

I begin with the Chinese silk simile. What was known about silk production in antiquity, and when it was known, is a matter of some debate, made all the more confusing because there were in fact two types of silk known in the ancient world: one was the true Chinese import, and the other was a product from Asia Minor and India, made from certain types of cocoons scraped from trees and then worked like linen. Aristotle, who provides the fullest early description of silk production, appears to have conflated the two types.[61] More important for Ovid, however, is the immediate literary example provided by Virgil, who seems to have reproduced

---

61. *HA* 5.19.551b; cf. Pliny *NH* 11.75–77. The provenance of the silk-producing insect described by Aristotle is the subject of some debate: see G.M.A. Richter, "Silk in Greece," *AJA* 33 (1929): 27–33, and W.T.M. Forbes, "The Silkworm of Aristotle," *CP* 25 (1930): 22–26.

the Aristotelian conflation. In the second *Georgic,* Virgil uses the expression *vellera depectere* to characterize the Seres' mode of silk production as akin to the combing or carding of cotton (*quid nemora Aethiopum molli canentia lana, / velleraque ut foliis depectant tenuia Seres?*, Geo. 2.120–21).[62] It is likely that Ovid has Virgil's use of the rare word *depectere* in mind as he uses the image of working in silk to describe long and luxurious hair.[63] This association might also help to explain what is otherwise a very strange description of hair later in Ovid's poem. At line 23, Ovid tells us that Corinna's locks were *graciles* and *lanuginis instar*—that is, like woolly down. This comparison of a woman's hair with *lanugo* is unparalleled in extant literature.[64]

The imagery of spun thread and textiles (*vela*)[65] is an apt, if not entirely logical, introduction to the subject of the second simile, the spinning spider. In the hexameter, Ovid's point seems to be that Corinna's hair is fine like a spider's thread; but the pentameter seems at best superfluous. In fact, Ovid recalls here a literary commonplace—that the spider is free to pursue its busy work wherever something is not cared for. Variations on this commonplace are found in ancient poetry from Homer and Bacchylides to Catullus and Propertius.[66] While creating a simile that substantially recalls this conventional imagery, however, Ovid uses it in a way that evokes a purely Hellenistic tradition of the spider as artist, master of a laborious and fine craft. In fact, Ovid's use of the image evokes the highly prized qualities of Hellenistic literary artistry, so well known from discussions of Callimachean programmatic language.[67] Of particular relevance here is a fragment from Callimachus' *Hecale,* in which a cloak held by golden brooches is called the work of spiders on account of its fineness (*SH* 285.10–12 = Hollis 42.4–6 = fr. 253 Pf. 10–12):

---

62. On cotton, see Theophr. 4.7.7 and the Pliny passage cited in n. 63 in this chapter.

63. Virgil is the first to use *depectere* in the sense *pectendo demere:* see *TLL* 5.1, col. 563.5. Pliny follows Virgil at *NH* 6.54 (*perfusam aqua* **depectentes frondium caniciem**), although he confuses two Chinese textiles, silk and cotton.

64. See *TLL* 7.2, col. 937.5–18.

65. See McKeown, ad loc., suggesting that Ovid's unusual *vela* may be a variation on Virgil's *vellera tenuia* at Geo. 2.121; note also Ovid's use of the adjective *tenues* in line 5.

66. See Bacch. fr. 4.31; Theocr. Id. 16.96; Cat. 68.49–50; Prop. 2.6.35–36. Cf. Prop. 3.6.33, modeled on Homer Od. 16.34.

67. See E. Reitzenstein, "Zur Stiltheorie des Kallimachos," in *Festschrift Richard Reitzenstein,* ed. E. Fraenkel, H. Fränkel, et al. (Berlin and Leipzig, 1931), 25–40; cf. M. Poliakoff, "Clumsy and Clever Spiders on Hermann's Bridge: Catullus 68.49–50 and *Culex* 1–3," *Glotta* 63 (1985): 248–50.

μέμνημαι καλὴν μὲν α [
ἄλιλͺικα χρυσείησιν ἐεργομένην ἐνετῆσιν,
ἔργον ἀιραͺχνάωͺιν . .]ͺ . . . . [⁶⁸

[I remember . . . a lovely garment closed with golden brooches, the work of spiders . . .]

Ovid has combined a commonplace with an Alexandrian conceit to describe Corinna's hair. In this connection, consideration of a rather confused comment by Servius (on the aforementioned *Geo.* 2.121) may help to explain the logic underlying Ovid's move from silk to spiderwebs. Servius notes that *sericum* is produced by certain worms who spin their thread in a manner like that used by spiders: *apud Aethiopiam, Indos et Seras sunt quidam in arboribus vermes et bombyces appellantur, qui in aranearum morem tenuissima fila deducunt, unde est sericum.*⁶⁹

The color simile with which Ovid continues is an erudite and original effect as well. Trees are familiar enough as the subjects of extended similes, particularly when individual heroes are compared to felled trees.⁷⁰ But this instance is quite different and is to my knowledge a novelty. Ovid is concerned not with what happens to the tree or with its sturdy character but instead with the color of its flesh when stripped of bark. The design that has gone into this comparison is obvious: the chiastic word order of epithet-epithet-substantive-substantive in the hexameter, *clivosae madidis in vallibus Idae,* recurs in the pentameter, with *ardua derepto cortice cedrus;* and the whole simile is framed by a coordinating relative and a verb.⁷¹ The reference to cedar is itself exotic and is unparalleled in ancient poetry, although it is possible that Ovid had a learned model in mind. We do know that confusion over the identity of the tree or trees so named was notorious even in antiquity.⁷² Particularly relevant to Ovid's cedar, however, is the description given by Theophrastus (*HP* 3.11.4) not of the cedar but of the smooth-barked mountain ash (*fraxinus*): this type grows mostly in deep

---

68. The text printed here is that which appears in *SH;* cf. A.S. Hollis, ed., *Callimachus: Hecale* (Oxford, 1990), ad loc. Pfeiffer, ad loc. notes that what is being described is probably a *vestis picturata,* i.e., an "ecphrastic" garment; see also Thomas, "Callimachus, the *Victoria Berenices,* and Roman Poetry," 105–11. We need not look for this implication in Ovid's simile, however; the spider as artist is the important image in Ovid's fleeting sequence of pictures.

69. Servius may have been reading Pliny: see *NH* 11.76. See also n. 63 in this chapter.

70. See Clausen, *Virgil's Aeneid,* 50–52.

71. The epithet *clivosus* is itself likely to be a Virgilian import into poetry from the agricultural lexicon: see *Geo.* 1.108 and 2.212; Bömer, "Ovid und die Sprache Vergils," 277–78.

72. See Theophr. *HP* 3.12.3 on the confusion over the two known types of cedar, Lycian and Phoenician.

ravines (Theophrastus' βαθυάγκη parallels Ovid's *clivosae . . . in vallibus Idae*) and in damp places (ἔφυδρα parallels Ovid's *madidis*); this ash is also lofty (ὑψηλή parallels *ardua*) and has pale wood (τὸ ξύλον ἔχουσα λευκόν) and reddish bark (τῇ χρόᾳ πυρρόν). Of this same ash Pliny tells us that the one that grows on Trojan Ida is so much like the cedar that when its bark has been removed, it deceives potential buyers (*NH* 16.62). Ovid's cedar appears to be a conflation based on this traditional confusion; the reference to Ida thus becomes not just an otiose descriptive detail but a casual index of Ovid's learning.[73]

What is the point of this rather pronounced display of learning? I have already suggested the irony of so elaborate a verbal picture developed to describe something that no longer exists; but it may well be wondered whether we are really dealing simply with one of those displays of technique for which Ovid is so often criticized. I suspect that when taken together, Ovid's allusions to Virgil and the scientific writers, among others, should lead us to another conclusion. In crafting these hyperbolic similes to describe the unheard-of—and now unseeable—marvel of his *puella*'s hair, Ovid suggests that we are to think of this phenomenon much as we would the θαύματα of ancient ethnography. Indeed, the *Georgics* passage mentioning the Seres and their remarkable textiles occurs in just such a list of marvels to be found in faraway lands;[74] and the mention of the rare cedar located on distant Ida is a typical artifact of ethnographical lore. Even the *Hecale* passage previously cited has a contextual analogy to offer: it occurs in a fragment in which the poor and aged Hecale recalls more prosperous days—a prosperity typified by the marvelous cloak she once saw but that, like Corinna's lovely hair, is long gone.[75]

The apparently disparate imagery of the three similes, then, leads us in all three cases to the same *tertium comparationis,* the θαύματα of distant times and places. At the same time, Ovid's choice of diction provides another type of cohesion to the simile sequence. Although Ovid begins by describing the texture of Corinna's hair and only later moves on to its color, his ethnographical epithet for the Seres in line 6, *colorati,* anticipates the focus on color in lines 9–12.[76] Ovid's suggestion of correspondences that cut across or connect the individual comparanda is analogous,

---

73. McKeown, ad loc., following Lee, identifies Ovid's cedar with a species of juniper; but the evidence put forward is not conclusive.

74. See Thomas, *Geo.,* ad loc.

75. See Hollis, *Hecale,* on fr. 42; cf. also Hecale's μέμνημαι (10) with Ovid's *dicebam* (1).

76. On such epithets as a feature of ancient ethnography, see Thomas, *Geo.,* on 2.115, *pictosque Gelonos.*

although not identical, to what David West identifies as the "multiple-correspondence simile." In a pair of articles on the *Aeneid,* West demonstrates that Virgil's similes "contain *many* details which correspond to details in the surrounding narrative";[77] in other words, Virgilian similes interact on multiple levels with their context.[78] Ovid's technique is equally sophisticated and invites comparison of correspondences not just from narrative to simile and vice versa but from one simile to another within this series.

Note, last of all, that while thus emphasizing the color of her hair, Ovid manages never to tell us what color it in fact is. This extended simile taken as a whole, then, is a bit of brilliant deception: while purporting to illustrate the exotic quality and color of Corinna's hair, in fact these features are only hinted at in the most elusive and tantalizing way, and meanwhile even the tree whose bark recalls the color of Corinna's lost hair conceals its identity. Both her hair and her hair loss seem as fantastical as they are remarkable; and Ovid becomes not simply an elegist but a paradoxographer as he composes this extended simile.

The three extended similes considered thus far show the range of Ovid's interest in the device. Now I want to turn my attention more fully to the possibilities of multiple correspondence as exploited by Ovid. It is already evident that in composing extended similes, Ovid prefers to build up a comparison not out of one detailed image spun out over six or eight verses but out of the juxtaposition of a series of similar images, often related to each other in the most quirky or unexpected of ways. While clearly related to patterns for cataloguing exempla, such collocations of extended similes have an effect all their own: they are often disconcerting, distracting, and deceptive. *Am.* 1.7 is a tour de force of rhetorical deception, in which the accumulation of images is so relentless as to be almost chaotic; yet the composition as a whole is held together by the multiple correspondences running through the series of images found here. This elegiac poem exploits the possibilities of analogy more fully than any elegy since Catullus 68; but even as he follows Catullus' precedent, Ovid achieves an effect entirely alien to Catullan elegy.[79]

---

77. "Multiple-Correspondence Similes in the *Aeneid,*" *JRS* 59 (1969): 40–49, and "Virgilian Multiple-Correspondence Similes and Their Antecedents," *Philologus* 114 (1970): 262–75. The quotation is from the first of these, p. 40.

78. In his valuable discussion of Virgil's similes, Lyne, *Words and the Poet,* is critical of West for not making more of their narrative function: see 63–99 and especially 64 n. 7. Lyne's idea that similes can substitute for narrative and his development of the concept of "trespass" in simile imagery are useful extensions of West's work, and I have incorporated them into what follows.

79. See Feeney, "Limits of Analogy."

In *Am.* 1.7, Ovid ranges along the entire continuum of analogy, using a variety of exempla, short comparisons, and extended similes. After bemoaning his display of uncontrolled *furor,* Ovid charges himself with the same sort of crazed behavior shown by Ajax in his slaughter of the sheep or by Orestes on his mother's murder (7–10). Precisely because these tragic characters and their actions are so well known, Ovid's equation of himself with them is ludicrous—a condition made all the more apparent after Ovid indicates that, in raising his hands (*temeraria bracchia,* 3; *vesana . . . manu,* 4) against his *puella,* his assault has done little more than disturb her hairdo (*digestos potui laniare capillos,* 11). His would-be heroic madness has driven him to this state; and so the subsequent hyperbole of his wish to be without hands (23–26) and of his curse (*quid mihi vobiscum, caedis scelerumque ministrae?,* 27) is as predictable as it is exorbitant. The operatic pitch of Ovid's self-reproach leads to a third exemplum, and another Homeric hero, Diomedes. Like him, Ovid has struck a goddess; but Ovid's actions are far more loathsome, for while Diomedes struck a divine enemy, Ovid has wounded someone he loves (31–34).

These would-be heroic exempla are complemented by a sequence of similes in which the *puella* is compared to three mythological heroines (13–18):

> **sic formosa fuit; talem** Schoeneida dicam
> Maenalias arcu sollicitasse feras;
> **talis** periuri promissaque velaque Thesei   15
> flevit praecipites Cressa tulisse Notos;
> **sic,** nisi vittatis quod erat, Cassandra, capillis,
> procubuit templo, casta Minerva, tuo.

[Thus was she beautiful; I would say that the daughter of Schoeneus, who pursued the beasts of Maenalus with a bow, was so; so was the Cretan girl, who wept that the headstrong west winds had carried off both the promises and the sails of perjuring Theseus; so was Cassandra, who lay prostrate, chaste Minerva, in your temple—except that her hair was tied up in a priestess' fillet.]

This extended simile, like that with which *Am.* 1.10 opens, shows through its structure the legacy of the exemplum catalogue. In addition, it displays the usual Alexandrian learning and allusiveness: the Greek patronymic *Schoeneida* for Atalanta and the epithet *Maenalias* evoke two different versions of the Atalanta myth in one couplet;[80] the allusion in 15–16 to Ariadne's appearance at Catullus 64.58–67 recalls that passage's visual emphasis; and the qualification regarding Cassandra's hair in the words *nisi vittatis quod erat . . . capillis* corrects the picture of her offered by Virgil at *Aen.* 2.403–6 (*ecce trahebatur **passis** Priameia virgo / **crinibus** a templo Cassandra adytisque Minervae / ad caelum tendens ardentia lumina frustra, / lumina, nam teneras arcebant vincula palmas*).[81] Yet all of this learning and style is put to very mundane use, its point being simply that the *puella* is beautiful even with her hair in disarray (*sic formosa fuit,* 13), just as the earlier heroines were; any other particular aptness is left unexplored. Like Ajax, Orestes, and Diomedes, the three women mentioned here have a sort of all-purpose application that deflates the very emotionality these analogies seem intended to emphasize, and their appearance within an extended simile bespeaks an almost timeless cliché about pretty girls looking even prettier when in jeopardy.[82]

The narrative of 1.7 is obviously ironic;[83] it also has obvious visual potential, which Ovid goes on to exploit with yet another set of similes (51–58):

> astitit illa amens albo et sine sanguine vultu,
>   caeduntur Pariis qualia saxa iugis;
> exanimes artus et membra trementia vidi,
>   ut cum populeas ventilat aura comas,
> ut leni Zephyro gracilis vibratur harundo   55
>   summave cum tepido stringitur unda Noto;
> suspensaeque diu lacrimae fluxere per ora,
>   qualiter abiecta de nive manat aqua.

---

80. See McKeown, ad loc.

81. On all three comparanda, see McKeown, ad loc. On Cassandra's hair, see also R.G. Austin, ed., *Aeneidos liber secundus P. Vergili Maronis* (Oxford, 1964), ad loc.; Davis, "*Exempla* and Anti-*Exempla*," 415–16. Cf. also *Am.* 1.9.37–38: *summa ducum, Atrides visa Priameide fertur / **Maenadis** **effusis** obstipuisse **comis.*** J. Morrison, "Literary Reference and Generic Transgression in Ovid, *Amores* 1.7: Lover, Poet, and *Furor*," *Latomus* 51 (1992): 571–89, discusses many of the same points but interprets them somewhat differently, seeing virtually all allusions in this poem as equally weighted references.

82. Again, a favorite vehicle of Ovidian irony: *prima inter pares* is Daphne, at *Met.* 1.497–502, 525–30 (. . . *auctaque forma fuga est*).

83. See H.A. Khan, "*Ovidius Furens*: A Revaluation of *Amores* 1,7," *Latomus* 25 (1966): 880–94.

[She stood there in turmoil, her face white and bloodless, like the stones that are cut on the yokes of Paros; I saw her lifeless limbs tremble, as when a breeze fans the poplar's tresses, as when a slender reed is shaken by a gentle west wind or the very top of the wave is grazed by a mild south wind. Tears stayed in her eyes for a long time and then flowed down her face, as when water thrown off by melting snow finally flows.]

By this time, we expect something trite and superficial; but in these lines Ovid's style is quite different from what has proceeded them. The *puella* has just been struck; in describing her reaction, Ovid leads us through a sequence of five similes. First, she is stunned; she stands unmoving, the blood drained from her face, and Ovid lingers for a moment to compare her pallor to the color of Parian marble. Then she begins to tremble; her trembling is described in quick succession as like the leaves of the poplar, like a reed, like the surface of a wave grazed by the wind. At last her tears begin, falling like the water released by melting snow.

Barsby's response to all this—a response that is not at all atypical—is not enthusiastic. He finds the comparison of the *puella*'s complexion to Parian marble "not particularly apt," for reasons I shall return to shortly; he compares the melting snow simile to *Od.* 19.204–8, where Penelope's tears are likened to melting snow (τῆς δ' ἄρ' ἀκουούσης ῥέε δάκρυα, τήκετο δὲ χρώς. / ὡς δὲ χιὼν κατατήκετ' ἐν ἀκροπόλοισιν ὄρεσσιν, / ἥν τ' Εὖρος κατέτηξεν, ἐπὴν Ζέφυρος καταχεύῃ / τηκομένης δ' ἄρα τῆς ποταμοὶ πλήθουσι ῥέοντες· / ὡς τῆς τήκετο καλὰ παρήϊα δάκρυ χεούσης); and he offers a comprehensive interpretation: "What is noteworthy about all five similes is that they are taken from inanimate and unfeeling nature: Ovid is fascinated by the appearance of the girl but shows no awareness of her emotions in his choice of illustrations."[84] While more approving of the passage, McKeown expresses real confusion about the function of the simile series, which he finds effective in a way not at all congruent with Barsby's interpretation: "It serves the same purpose as the triple comparison in 13ff., that of humorously exaggerating the solemnity of the scene. It also heightens the tension by delaying the girl's outburst of tears . . . , thus making the outburst dramatically more effective."[85] Which is it? Is the passage otiose and in bad taste, or is it a combination of humorous and tension provoking? Neither of these choices considers the integrity of the passage, either as a whole or as part of a highly affective elegy; and

84. Barsby, *Am.*, 89.
85. McKeown, on 53–56.

while McKeown rightly notices the abundance of analogy in the poem, his treatment of it simply as exaggeration misses the nuanced variations of Ovid's style.

It will be helpful to look again at the composition of the passage itself. Ovid has distributed the five terms of the simile symmetrically over eight lines, with one comparison in both the first and the last couplets, and with three shorter comparisons distributed over the two central couplets. As with the triple Homeric simile discussed earlier in this chapter, seemingly disparate illustrative analogies contribute to an overall visual unity further emphasized by Ovid's assertion of autopsy (*vidi,* 53).[86] Together, these similes illustrate three aspects, or stages, of the *puella's* response: her stunned pallor, her trembling, and her tears. They have a cumulative effect, particularly since the three central similes suggest the gradual increase of her trembling and build slowly to the eventual climax of her tears, *suspensae . . . diu.*[87] There is nothing to laugh at in the passage; and *pace* Barsby, this simile sequence is exquisitely sensitive to the emotional changes that occur within the *puella* and that are reflected in her appearance.

Of particular interest are the correspondences of imagery between the first and last similes, those that compare the *puella's* motionlessness and pallor to Parian marble and her tears to melting snow. Separated as they are by the three delicate similes describing her trembling, these two similes may at first appear as polarized in imagery as they are in placement. Ovid exploits a traditional connection, however, so that the gradual transition from stasis to movement in this passage is seamlessly naturalistic.[88] Again, West's description of the multiple-correspondence simile is applicable to this situation, as we see the movement of correspondences in this series of similes paralleled by the *puella's* own movement.

The *puella's* state of petrifaction is essential to Ovid's simile. Comparison of the sorrowing woman to a figure frozen in stone has admirable predecessors, including Euripides' Medea (*Med.* 28) and Catullus' Ariadne (*saxea ut effigies bacchantis,* 64.61). Two others, however, are even more apposite. In his hymn to Apollo, Callimachus describes Niobe as ὁ δακρυόεις πέτρος (*h.* 2.22) and as marble instead of woman (μάρμαρον ἀντὶ γυναικὸς ὀϊζυρόν τι χανούσης, *h.* 2.24). This description is based on an athetized passage at Homer *Il.* 24.614–17, of interest to a scholar like

---

86. See my earlier comments, in n. 20 in this chapter, on Ovid's use of *vidi* at 1.2.11.

87. McKeown, ad loc., calls *diu* a "dramatically convincing detail."

88. For Ovid's fondness for asyndetic groupings of the comparative *ut,* see Goold, "*Amatoria Critica,*" 61.

Callimachus because of its notoriety.[89] Ovid, however, does not describe the cut marble as weeping. Instead, he separates the two aspects of the image, so that the *puella* herself weeps; her tears will eventually become the subject of the final simile. For these tears, as Barsby suggests, Homer's Penelope is the prototype; and so the *puella* is a conflation of Niobe and Penelope—the former frozen like stone, the latter melting like snow—as Ovid moves from a static to a dynamic portrait of her. The underlying link between the two similes is color: the whiteness of the snow is anticipated by the renowned whiteness of Parian marble. As I noted earlier, Barsby criticizes the Parian marble simile as not apt, apparently because elsewhere in ancient literature comparison with Parian marble generally focuses on the gleaming brilliance of the stone. In Horace *Odes* 1.19, for example, the brilliance of Glycera's complexion is greater than that of Parian marble and inflames Horace (*urit me Glycerae nitor / splendentis Pario marmore purius,* 5–6).[90] Ovid, however, is interested not just in the *puella*'s color—although that is an important point—but also in her state of petrifaction; and in comparing her to Parian marble, he evokes a brief memory of one other model, Dido in the underworld (*nec magis incepto vultum sermone movetur / quam si dura silex aut* **stet Marpesia cautes,** *Aen.* 6.470–71). Marpessos is a mountain on the island of Paros; in comparing her to Marpessan, or Parian, stone, Virgil emphasizes Dido's motionlessness (*stet*) while only hinting indirectly at her pallor.[91] Similarly, Ovid emphasizes the *puella*'s petrifaction (*astitit*) and avoids direct reference to the marble's color, instead comparing it with the *puella*'s pallor: *albo et sine sanguine vultu.* The epithet *albus,* according to Servius at least,[92] is far different from *candidus: aliud est candidum esse, id est quadam nitenti luce perfusum, aliud album, quod pallori constat esse vicinum.*[93] Last but not least, Ovid points to his own role in the events represented by this extended simile, with the verb *caeduntur.* McKeown observes that while *caedere* is the regular term for quarrying, "[t]he general sense 'strike' . . . comes readily to mind and makes the simile the more apposite."[94] In other words, the verb

89. See F. Williams, ed., *Callimachus: Hymn to Apollo* (Oxford, 1978), on 22.

90. Other examples include Pindar *Nem.* 4.81; Theocr. *Id.* 6.38; Virg. *Geo.* 3.34, *Aen.* 1.593, and *Aen.* 3.126; Hor. *Odes* 1.14.19–20. Cat. 64.100, *magis fulgore expalluit auri,* is an interesting and odd combination of the two emphases.

9!. See Servius, ad loc.; cf. Norden, ad loc. See also S. Skulsky, "The Sibyl's Rage and the Marpessan Rock," *AJP* 108 (1987): 72–73.

92. On *Geo.* 3.82. Cf. Hor. *Epod.* 7.15, *albus pallor.*

93. I suspect that Ovid wanted to conflate here Virgil's Dido of Parian marble and his description, at *Aen.* 3.126, of the island of Paros as snowy (*niveamque Paron*).

94. McKeown, ad loc.

takes on an association reflective of its context in addition to its primary descriptive function: the *puella* resembles Parian marble not only in color but also because she has been struck.

This simile sequence, then, is anything but one-dimensional; and although much of it is clearly evocative of Homeric and Alexandrian poetry, little or nothing here can be pinned down as strictly imitative or precisely referential. Instead, Ovid seems primarily interested in the suggestiveness of poetic memory and, as I have mentioned before, in visual effectiveness. To achieve these goals, he relies on accumulation of detail, symmetry, and movement. Zanker has identified *enargeia,* or literary pictorialism, as one of the major manifestations of realism in Hellenistic poetry;[95] the design of Ovid's simile is a trompe-l'oeil masterpiece in this tradition. Very little really happens, the movements and changes described are all but imperceptible, yet the overall effect is intensely vivid. By alluding to other literary "pictures," especially similes, and by recalling women sculpted, as it were, in stone, Ovid creates a portrait of his *puella* that is at once purely literary and visually realistic.

Before leaving this simile, I want to point to one other contextual detail that indicates how it is intended to complement the larger analogical pattern of the poem. In the lines immediately preceding the extended simile, we find a rush of imagery extending over three quasi-enjambed couplets, in a sequence very much unlike the gradual and controlled detection of movement and sensation that follows (43–48):

> denique si tumidi ritu torrentis agebar
>   caecaque me praedam fecerat ira suam,
> nonne satis fuerat timidae inclamasse puellae   45
>   nec nimium rigidas intonuisse minas
> aut tunicam a summa diducere turpiter ora
>   ad mediam (mediae zona tulisset opem)?

[In short, if I was being driven like a swollen torrent and blind fury had made me its prey, would it not have been enough to shout at the timid girl and to thunder less-than-binding threats or to sunder her tunic

---

95. Zanker, *Realism in Alexandrian Poetry,* esp. 39–41. It is worth noting that Eustathius, commenting on the first extended simile in the *Iliad* (beginning at 2.87), sees *enargeia* as one important function of similes (Eust. *Il.* 176, lines 20–25 = M. van der Valk, ed., *Eustathii Commentarii ad Homeri Iliadem Pertinentes* [Leiden, 1971], 1.270, lines 23–29): see also Richardson, "Literary Criticism," 276–80.

shamelessly, from its top edge to her midriff (her girdle would have protected her at the midriff)?]

Ovid breathlessly laments his outburst and wonders why he did not resort to more typically elegiac behavior—shouts, threats, and the tearing of clothes. The whole passage opens with a short simile, *tumidi ritu torrentis,* evocative of comparisons used by Homer to describe both Ajax and Diomedes (*Il.* 11.492–95 and 5.87–88), two of the heroes to whom Ovid had compared himself previously in this poem.[96] Ovid uses this comparison to characterize the anger that drove him to action—and the movement of the passage appropriately runs on, like a torrent swollen beyond the limits of its riverbed. The image of a torrential flow rushing out of control is programmatic, too: as Ovid begins to equate himself with the heroes of epic, he behaves like the "Assyrian river," described by Callimachus' Apollo to Phthonos as a great stream which carries with it much trash (*h.* 2.108–9): Ἀσσυρίου ποταμοῖο μέγας ῥόος, ἀλλὰ τὰ πολλά / λύματα γῆς καὶ πολλὸν ἐφ᾽ ὕδατι συρφετὸν ἕλκει.[97]

The couplet beginning with *at nunc* at 49 (*at nunc sustinui raptis a fronte capillis / ferreus ingenuas ungue notare genas*) brings Ovid up short, as he reflects upon the results of that outburst; and the way in which our quintuplet of similes begins, with *astitit illa,* throws his surge of epic violence into sharp contrast to the *puella*'s petrifaction. Her gradual return to emotion and movement is then aptly characterized as a trickle, not a torrent. Ovid juxtaposes the short simile describing himself, meant to capture an indiscriminate rush of action, with the five fully developed similes that document in detail every stage of her response. The overall effect is not just remarkably cinematic; it also characterizes Ovid's artistic control over his medium and is a harbinger of the very real transformations, of women in particular, that will be at the heart of the *Metamorphoses.* The whole episode is carefully, dramatically, and masterfully assembled.

But how does it fit into this poem? Our investigation of the abundance of analogy in *Am.* 1.7, and especially of the extended and multidimensional simile there, has uncovered a rich array of inspirational models; but it is worth reflecting as well on the end result. It would be easy, and typical

---

96. McKeown, ad loc., notes the Homeric cast of Ovid's simile.

97. On the programmatic status of this imagery, see, inter alios, Wimmel, *Kallimachos in Rom,* 222–25; Clausen, "Callimachus and Latin Poetry," 189. Cf. A. Suter, "Ovid, from Image to Narrative: *Amores* 1.8 and 3.6," *CW* 83 (1989): 17–20; Morrison, "Literary Reference and Generic Transgression," 588 n. 36.

of current Ovid criticism, to stop here; but it remains to be wondered not only why this poem is so full of allusive analogies from the entire continuum but also how they work together as part of an organic whole. The five-part simile just discussed is clearly the emotional climax of the poem; ten lines later, Ovid brings the scene to a close. Meanwhile, however, we should not forget what preceded these similes, particularly the mythological similes and exempla that were so obviously tongue-in-cheek. If we do as Barsby does and simply disparage as overdone the five-part simile describing the *puella*'s pallor and tears, we attribute to Ovid a lack of narrative control belied by the extended simile itself, with its wonderful sense of symmetry and movement. A better solution, it seems to me, is to consider the poem in its entirety as a comment on Ovid's literary love affair and his attitude toward his poetry. Just as his similes are intellectualizing devices, so is his love affair a primarily literary endeavor; and as he captures his *puella* in images borrowed from others, she becomes a metaphor for the *Amores* as a whole, inscribed as they are with a distinctive Roman poetic tradition that transcends genre. The excess of his similes plays a central role in signaling the literary nature of Ovid's love affair.

In the preceding pages I have pursued a wide-ranging examination of the dominant stylistic features and general literary effect of analogy, especially of the extended and multidimensional similes, in the *Amores*. Let us now pull together at least some of the variegated threads running through this discussion. First, the extended simile itself is not entirely new to elegy by any means, but as it is used by Ovid it is rearticulated in a manner that recalls the affinity between simile and exemplum while at the same time evoking the world of epic to which his elegy is in stark (and intended) contrast. Second, the visual emphasis of these similes gives to Ovid's elegy a realism that paradoxically marks the literary nature of Ovid's elegiac love.[98] In narrative terms, Ovid's fondness for similes as vehicles for realism heightens the deceptions that ultimately end his love affair: the blurred or negative image can be particularly useful in helping Ovid to illustrate his own amatory illusion. Finally, we have considered the variety of ways in which Ovid's extended similes interact not only with the contexts in which they appear but also with the tradition that shapes them. As in the preceding chapter, here too we have seen the particular, though not exclusive, prominence of Virgil and Callimachus in Ovid's poetic memory; and again

---

98. See further my discussion in chap. 4.

we have seen striking evidence for the vitality of the tradition in which Ovid writes. Most important, the extended similes examined here testify to Ovid's transcendence of imitativeness in the *Amores,* even as they transcend the conventional boundaries of elegy. I began this discussion by dismissing generic propriety as a valid criterion for Ovid's poetic success, and I have mentioned a number of critics who find Ovid's extended similes unfortunate at best. I have aimed for a different perspective on this feature, a perspective in which propriety yields to effectiveness as a primary criterion for the evaluation of literary success, and in which Ovid's revisions of epic are themselves reflective surfaces mirroring the literary past in the framework of modern poetry. I turn now to Ovid's self-portrait as reflected in the *Amores.*

Chapter 4

From Authenticity to Irony: Programmatic Poetry and Narrative Reversal in the *Amores*

est tibi agendus amans
Ovid *AA* 1.611

In the preceding chapters I have pursued clues provided by Ovid himself to escape from the critical labyrinth of genre and imitation that has imprisoned the *Amores*. But is the creature found at the center of this maze really just a monstrous hybrid? We have seen the inadequacy of labeling the *Amores* Propertian parody or imitation; we have seen as well that Ovid's comprehension of the Augustan legacy is both vast and precise. In the last two chapters especially, I have shown how the poetry of Virgil, Callimachus, and many other predecessors has left its indelible impression on Ovid in the *Amores*. But this is not yet the place to stop our discussion of the collection. The creative processes that give the *Amores* their shape tell only a part of the story; I want to turn now to consider what the *Amores* are about.

So baldly put, the idea is at first stunning: are the *Amores* really *about* anything at all? When Ovid makes reference to Homer, Virgil, and other poetic models in, for example, the blushing simile of *Am.* 2.5, discussed in chapter 3, we do not simply end up with a poem about Homer, Virgil, and the others. Likewise, the premise that the *Amores* are in any substantial sense, parodic or otherwise, about Propertian elegy does not withstand serious scrutiny. While Ovid clearly does not ignore Propertius—he probably would have been unable to do so completely even if he had tried—his efforts in many ways look beyond Propertius' model and offer us instead a vision of elegy that confounds generic boundaries even as it complicates simplistic definitions of imitation. It is thus misleading to claim that elegy itself is Ovid's topic, although many have done so; generic entropy ensues

in this reading, as the poems apparently turn in on themselves and consume the elegiac genre even as they embody it. Rather, as we have already
seen, elegy undergoes a continual process of redefinition and expansion in
Ovid's hands, in the process serving as a means to a distinct end. The purpose of this chapter and the following one is to suggest what this end is.

I want to begin by focusing on the central theme of the *Amores*. Most
readers, attending to conventions of genre, would identify love as this central theme; yet when readers do so, they are perforce led quite quickly to
the conclusion that, since the *Amores* are only superficially about love and
since Corinna is so evidently an artificial construct, the poems themselves
are artificial and superficial constructs. Of course, on one level the same
thing could be said about virtually every poem by every poet; yet the insub-
tantiality of Ovid's love has, as we saw earlier, earned his *Amores* few
admirers not inclined to read them as fundamentally derivative. Once
generic determinism has been surmounted, however, a second look at the
Amores suggests that another theme besides love and another character
besides Corinna are really of primary importance to Ovid: the theme of
poetry writing and the character of the poet. The following discussion will
illustrate how Ovid uses the format of elegy to create for himself a literary
autobiography of sorts, using the three-book design of the collection to
create a narrative about his early career.

One of the most striking and paradoxical features of the *Amores* is a
phenomenon that, for lack of a better term, I call Ovid's "realism." By this
term I do not mean to imply a special interest on Ovid's part in reflecting
in his poetry the *Realien* of everyday experience as he witnessed and lived
it; the *Amores* are not primarily documents providing data for the social
historian. In fact, virtually all the available "evidence," if we can call it that,
would suggest that the amatory setting of the *Amores* is more fundamentally conventional, and has far less of a basis in any historical reality, than
do the love poems of any other Roman elegist.[1] The strongest witness to

---

1. The eighties and early nineties have seen the renewal of debate on the "reality "of
Augustan elegy among many scholars. On the the "real" side are such scholars as Lyne (*Latin
Love Poets*) and J. Griffin (*Latin Poets and Roman Life* [Chapel Hill, 1986]), the latter of
whom is taken to task for his sociological/biographical reading of elegy by R.F. Thomas,
"Turning Back the Clock," *CP* 83 (1988): 54–69; cf. also the review of Griffin by R.G.M. Nisbet in *JRS* 77 (1987): 165–73. The continental view of Veyne, *Roman Erotic Elegy*, represents
the opposite extreme, with its insistence on discourse analysis (cf. the sympathetic review by
M. Wyke, "In Pursuit of Love, the Poetic Self, and a Process of Reading: Augustan Elegy in
the 1980s," *JRS* 79 [1989]: 165–73). Not surprisingly, neither side in the debate has much
interest in the *Amores*, focusing instead almost entirely on Propertius and, to a lesser degree,

this is the fictive character of Corinna herself; from the mise-en-scène of the opening poems, in which Ovid openly admits that he is without a beloved, to the absence of Corinna's name from Apuleius' list of amatory pseudonyms (*Apol.* 10), the reality of Corinna's existence remains unprovable, if not unbelievable.[2] Indeed, the name *Corinna* itself may be intentionally vague; McKeown comments that "Corinna is cognate with κόρη and can always be replaced with *puella,* which has exactly the same prosody."[3] A second, less frequently remarked factor contributing to the collection's detachment from the historical environment in which it circulated is the evident absence of a patron; while three of the elegies are addressed to men apparently of Ovid's acquaintance (1.9 to Atticus, 2.10 to Graecinus, and 2.18 to Macer), there is no evidence in the extant second edition of the *Amores* for the existence of a powerful friend to whom Ovid might have dedicated his first foray into the elegiac arena.[4] I shall return to this point later in this chapter, to discuss more fully its implications for our reading of the *Amores;* for now, it is simply worth drawing attention to the fact that this absence complements the absence of a real woman behind Corinna.

Tibullus. A refreshing and valuable alternative, therefore, is the approach demonstrated by Conte, "Love without Elegy"; although my reading of the *Amores* differs from his on many individual points, it will be evident that I share his belief that Ovid's irony creates a fundamental split between Ovid's roles as poet and as lover: see my subsequent discussion in the text.

2. See the full survey of this topic by McKeown, 1:19–24. McKeown considers Corinna a persona for an intentionally unidentifiable mistress; while I agree on Ovid's intentionality, I shall suggest in this chapter that the labeling of Corinna as "persona" is not only unnecessary but even misleading.

3. McKeown, 1:21.

4. See McKeown, 1:24–25. As he shows, in this way as in many other ways Ovidian practice is radically different from that of Propertius, who involves others in his amatory drama from the very start.

White, *Promised Verse,* 239–48 provides a list of all the friends addressed or mentioned by name in Ovid's poetry and offers prosopographical information for each. In fact, as White comments in introducing the list, "[t]he great majority of Ovid's friends are known to us from his references to them in poems he wrote late in life," i.e., from the exile poetry. In almost all of the references in *Tr.* and *Pont.* to Messalla Corvinus and his two sons, Messallinus and Maximus Cotta, however, Ovid is at pains to indicate that their friendship and support has been of long standing, i.e., has long preceded his exile: see, e.g., *Tr.* 4.4.27–32; *Pont.* 1.7.27–30, 2.2.1 and 97–98, 3.5.7, and 2.3.69–78. *Pont.* 2.3.75–78 suggest that Messalla was Ovid's first literary supporter: *me tuus ille pater, Latiae facundia linguae / cui non inferior nobilitate fuit, / primus, ut auderem committere carmina famae, / impulit: ingenii dux fuit ille mei* (the addressee here is Maximus Cotta).

I have for convenience's sake used the term *patron* here in the sense in which it is commonly used by scholars, although I am persuaded by White that the terms *patron* and *patronage* misrepresent the social context in which Augustan poets and their powerful friends mingled: see *Promised Verse,* esp. 3–34. The designation *powerful friend* is a far more useful alternative.

By the term *realism* I mean instead that feature of Ovid's poetry we may wish to call its tangibility, or concreteness, or visual effectiveness— its *Wirklichkeitsbild,* to borrow Reitzenstein's term.[5] Ovid often narrates as literal fact something that in other poets' work had remained a purely linguistic metaphor;[6] and in so doing, he uses mimesis to invest his fiction with immediacy. In using a term like *mimesis,* I am well aware that this effect, in its many components, is illusory—or, as the semeioticians would have it, that words are arbitrary signs, and that the world described by Ovid is no more tangible or concrete for the illusory signs he employs. From the very outset of the *Amores,* Ovid himself makes it clear that even the most detailed description of Corinna's physical presence, such as that provided in 1.5, is nothing more than a mimetic fantasy. His work would thus appear to be even less "realistic," as it is even less "sincere," than that of his elegiac predecessors. As we consider Ovid's narrative innovations in greater detail, however, I believe that both these terms will invite further and more subtle definition: charges of "lack of realism" and "superficiality" in the *Amores* reflect a reading of these poems that is itself superficial. Attention given instead to the collection's dominant features as a narrative about the poet himself will clarify the relationship of Ovid's mimetic accomplishment to the Augustan literary tradition.

Before we pursue the details of his narrative technique, however, it will be useful to recall for the sake of comparison the narrative status of several other poetry collections involving an amatory autobiography, since I believe that it is the rule that makes Ovid's narrative in the *Amores* both possible and exceptional. Propertius is of course the most obvious comparandus; and we have already explored in some detail the basis for the claim that Ovid simply hollowly imitates Propertius, even offering us a three-book collection to rival Propertius' first three books, all focusing on Cynthia.[7] Again, just like Propertius, Ovid is a product of the Hellenistic aesthetic tradition and so employs a program rich in Callimachean clichés: a *recusatio* at the opening of each book; a programmatic statement or other sort of *sphragis* at or near[8] the close of each book; and programmatic imagery liberally sprinkled elsewhere in the collection, betokening

---

5. See E. Reitzenstein, *Wirklichkeitsbild und Gefühlsentwicklung bei Properz,* Philologus Suppl. 29 (Leipzig, 1936), 35, on the connection between narrative and *Wirklichkeitsbild* in Propertius.
6. See Suter, "Image to Narrative."
7. On the problem of book division in Propertius, see n. 31 in this chapter.
8. On the close of book 2, see my discussion in chap. 5.

Ovid's aesthetic heritage and allegiance. Catullus, too, as potent predecessor and role model for the Augustan elegists, provides a likely basis for comparison, particularly in his extremely articulate and self-conscious recognition of the difference between poetry and life and in his consummate ability to transcend this difference through language.

This catalogue of similarities could continue for some time; yet the differences have received far less attention and are crucial to a grasp of Ovid's narrative innovation in the *Amores*. First, unlike any other collection we know of with the exception of Horace's *Odes* 1–3,[9] the three books of *Amores* as we have them appeared simultaneously, in a collection intended to be read and comprehended together and in their present sequence. I shall return shortly to the question of the second edition and its implications for interpretation; at this point, it is important to give due consideration to the fact that Ovid packaged the poems in this way. The consequences of this fact for a reading of the *Amores,* relatively simple yet far-reaching, have received scant attention in the critical tradition.[10] The three books present us with a completed story, a beginning, middle, and end, in three acts, if you will; closure is implicit in the opening, and at the close we do indeed discover that the end of the love affair is paralleled by the end of the collection. The synonymy between Ovid's love and his "loves," between his *amor* and the *Amores,* is more than a linguistic pun; form and content are not simply complementary in this collection, but constantly determine and define each other.[11]

One exemplary comparison will, I think, capture the difference. Propertius 1.1 is universally admired for its masterful articulation of the subjective ethos of elegy, even by those who recognize in it as well the voice of Alexandrian aesthetics.[12] His *puella,* Cynthia, is cast in the role of Muse; and together with her partner Amor, she subjugates Propertius to her love (1.1.1–6):

---

9. On the likelihood that *Odes* 1–3 were published simultaneously, see Nisbet and Hubbard, 1:xxxv–xxxvii; White, *Promised Verse,* 157.

10. In "Ringing Down the Curtain on Love," *Helios* 12 (1985): 21–28, W.R. Johnson emphasizes the necessity of reading the collection as we have it, in revised form, and making sense of its structure and design; but the remainder of Johnson's analysis diverges widely from mine. McKeown, 1:90–102, argues against any significant "chronological" ordering in the *Amores;* but see L. Cahoon, "The Bed as Battlefield: Erotic Conquest and Military Metaphor in Ovid's *Amores,*" *TAPA* 118 (1988): 293–307.

11. See A.M. Keith, "*Corpus Eroticum:* Elegiac Poetics and Elegiac *Puellae* in Ovid's *Amores,*" *CW* 88 (1994): 27–40, who focuses on Ovid's movement away from Corinna in book 3.

12. E.g., Allen, " 'Sincerity' and the Roman Elegists," 253–77; cf. also idem, "Sunt Qui Propertium Malint," 107–48; Ross, *Backgrounds to Augustan Poetry,* 59–70.

Cynthia prima suis miserum me cepit ocellis,
   contactum nullis ante cupidinibus.
tum mihi constantis deiecit lumina fastus
   et caput impositis pressit Amor pedibus,
donec me docuit castas odisse puellas   5
   improbus, et nullo vivere consilio.

[Cynthia was the first to capture poor me with her eyes: I had never been touched before by desire. Then Love cast down my look of stubborn pride and with his feet pushed down my head, until he taught me to hate chaste girls, shameless god that he is, and to live without purpose.]

The *furor* (7) that results is inescapable; even the mythical paradigm offered by the devoted Milanion (9–16) is useless.[13] Neither magic nor medicine offers a solution (19–28), nor does escape (29–32). Propertius is dominated by his love and can only warn others to avoid his fate (33–38). Trapped as he is in love, his only resort is to poetry; his *furor* is ironically what gives him an elegiac voice. Conte's description of the essence of elegiac love is apt: ". . . the code of elegy . . . demands that the lover-poet be a patient reluctant to be cured: he loves his suffering not only as the substance but above all as the very condition of his poetry-writing, for to live without the suffering of love would mean that the poet remained wordless, no longer a poet."[14] So it is from the outset of the Monobiblos: love constitutes Propertius' program and creates poetry; and what this poetry creates in turn is the expression of the lover's love.

Amores 1.1 is fundamentally different.[15] I shall return presently to consider it in more detail; but with the Propertian predecessor in mind, we may note immediately that Ovid describes himself as a poet with an abundance of poetry but without love. When Cupid intervenes to change this poet's theme, the situation degenerates further: now the poet has neither poetry nor love. Only when set aflame by Cupid's arrow does Ovid's poet begin to experience love (paradoxically, a love with no object), and thus he is restored to his identity as poet. From this brief description we can see that Ovid has reversed the cause-and-effect relationship implicit in Propertius:

---

13. On the role of the Milanion exemplum in Propertius' statement of poetic allegiance, see Ross, *Backgrounds to Augustan Poetry,* 61–65; Rosen and Farrell, "Acontius, Milanion, and Gallus," 241–54.

14. Conte, "Love without Elegy," 446–47; cf. also 448.

15. See Keith, "*Amores* 1.1," 340–42, and my discussion of *Am.* 1.1 later in this chapter.

now, poetry creates a programmatics of love; and this program enables the poet to establish a literary presence for himself.

With this comparison in mind, we can now return to the narrative character of the *Amores* and make better sense of the nuances of Ovid's innovation. Albeit using a different critical framework, Reitzenstein captured the novelty of Ovid's achievement in the *Amores* in terms strikingly similar to mine when he observed that, by inverting the usual programmatic relationship of life to poetry, Ovid creates the illusion that his elegy exists despite, not because of, his inspiration.[16] I want to take this observation a step further and propose that the illusion achieved is as ironic as the strategies used to achieve it: while suggesting that poetry shapes a poet's life regardless of his intentions, Ovid uses the life described in the *Amores* to assert his control over elegiac inspiration. The result is what I shall call here *narrative reversal,* as poet and poetry take the place formerly held in elegy by lover and love.

The word *reversal* also suggests that there are two sides or aspects to the narrative of the *Amores;* and this suggestion in turn allows for a refinement on my earlier observation that the three books of the *Amores* are a completed story. I propose that we see in the *Amores* two narratives running parallel to each other and at times merging: in addition to inventing the narrative of his affair with Corinna, Ovid describes the creative process into which he is initiated as poet, willy-nilly, by Cupid. Not surprisingly, readers who come to the *Amores* with a generic focus derived from Propertius and Tibullus are likely to look first to Ovid's amatory narrative, because of the obvious comparisons to be made; and it is of course in this narrative that Ovid's flagrant disregard for sincerity is so apparent. To these same readers, meanwhile, the programmatic material seems nothing other than an artificial superstructure whose sole function is to alert us to the fiction of all that follows. I believe instead that in inverting the expectations of his audience, Ovid sets out to exploit the inevitability of comparison with the other elegists. I want to focus attention, therefore, on how Ovid tells two complementary narratives, setting up a realistic story about a poet's conversion to and initiation into elegy as counterpart and contrast to the Corinna narrative. As creator of both stories, Ovid is both intimate and detached: using the character of the poet to serve as intermediary between his audience and the lover he invents, he

---

16. E. Reitzenstein, "Das neue Kunstwollen in den Amores Ovids," *RhM* 84 (1935): 67–73 (= *Ovid,* ed. M. von Albrecht and E. Zinn, Wege der Forschung 92 [Darmstadt, 1968], 211–18).

draws his readers into the creative process even as he puts his amatory fiction at a second remove.[17]

How are we to understand Ovid's double role in the *Amores*, as both aspiring poet and lover of Corinna? Virtually all modern critics of the collection talk in terms of Ovid's assumed "persona" of *poeta-amator*, with the two sides of this identity seen as inseparable. I too shall suggest that there is often a strong identification of poet with lover, and vice versa, in the *Amores;* but I believe it is crucial that we see them from the outset as separable identities—Ovid certainly does[18]—and that we understand their mutual identification as part of the plotting of the *Amores*. Furthermore, while persona theory has generally proven to be a beneficial remedy to the earlier fashion for biographical criticism in Latin poetry studies,[19] I believe that in this particular case it has played a central role in diminishing our ability to read the *Amores* without generic prejudice. The insistence that the central character of the collection is a cynical *poeta-amator*—"your basic sado-masochist pretending to be a total masochist," in one scholar's extreme formulation[20]—has been appealing to many, even though it leads us back almost inevitably to the sort of reductive conclusions that we saw hampering our view of the *Amores* earlier.[21] Because persona theory is

17. In referring to the narrator or the poet in the *Amores,* I mean the first-person narrator-focalizer created (but only implicitly fictionalized) by Ovid to deliver the narrative of the *Amores;* when I refer to the lover, I mean the explicitly fictional identity Ovid gives to himself as a character or actor within his own poetry. See further n. 23 in this chapter.

18. In fact, this separation was noted over three decades ago, in a study of Ovid's portrayal of the *lena* in *Am.* 1.8, O. Kratins' "The Pretended Witch: A Reading of Ovid's *Amores,* I.viii," *PhQ* 42 (1963): 151–58. Cf. also F. Bertini, trans., *Ovidio: Amori,* 2d ed. (Milan, 1988), xv, on Ovid's "duplice punto di vista: quello del poeta-innamorato e quello dell'autore-Ovidio": "Il primo è il protagonista di ogni singola vicenda . . . vive solo in funzione del suo amore; il secondo valuta con ironico e scettico distacco le passioni del suo *alter-ego* e ne sorride con superiorità." Neither Kratins nor Bertini, however, proceeds to connect this observation with a reading of the *Amores* as narrative.

19. For a good introduction to the topic, see R.C. Elliott, *The Literary Persona* (Chicago and London, 1982). M. Winkler, *The Persona in Three Satires of Juvenal* (Hildesheim and New York, 1983), 1–12, clearly describes the application of persona theory to satire, and J.T. Davis, *Fictus Adulter: Poet as Actor in the Amores* (Amsterdam, 1989), is a recent illustration of its application to Ovid.

20. Johnson, "Ringing Down the Curtain on Love," 22.

21. W. Ginsberg, *The Cast of Character* (Toronto, 1983), 19–47 is an interesting, if only partially satisfying, exception: his discussion is unusual in observing that Ovid's poet is the central character of the *Amores,* but he fails to proceed from this observation to anything other than a superficial discussion; for Ginsberg, Ovid's lover is pure elegiac parody. Cf. also Conte, "Love without Elegy," 452, who continues to use the persona metaphor but who characterizes Ovid as " 'impersonating' the role of the elegiac lover." He thus reaches a conclusion very similar to mine, although his use of persona theory places more emphasis on the lack of authenticity in the *Amores* than I think is necessary or helpful.

premised on the assumption of a "mask" or "pose" by the author, it tends to set up a dichotomy between "false" and "true" voices that has even caused one recent interpreter to resort to an oddly moralistic view of the *Amores,* distinguishing between the deceptive and self-deceptive *poeta-amator,* on the one hand, and an ethical poet Ovid, on the other, whose reductive aim, according to this reading, is to indict the genre and the persona even as he uses them.[22] A more helpful and, I believe, more meaningful approach is offered by the attention to perspective and focalization that is the centerpiece of contemporary narratology. This approach allows us to recognize not only two narratives but also two central characters in the *Amores:* first, and hierarchically more important, is the programmatic or framing narrative, featuring the poet; entirely embedded within the first narrative is the amatory one, featuring the lover as central player.[23] The

22. Cf. L. Cahoon, "A Program for Betrayal: Ovidian *Nequitia* in *Amores* 1.1, 2.1, and 3.1," *Helios* 12 (1985): 38–39: ". . . the poet betrays himself by pretending to be someone else—by posing as a lover. This self-deception leads him to seduce, exploit, manipulate, and betray those whom he pretends to love. Poetry that similarly seduces and manipulates its readers ends up by betraying the values that make the social order cohere. . . ." Cf. also her article on *Am.* 2.6, "The Parrot and the Poet: The Function of Ovid's Funeral Elegies," *CJ* 80 (1984): 27–35, and my discussion of this elegy in chap. 5.

23. *Quot narratologi, tot nomina:* readers should be advised that I here draw on the language of narratological theory. A brief foray into this literature will make it evident that virtually every single theorist finds it necessary or expedient to adapt and modify the terminology used by his/her predecessors; I therefore want to indicate that in using the term *embedded narrative* and several other narratological concepts in this chapter, I am following the general model established by G. Genette, *Narrative Discourse: An Essay in Method,* trans. J.E. Levin (Ithaca, 1980), and pursued by I.J.F. deJong in *Narrators and Focalizers: The Presentation of the Story in the Iliad* (Amsterdam, 1987). I have chosen not to employ the terminology of Genette's distinction between narrator and focalizer as refined by deJong, mainly because the *Amores,* unlike the *Iliad,* present us with a first-person narrative; but it might be possible to follow their example and distinguish between the poet as "primary narrator-focalizer" and the lover as "secondary narrator-focalizer." I think, however, that Ovid's constant blurring of this distinction in the *Amores*—a distinction he has himself created—is easily made evident without jargon, since the range of characters represented in the *Amores* is so much more restricted than that which we find in Homeric epic.

On the concept of embedded narrative, see also M. Bal, "Notes on Narrative Embedding," *Poetics Today* 2 (1981): 44–45: "Within its own proper limits, narrative communication presents a narrative subject called the *narrator* who proffers sentences, the direct content of which is a vision. This vision or presentation is the act of another subject who is *contained* relative to the first subject (the narrator), and this second subject is the focalizer. The identity of the focalizer can coincide with that of the narrator, but does not necessarily do so. As subject of its vision, this focalizer presents a history or diegesis. This history is the act of another subject, usually plural, which is the agent of the events which compose the history and whom we call the *actor.* . . . In other words, the narrator speaks the text whose content is the narrative; the focalizer presents the narrative, whose content is the history; the history is acted out by the actors."

remarkable interdependence of these two narratives makes the *Amores* something distinctively new in the Roman elegiac tradition.

This approach to the narrative of the *Amores* not only has the advantage of defining the collection's character more comprehensively; it also allows us to proceed further with Reitzenstein's reading of the *Amores* as ironic illusion. The poet's reversal of our narrative expectations gives him the ability both to describe an emotional outburst on his own part and to remain detached from the amatory narrative, refocusing our attention on his control of the medium. As Conte remarks:

> . . . [Ovid's irony] is the sign of a critical consciousness that observes the text's formation from outside and reveals its implicit practices. Ovid keeps the traditional elegiac poet-lover alive by separating onto two different textual levels the two functions that earlier had coincided: as lover, he shares the same status as the other elegiac personas; as poet, he possesses the code and takes advantage of this privilege to govern the play of the personas from above.[24]

Ovid's poet often employs some sort of ironic strategy precisely at the point when the two narratives of the *Amores* seem most likely to merge and when poet and lover are most likely to be identified with each other. As I noted earlier, the programmatic material in the collection is generally treated as extraneous; not only do I intend to treat it as the primary narrative of the *Amores,* but, as will become apparent as I proceed, I mean to extend the boundaries of the term *programmatic* to include not only the poems in which Ovid's poet takes center stage to talk about his literary career but also a number of poems in which the lover and the poet are closely identified. We shall see that Ovid uses realistic irony to control the "authenticity" of emotional abandonment and to invert our response to the narrative. This realism encourages us to read the programmatic narrative as the "true" story of the *Amores,* described as it is in vivid and concrete images.[25] Cupid's theft of a foot from the opening of the poet's would-be epic (1.1.1–2) turns conventional metaphor into something tan-

---

24. Conte, "Love without Elegy," 453; cf. also 455–56, 458–59. Note that in Conte's view as expressed in the last section of this quote, the poet persona he sees Ovid using is a sort of deus ex machina. While Conte's division of lover and poet into two separate roles is useful, I believe that this emphasis on artificiality downplays too much the centrality of programmatic poetry to the narrative of the *Amores:* see my relevant discussion later, in chap. 5.

25. Cf. my earlier discussion, in chap. 3, of the epic torrent simile in *Am.* 1.7, and cf. my later discussion, in chap. 6, of *Am.* 3.6.

gible, even as it reverses the illusion of sincerity so central to the amatory narratives of Propertius and Tibullus. Ovid the poet is not interested in having us "believe" in Corinna or even in her lover; but he does want to persuade us of the centrality of the poet and his poetry to the narrative of the *Amores*. As we move through the collection from beginning to end, the lover is instantiated only to disappear gradually from view; the poet, in contrast, is ever present, not only "surviving" the amatory narrative, but also using it to create a new poetic self.

Finally, a reading of the *Amores* as a sort of plotted narrative with beginning, middle, and end and with the embedding of one story within another offers yet another opportunity to view these poems through a lens that avoids the generic labyrinth. We have already seen, especially in my discussions in chapters 2 and 3, that it is Ovid's intent repeatedly to move beyond the boundaries conventional to elegy even as he uses the traditions of Augustan poetry to create a literary identity for himself. By looking at the *Amores* as a plotted sequence with narrative embedding, we can add to our understanding of Ovid's aims: the narrative of the *Amores* has as much in common with the plotting of the *Aeneid* as it does with the episodic autobiography typical of an individual elegy by Propertius or Tibullus. From the opening of 1.1, in fact, we see Ovid's bold willingness to compare his accomplishment with Virgil's: he uses a reference to the opening of the *Aeneid* (*arma gravi numero violentaque bella*)[26] to show that the dominant plot of the *Amores* is the poet's conversion to elegy.

First, however, let us look at what precedes even this reference. Given the fact that otherwise Ovid the narrator almost entirely dominates the framing narrative of the *Amores,* it is striking that the first characters to speak as we begin book 1 are the three books of poems themselves. They take shape before our eyes as they begin the *Amores* with a four-line epigram prefaced to the collection:

> Qui modo Nasonis fueramus quinque libelli,
>   tres sumus: hoc illi praetulit auctor opus.
> ut iam nulla tibi nos sit legisse voluptas,
>   at levior demptis poena duobus erit.

[We who had just recently been the five books of Naso are now three: the author preferred the present collection to the previous one.

---

26. See Keith, "*Amores* 1.1," 328–36.

Although you may now get no pleasure in reading us, at least, with two books removed, your suffering will be lighter.]

Speaking on behalf of their creator, the books invite us to read (*legisse*), and they explain that, though once five in number, they have now become three. We are to assume that they have been somehow improved, for they promise that, although there can still be no guarantee of pleasure in the reading, there is bound to be less suffering than previously. Meanwhile, there is no mention of a Muse, no Apollo, no other appropriate figure of inspiration, not even Corinna or a *puella* like her. No allegory or metaphor directs Ovid to his work; instead, the *libelli* address the poet's very pragmatic concerns, his own preference and a desire to please his audience. This in itself is a realistic turn of events: Ovid is not marked at the outset as a man especially chosen as the mouthpiece of a Muse but appears instead as an accomplished poet whose primary goal is apparently not to commit his love to verse but rather to write a successful poetry collection. And his accomplishment quite literally speaks for itself, using the conceit of a second edition to guarantee a favorable reading.

It may well be objected at this point that the prefatory epigram is simply an afterthought, not really a part of the collection at all and of no particular literary consequence. It is generally treated as such, having only the explanatory value of a table of contents, and providing a useful, though frustrating, bit of information about Ovid's literary career.[27] This documentary value has so dominated our reading of the epigram that its literary nature has been all but unexplored; it seems worthwhile, therefore, to look at these four lines somewhat differently. I shall set aside questions concerning the dating of the two editions and their relative contents as problems already abundantly, if not satisfactorily, engaged elsewhere; such questions do not really help us to understand the text as we have it before

---

27. The scholarly discussion of the two editions, complicated by the identification of the *artes amoris* mentioned at *Am.* 2.18.19, has been as extensive as it is inconclusive. In addition to the much cited article by A. Cameron, "The First Edition of Ovid's *Amores*," *CQ* 62 (1968): 320–33, and the fine survey of the debate provided by Jacobson, *Ovid's Heroides,* 300–318, see the discussion by Knox, *Ovid's Metamorphoses,* 3–4. After a brief hiatus the discussion has reemerged with renewed vigor in two articles by Murgia, who suggests a more elaborate publication history for the *Amores* than has previously been detected: see "The Date of Ovid's *Ars Amatoria* 3" and "Influence of Ovid's *Remedia amoris.*" Murgia's chronology has not been met with much enthusiasm, however; for another novel (but to me unconvincing) hypothesis, see F. della Corte, "Gli 'Amores' di Ovidio Ripudiati," in *Kontinuität und Wandel: Lateinische Poesie von Naevius bis Baudelaire, Franco Munari zum 65. Geburtstag,* ed. U.J. Stache, W. Maaz, and F. Wagner (Hildesheim, 1986), 70–78. Meanwhile, in the absence of solid documentary evidence, no hypothesis is likely to clarify with full adequacy the editorial history of the collection: so argues McKeown, 1:74–89.

us. Ovid chooses to introduce himself and his poetry to the reading public in these lines; why, then, does he not speak for himself (e.g., *ille ego qui . . .*) but instead entrust his introduction to these talking books?[28] In one sense, of course, these poems and books of poems *are* Ovid. Thus, in speaking for him, they speak with his voice (as he does with theirs), and his name (*Nasonis*) appears prominently in their opening words. As they assume voice, so they assume form, and they thus become tangible, which narrative normally is not.[29]

Although the meaning and nature of publication and the distribution of published materials in the ancient world continue to be subjects of scholarly debate and speculation,[30] the *libelli* address what may be a very real circumstance in telling us that the former five books have now been reduced to three. That a poet's work may have gone through more than one edition is a likelihood in and of itself, especially if the work found more than fleeting favor; we may also imagine cases in which a collection of poems would be revised and edited for joint publication, having previously appeared individually or in smaller units, such as individual books.[31] An

---

28. Conte, *Rhetoric of Imitation,* 84–87, suggests that Ovid's prefatory epigram is modeled on the epigram prefaced to some editions of Virgil's works. Arguments against the authenticity of the Virgilian opening, however, seem conclusive: see E. Brandt, "Zum Aeneisprooemium," *Philologus* 83 (1927): 331–35, and G.P. Goold, "Servius and the Helen Episode," *HSCP* 74 (1970): 128, the latter of whom suggests that both epigrams are post-Ovidian fakes.

29. Catullus' *libellus* is made equally tangible by his description of it as *lepidum novum libellum / arida modo pumice expolitum* (1.1–2); in this case, however, the book does not speak for itself but remains objectified as a *donum*. A closer parallel is provided not only by the "sepulchral" epigrams of the Greek Anthology but by the "talking books" and the like of Hellenistic poetry: see P. Bing, *The Well-Read Muse: Present and Past in Callimachus and the Hellenistic Poets,* Hypomnemata 90 (Göttingen, 1988), 29–35 and 58–63.

30. See the discussions by E.J. Kenney, "Books and Readers in the Roman World," in *The Cambridge History of Classical Literature,* vol. 2, *Latin Literature,* ed. E.J. Kenney and W.V. Clausen (Cambridge, 1982), 3–32, esp. 15–22, and R. Starr, "The Circulation of Literary Texts in the Roman World," *CQ* 37 (1987): 213–23, esp. 218–19 on different versions of the same work. Cf. also K. Quinn, "The Poet and His Audience in the Augustan Age," *ANRW* 2.30.1 (1982): 75–180.

31. Such may be the case with Propertius, for example, the first three books of whose work may well have been brought together for joint publication on the example of Horace *Odes* 1–3. That the Monobiblos originally appeared independently is obvious, however, from the self-sufficient design of the book and from the fact that it seems to have won for Propertius the friendship of Maecenas thereafter. The publication circumstances of the remaining books, however, remain thorny problems: see O. Skutsch, "The Second Book of Propertius," *HSCP* 79 (1975): 229–33; G.O. Hutchinson, "Propertius and the Unity of the Book," *JRS* 74 (1984): 99–106. For the likelihood that Ovid's collection comprised three separate *volumina,* see McKeown, 2:3.

apt analogy for Ovid's situation with the *Amores* can be drawn from the history of Hellenistic, rather than Roman, publication. We know that Callimachus' *Aetia* was revised and that much new material (including, possibly, a new prologue)[32] was added for a much later second edition.[33] A decade ago, Peter Knox suggested that Callimachus' substantial revision of the *Aetia* included the addition of the last two books;[34] if we agree with the plausibility of this scenario, the editorial history of Callimachus' poem offers anything but a straightforward equivalent to Ovid's reduction of the size of the *Amores*. I suggest nonetheless that the trimming of the *Amores* implied by the epigram is in fact intended to have a distinctly Callimachean character to it, as it recalls by example the precept handed down to us by a number of Callimachean testimonia, μέγα βιβλίον μέγα κακόν (Call. fr. 465 Pf.); the collection tells us that it is made better insofar as it has been made smaller.[35] To emphasize this fact, Ovid introduces an element of humor that is as typical as it is subtle: the *libelli* refer to him, their composer, as *auctor*. Elsewhere in the *Amores,* Ovid avoids this designation for himself, using instead the more usual *poeta* or the lofty *vates*.[36] The word *auctor* is used frequently in Latin literature to mean "author" (i.e., of a literary work), and Ovid intends it to have that meaning here; but that another, more literal meaning was recognized and appreciated, although rarely exploited, in the Augustan period is indicated by Virgil's use of the word at *Geo.* 1.27 (*auctorem frugum tempestatumque potentem*), a line on which the anonymous author of the *brevis expositio* comments: *auctor ab*

---

32. But see now Cameron, *Callimachus and His Critics,* esp. chapters 4–6, and idem, "Genre and Style in Callimachus," 305 n. 1.

33. Pfeiffer's theory about the revision of the *Aetia* about twenty-five years after the first edition is set forth in 2:xl–xliii. P.E. Knox, "The Epilogue to the *Aetia,*" *GRBS* 26 (1985): 59–65, makes a convincing argument for the addition of the entire last two books; along the way, he also notes the striking similarities between the *Aetia* epilogue and *Amores* 3.15, each the *sphragis* to its collection and each likely, he believes, to have predated in composition the second edition to which it is appended.

34. Knox, "Epilogue to the *Aetia*"; cf. Cameron, *Callimachus and His Critics,* 156–60.

35. Reitzenstein, "Das neue Kunstwollen," 86 n. 1, has been the only critic to observe this parallel, even tentatively: "Es ist, als ob er das humoristisch μέγα βιβλίον μέγα κακόν auf sein Werk anwenden wollte." Cameron, *Callimachus and His Critics,* 52, offers a different interpretation of these words.

36. *Poeta* occurs five times and *vates* eighteen times in the *Amores;* of these, all but one (at 3.6.17) are used of Ovid the poet or of the group of poets with whom he associates himself. The other three examples of *auctor* in the *Amores* (at 1.3.8, 2.6.34, and 3.13.22) do not serve as literary designations; similarly, the four examples of the word in Propertius are not used to mean "poet." Cf. the discussion of *poeta* and *vates* in the *Amores* by J.K. Newman, *The Concept of Vates in Augustan Poetry,* Collection Latomus 89 (Brussels, 1967), 100–105.

augendo dictus.[37] Again, the possibility remains that, with the second edition, Ovid took the opportunity to add new material to the collection; but the indication that five books have been made three leads inevitably to the inference, however well founded, that the overall girth of the collection has been reduced, not increased. Ovid's designation as *auctor* humorously contradicts the claims to judicious editing made by the *libelli* on his behalf. More important, this playful contradiction sets up our expectations that what lies ahead is offered in a spirit of humorous detachment, so that we may derive greater enjoyment (*voluptas*) from the reading process. We may even wonder, however momentarily, if the so-called first edition ever existed in any form other than as fiction.[38]

In calling himself *auctor* in so ironic a context, Ovid also arouses our expectations concerning the role he will play in the *Amores:* what sort of an elegist is this, after all, whose first reference to himself suggests a poet objectively reflecting on his own work to improve its marketability and popular appeal? This is very different from the opening to the first three books of Horace's *Odes,* for example, in which the poet begins by drawing attention to the gracious and benevolent friendship of Maecenas, ostensibly so important to the poet's task. I have already noted that there is apparently no powerful friend to whom Ovid looks for guidance or inspiration in the writing of the *Amores;* this fact is particularly striking when we consider that the producing of a second edition might well have given Ovid the opportunity to dedicate the collection to an important admirer of the poems in their earlier edition.[39] The absence of such a dedicatee may invite any number of speculative explanations: one among them is the possibility that, in excluding such a personage from the world of the *Amores,* Ovid means to assert his unchallenged authority as poet over the elegiac fiction he has created. Again, even before we know what these books contain (the only hint that amatory poetry lies ahead is contained in the general promise of *voluptas*), we know that their author Naso has manipulated the contents in some unspecified manner. This epigram is thus Ovid's first manifesto of his own detachment from the

---

37. See McKeown, ad loc.

38. Cameron, *Callimachus and His Critics,* 115, comments, "Ovid's *Amores* is perhaps the only certain case of a revised ancient poetry book"—but his *perhaps* betrays an inescapable lack of certainty on the subject.

39. We might compare the situation we have in the *Ars Amatoria,* in which Ovid appears to have intruded into the narrative, perhaps after its completion, his digression on Gaius' forthcoming campaign against the Parthians: see White, *Promised Verse,* 198–99. See also my n. 4 in this chapter.

story to follow: he controls it, not it him; and the books themselves are the remarkably mimetic results of his work. They in turn make the idea of a second edition so realistic that we overlook the possibility that no first edition ever existed. The books' mimetic skill exists despite themselves, in other words, and so embodies the irony of what is to follow as Ovid the lover becomes enthralled with the creation of Ovid the narrator. The irony of this programmatic epigram is an appropriate introduction to Ovid's realism.

It will be useful to begin the book proper as Ovid does and consider the opening program of *Amores* 1. Interestingly, it is difficult to distinguish the programmatic story line from the amatory plot and so to decide where to put the dividing line between these two threads in Ovid's narrative. It is my intention temporarily to impose, therefore, on my readers' indulgence, in suggesting as a working hypothesis that the program proper is contained in *Am.* 1.1–3.[40] My reasons for this suggestion will manifest themselves as we proceed, and I hope that they will show, to the extent possible, that such is indeed the case; at the same time, I want to emphasize my own belief that the distinction between program and plot is constantly being tested and challenged by Ovid. Thus, any attempt to read *Am.* 1.1–3 as "the program" proper will fail; rather, I want to draw attention to how Ovid uses this opening to establish a modus operandi in which programmatic concerns and amatory material take on each other's characteristics.

Am. 1.1 begins as a first-person narrative, as the poet describes his desire to suit ostensible meter (dactylic hexameter) to would-be theme (epic). Cupid's abrupt appearance redirects the poem, however, and the poet reproaches him directly for eight of the poem's fifteen couplets. Even as the poet speaks, he uses the new meter forced on him by Cupid; and however much he may dismiss Cupid's epiphanic intrusion through the

---

40. Not a novel suggestion in and of itself: among many others, see, e.g., Reitzenstein, "Das neue Kunstwollen," 62–76; A.-F. Sabot, *Ovide poète de l'amour dans ses oeuvres de jeunesse: Amores, Héroïdes, Ars Amatoria, Remedia Amoris, De Medicamine Faciei Femineae* (Paris, 1976), 67–68 (Sabot in turn traces the idea to M. Pohlenz, "De Ovidi carminibus amatoriis" [Diss. Göttingen, 1913], 8); Kenney, "Ovid," in *The Cambridge History,* 420; Davis, *Fictus Adulter,* 62; McKeown, 1:92–93; L. Athanassaki, "The Triumph of Love and Elegy in Ovid's Amores 1,2," *MD* 28 (1992): 127–28; F. Cairns, "Imitation and Originality in Ovid Amores 1.3," *PLLS* 7 (1993): 101–22; J.F. Miller, "Reading Cupid's Triumph," *CJ* 90 (1995): 291. J. Moles, "The Dramatic Coherence of Ovid, *Amores* 1.1 and 1.2," *CQ* 41 (1991): 551–54, makes a succinct and strong argument for the dramatic continuity of the first two poems; see further n. 41.

distancing effect of *dicitur* (4),[41] the obvious fact is that Ovid's poet proceeds from tentative beginnings in the first couplet (*parabam* / *edere*) to a fluent inversion of the *recusatio* in his speech to Cupid. When all is said and done, we discover that the poet's complaint really has two sides: not only does he resent Cupid's metrical interference (*cum bene surrexit versu nova pagina primo,* / *attenuat nervos proximus ille meos,* 17–18), but he is also lacking the appropriate material (*nec mihi materia est numeris levioribus apta,* / *aut puer aut longas compta puella comas,* 19–20). In other words, what the poet had been doing (epic) is easier than what Cupid now forces on him, not least because Ovid's poet simply has no real subject matter for elegy at hand.

As in the opening four lines of the poem, again in 21–24 Cupid puts a speedy end to Ovid's epic pretensions. Using bow and arrow, he inflicts on Ovid both the physical wound of love and a metaphoric source of elegiac *materia:* "*quodque canas . . . opus*" (24). Within the course of one couplet, Ovid recognizes what has happened, dubs himself an elegiac lover in the Propertian tradition (*me miserum!*),[42] and begins to burn with passion. But even as he acknowledges his new condition (*uror*), he describes a strangely detached sort of passion: *et in vacuo pectore regnat Amor* (26). Barsby glosses *in vacuo pectore* as "in my once empty heart," but McKeown offers a more literal, if superficial, alternative: though love now rules him, Ovid has yet to find an object for his passion.[43] It is therefore appropriate that this poem end rather abruptly, and it does (27–30): Ovid claims the elegiac meter for his own and bids farewell to epic, asking his Muse to adorn herself appropriately for the changed situation. However brave this concluding invocation, we suspect that Ovid will indeed need all the help he can get.

---

41. Moles, "Dramatic Coherence," 553, comments that *dicitur* is an example of a distancing formula, "whereby the writer does not commit himself to the veracity of certain material, particularly when it is of a supernatural character. He thus avoids violation of the canons of realism or the charge of personal naiveté." Thus, Moles continues, "the rationalising Ovid" distances himself from the historicity of Cupid's epiphany; "on the other hand, Ovid the dramatic character, the hapless victim of the divine epiphany, has naturally forgotten this by the end of the poem. . . ." Moles' "rationalising" Ovid is akin to the narrator, while his "dramatic character" Ovid is what I have here called the lover. Thus, Moles characterizes as "schizophrenia of attitude" (554) the relationship between Ovid's two parallel narratives.

Keith, "*Amores* 1.1," 340–42, believes that *dicitur* (along with *surripuisse,* 4) indicates a specific reference to Propertius 1.1.1–4; but this otherwise attractive suggestion founders in asking us to read Ovid's *Cupido* as modeled on a personification of *cupidinibus* at Prop. 1.1.2.

42. See Keith, "*Amores* 1.1," 343.

43. Barsby, *Am.,* ad loc., and McKeown, ad loc.; see also Moles, "Dramatic Coherence."

Am. 1.1 concludes, then, on a paradoxical note: the poet is now a lover without a beloved. Armed as he is for epic composition, he has been caught unprepared for Cupid's assault. Ovid immediately makes the evident detachment of his narrator not only a technique of narrative but an element in the plot of his story: he pretends to know as little as (or even less than) his readers about the story to follow, and he has just enough forethought to turn to the Muse for help. Thus, Ovid the lover has not yet been fully invented; he can speak to us only as narrator of a tale about literary frustration and aspiration.

Am. 1.2 proceeds from this point, as Ovid feels himself becoming a lover. Ironically, all his reading cannot help him; as the poem opens, he is unable to diagnose his own symptoms (1–6):

> Esse quid hoc dicam, quod tam mihi dura videntur
>   strata, neque in lecto pallia nostra sedent,
> et vacuus somno noctem, quam longa, peregi,
>   lassaque versati corporis ossa dolent?
> nam, puto, sentirem, si quo temptarer amore—   5
>   an subit et tecta callidus arte nocet?

[What should I say this is, that the mattress seems so hard to me, and my covers do not stay on the bed, and I have gone through the night, long as it is, without sleep, and my bones ache, weary from tossing and turning? For I would feel it, I think, if I were being teased by some love—or is love skillful at coming stealthily and injuring me with hidden machinations?]

Can Ovid really be this ingenuous? The condition he describes is a highly unoriginal case of lovesickness; and as he acknowledges (5), he would be likely to recognize it (*sentirem*) if it were indeed love. We can see in this comment that Ovid the poet and Ovid the lover now coexist, although they have not yet been assimilated to each other; the "conversational aside"[44] *puto* draws out the suggestion that Ovid the poet is quizzically scrutinizing his odd predicament, as if it were happening to someone else. Meanwhile, for the poet love remains such an unknown quantity that he is surprised at its insidiousness (6). With the next couplet, the poet recognizes what the lover has begun to experience: this is indeed love (*sic erit: haeserunt tenues*

---

44. This term is McKeown's, ad loc.

in corde sagittae, / *et **possessa** ferus **pectora** versat Amor,* 7–8). The heart
that had been empty in the previous poem is now occupied, if only by the
abstraction Amor; without a *puella* in sight, Ovid's poet may be forgiven a
momentary lapse. As if in recognition that he is now both poet and lover,
he uses a plural verb in the first person to consider the appropriate course
of action: *cedimus . . . ?* / *cedamus* (9–10).

Ovid's surrender is both amatory and literary, as befits his parallel narratives; but in his case, the two factors struggle against each other, as the
poet only unwillingly, but necessarily, creates an amatory fiction. A valuable comparison can be drawn with a poem to which I have already
referred in a different context,[45] Catullus' description of the aftermath of
his *ludus poeticus* with Calvus (50.7–17):

> atque illinc abii tuo lepore
> incensus, Licini, facetiisque,
> ut nec me miserum cibus iuvaret
> nec somnus tegeret quiete ocellos,   10
> sed toto indomitus furore lecto
> versarer, cupiens videre lucem,
> ut tecum loquerer simulque ut essem.
> at defessa labore membra postquam
> semimortua lectulo iacebant,   15
> hoc, iucunde, tibi poema feci,
> ex quo perspiceres meum dolorem.

[And I departed from there inflamed, Licinius, by your charm and wit,
so that food could not help poor me nor could sleep cover my eyes with
rest, but wild with passion I tossed all over my bed, desiring to see the
light of day, so that I might speak with you and at once be with you. But
after my limbs, weary from the struggle, lay half-dead in my small bed,
I made this poem for you, charming friend, so that you might learn from
it my torment.]

Catullus is fully aware of the cause of his passion and uses erotic imagery
to capture the essence of his intellectual excitement; at the same time, he
uses the imagery of sleeplessness to recall an important Callimachean

---

45. See chap. 2.

metaphor for poetic labor, ἀγρυπνία.[46] Ovid's poet, in contrast, is only frustrated by his sleeplessness; his wakefulness has not led him to poetic insight. Thus, even now he is unable to offer his audience a *puella;* instead, after cataloguing a few exempla intended to help him resign himself to his situation, he devotes the remainder of the poem (18–52) to a description of Cupid's triumphal procession, with the conquered lover in tow.

The scene the poet describes is again premised on a reversal or inversion of an elegiac convention, *militia amoris.* This inversion works on two levels. First, although the military scenario is a cliché, we would expect to find the lover casting himself in the role of soldier (as indeed he does in 1.9, to which I shall return later in this chapter), but instead Cupid is the *triumphator,* while the lover Ovid is one of the vanquished whom Cupid will parade into the city in his triumphal procession. Second, simply by detailing at such length the components of Cupid's triumphal procession, Ovid makes literal a scene that, like all the other conventions associated with *militia amoris,* we would expect to be depicted only as metaphor. Barsby comments on this long description that "its tendency to labour a point at length [is] . . . a foretaste of what is to come,"[47] clearly echoing the ancient verdict that Ovid is *nimium amator ingenii sui;* but while he notes the technique, Barsby overlooks its realistic effect, modeled as it is on authentic triumph imagery.[48] Even the wound received from Cupid's sure arrow in 1.1 is no idle image; rather, it is a physical token of his struggle with the victorious god (*ipse ego, praeda recens, factum modo vulnus habebo,* 1.2.29). The poet still has no *puella* to love; but all the other ingredients for an elegiac career are now in place, and he closes the poem by asking Cupid to be merciful. For his part, Cupid can be expected to be so; after all, as we are reminded by the reference to Cupid's close relative (*cognati . . . Caesaris*) in the final couplet, this divinity has a reputation to maintain.[49]

At last in 1.3 Ovid's *puella* appears on the scene; but though the poet is now fully prepared to love her, she, it seems, will need some persuading.

---

46. See R.F. Thomas, "New Comedy, Callimachus, and Roman Poetry," *HSCP* 83 (1979): 195–205; cf. M. Buchan, "Ovidius Imperamator: Beginnings and Endings of Love Poems and Empire in the *Amores,*" *Arethusa* 28 (1995): 58–60.

47. Barsby, ad loc.

48. See G.K. Galinsky, "The Triumph Theme in the Augustan Elegy," *WS,* n.s., 3 (1969): 75–107; G. Moretti, "Trionfi d'amore: Due note esegetiche ad *Amores* 1,2," *Maia* 46 (1994): 47–49; Miller, "Reading Cupid's Triumph," 287–94.

49. See F.D. Harvey, "Cognati Caesaris: Ovid *Amores* 1.2.51/2," *WS,* n.s., 17 (1983): 89–90.

This poem opens, therefore, with a prayer that this *puella* will at least allow herself to be loved (*a, nimium volui: tantum patiatur amari; / audierit nostras tot Cytherea preces,* 3–4). At this point, we see the almost total integration of lover and poet: most of the remainder of the poem is taken up with a sort of advertisement, as the lover declares his *fides* and explains, with due humility, why the *puella* should love him in return. The reason is simple: he is a poet (*at Phoebus comitesque novem vitisque repertor / hac faciunt,* 11–12) and so will use his poetry to celebrate her and their love (19–20):

> te mihi materiem felicem in carmina praebe:
>   provenient causa carmina digna sua.

> [Offer yourself to me as fruitful subject matter for poetry: poems worthy of their subject will come forth.]

As a result, she and he together will become immortal, she through his poetry, and he through his love for her (25–26):

> nos quoque per totum pariter cantabimur orbem
>   iunctaque semper erunt nomina nostra tuis.

> [And we shall be sung of equally throughout the world, and my name will always be joined to yours.]

This conclusion is a fitting culmination to the sequence of poems 1.1–3, in which the poet details his parallel conversions to elegy and to love—fitting, that is, if we overlook the imagery he uses to illustrate and underline the fame that will result from his *fides*. In 21–24, the poet alludes to three women whose love affairs have caused them to be immortalized in verse:

> carmine nomen habent exterrita cornibus Io
>   et quam fluminea lusit adulter ave
> quaeque super pontum simulato vecta iuvenco
>   virginea tenuit cornua vara manu.

> [Io, terrified by her own horns, is famous from song, as is she whom the wife-cheater deceived in the shape of a water bird, and she who was car-

ried across the sea on a counterfeit bull, as she held its widely set horns with her virginal hand.]

Io, Leda, and Europa—all were seduced by Jupiter *adulter* and then abandoned. The immortality they gained through his lust was sorely won, and we can far more easily, and transparently, see them as hapless victims of circumstance than as beneficiaries of amatory *fides*.

These exempla, standing at the culmination of the poet's introductory program, have generally been seen as humorous and as typical of just the sort of self-deflating material that invites some critics to call the *Amores* a parody.[50] The effect is indeed humorous, as the poet undermines by implication the theme of *fides* on which this poem is otherwise premised; but I submit that the cause of this effect is not an impulse to literary burlesque but rather the continuing and intentional dissonance between narrator-poet and lover. Much as Ovid attempts to transform himself into the lover in the embedded narrative of the *Amores,* he remains the central character in the framing story about his career as poet. Ovid the poet speaks through the rhetoric of these exempla, seeking literary analogies for his literary *puella.* His selection of examples cannot help but contradict the declaration of *fides* made by Ovid the lover, and so it permits him to maintain his ironic detachment even when his own fame as poet is under discussion.

The sequence of three elegies with which the *Amores* opens leads us through the creation and development of two parallel plots centered on two complementary characters, the narrator-poet and the lover. In the course of these three poems, we see these two characters take shape, interact, and at times even identify with each other. As the end of 1.3 suggests, however, these two players can never be fully integrated: the poet is conscious of his literary past even as the lover attempts to invent the conventions of amatory poetry anew. This tension transcends both narratives to become the dominant plot of the *Amores.*

Let us turn now to consider three poems from book 1 in which the narrator creates a biography for Ovid the lover: *Am.* 1.5, 1.7, and 1.9. These elegies are not placed immediately adjacent to one another but are separated by a paraclausithyron (1.6) and a portrait of the *lena* Dipsas (1.8).

---

50. See my introduction. See also K. Olstein, "*Amores* 1.3 and Duplicity as a Way of Love," *TAPA* 105 (1975): 241–57.

Nonetheless, their relative proximity and their interconnected narrative invite us to follow the progress of both poet and lover further into the amatory fiction, as Corinna herself finally appears. I may seem temporarily to have wandered far afield from both realism and programmatic considerations, but in fact they will emerge in due course as implicated in the current discussion. Ovid the narrator-poet is never far distant from Ovid the lover, yet the poet is never fully overtaken by the lover—at least not for very long; and even in what are ostensibly nonprogrammatic contexts, the narrator uses realism to draw attention to the literariness of his love.

Am. 1.5 opens ecphrastically: *aestus erat.* Ovid proceeds to describe himself lying in bed—presumably, the same bed in which he was unable to find rest in the opening of 1.2. The window is partly open, and the dim light it produces provokes a triple simile (4–6). Only in 7–8 do we get an inkling of the purpose for this big buildup: this is the perfect sort of light for *puellae* who wish to conceal their own shyness (or preserve an appearance of modesty). The stage is set for an apparition, in "an atmosphere of poetic suggestiveness and mystery."[51] And so Corinna enters, into both the lover's bedroom and the narrator's poetry: *ecce, Corinna venit* (9). It seems natural that, after so long a wait, this would-be love affair should be consummated as quickly as possible; and so it is, in short order, after a pause of only two couplets, in which Ovid provides us with a description of her physical appearance and a comparison of her with the legendary Semiramis and Lais (9–12):

> ecce, Corinna venit tunica velata recincta,
>   candida dividua colla tegente coma,   10
> qualiter in thalamos formosa Semiramis isse
>   dicitur et multis Lais amata viris.

[Look!—Corinna enters veiled in an unbelted tunic, with her hair parted and covering her white neck, just as lovely Semiramis is said to have looked when going into the bedchamber, and Lais, beloved of many men.]

The narrative function of these lines is worth considering. Ovid provides visual details about Corinna's appearance, mentioning in short order her tunic and the way her hair is arranged on her neck. Both details are realis-

---

51. Hinds, "Generalising about Ovid," 11.

tic and persuasively evoke her presence through language. The simile, however, is another matter: if anything, it distracts us from the scene before us, instead inviting comparison with other unseen, but lovely, women. Most important, it is an explicitly literary device, at least briefly detaching both Ovid and his reader from the scene at hand and evoking in its place other women and other loves. These two couplets are an amalgam of the different perspectives of lover, whose Corinna is immediate and physical, and of narrator, whose view of Corinna is refracted through similes.

The literary nature of this opening goes even further. A number of scholars have suggested that the beginning of 1.5 is actually modeled on literary descriptions of divine epiphanies;[52] and Hinds has argued that the epiphany of Catullus' *candida diva* Lesbia as she steps across the threshold (68.70) is recalled by a verbal pun in Ovid's words *candida dividua*.[53] If these suggestions are correct—and I believe they are—then even the part of this poem's opening that we are most likely to identify as documentary can be seen as a product of the literary past. The mise-en-scène, the similes, even the appearance of Corinna—all result in an encounter that, for all its vividness, simultaneously recalls the countless *amores* of the poetic past and emanates from them.

As if in recognition of a need to make Corinna real, the poet's first action is to strip her of the tunic in which she appeared: *deripui tunicam* (13). The distancing effect of the simile dissolves as Ovid looks for the authentic *puella,* thinly veiled by the elegiac past. The abruptness of his action has been taken by some as violent, and indeed it is:[54] but he himself attempts to diminish this implication of his action by characterizing the ensuing struggle as a self-betrayal on Corinna's part (*quae, cum ita pugnaret tamquam quae vincere nollet, / victa est non aegre proditione sua,* 15–16). Even as he describes Corinna's *proditio ipsius,* however, the lover cannot resist resorting to the language of literary convention. As Corinna reacts to her lover's approach, the tussle between them is constructed as an

---

52. See W.S.M. Nicoll, "Ovid, Amores I 5," *Mnemosyne* 30 (1977): 40–48, who suggests that the opening of the poem and the description of Corinna's epiphany are meant to recall Virgilian apparition scenes; T.D. Papanghelis, "About the Hour of Noon: Ovid, *Amores* 1,5," *Mnemosyne* 42 (1989): 54–61, who endorses the idea that Corinna's epiphany effects a sort of *Dichterweihe*. Also, cf. McKeown on lines 1–8.

53. Hinds, "Generalising about Ovid," 7–9.

54. Although the reading *deripui* gives us a less violent scene than does the alternative found in some manuscripts, *diripui:* see McKeown, ad loc. On violent rapes in Ovid, see L.C. Curran, "Rape and Rape Victims in the *Metamorphoses,*" in *Women in the Ancient World: The Arethusa Papers,* ed. J. Peradotto and J.P. Sullivan (Albany, NY, 1984), 263–86. See also Cahoon, "The Bed as Battlefield."

example of *militia amoris,* replete with the most obvious military diction: *pugnaret, vincere, victa est, proditione.* This language is distinctly prosaic; it is nonetheless used here in the service of elegiac tradition.[55]

In 17–24, the false struggle is over. The poet gazes at Corinna's uncovered body and offers a catalogue of her remarkable features. His one real action so far in this poem (*deripui*) has given him his one opportunity to abandon his detachment. As if to reclaim this involvement, Ovid's poet now not only looks at Corinna's body but touches it (*vidi tetigique,* 19): the lover struggles to infuse Corinna's epiphany with realism. By the end of the poem, however, this realism once again gives way to detachment, as the narrator gives the encounter elegiac shape. *Singula quid referam? nil non laudabile vidi* (23), summarizes the poet as he steps back, no longer enthralled by her immediacy. He then asks, *cetera quis nescit?* (25), knowing full well that for the reader of elegy, there is no mystery or suspense in the embedded amatory narrative, however much the narrator may have attempted to introduce this ingredient into the poem's opening lines.[56] In praying for many similar days at the close of this elegy (*proveniant medii sic mihi saepe dies,* 26), the poet reminds us that such is indeed possible: the singularity of an authentic love can be replicated *ad infinitum* in his verse should he wish it.

Critics have by turns found *Am.* 1.5 either typical of Ovidian excess or a tour de force, because in both cases they have been struck by the concreteness of Ovid's descriptions, his attention to detail, and his desire to move beyond the usual decorum of elegiac love scenes.[57] As we observe the interaction of poet and lover, it becomes apparent that both readings miss the mark: for Ovid, the poem embodies a mutual relationship between amatory and literary success and failure (the two coexist). As the lover describes his experience, he uses the language and voice of the poet, for whom love is a literary phenomenon. The would-be realism of the scene is necessarily clad in the fabric of tradition; try as the lover may to strip this

---

55. On the diction of 15–16, see McKeown, ad loc. For the convention of *militia amoris,* see E. Thomas, "Variations on a Military Theme in Ovid's Amores," *G&R* 11 (1964): 151–65; P. Murgatroyd, "Militia amoris and the Roman Elegists," *Latomus* 34 (1975): 59–79; Cahoon,"The Bed as Battlefield"; and the works cited in my nn. 62 and 63 in this chapter.

56. On the "amusingly abrupt ending " of 1.5, see also McKeown, on 25–26 (and 1:71), and see Reitzenstein, *Wirklichkeitsbild und Gefühlsentwicklung,* 92–93, comparing *Am.* 1.5 with Prop. 2.15.

57. Hinds, "Generalising about Ovid," 4–6, provides a valuable comparison of the two dominant schools of thought, typified by Williams, on the one hand (1.5 is overly explicit), and Lyne, on the other (1.5 is suggestive but shallow). See also N.P.C. Huntingford, "Ovid *Amores* 1.5," *AClass* 24 (1981): 107–17.

love affair of convention, its form is a metaphor for the past. The emergence of Corinna into the *Amores* represents the challenge Ovid has set for himself to transcend the boundaries of elegiac mimesis.[58]

Am. 1.7 develops this challenge far more fully than had 1.5, by taking both violence and visual effect to new extremes. The poem opens neither in medias res nor with the dramatic suspense of 1.5 but rather after the fact, as the lover reflects remorsefully on his violence against his *puella: nam furor in dominam temeraria bracchia movit; / flet mea vesana laesa puella manu* (3–4). The remainder of this elegy, sixty-eight lines in all, offers a meditation on the consequences of his momentary outburst, and is an attempt to rationalize, if not to make sense of, his own culpability. The lover begins by cataloguing other poetic heroes whose *furor* has been celebrated in verse (Ajax and Orestes, 6–10), suggesting that since he too is a literary hero, his *furor* is somehow exonerated. Momentarily acknowledging that his deed was really no heroic act of vengeance but rather a lover's loss of temper, he describes in one verse what he actually did—*ergo ego digestos potui laniare capillos?* (11)—only to turn this detail too to the service of an heroic scenario. The *puella*'s beauty in disarray is to be compared favorably, he maintains, to that of Atalanta while hunting, that of Ariadne when abandoned by Theseus, or even that of Cassandra at the fall of Troy.

The poet repeatedly invokes exempla to give his *furor* meaning; but repeatedly, the exempla fail.[59] He abandons them briefly, therefore, and turns his attention to his guilty hands and arms (19–30)—if only they can take the blame for him. Again a self-serving exemplum intrudes: both Diomedes and he are guilty of striking goddesses—though, in the spirit of one-upmanship, Ovid's poet notes that Diomedes' crime was less outrageous than his own (*et minus ille nocens,* 33). Making the most of the situation's irony, the poet then describes an imaginary triumphal procession, with the *puella* his bruised captive and himself as victorious general (35–42): his empty victory revises that depicted in *Am.* 1.2, when he was a captive of the triumphant Cupid.

To this point, the poem has proceeded as a series of ironic reversals on itself: in Ovid's simultaneous lamentation and inflation of his act, we see both the inescapability of elegiac convention sensed by the poet and the

---

58. See Keith, "*Corpus Eroticum,*" 29–33.

59. See my chap. 3 for a fuller discussion of Ovid's use of exempla. Morrison, "Literary Reference and Generic Transgression," 583, distinguishes between two characters or roles played by Ovid in this poem, Ovid the lover and Ovid the poet; but Morrison's view of the portrayal of *furor* here differs widely from mine.

lover's desire for shocking realism. As poet-narrator, Ovid constructs the narrative of his experience out of literary tradition; the experience is thus embedded in the language of poetry. We see this most vividly as the poem culminates with a description of what should have happened but did not (43–48):

> denique si tumidi ritu torrentis agebar
>> caecaque me praedam fecerat ira suam,
> nonne satis fuerat timidae inclamasse puellae   45
>> nec nimium rigidas intonuisse minas
> aut tunicam a summa diducere turpiter ora
>> ad mediam (mediae zona tulisset opem)?

[In short, if I was being driven like a swollen torrent and blind fury had made me its prey, would it not have been enough to shout at the timid girl and to thunder less-than-binding threats or to sunder her tunic shamelessly, from its top edge to her midriff (her girdle would have protected her at the midriff)?]

He should have shouted and threatened (but not too harshly), and he should have torn the front of her tunic. Then his assault would have remained reasonable; that is, it would not have surpassed the horizon of elegiac expectations. Instead, the lover confesses at last, he not only mussed her hair but also scratched her cheeks (49–50):

> at nunc sustinui raptis a fronte capillis
>> ferreus ingenuas ungue notare genas.

[But now I have allowed myself to pull her hair away from her forehead and—brute that I am!—to scratch her tender cheeks with my fingernails.]

The lover's *furor* has made him lose control of his love, however momentarily; but like his love, his *furor* too is a literary fiction. It is telling that, throughout this long elegy, his outburst remains unmotivated; though he dwells at length on his behavior after the assault, he gives no explanation or rationale for its cause. It simply provides the poet with the occasion for a poem.

Having described not only what he should have done but also what he did, the narrator turns our full attention at last to the *puella,* whose reaction to the blow is elaborated in a series of similes (51–58). Like the description of Corinna's physical beauty in 1.5, these lines reflect the lover's desire to evoke as vividly as possible the reality of his beloved: her face (*albo et sine sanguine vultu,* 51), her limbs (*exanimis artus et membra trementia,* 53), and the tears on her cheeks (*suspensaeque diu lacrimae fluxere per ora,* 57) inspire a succession of fleeting images whose purpose at least in part is to capture the intensity of the *puella*'s trauma.[60] Of course, it is the poet-narrator, rather than the lover, who focuses our attention through the rhetoric of similes; and so the *puella* remains mute even as he attempts to infuse her with life.

The lover then tries a last time to make the *puella* respond, describing his sorrow with an unusual image (*sanguis erat lacrimae, quas dabat illa, meus,* 60) and asking that she strike him in turn (63–66). But at the close of the elegy (67–68), it is the poet who has the last word; and as he speaks, the irony of his attempts at realism is palpable:

neve mei sceleris tam tristia signa supersint,
    pone recompositas in statione comas.

[And, lest the sad marks of my crime remain, rearrange your hair and put it back in place.]

With the poem, Ovid's *furor* has come to a close; and so he invites the *puella* to repair her coiffure so that no signs of his outburst may remain. The slight hint of military imagery in *in statione*[61] may well be intended to suggest that it will be safer for the both of them to return to an arrangement in which *militia amoris* is the only sort of warfare in which they engage. Meanwhile, the lover's mock heroics earlier in 1.7 serve as a reminder that the poet has in fact been bidden not to write heroic epic at all. When he persists in invoking the epic paradigm for inspiration, the consequences for his elegiac love step outside the boundaries of elegy.[62]

The reversals between lover and narrator out of which 1.7 is constructed reflect Ovid's interest in the relationship between his two narratives. The lover struggles to articulate the reality of experience, but the only language he can use is that provided by the poet, the artifices of poetry. The hierarchical relationship between poet and lover, which the poet domi-

---

60. See my discussion of this simile earlier, in chap. 3.
61. Cf. Barsby, *Am.,* ad loc., and McKeown, ad loc.
62. See Morrison, "Literary Reference and Generic Transgression," 588; for other discussions of irony in 1.7, see Khan, "*Ovidius Furens*"; B.E. Stirrup, "Irony in Ovid Amores I 7," *Latomus* 32 (1973): 824–31; S. Gössl, "Ovid, Amores I 7," *GB* 10 (1981): 165–80.

nates, insures that the explicitly artificial frame for erotic experience depicted through verse and poetic language will inevitably control, and to some extent skew, our view of that experience. The *Amores* are not representations of experience shaped and transformed by poetry but poetry evoking the poetic memory as a source of fictional inspiration.

In *Am.* 1.9, Ovid takes this reversal of frame and picture to its logical extreme, turning inside out a number of otherwise mutually exclusive elegiac topoi in order to defend his status as both lover and poet of love.[63] The cliché of love as war, a fundamental equation in amatory elegy, is used repeatedly by the lover to describe his love affair, just as it had been used not only by the other Roman elegists but by the very creators of Greek lyric.[64] We have already seen it play a prominent role in the erotic encounter of 1.5 and the would-be heroics of 1.7. Meanwhile, another strand of imagery in which war plays a central metaphorical role can be traced back to Callimachus' earliest Roman heirs: that is, the association of war, as epic theme, with non-Callimachean aesthetics. We have already seen this metaphor, too, play an important role in the *Amores,* particularly in 1.1 and 1.2, as the poet takes up Cupid's poetic commission. There is thus an obvious, but previously elided, contradiction between the Roman elegists' espousal of an antiheroic aesthetic, on the one hand, and a system of images inextricably bound up with and derived from the broader traditions of Greek and Latin amatory poetry, on the other. In *Am.* 1.9, Ovid exploits his double identification as poet and lover to polarize these two views of the relationships between love and war and between love and poetry, the concerns of lover and narrator, respectively.

The poem opens with a typically Ovidian rhetorical flourish, the "circular" couplet:[65]

Militat omnis amans, et habet sua castra Cupido;
  Attice, crede mihi, militat omnis amans.

---

63. See Conte, "Love without Elegy," 444. For a recent and complementary discussion of *Am.* 1.9, see J.C. McKeown, "*Militat omnis amans,*" *CJ* 90 (1995): 295–304.

64. For a survey of the topos, see A. Spies, "Militat omnis amans: Ein Beitrag zur Bildersprache der antiken Erotik" (Diss. Tübingen, 1930); and for the sophisticated deployment of the metaphor in early Greek lyric, see L. Rissman, *Love as War: Homeric Allusion in the Poetry of Sappho* (Koenigstein/Ts., 1983).

65. So called by Barsby, *Am.,* on 1.4.13–14; see also Barsby, *Am.,* ad loc., and McKeown, ad loc.

[Every lover is a soldier, and Cupid has his camp; believe me, Atticus, every lover is a soldier.]

Commentators have duly observed that this is one of the very few elegies in the collection with an external addressee (i.e., an addressee other than the gods, Corinna/*puella,* or Ovid himself).[66] The identity of this Atticus is unknown, although it is of course a subject of speculation;[67] worthy of equal consideration is the fact that the poet invents an addressee at all. In explicitly summoning a third party to hear his proof of the logical proposition *militat omnis amans,* the poet increases the odds of exposing its contradictory nature. The imaginary presence of a third party as audience nonetheless allows Ovid to conflate his roles as poet and lover and so to erase temporarily the dividing line between primary and embedded narratives. As *praeceptor amoris,* Ovid's poet stands both inside and outside his story.

The poem proceeds through a long series of balanced and varied couplets, in each of which the poet draws a parallel between the characteristics appropriate to lovers and those appropriate to soldiers: youth (3–6); vigilance and sturdiness (7–10); endurance in the face of the elements (11–16); and tactical acuity (17–28). Last but not least is resilience, needed in the face of constant uncertainty (29–30):

Mars dubius, nec certa Venus: victique resurgunt,
    quosque neges umquam posse iacere, cadunt.

[Mars is unreliable, and Venus is not sure: those who have been defeated rise again, and those who you would say can never lie low, fall.]

The parallelism between love and war is carried to an extreme in this couplet, as the two gods who preside over the domains of war and love, respectively, are themselves paralleled. The metaphor making love a sort of erotic warfare, conventional as it is, is abandoned in favor of a concrete and obscene literalism: the double entendres *victi . . . resurgunt, iacere,* and *cadunt* not only violate the decorum of heroic verse but also subordinate the language of war to that of love.[68]

---

66. See my n. 4 in this chapter.
67. See McKeown, ad loc.; White, *Promised Verse,* 204.
68. For the obscene interpretation of Ovid's diction, see McKeown, ad loc.

Having demonstrated the laboriousness of love, the poet now dismisses *desidia* from the language of those who would criticize him (31–32):

> ergo desidiam quicumque vocabat amorem,
>   desinat: ingenii est experientis Amor.

[Whoever called love laziness, therefore, should stop: Love has an industrious nature.]

To prove his point, he turns to a catalogue of exempla appropriately drawn from heroic epic: Achilles inflamed by Briseis (33–34), Hector battling for Andromache's sake (35–36), Agamemnon overcome by the loveliness of Cassandra (37–38); even Mars captured by his own captivation (39–40). Like the exempla with which *Am.* 1.3 drew to a close, however, these too invite second thoughts: even a reader only superficially acquainted with the plots of the *Iliad,* the *Odyssey,* and the major Greek tragedies would be likely to know that Achilles' love for Briseis in fact kept him from war; that Hector returned to battle, and sure death, against the wishes of his wife; that Agamemnon's infatuation with Cassandra caused him to be less wary than he might otherwise have been and so resulted in his death; and that Mars' flirtation with Venus caused him quite literally to be captured. Yet the poet cites these heroes as role models who prove the irrelevance of *desidia* to the lover's life! The exempla themselves suggest that love and *desidia* are virtually synonymous.

The poem closes with an explicit reminiscence of the opening of 1.5, the poem in which the lover had first introduced Corinna by name and in which they had first consummated their love. Yet the setting that had in the previous poem seemed the most conducive for love—and which the poet had wished might be frequently replicated (*proveniant medii sic mihi saepe dies,* 1.5.26)—now is made to symbolize the life the poet led before love entered his life (1.9.41–44):

> ipse ego segnis eram discinctaque in otia natus;
>   mollierant animos lectus et umbra meos;
> impulit ignavum formosae cura puellae,
>   iussit et in castris aera merere suis.

[I was lazy and born for a life of dissolute leisure; bed and shade had softened my spirit; but love for a beautiful girl aroused me, listless as I was, and ordered me to earn my pay in his camp.]

With wonderful irony, the poet suggests that the very *otium* that enabled him to become a lover in the first place has itself been overtaken and replaced by *militia amoris*. McKeown observes that the *vita umbratilis* described here is frequently associated with literary pursuits;[69] we may think also of the central role played by *otium* in the aesthetics of earlier Roman love poetry.[70] In taking the convention of *militia amoris* to an extreme that is as absurd as it is logical, then, Ovid lays bare the fundamental flaw in the topos: while the poet may find such imagery unavoidable for depicting love, the lover who becomes a soldier in verse faces ultimate defeat. In the words *Qui nolet fieri desidiosus, amet* (46), the juxtaposition of *desidiosus* and *amet* visually contradicts the distance between them that the poet's argument would suggest. Having perforce abandoned epic, with its military subject matter, the lover finds himself constrained by the poet—under the circumstances, paradoxically—to enact a war that parallels the real thing even as it rejects it.

The sequence of *Am.* 1.5, 1.7, and 1.9 is hardly haphazard. As the previous poems in the collection become part of a given poem's past, they are not only remembered but also rewritten: thus, the love play of 1.5 becomes the violence of 1.7, the erotic immediacy of 1.5 becomes a scene of past *desidia* in 1.9, and the assault of 1.7 in turn becomes a part of the cliché of 1.9. The realism of scenes and actions when first depicted, already qualified by the narrator's control of the narrative, gives way in retelling to the detachment of literary framing. In each poem, Ovid invokes a lover to act in and speak of his love; but this lover is the creation of the poet, who uses the literary past to invent anew the lover's amatory experience. The resulting realism derives its meaning from Ovid's poetic memory.

The embedding of an amatory plot into a narrative about becoming a poet reflects a distinctively Ovidian approach to elegy. The project Ovid has set for himself is as bold in its own way as was Callimachus' when the latter set out neither simply to reject the past (for this would indeed have been relatively simple) nor to echo it hollowly (the choice of many) but rather to use the past to create a literary future. Like many others, Ovid asks himself: how does one say anything new in poetry in the post-Virgilian age? As I argued earlier in this book, he sees himself quite naturally as part of a continuum and so makes the literary past his own; but at the same time he strikes out on a new path, to find new ways to articulate his voice

---

69. McKeown, ad loc.

70. See R.I. Frank, "Catullus 51: *Otium* versus *Virtus*," *TAPA* 99 (1968): 233–39, and C. Segal, "Catullan *Otiosi*: the Lover and the Poet," *G&R* 17 (1970): 25–31; cf. J.M. André, *L'otium dans la vie morale et intellectuelle romaine* (Paris, 1966).

and let it be heard. In the *Amores,* he offers us a new type of elegy, in which love is not an end but a means. This relationship between style and substance is itself a legacy of Callimachus; but in claiming it for himself, Ovid personalizes it, giving the narrator his own name.

Chapter 5

Ovid's Narrative of Poetic Immortality

sunt etiam qui nos numen habere putent
Ovid *Am.* 3.9.18

We saw in the preceding chapter that the programmatic narrative, rather than the amatory fiction, is the authentic story of the *Amores.* Detached as Ovid is from the embedded narrative about his love for Corinna, he creates a close identification with the narrator-poet who carries his name. Thus, when he imagines the immortality that will proceed from his poetic success, the poet engages us in the dominant plot of the *Amores,* which is to carve out a distinctive role for himself in the Roman poetic tradition. Like the other elegists, Ovid takes advantage of the first-person narrative style of elegy to envision the immortality he will achieve after death through his verse; but unlike them, he does not see his immortality resulting from a romantic death wish but instead uses a combination of detachment and realism to reflect on his fate. The sense of literary fate that emerges is both subtler and more complex than those offered by the other elegists, as Ovid looks at his own work in the *Amores* with the double vision of poet and lover. In this chapter, I intend to show how Ovid's poetic immortality becomes central to the plot of the *Amores.*

A first indication of Ovid's more complex attitude toward the subject is evident in the fact that the transcendence of death through poetic immortality is the central theme of three elegies in the collection. In 1.15, the poet takes center stage, all but abandoning both the lover and the amatory diegesis of the *Amores,* as he considers the phenomenon of immortality conferred by poetry; in 2.6, the embedded narrative resumes, as the lover presides over the funeral of his gift to Corinna, a parrot, who, much like a poet, is destined to transcend death through poetry; and in 3.9, the poet reemerges, to mourn the passing of a colleague who has merited poetic

165

apotheosis for his paradigmatic contributions to elegy. We saw in my discussion in chapter 4 that, even though poems on related themes may not be immediately juxtaposed, Ovid sometimes returns more than once to themes and scenes featured in earlier poems, in order to recast and problematize the previous episode; he is particularly fond of doing so through a change of perspective from one poem to another.[1] As his recollection of his own poetry becomes part of the elegiac tradition and part of his, and our, poetic memory, Ovid exploits the technique of ironic reversal by modifying his perspective in successive poems. In the sequence of three poems to which we now turn, Ovid establishes a vision of poetic immortality only to revise it, and so he revises our expectations of him.

In *Am.* 1.15, Ovid speaks as a poet triumphant at the close of his first book. The structure of the poem is worth noting, since it indicates how Ovid can transform even a seemingly straightforward theme into a very personal *sphragis.* The poet begins with a six-line address to Livor, marked by emotive enjambment.[2] A preemptive response to Livor's presumed charges—namely, that Ovid is wasting his time on poetry and should instead, like any good Roman, engage in military service or a legal career— comes in the next couplet and is suitably abrupt: *mortale est, quod quaeris, opus* (7). The thematic importance of reversal to Ovid's narrative is suggested by the way in which this scene recalls the confrontation and challenge with which *Am.* 1.1 opened;[3] the tables have turned, and now Ovid is the one championing elegy, while Livor urges on him the works of war— not poetry in this case, but the military life itself. As Ovid goes on to claim *fama perennis* for himself, he gives to his literary achievement the first of four couplets (7–14), in each of which one poet is said to have legitimate claim to literary immortality:

> mortale est, quod quaeris, opus; mihi fama perennis
> quaeritur, **in toto semper ut orbe canar.**
> **vivet** Maeonides, Tenedos **dum** stabit et Ide,
> **dum** rapidas Simois in mare volvet aquas;   10
> **vivet** et Ascraeus, **dum** mustis uva tumebit,
> **dum** cadet incurva falce resecta Ceres.

---

1. See my further discussion later in this chapter, in the text and n. 45, on paired poems.

2. On this extended period, see McKeown, ad loc. and 1:108 n. 3.

3. D.W.T. Vessey, "Elegy Eternal: Ovid, *Amores,* I.15," *Latomus* 40 (1981): 607, notes that 1.15 balances 1.1–2, restating and revising many of the themes begun in the earlier poems; but Vessey's reading generally belongs to the "parody" school of Ovidian criticism.

Battiades **semper toto cantabitur orbe:**
    quamvis ingenio non valet, arte valet.

[The work that you ask for is destined to die; I seek eternal fame, so that
I may be sung of throughout the world. The Maeonian poet will live as
long as Tenedos and Ida stand, as long as Simois rolls her swift-moving
waters into the sea; the Ascraean poet will live as long as the grape
swells with must, as long as Ceres is cut with a curved sickle and falls to
earth. The poet descended from Battus will always be sung throughout
the world: though weak in inspiration, he is powerful in technical skill.]

The four poets with whom the poet begins—himself, Homer, Hesiod, and
Callimachus—are not randomly chosen; rather, by using a combination of
stylistic repetition and variation in these lines, Ovid as poet implies that
these four are closely linked. The bond between the two central poets in
this group, Homer and Hesiod, is emphasized by the placement of *vivet* at
the opening of two successive couplets; in each instance *vivet* is followed by
two temporal clauses beginning with *dum,* the second of which fills the
entire pentameter. The couplets describing Ovid and Callimachus, meanwhile, are balanced by the close verbal echo between *in toto semper ut orbe
canar* and *semper toto cantabitur orbe.* The poet thus gives added emphasis
to the parallelism between himself and Callimachus that is already implicit
in his rebuke to Livor.[4]
    Then follow four couplets with a slightly different design (15–22):

nulla **Sophocleo** veniet iactura cothurno;   15
    cum sole et luna semper **Aratus** erit.
dum fallax servus, durus pater, improba lena
    vivent et meretrix blanda, **Menandros** erit.
Ennius arte carens animosique **Accius** oris
    casurum nullo tempore nomen habent.   20
Varronem primamque ratem quae nesciet aetas
    aureaque Aesonio terga petita duci?

[No loss will come to Sophoclean tragedy; as long as there are sun and
moon, there will always be Aratus. Menander will live as long as there
are tricky slaves, severe fathers, naughty bawds and seductive whores.

---

4. On Callimachus' personifications of envy, see McKeown, ad loc.; Wimmel, *Kallimachos
in Rom,* 61–64, 302.

Ennius, though lacking in technical skill, and Accius, with his inspired mouth, will have names that never fade; and what age will not know Varro, and the first ship, and the golden fleece sought by the Aesonian leader?]

Six poets are mentioned, two in the first and third couplets and one in the second and fourth; the first threesome composed in Greek, the second threesome in Latin. Lest the parallel design become too repetitious, however, the poet avoids reusing the same temporal expressions and instead offers a series of ingenious variations: *nulla iactura; semper erit; dum vivent, erit; casurum nullo tempore; quae nesciet aetas . . .* ? The overall effect is that of randomness, dispelled only by careful reading.

With the next four couplets, the poet returns to the pattern with which he had begun his catalogue, mentioning one poet in each (23–30):

> carmina sublimis tunc sunt peritura **Lucreti,**
>   exitio terras cum dabit una dies.
> **Tityrus et fruges Aeneiaque arma** legentur,   25
>   Roma triumphati dum caput orbis erit.
> donec erunt ignes arcusque Cupidinis arma,
>   discentur numeri, culte **Tibulle,** tui.
> **Gallus** et Hesperiis et **Gallus** notus Eois,
>   et sua cum **Gallo** nota Lycoris erit.   30

[The poems of the eminent Lucretius will die only when one day brings the earth to destruction. [The poems concerning] Tityrus, and the crops, and the arms of Aeneas will be read as long as Rome rules the world over which she has triumphed. As long as there are fires and bows, the weapons of Cupid, your verses, elegant Tibullus, will be studied. Gallus will be known to the inhabitants of the West and to those of the East; and with him will be known his Lycoris.]

Again the poet relies on variation of temporal expressions to avoid repetitiousness and does not resort to conspicuous verbal echo; but a parallelism of sorts is again evident, with the first two couplets describing two epic poets (although of course the *Eclogues* and *Georgics* are equally important in the description of Virgil, the only poet in the entire catalogue given neither name nor patronymic nor geographic designation), and with the second two describing elegists. The poet simultaneously offsets this pairing with another pattern, in which the first and third poets are each mentioned once, while Virgil and Gallus each earn triple identification—Virgil through the listing of his three works, Gallus through the threefold repetition of his name. Ovid also incorporates into each couplet a feature of style or diction intended to recall the work of the poet being described: thus, *exitio terras cum dabit una dies* looks not only to the long-lasting sublimity of the *de Rerum Natura* but to its subject matter, the workings of the cosmos, with a reference to the eventual destruction of the world heralded by Lucretius (*DRN* 5.92–95; see especially the wording of line 95: *una dies dabit exitio*). With *Tityrus, fruges,* and *Aeneia arma,* Ovid refers precisely to the openings of each of Virgil's works: *Tityre* is the first word in the first *Eclogue,* the first *Georgic* opens with *quid faciat laetas segetes?*, and the first book of the *Aeneid* with its dual reference to *arma* and Aeneas (*virumque*). Fire and the bow, the weapons of Cupid, figure prominently in Tibullan elegy (cf., e.g., 2.6.15–16). Both the mention of his beloved Lycoris and the wording used to describe the extent of Gallus' fame (*et Hesperiis et . . . notus Eois*) must refer to Gallus' own words, as we can see from the parallel Propertian reference to Gallus at 2.3.43–44, *sive illam Hesperiis sive illam ostendet Eois, / uret et Eoos, uret et Hesperios.*[5] Finally, the overall balance of the catalogue is enhanced by the fact that all the poets in this group are Roman; aside, of course, from himself, the opening foursome is Greek.

After this catalogue, the poet builds to a crescendo with a twelve-line conclusion, meant to complete his response to the charges lodged by Livor in the opening of the poem. The twelve lines (31–42) consist of three four-line units, each focusing on one aspect of the poet's claim to poetic immortality. First, the poet provides a list of a number of entities whose longevity is as nothing compared to that of *carmina;* next, he indicates that his calling is no common one, but that he is to be granted the sort of *Dichterweihe* that is the mark of the truly inspired poet, with water from the Castalian spring, served by none other than Apollo himself, and an initiatory wreath of myrtle to wear in his hair; and finally, he predicts the *honos* that will accrue to him after death and, indeed, his own immortality through the survival of his verse.

This elegy is an elegant but fundamentally conventional depiction of a poet's desire to ensure his immortality. With the formal design of the poem so dominant, the poet's placement of himself first in the catalogue of

---

5. See McKeown, ad loc., on all of these references.

immortals is a bold touch. Yet the poem has a paradoxical effect: it does little to advance the poet's claim to originality, although it amply demonstrates his mastery of technique. This poem has therefore received very little discussion, being generally and quickly dismissed as just the sort of set piece one would expect at the close of the first book;[6] and because it does not sustain the amatory narrative in any way, it appears to have little besides programmatic value. If we read the poem not in isolation, however, but as the first of three acts in Ovid's exploration of literary immortality, it becomes more comprehensible. As we move on to the other two poems in this sequence, we shall see that the poet envisions his contribution in terms less predictable than this elegy alone might suggest.

Am. 2.6, with its debt to ancient rhetoric and its dedication to a frivolous subject, is generally considered either a spiritless set-piece or an unfortunately tedious reworking of a Catullan gem.[7] It shares with 1.15 the interest in formal design so typical of Ovid, and it once again makes prominent his lack of concern for the illusion of sincerity. This poem, however, participates in both the primary and the embedded narratives of the *Amores.* As Ovid describes the bird that he gave as a gift to Corinna (*ut datus es,* 19; *extremo munus ab orbe datum,* 38), the lover's identification with the beloved, late-lamented pet gradually gives way to and is subsumed in the narrator-poet's identification of the *psittacus* with a poet.[8] In setting up a sequence of identifications between lover and parrot, on the one hand, and parrot and poet, on the other, Ovid uses the realism of amatory narrative to explore the paradox of originality within a poetic tradition.

Hinds has urged anew[9] that we recognize in the opening words of *Am.*

---

6. See, e.g., Vessey, "Elegy Eternal"; see also Farrell, *Vergil's Georgics and the Traditions of Ancient Epic,* 339–41. Unusual for a willingness to take 1.15 as something other than a string of clichés is the attempt by F. Stoessl to argue that this poem should be read as a political as well as a literary manifesto; his suggestion that Livor represents both Callimachean Phthonos and Augustus Caesar, however, is not persuasive: see "Ovids Lebensentscheidung," in *Festschrift K. Vretska,* ed. D. Ableitinger and H. Gugel (Heidelberg, 1970), 250–75.

7. For the bibliography on this poem, see the works cited in my article "The Death of Corinna's Parrot Reconsidered: Poetry and Ovid's *Amores,*" *CJ* 82 (1987): 199–207. See also D. Parker, "The Ovidian Coda," *Arion* 8 (1969) 94–95. Much of the following discussion was inspired by ideas formulated in my earlier article, although the approach presented here moves beyond many of the ideas first developed there.

8. Here I disagree with K.S. Myers, "Ovid's *Tecta Ars: Amores* 2.6, Programmatics, and the Parrot," *EMC* 34 (1990): 367–74, who calls the entire poem "programmatic" and the bird's poetic nature "Callimachean." I shall argue here that the parrot's poetic identity is revealed only in the course of the poem—and that no parrot is as much like a poet as a dead parrot.

9. The suggestion has been made by others: see, e.g., J. Ferguson, "Catullus and Ovid," *AJP* 81 (1960): 337–57.

2.6—*psittacus, Eois imitatrix ales ab Indis*—a challenge by the poet to compare his *psittacus* with the *passer* of Catullus: in his view, the word *imitatrix* signifies the existence of another, earlier entity that inspires this bird.[10] Let us begin, therefore, by recalling the death of the *passer* (Catullus 3):

Lugete, o Veneres Cupidinesque,
et quantum est hominum venustiorum:
passer mortuus est meae puellae,
passer, deliciae meae puellae,
quem plus illa oculis suis amabat—   5
nam mellitus erat suamque norat
ipsam tam bene, quam puella matrem,
nec sese a gremio illius movebat,
sed circumsiliens modo huc modo illuc
ad solam dominam usque pipiabat: 10
qui nunc it per iter tenebricosum
illud, unde negant redire quemquam.
at vobis male sit, malae tenebrae
Orci, quae omnia bella devoratis:
tam bellum mihi passerem abstulistis.   15
o factum male! o miselle passer!
tua nunc opera meae puellae
flendo turgiduli rubent ocelli.

[[1] Mourn, o Venuses and Cupids, and however many elegant mortals there are: the sparrow of my girl is dead, the sparrow, my girl's delight, which she loved more than her eyes. For he was a sweet one, and he knew his mistress as well as a girl knows her mother; nor did he move from her lap, but hopping about, now here, now there, he chirped always to his mistress alone.

[11] He now travels along that gloomy path from which they say no one returns. I curse you, evil shadows of Orcus, who devour all lovely things: such a lovely sparrow have you stolen from me. O dire deed! O poor little sparrow! Because of you my girl's eyes are now red and swollen from weeping.]

---

10. Hinds, "Generalising about Ovid," 7.

That the lover's parrot in *Am.* 2.6 hearkens back to the earlier *passer* is an inference that can hardly be avoided. Each of the two openings envisions a sentimental funeral procession of like-minded mourners; and Hinds is right, I think, to point to the importance of the word *imitatrix* in Ovid's poem as signifying not just literally but also symbolically the imitative essence of Ovid's *psittacus*. At the same time, it is important to observe that some telling differences separate Ovid's bird from that of Catullus; and while some of these differences may appear to make Ovid's poem only a travesty, I shall argue in what follows that, because in the Ovidian narrative the parrot is identified not only with Corinna's lover but also with her poet, Ovid is able to give to the earlier erotic imagery associated with Catullus's *passer*[11] another level of associations, which reflect not on the embedded narrative but on the predicament of a poet whose adherence to tradition is his claim to immortality.

Having begun with a reference to the most remarkable feature of Corinna's exotic parrot, its voice, the lover continues to invoke this characteristic of the bird throughout 2.6, with *vox . . . ingeniosa* at 18, *garrulus* at 26, *sermonis amore* at 29, *loquax humanae vocis imago* at 37, and *ora . . . docta loqui* at 62. Of course, this emphasis itself is not surprising: along with its color, breadth of tongue, and hardness of beak, the φωνή ἀνθρωπίνη of the *psittacus* is, understandably, the focal point of all ancient descriptions of this curious and exotic bird.[12] It is rather what happens to the parrot in the course of the poet's funeral eulogy that invites direct comparison of poet and parrot. Even as the lover mourns the dead

---

11. Some have argued for an obscene reading of the *passer* poem: for a defense of this interpretation, see R.F. Thomas, "Sparrows, Hares, and Doves: A Catullan Metaphor and Its Tradition," *Helios* 20 (1993): 131–42. Thomas' reading, while attractive, is not airtight; and it may be worth noting that Ovid, who elsewhere in the *Amores* does not hesitate to make explicit and humorous reference to his own sexual impotence (*Am.* 3.7; see the discussions by R.F. Thomas, in " 'Death,' Doxography, and the 'Termerian Evil' (Philodemus, *Epigr.* 27 Page = *A.P.* 11.30)," *CQ* 41 [1991]: 133, and A. Sharrock, "The Drooping Rose: Elegiac Failure in Amores 3.7," *Ramus* 24 [1995]: 152–80), does not hint at an obscene reading of 2.6; yet had the Catullan ancestor of the *psittacus* invited double entendre, we might well expect Ovid's parrot to do the same. Instead, Ovid saves the suggestiveness of self-identification with a possession dear to his beloved for 2.15, in which he wishes to be the gold ring worn by Corinna: see esp. 2.15.25–26; E. Courtney, "Some Literary Jokes in Ovid's *Amores*," in *Vir bonus discendi peritus: Studies in Celebration of Otto Skutsch's Eightieth Birthday*, ed. N. Horsfall, *BICS* Suppl. 51 (London, 1988), 18–20, and Booth's discussion of the poem.

12. The *psittacus* is first mentioned in Ctesias' *Indica*, *FGrHist* 688 F 45. See also Arist. *HA* 8.597b25; Paus. 2.28; Arrian *Ind.* 1.15.8; Solin. 53; Pliny *NH* 10.117; Apul. *Flor.* 12. And see Sir D'A.W. Thompson, *A Glossary of Greek Birds*, 2d ed. (London, 1936), 335–38, and Wotke, *RE* 36.2: 926–32, s.v. *Papagei*.

bird, he arouses our curiosity about the fates of both Corinna's lover and the poet who gives the lover voice. Before we proceed, it is worth pausing for a moment here to note how different Catullus' *passer* is: although as he plays in the *puella's* lap we can easily see that he is a surrogate of sorts for Catullus, there is no suggestion in Catullus' poem that Lesbia's bird is poetic. However anthropomorphized Catullus' description of the *passer* may otherwise be, the only reference to the bird's voice is contained in the nonanthropomorphic *pipiabat* (10).[13]

The parallel between parrot and poet will finally be brought to the foreground when Ovid describes the parrot's funeral and afterlife. Before we turn to the close of the elegy for its moving funerary commemoration and underworld scene, however, we should note how the prior parallel between parrot and lover controls Ovid's description of the bird while it is alive. After the opening invocation to *piae volucres* to mourn their lost fellow (1–12), the central portion of the poem (13–32) is taken up with an emotional catalogue of all those qualities that made the *psittacus* a remarkable, almost human, pet, and with a lavish development of the theme that only the good die young (33–48). This lament culminates with a reference to the prayers said in vain by the *puella* on her *psittacus'* behalf (43–44) and with the brief but apt farefell to Corinna uttered as the bird's dying words (48). Particularly at this point, then, the parrot is cast in the role of surrogate for the lover: the *pia vota* carried off by the stormy wind Notus are reminiscent of the prayers a lover is wont to say vainly on behalf of his or her beloved,[14] and the parrot's dying words, *"Corinna, vale,"* are clearly something it has learned by mimicking the lover himself. Thus, as we see the little bird depart for the underworld, its sentimental anthropomorphism suggests that it is a stand-in for Corinna's lover.

The parrot's journey to the underworld begins the bird's metamorphosis into an accomplished poet as well. In death, the *psittacus* presides over an Elysium inhabited exclusively by birds (49–58):

colle sub Elysio nigra nemus ilice frondet
  udaque perpetuo gramine terra viret.   50

---

13. Columella 8.5.14 uses this verb of chicks (*pulli*); cf. Var. *Men.* 3, using the related *pipare* of a *gallina*. *Pipiare* is used by Tertullian of children; and at Lucil. 1249 Marx (= 1266 Krenkl) the subject of the verb cannot be determined (but, in any case, if used of a human, it is likely to be done so with humorous intent). Cf. also the definition of *pipatio* provided by Festus p. 235 Lindsay: *clamor plorantis lingua Oscorum.*

14. See Booth, ad loc., and *Am.* 1.4.12, 2.8.20; cf. Cat. 30.10 (and Fordyce, *Catullus,* ad loc.) and Tib. 1.4.21 (and Smith, *Tibullus,* ad loc.).

si qua fides dubiis, **volucrum locus ille piarum**
    dicitur, obscenae quo prohibentur aves.
illic **innocui** late pascuntur **olores**
    et **vivax phoenix,** unica semper avis;
explicat ipsa suas **ales Iunonia** pinnas,   55
    oscula dat cupido **blanda columba** mari.
psittacus has inter nemorali sede receptus
    convertit volucres in sua verba pias.

[Beneath the Elysian hill there is a grove leafy with black oak, and the moist earth flourishes with grass that never fades. If there is any trustworthiness in doubtful things, that is said to be the home of faithful birds, a place from which ill-omened birds are excluded. There graze far and wide harmless swans and the durable phoenix, always one-of-a-kind; Juno's bird herself, the peacock, spreads her feathers there, and the gentle dove gives kisses to her loving mate. Received among these birds in their shady home, the parrot attracts the faithful birds to his words.]

The exclusivity of this avian Elysium is among several distinctive features of this scene that will be best understood when we compare it presently with another underworld scene in *Am.* 3.9. We may note in passing, however, that, again unlike Lesbia's *passer,* Corinna's *psittacus* descends not to the gloom of Hades (cf. *iter tenebricosum / illud* and *malae tenebrae / Orci, quae omnia bella devoratis,* Cat. 3.11–12, 13–14) but to an Elysium of sorts, reserved for only the best birds. As befits an epicedion,[15] Ovid emphasizes the *pietas* of the dead by using the phrase *piae volucres* twice here (at 51 and 58; cf. also 3), once in contrast with *aves obscenae* (52). Again, just as the other *piae volucres* continue to do in death what they did in life, so the *psittacus* continues to speak; and like a sort of Orpheus, he draws all those who hear him into his audience. A parallel for this image occurs in a poem in the Palatine Anthology (*AP* 9.562) that Ovid may have known, in which Crinagoras[16] describes a pet parrot that escapes into the woods and there, like Orpheus, instructs the other birds to cry, "Hail, Caesar!" I have already

15. The best general discussion of the epicedion is by Norden, on *Aen.* 6.868–86; see also E. Thomas, "A Comparative Analysis of Ovid, *Amores,* II,6 and III,9," *Latomus* 24 (1965): 599–609.

16. Or Philippus: see A.S.F. Gow and D.L. Page, eds., *The Greek Anthology: The Garland of Philip* (Cambridge, 1968), 2:232. Gow and Page prefer the ascription to Philippus on the basis of style and contents but leave it among the epigrams of Crinagoras. O. Weinreich, "Der Papagei und sein Caesar have," *Tübinger Beiträge zur Altertumswiss.* 4 (1928): 113–25, argues

suggested that, in uttering the words *"Corinna, vale,"* the parrot is imitating the lover; and just as this lover exists within the framework of the poet's narrative, so the parrot too is a creature of elegy. Comparison of this *psittacus* with the other talking birds described in ancient literature is significant: typically, such talking birds are given as gifts to the emperor and speak appropriately, as imperial subjects. Macrobius (*Sat.* 2.4.29–30) records that several birds, including a *psittacus,* were brought before Octavian to praise him as victor after Actium. Pliny, perhaps aware of the same or a similar anecdote, reports that hailing the emperor is a common parrot pastime: *imperatores salutat* (*NH* 10.117). In comparison, the only audience for Corinna's parrot is not public but private, not the emperor but its mistress. Thus, we can be sure that the parrot is no generic poet impersonator but has specifically chosen elegy, with its many-layered rejection of war and the military life, as its favored form of self-expression.

Its last words are those of a poet who was a lover in life; its afterlife is that of a poet; we might well expect its tomb and epitaph to be those of a poet as well. And as the elegy draws to a close, we indeed discover that the Hellenistic and elegiac preferences of this bird are expressed in the details of its funeral arrangements. In the last four lines of the poem, the lover remarks on the size of the parrot's tumulus and monument and then relates the parrot's epitaph verbatim, so that the bird may speak even from the grave (59–62):

ossa tegit tumulus, tumulus pro corpore magnus,
    quo lapis exiguus par sibi carmen habet: 60
COLLIGOR EX IPSO DOMINAE PLACUISSE SEPULCRO.
ORA FUERE MIHI PLUS AVE DOCTA LOQUI.

[A mound covers his bones, a mound large for the size of his body; on it, a small stone displays a couplet its size: FROM THIS BURIAL YOU MAY GATHER THAT I WAS PLEASING TO MY MISTRESS. MY ORAL ABILITIES FAR SURPASSED THOSE OF THE COMMON BIRD.]

A description of the funeral is a standard element in the epicedion; this description, however, is remarkable. First of all, the lover uses the peri-

---

for Augustan dating and prefers the ascription to Crinagoras. If Crinagoras is the author, it is possible that Ovid knew this epigram or that Crinagoras knew Ovid's elegy; I do not think, however, that either poet can be shown to be imitating the other.

phrasis *tumulus pro corpore magnus* to emphasize the slight size of the tomb. The appropriateness of the tumulus' size to the bird's stature is complemented by the fact that the site is marked with a small stone, on which is a suitably slender epitaph. An appreciation of the unusual character of this elaborate though brief description can be gained by comparison with one of the numerous Hellenistic pet epitaphs that are likely to have provided a general precedent for *Am.* 2.6 (as well as for Catullus 3), *AP* 7.198 (Leonidas of Tarentum).[17] In this poem, a deceased ἀκρίς remarks that the slight size of its monument is not meant to suggest that the creature was little loved by its mistress; the woman is rather to be commended (αἰνοιής, 3) for not disowning (οὐδὲ . . . ἀπανήνατο, 7) the creature after death. The pathos of this epigram is underlined by the reference twice, once in the first couplet and once in the last, to the smallness of the monument: μικρὸς ἰδεῖν . . . / λᾶας ὁ τυμβίτης (1–2); τὼλιγον . . . σᾶμα (8). In the parrot's case, in contrast, a small tomb is not something demanding apology or explanation; although the bird, like the ἀκρίς, interprets its burial as a sign of its mistress' fondness (*colligor ex ipso dominae placuisse sepulcro*), there is no suggestion in *Am.* 2.6 that the smallness of mound, tomb, and epitaph is to be interpreted as a slight on the *psittacus*.

For Corinna's parrot, then, smallness has not a pathetic but a positive connotation; this unusual twist is but one of the numerous factors contributing to the poetic nature of the bird.[18] A noteworthy parallel appears in Propertius 2.13b, where throughout his funerary fantasy the poet expresses his preference for the small and simple (19–26, 31–36). While it is conventional in funerary poetry to describe the tumulus or grave as pathetically small, sometimes too small for the person buried within,[19] smallness is a desirable characteristic in Propertius' fantasy. He aims not to evoke

---

17. See A.S.F. Gow and D.L. Page, eds., *The Greek Anthology: Hellenistic Epigrams* (Cambridge, 1965), 2:90–91, 330–32.

18. In connection with the Alexandrian connotations of small size, Myers, "Ovid's *Tecta Ars*," 373, mentions Callimachus *Epigr.* 11 and its discussion by Gow and Page, *Hellenistic Epigrams,* 2:192: U. von Wilamowitz-Moellendorff, *Hellenistische Dichtung in der Zeit des Kallimachos* (Berlin, 1924), 2:121 had suggested that this sepulchral epitaph for Theris the Cretan was a model for *Am.* 2.6.59–60, beginning as it does with an apparent play on the word σύντομος (the epitaph must be brief because Theris himself was abbreviated in stature or because Theris was not much of a talker). While Ovid does little if anything in 2.6 to evoke this model with precision, we may well consider it a feature of the poetic memory informing this elegy.

19. See Nisbet and Hubbard, 1:321–22 (on *Odes* 1.28.2–3).

pathos but, as Wilkinson has suggested,[20] to describe a funeral in keeping with the Alexandrian character of his work. Propertius has adapted Callimachean literary terminology to the metaphor of poetry as monument: his most lasting memorial is to be not a grave but his elegies. When Ovid's lover describes the parrot's last resting place in similar terms, it is reasonable to suppose that we are meant to recall Hellenistic pet epitaphs, on the one hand, and the Callimachean connotation of smallness (τὸ κατὰ λεπτόν) as part of an artistic creed, on the other.[21] In other words, this parrot has become in death much more like an Alexandrian poet than like the typical pets of Hellenistic epigram, and it has become much more like the human poet of the *Amores* than like Lesbia's cherished playmate.

The suggestion of a similarity between parrot and poet, as well as of a similarity between parrot and lover, is reinforced by the bird's epitaph. Several imaginary epitaphs appear in Roman elegy; both Propertius and Tibullus, in imagining their own deaths, provide their own sepulchral addresses to passersby (Prop. 2.13b.35–36; Tib. 1.3.55–56). It is worthwhile, therefore, to look at the diction and style of the parrot's epitaph carefully. As I noted earlier, the *psittacus* addresses us in the first person (*colligor; ora fuere mihi*). Thus, the bird that spoke in life speaks also in death, to express its deathless devotion to Corinna. The words in which it does so are an odd mixture of the exotic and the clichéd, the pompous and the punning: *colligor* with the infinitive (*placuisse*), for example, is a novelty here; in classifying this occurrence of *colligere* among instances where the verb connotes *ratiocinari,* the *Thesaurus Linguae Latinae* indicates that this is a unique example of the verb used in the nominative-with-infinitive construction.[22] *Placuisse,* meanwhile, is a double entendre: in addition to its standard meaning, this verb frequently assumes an erotic connotation in comedy and elegy.[23] This double entendre is further reinforced by the juxtaposition of *placuisse* with *dominae*—the ubiquitous presence of the *domina* in amatory poetry, especially elegy, speaks for itself. In other words, the *psittacus* describes its behavior with a word we would normally expect, in elegy, to be used by a lover, and it calls its owner by a name normally indicative, in elegy, of a lover's mistress.[24]

20. L.P. Wilkinson, "The Continuity of Propertius ii.13," *CR,* n.s., 16 (1966): 142–43.

21. See Reitzenstein, "Zur Stiltheorie des Kallimachos," 31–35.

22. *TLL* 3, col. 1617.10–11 and col. 1618.23–24, s.v. *colligo.*

23. See, e.g., K. Preston, *Studies in the Diction of the Sermo Amatorius in Roman Comedy* (Chicago, 1916), 28; Pichon, *De sermone amatorio,* 234.

24. Note also the ambiguity of the possessive adjective in line 19, *nostrae placuisse puellae.*

In the pentameter, *docta loqui,* like the infinitival construction in the previous line, is a Grecism; *doctus* with an infinitive is exclusively poetic diction, not appearing in prose until Tacitus.[25] The parrot thus suggests, by its choice of words, that it is a neoteric bird, for *docta* evokes the learning of an Alexandrian poet. The literary characterization of the *psittacus* culminates in its use of the phrase *plus ave:* as Guy Lee has noticed,[26] we have here another play on words, in which *ave* may be understood either as the ablative of *avis* or as the greeting *ave.* In other words, Corinna's parrot had more vocal ability than the average bird, or Corinna's parrot was trained to say more than "Hello." Certainly the epitaph itself is meant to illustrate the bird's artistic eloquence, taking as it does the form of a perfect elegiac couplet.

The lover of *Am.* 2.6 styles the parrot as his would-be poetic alter ego: loving and beloved by Corinna, it embarks on a poetic afterlife following its merely mortal death. As in 1.15, so here the immortality bestowed by poetry guarantees the deceased's transcendence of death; and yet, as in 1.15, the parrot itself gives us very little to go on. In the earlier poem, Ovid as poet had established—or at least asserted—a place for himself in a proud tradition; in this poem, he uses the lover/poet/parrot analogy to look at the burden of that tradition. On the one hand, we see in the course of this poem the almost complete merger of amatory and poetic narratives, as the lover uses literary convention to become a poet himself and so to complete the round of identifications between and among lover, parrot, and poet. On the other hand, the lover's portrait of a parrot whose major skill is mimicry—the very parrot that, insofar as it is the lover's love token to Corinna, is a stand-in for the lover himself—blurs the distinction between love poetry and parrotry. As the lover-poet immortalizes in verse another would-be poet, which can after all only mimic what it has learned from the lover-poet himself, Ovid scrutinizes the relationship between allusion, imitation, poetic memory, and creativity in the formation of a Roman poet. The problem raised implicitly in 1.15 is not resolved at all; instead, it is made explicit in 2.6, even as it is a source of rueful humor for Ovid's

---

25. See *TLL* 5.1, cols. 1760–61; see also Tränkle, *Die Sprachkunst des Properz,* 73.

26. [A.]G. Lee, trans., *Ovid's Amores* (New York, 1968), 189. Booth, ad loc., is inclined to reject this double entendre on the grounds that the ablative *ave* ends with a short vowel, while the imperative *ave* ends with a long vowel. Vowel length, however, appears to have played little role in the punning and etymologizing of the Romans: see F. Ahl, *Metaformations: Soundplay and Wordplay in Ovid and Other Classical Poets* (Ithaca and London, 1985), 54–60, and J. O'Hara on Virgilian wordplay and etymologizing, in *True Names: Vergil and the Alexandrian Tradition of Etymological Wordplay* (Ann Arbor, 1996), 61–62.

poet. The lover carries on the amatory narrative of the *Amores* even as the poet comments on the fate of this narrative, using the *psittacus* to mediate the strong identification between the two.

Not until book 3 does Ovid offer a resolution, not in a poem on behalf of himself or featuring another elegiac poet's death fantasy, but rather in an epicedion on behalf of a much admired colleague in elegy, Tibullus. Much as in the case of the opening epigram, 3.9 has often been taken quite literally at its word, and it has been used in documentary fashion. Since scholars believe the poem is most likely to have been written not long after Tibullus' death, an event that itself can be independently dated to 19 B.C., it has become first and foremost an aid to dating the *Amores*.[27] Indeed, it is helpful in dating the collection: there is no reason not to assume that this poem was written in some proximity to Tibullus' death, and there is certainly no reason to assume that it it is entirely fantastical, like the death fantasies that Propertius and Tibullus wrote for themselves. At the same time, however, we should recognize that the poem's documentary value is no substitute for interpretation. The question remains: why is a poem commemorating Tibullus' death among the fifty elegies selected for inclusion in the second edition of the *Amores*? I believe that Ovid chooses to use this format—to include one poet's memorialization of another in his own collection of elegies—to conclude his exploration of the struggle begun in book 1 between lover and poet, between tradition and innovation, and between the literary past and his own poetic future.

Scholars have long observed that much of the diction and style of *Am.* 3.9 is reminiscent of Tibullus' work.[28] Yet the meaning of Tibullus' influence on Ovid has been less easily determined, and here as elsewhere it is easiest to explain—and explain away—the Tibullan features of 3.9 as "parody."[29] But this conclusion, too, so easily reached in some ways, is a rather hollow victory; after all, what would the point of such a parody be? If it is to make light of the idea of immortality through poetry, we have seen this topic already treated in 2.6, in a way that is both light-hearted and thought provoking; but both of these effects result precisely because of the self-reflexivity of the poem, and because of the self-identification with the parrot that Ovid's lover-poet invites. The same topic would have a far dif-

---

27. See McKeown, 1:79; Smith, *Tibullus,* 30–31. See also Cameron, "The First Edition of Ovid's *Amores,*" 331, and Jacobson, *Ovid's Heroides,* 305.

28. Well documented by Munari, *Amores,* ad loc.

29. The most recent example is C.A. Perkins, "Love's Arrows Lost: Tibullan Parody in *Amores* 3.9," *CW* 86 (1993): 459–66.

ferent and even grotesque effect if used in an ad hominem manner; and
however much Ovid may delight in the grotesque elsewhere in his poetry,
there is absolutely no reason to suppose that Tibullus would be a target sin-
gled out for this dubious distinction by the poet of the *Amores*. I propose
instead a reading that recognizes the delicate balance in this poem between
sentiment and cleverness, and that refrains from labeling reference as parody. This poem, too, is reflexive, and it invites us to identify the poet of the
Amores with his subject, Tibullus; in so doing, it affirms for us and for
Ovid that poetic immortality and literary Elysium need not be reserved for
parrot-poets alone.

In this elegy, Ovid displays a sensitivity both to literary convention and
to the possibility for stylistic innovation within the framework of the epicedion. The six lines with which the poem opens are typical of the care Ovid
takes with the nuances of sentiment implicit in his theme: what his poet
offers is at once a sentimental memorial to a dead poet and a stylish tribute to that poet's enduring literary achievement:

> Memnona si mater, mater ploravit Achillem
>   et tangunt magnas tristia fata deas,
> flebilis indignos, Elegia, solve capillos:
>   a, nimis ex vero nunc tibi nomen erit!
> ille tui vates operis, tua fama, Tibullus   5
>   ardet in exstructo corpus inane rogo.

[If Memnon's mother wept, if his mother bewailed Achilles' loss, and if
sad fates move even great goddesses, tearfully loosen your hair, Elegy,
undeserving as it is [i.e., as you are] of such sorrow: ah, too true will
your name now be! That poet of your craft, your source of fame, Tibullus, now burns, a lifeless body, on the funeral pyre built for him.]

The first line is a gem of design: the heroes' names in first and last position
(emphasized by the postponement of *si*) and the repetition of *mater* at the
major caesura give the line an elegant balance at odds with its sad subject;
and *ploravit,* appropriate as it is not to epic diction but to that of lyric and
elegy, introduces a note of intimacy into the epic scenery.[30] In the second
line, the poet underlines the importance of an intimate tone in this context
by reminding us that the mothers described in the first line are no ordinary

---

30. See Axelson, *Unpoetische Wörter,* 28–29; cf. Watson, "Axelson Revisited," 439.

women but goddesses, who are indeed touched by the loss of their sons; and then, in a transition emphasized by the enjambment of the first and second couplets, he invokes Elegia, whose loss of Tibullus is implicitly paralleled to a mother's loss of a son. Ovid's poet thus invents a sort of elegiac family tree, reminiscent of poetic genealogies like that Virgil provides for Gallus in the sixth *Eclogue*,[31] but centering on a distinctly Ovidian paradox: the lament of a mother whose survival is predicated on the death of the very son whose work she has brought into being.

The personification of Elegia in 3.9 also recalls another scene in book 3, one to which I shall return presently; here, the poet uses her presence to signal the vital relationship between style and content, the intimate connection between a poet and his theme, narrator and narrative. By providing her name's etymology,[32] the poet also points to his own virtuosity and thus his appropriateness as heir to Tibullus: he is Elegia's second son, if you will. But Ovid's poet is no slavish imitator; and even as he memorializes Tibullus, he indulges in a deliberately flamboyant mixture of styles, which combines reminiscence of particular Tibullan phrases and episodes with this poet's own poetic voice. The use of exclamatory *a!* to open the otherwise learned line 4 exemplifies the poet's combination of close identification with and narrative detachment from his theme: the result is a subtle blend of pathos and scholarship.[33] This interplay of style and sentiment recurs in the third couplet, where the hexameter is devoted in its entirety to naming Tibullus,[34] while the pentameter somberly depicts the cremation of his corpse.

Although Tibullus' death is his theme, the poet now moves away from specific mention of the dead elegist. Instead, he offers a portrait of the grieving Cupid, a description rich in Hellenistic detail and pathos.[35] The ostensible point of this description is to compare Cupid's mourning for Tibullus with the loss Cupid felt at the death of his brother Aeneas (13–14):

---

31. See Ross, *Backgrounds to Augustan Poetry,* 18–37, developing Stewart, "The Song of Silenus," and Elder, "*Non iniussa cano.*"

32. Cf. Suda s.v.; Etym. Mag. 326, 57; and R. Maltby, *A Lexicon of Ancient Latin Etymologies* (Leeds, 1991), s.v.

33. On exclamatory *a!* see Ross, *Style and Tradition in Catullus,* 51–53; cf. A. Kershaw, "Emendation and Usage: Two Readings of Propertius," *CP* 75 (1980): 71–72.

34. Complete with a so-called schema Cornelianum: see Skutsch, "Zu Vergils Eklogen," 198–99. Solodow, "*Raucae, tua cura, palumbes,*" renames this device "inserted apposition" and, at 137, comments on its "stylishness."

35. See the description of Cupid in *AP* 12.144 (Meleager), and see Tib. 2.6.15–16.

fratris in Aeneae sic illum funere dicunt
   egressum tectis, pulcher Iule, tuis.

[They say, fair Iulus, that thus did he depart from your halls at the death
of his brother Aeneas.]

The vocative *pulcher Iule* is a deliberate touch, introducing a reminiscence
of Virgil's Iulus not just by name but by the Virgilian epithet *pulcher*,[36] but
Ovid's poet uses this Virgilian reference in a non-Virgilian context, with
allusion to a tradition about Aeneas not recorded in the epic.[37] Whoever
the subjects of the Alexandrian footnote[38] *dicunt* may be, they do not
include the poet with whose work Iulus is most immediately identified. At
the same time, the Ovidian poet's association of Tibullus with Aeneas reinforces the suggestion that the dead poet, already part of the poetic memory
in the broadest sense of that term, has now become not only a writer of
elegy but also its theme.

    Having mentioned the mothers of Memnon and Achilles, Tibullus' lit-
erary alma mater, Elegia, and Cupid's fraternal mourning of Aeneas, the
poet continues to develop the familial theme by bringing in Venus, mother
of both Cupid and Aeneas. In lines 15–16 Venus in turn becomes a mourning woman, lamenting the death of Tibullus just as she had previously
lamented that of her lover Adonis, here allusively unnamed. The parallelism between Elegia and Tibullus, on the one hand, and Venus and Adonis, on the other, is explicit insofar as the two females lament young males
dear to them; but there is a further parallel, too, between Tibullus and
Adonis, the first a poet and the second a lover: *both* are beloved by Venus.
Thus, the series of mythic and imagistic associations with which the poem
opens culminates by linking Tibullus with two maternal surrogates, one of
whom inspires his poetry, the other his love. In the poetic genealogy into
which he is introduced, his roles as poet and as lover, like the patron goddesses of his poetry and of love, are virtually interchangeable.

    In addition to reminding us that Tibullus is first and foremost to be
numbered among poets, Ovid's poet makes a place for himself in that select
group (17–18):

---

36. Iulus is called *pulcher* four times in the *Aeneid,* at 5.570, 7.107, 9.293, and 9.310. Cf. my
discussion of this Virgilian formula earlier, chap. 2 n. 5.

37. Cf. M. von Albrecht, *EV* 3:907, s.v. *Ovidio.*

38. See Ross, *Backgrounds to Augustan Poetry,* 78; cf. Horsfall, *L'epopea,* 117–33.

at sacri vates et divum cura vocamur,
  sunt etiam qui nos numen habere putent.

[But we poets are said to be holy and the care of the gods, and there are even those who think that we have divine power.]

This is the first of three occasions in this poem on which the poet-narrator makes reference to himself: momentarily, he joins Tibullus in their shared calling. But the poet does not press the comparison, preferring instead to let the fate of Tibullus speak for that of other poets as well. Such tactful reticence is at first surprising in the poet responsible for giving himself pride of place in *Am.* 1.15, but it is very much in keeping with the elegant but muted tone of this poem. When we observe that the other two instances in which the poet involves himself in this elegy (in the outburst *cum rapiunt mala fata bonos,* (*ignoscite fasso*) / **sollicitor** *nullos esse putare deos,* 35–36, and in the melancholy words *si tamen e **nobis** aliquid nisi nomen et umbra / restat* . . . , 59–60) are both formulaic features of the epicedion, the one nonformulaic instance in which he reminds us of his role as poet takes on added significance; I shall return to this point presently.

The poet devotes the next twelve lines (19–30) to extending Tibullus' poetic genealogy even as he laments the greedy inevitability of death. He catalogues the deaths of three eminent predecessors whose poetry could not save them in the face of death: Orpheus, Linus, and Homer. Parental sorrow made no difference to these men in their deaths (*quid **pater** Ismario, quid **mater** profuit Orpheo?,* 21; *et Linon in silvis idem **pater** 'aelinon'* . . . / *dicitur* . . . *concinuisse,* 23–24), even when their parents included Apollo himself and Calliope. Yet even as they have been plunged into black Avernus, their poetry survives the funeral pyre (27–28):

hunc quoque summa dies nigro submersit Averno:
  defugiunt avidos carmina sola rogos.

[The final day submerged even this one in black Avernus: poetry alone survives the greedy pyre.]

The poet's first two examples of this immortal poetry are the *Iliad* and the *Odyssey* (*Troiani fama laboris / tardaque nocturno tela retexta dolo,* 29–30); as he returns to the subject at hand, this pair is balanced by

Nemesis and Delia, likewise destined to achieve immortality. Like the mourning Elegia earlier in the poem, they live on in the form of Tibullus' poetry—as does he.

With this mention of the two loves who embody Tibullus' poetry, Ovid's poet begins a series of allusions to Tibullan themes that will continue through the remainder of the elegy (33–66). These themes include the worship of Isis; the possibility of death in Phaeacia; the mourning of mother, sister, Nemesis, and Delia for their lost Tibullus; and afterlife in Elysium. All these themes (except, of course, for the mourning of Nemesis, who does not appear until book 2) figure prominently in Tibullus 1.3, the poem in which that poet describes his imagined death in Phaeacia; I refer the reader to Munari, who catalogues the parallels thoroughly.[39] Most relevant to this discussion is how the poet has transformed Tibullus' fantasy into a real event; the very deliberate allusiveness of the poem is paradoxically realistic in a way that Tibullus' own death fantasy is not. That the poet here focuses on the death of a literary colleague, rather than on his own imagined death, enables him to achieve both the narrative detachment inherent in the use of a set form like the epicedion, with all of its particular stylistic demands, and a realism not available (or desirable) from the perspective of fantasy. Thus, the poet narrates the funerary ministrations of mother and sister simultaneously as allusions to Tibullus 1.3 and as real events (49–52):

> hic certe madidos fugientis pressit ocellos
>   mater et in cineres ultima dona tulit;   50
> hic soror in partem misera cum matre doloris
>   venit inornatas dilaniata comas.

[Here, to be sure, his mother pressed his wet eyes as he fled his body, and she made last offerings to his ashes; here his sister came, her hair disheveled and unadorned, to join in the grief of her wretched mother.]

---

39. See Munari, *Amores,* ad loc. It should be added that the poet does not limit himself to recollection of one poem only but in fact looks to several Tibullan death scenes: *Am.* 3.9.58 (*me tenuit moriens deficiente manu*), e.g., is closely modeled on Tib. 1.1.60. On this reference, see also G.A. Cornacchia, "Ovidio, *Am.* 3,9,58: Nota di lettura," in *Mnemosynum: Studi in onore di Alfredo Ghiselli* (Bologna, 1989), 101–2, who observes that in Ovid's epicedion, the appropriately named Nemesis has stolen from her rival a verse originally composed by Tibullus for Delia. As Cornacchia notes, this subtle allusion to Tibullus' poem is hardly a simple citation but is rather a brilliant use of reference by Ovid—who, I might add, himself "steals" the entire complex of reference and context from Tibullus.

By mentioning Tibullus' human mother—after her surrogates, Elegia and Venus—the poet returns to his genealogical theme, again blurring the distinction between Tibullus' poetry and his life. This effect is further heightened by the addition of Nemesis and Delia to the mournful scene at Tibullus' funeral pyre (53–58):

> cumque tuis sua iunxerunt Nemesisque priorque
>   oscula nec solos destituere rogos.
> Delia discedens 'felicius' inquit 'amata   55
>   sum tibi: vixisti, dum tuus ignis eram.'
> cui Nemesis 'quid' ait 'tibi sunt mea damna dolori?
>   me tenuit moriens deficiente manu.'

[Nemesis and her predecessor joined their kisses to those of your family, and they did not leave the pyre abandoned. Departing, Delia said, "I was loved more happily by you; you lived while I was your passion." To her, Nemesis said, "Why is my loss a source of grief for you? As he died, he held on to me with his weakening hand."]

With the addition of these three couplets, the poet imagines the four women together: mother, sister, and the two women celebrated in Tibullus' verse. Yet that the latter two have a different relationship to Tibullan narrative is signaled by the fact that, unlike Tibullus' blood kin, these women speak to bid their beloved farewell: as we read their words, we may recall the *libelli* that opened the *Amores* with their address to the reader. Nemesis and Delia are both the lovers of Tibullus and the poems Tibullus has written about them; they thus can speak with the words Tibullus has given them in bidding farewell to their poet and lover. In fact, Nemesis' use of words once written by Tibullus for his first lover, Delia, suggest that the power of poetry to flourish on its own has already begun to transcend the limitation of mortality imposed on the poet.

The scene of Tibullus' death is relieved at the close of the poem by his translation to Elysium. Even here, the poetic genealogy applies, as he joins the *numeri pii* of other poets (59–66):

> si tamen e nobis aliquid nisi nomen et umbra
>   restat, in Elysia valle Tibullus erit.   60
> obvius huic venies hedera iuvenalia cinctus
>   tempora cum Calvo, docte Catulle, tuo;

tu quoque, si falsum est temerati crimen amici,
    sanguinis atque animae prodige Galle tuae.
his comes umbra tua est, si qua est modo corporis umbra;   65
    auxisti numeros, culte Tibulle, pios.

[Nevertheless, if anything remains from us besides reputation and shade, Tibullus will be in the Elysian vale. You will come to meet him, learned Catullus, in company with your dear Calvus, your temples entwined with youthful ivy; and you, too, Gallus, if the charge of having insulted your friend is false, wasteful as you have been of your blood and your life. Your shade is a companion to these, as long as the shade of anybody exists; elegant Tibullus, you have enlarged the numbers of the faithful.]

As in death, so in the afterlife, Tibullus is to be remembered for his poetry; just as in death his poetic fantasy was realized, so after death he lives among poets. Ovid's poet follows his Tibullan model in translating the dead man to Elysium; but the character of this Elysium is somewhat different from that envisioned by Tibullus in his elegy 1.3. There, Tibullus had characterized himself not as a poet but as a lover; and it is because of this role that he is able to enter Elysium (*sed me, quod facilis tenero sum semper Amori, / ipsa Venus campos ducet in Elysios,* 1.3.57–58). Accordingly, the Elysium that Tibullus describes is one especially for lovers (1.3.59–66):

hic choreae cantusque vigent, passimque vagantes
    dulce sonant tenui gutture carmen aves;   60
fert casiam non culta seges, totosque per agros
    floret odoratis terra benigna rosis;
ac iuvenum series teneris immixta puellis
    ludit, et adsidue proelia miscet amor.
illic est, cuicumque rapax Mors venit amanti,   65
    et gerit insigni myrtea serta coma.

[Here dances and songs flourish, and birds wandering here and there produce sweet song from their slender throats; the crop, though untended, bears wild cinnamon, and the beneficent earth blooms with fragrant roses through all the fields; a row of youths combined with tender girls frolics, and love repeatedly joins in battle. In that place is every lover to whom greedy death has come, and on his distinguished head each one wears a myrtle wreath.]

As has been frequently noted, Tibullus is apparently the first not only to introduce erotic motifs to the underworld but also to create an Elysium exclusively for lovers.[40] In adapting this important scene for his own purposes, Ovid's poet maintains the feature of exclusivity even as he inverts the rationale for Tibullus' entry to this place—Tibullus is apparently to share the company only of other poets. For Ovid's poet, Tibullus was not simply a lover but also a poet of love; thus, in death Tibullus joins other love poets.

At this point, it is appropriate to get our bearings and to think about how, if at all, this poem alters the Ovidian poet's earlier claim to originality and immortality in 1.15. But another question requires even more immediate attention, and in answering it we will be better able to understand the change that has occurred in the narrative between 1.15 and 3.9: what are we to make of the thematic and structural similarities between 2.6 and 3.9? Is the role of tradition, particularly as he develops it in the figure of the perfectly mimetic parrot, so daunting for Ovid's poet—who, as Corinna's lover, identifies on two counts with the parrot—that he can do nothing other than mimic his predecessors? And is 3.9, then, really to be taken any more seriously than 2.6, or should it be read as a shadow of a shadow, formally and stylistically sophisticated but emotionally hollow? After all, like the *psittacus* before him, the poet Tibullus is also to be counted among *numeri pii* (66), although in his case this select group is limited to poets, including Calvus, Catullus, and Gallus. In describing these men as *pii,* the poet accords to Tibullus, as to the parrot, conventional funeral praise;[41] but unlike the Homeric heroes whose deaths were briefly evoked at the opening of 3.9, neither the parrot nor Tibullus has gained Elysium through heroism. Instead, Tibullus has done so through his conduct as lover and *Elegiae vates,* while it is for the parrot's verbal talents and devotion to Corinna that the deceased bird is rewarded. The central char-

---

40. F. Solmsen suggests that the Elysium of Prop. 4.7 is also inspired by Tibullus: see "Propertius in His Literary Relations with Tibullus and Virgil," *Philologus* 105 (1961): 283. See also A.A.R. Henderson, "Tibullus, Elysium and Tartarus," *Latomus* 28 (1969): 649–53; D. F. Bright, *Haec mihi fingebam: Tibullus in His World* (Leiden, 1978), 28–29; and F. Cairns, *Tibullus: A Hellenistic Poet at Rome* (Cambridge, 1979), 52.

41. Norden, on *Aen.* 6.878–81, discusses conventional elements in funerary praise.

acters of these two epicedia descend, then, to similarly exclusive Elysia, and by implication their fates are, if not identical, at least parallel; the poet thus suggests an equation of sorts between Corinna's parrot and the elegist Tibullus.

I have already mentioned that the shallow reading of 3.9 is tempting to many who wish to read the *Amores* as monotone parody; but I want to consider again the brief but strong assertion of communal identity among love poets that is spoken by the poet after his opening association of Elegia and Venus (17–18):

> at sacri vates et divum cura vocamur;
> > sunt etiam qui nos numen habere putent.

> [But we poets are said to be holy and the care of the gods, and there are even those who think that we have divine power.]

He counts himself among this group (*nos*); indeed, with Tibullus' passing he is their heir apparent.[42] Thus, I believe that we are to read *Am.* 3.9 less as a companion piece to 2.6[43] than as a revision of the earlier elegy, in which the Elysian aviary is replaced by the literary immortality that Tibullus—and others like him—have truly merited. Ovid's poet makes no mention of a future for himself in this blessed company; he focuses his attention instead on Tibullus. Nonetheless, the way in which he creates this memorial to Tibullus, transforming the earlier poet's work into his own, reveals the security with which Ovid's poet can now approach his continuing tradition. We find no declaration of feigned humility intended to evoke our sympathy for the epigone. Rather, the poet uses the rhetorical conventions of the epicedion to emulate an admired model even as he makes a place for his own innovations in the Roman poetic tradition. Seen in the aftermath of 1.15 and 2.6, *Am.* 3.9 resolves the inspirational dilemma posed earlier by Ovid's poet. The hyperbolic first place among poets that the poet claims for himself in 1.15 is replaced, in 3.9, with a fully developed poetic genealogy and a community of *numeri pii,* among whom the poet

---

42. The absence of Propertius from Ovid's literary Elysium has troubled some: among others, Barsby, *Am.,* 163 believes that Ovid deliberately excludes Propertius (and Horace) from the catalogue of 1.15 because they are still living; the reference to Tibullus at 1.15.27–28 would then date this poem to after 19 B.C. A similar case can be made for the absence of Propertius from 3.9.

43. Cf. E. Thomas, "Comparative Analysis."

enrolls himself even as he pays tribute to his past. We would not be far wrong if we were to see in 3.9 the death fantasy of Ovid's poet, but in a new form, as Ovidian realism takes the place of Alexandrian polemic.

I have already indicated my reasons for objecting to a reading of 3.9 as parody; the interpretation I have offered here is also at odds with several other critical perspectives. The voices of two familiar critics will be allowed to speak for the multitudes. Wilkinson says of 3.9: "The elegy on the death of Tibullus . . . is as conventional as it could be in form; it is full of traditional artificialities . . . ; and yet it pulses with indignation and pity. It is a passionate vindication of the value of poets in the world. . . . The feeling of solidarity among poets comes out in the closing lines." And Du Quesnay says, "the witty poem on Tibullus' death is a delightful tribute to the memory of a poet whom Ovid genuinely respected and admired, but clearly is not an emotional outpouring of grief at the death of a friend."[44] My reading acknowledges both the passion and the wit of 3.9; but I locate these effects too within the narrative that dominates the *Amores,* the first-person narrative of a poet who in the course of the three books of *Amores* goes from being a would-be writer of epic to being the heir apparent to the literary tradition symbolized by Tibullus' poetry and its place in the poetic genealogy of Roman Alexandrianism. This narrative is fictional; but its embrace of the amatory narrative of elegy authenticates the fiction and allows Ovid's poet-narrator to grant to Tibullus the immortality of a poetic afterlife.

In the preceding discussion of *Am.* 1.15, 2.6, and 3.9, we have observed a subtle but important instance of structural design in the *Amores:* each of the three books contains one elegy on the subject of a poet's death and immortality, and these three poems follow a progression of sorts, as Ovid's narrator locates himself within a literary tradition. In fact, such sequential ordering of poems connected by theme is a well-known feature of the *Amores,* although most attention has been paid to the striking pairs of contiguous elegies, like 1.11 and 1.12, on the exchange of *tabellae* between the lover and Corinna, or 2.7 and 2.8, revealing the lover's duplicity in his affair with Corinna's maid Cypassis.[45] My approach is broader and recom-

---

44. Wilkinson, *Ovid Recalled,* 74; Du Quesnay, "The *Amores,*" 3.

45. See K. Jäger, "Zweigliedrige Gedichte und Gedichtpaare bei Properz und in Ovids Amores," Diss. Eberhard-Karls-Universität (Tübingen, 1967); J.T. Davis, *Dramatic Pairings in the Elegies of Propertius and Ovid,* Noctes Romanae 15 (Bern and Stuttgart, 1977); C. Damon, "Poem Division, Paired Poems, and *Amores* ii.9 and iii.11," *TAPA* 120 (1990): 269–90. And cf., e.g., Du Quesnay, "The *Amores,*" 30–40, and P. Watson, "Ovid Amores ii.7 and 8: The Disingenuous Defence," *WS,* n.s., 17 (1983): 91–103.

mends that we see all the poems as relating to the dominant narrative plot of the *Amores,* the poet's invention of an embedded narrative about a first-person love affair with Corinna, and the consequences of this invention for his growth into the role decreed for him in 1.1 by Cupid. Just as there is a beginning, middle, and end to the love affair, so we see these components in the poet's narrative about his own fate; thus, poems like the three we have just considered replicate through their ordering the poet's literary journey.

These sequential orderings are like narrative threads running through the entire fabric of the collection; not only are there many such threads, but they of necessity cannot remain discrete from one another. Rather, they are interwoven, so that a given poem may well be part of more than one pattern in the larger fabric. In looking at 1.5, 1.7, and 1.9 as a narrative sequence,[46] for example, we focused on how the poet gradually arrives at a position of ironic detachment from his physical relationship with Corinna. We did not investigate, however, other facets of these poems' relationship to the larger whole: for example, the role of Corinna's entry in 1.5 in terms of the programmatic sequence with which the book opened, or the lover's assault in 1.7 in terms of the many other poems ostensibly about Corinna's hair. Similarly, in looking at 1.15, 2.6, and 3.9, we might also have juxtaposed the catalogue style of 1.15 with that of 2.18, describing the poet's work in progress, or we might have noted the similarity of 2.6 to another poem in the same book on a love token for the lover's *puella,* 2.15 (on a ring).[47] My reading is emphatically not intended to exclude other associations such as these; rather, by putting the individual elegies into a narrative framework, I have attempted to demonstrate, *multum ex parvo,* how the collection can be opened up to a more complex and satisfying interpretation than was previously available.

I shall close this chapter by considering a final group of elegies, keeping in mind as I proceed that the individual poems in this group can each be shown to belong to yet other groupings: this complexity is one of Ovid's many underrated accomplishments in the *Amores.* The poems I turn to now are 2.1, 3.1, and 3.15; and to provide a coda of sorts to my discussion, I shall look back again at my starting point, the prefatory epigram and opening poems of book 1. In beginning a "second reading," as it were, of the collection, I want to emphasize again how well plotted the *Amores* are

---

46. See chap. 4.
47. See n. 11 in this chapter.

and how strong their narrative sequence is: the close of the third book, in which poet and lover part ways again, invites us to recall, for the sake of comparison, the opening distinction between Ovid's two roles.

Am. 2.1, like the prefatory epigram, opens by providing the poet with a signature, giving his name, place of origin, profession, and theme (*Paelignis natus aquosis / ille ego nequitiae Naso poeta meae,* 1–2); but here he identifies himself straightforwardly as *poeta,* rather than with the ironic *auctor* of the epigram, and the ensuing discussion of his calling is appropriately solemn. He reports that he is now under divine orders (*hoc quoque iussit Amor,* 3), but instead of resisting the power of divine inspiration, as he had done in 1.1, here he expresses no unwillingness or hesitation; and at the poem's close, he reaffirms his inspirational relationship with *Amor* in positive terms (*ad mea formosos vultus adhibete, puellae, / carmina, purpureus quae mihi dictat Amor,* 37–38). The solemnity of the poet's stance is emphasized by the fact that he here assumes the responsibilities of a *vates,* called on to compose a gentle but powerful poetry.[48] The language of line 3, *procul hinc, procul este, severi*—like Virgil's solemn *procul, o procul este, profani* (*Aen.* 6.258) and its Callimachean model, ἑκάς, ἑκὰς ὅστις ἀλιτρός (*h.* 2.2)[49]—is our first indication that the poet is preparing for this role. He will eventually expand on it more fully in the second half of the poem, with praise of the power of *carmina* (emphatically repeated four times, with anaphora and polyptoton, in 23–28)[50] and with a statement of its rewards (*at facie tenerae laudata saepe puellae / ad vatem, pretium carminis, ipsa venit,* 33–34). But the extended solemnity of the beginning and end of this poem is at odds with its center, where both the poet and his pretensions are undone by his *amica* (17). Consider the organization of the poem: two fully developed sections (1–14, 23–38) are used to advance conventional programmatic ends, as the poet proclaims his calling and rejects epic themes (the gigantomachy in 11–14 and the Trojan War in 29–32). In the central section, however, conventions disappear as realism very literally intrudes and as the poet again finds himself perforce becoming a lover (15–22):

in manibus nimbos et **cum Iove fulmen** habebam,   15
    quod bene pro caelo mitteret ille suo.
clausit amica fores: ego **cum Iove fulmen** omisi;

---

48. See Newman, *The Concept of Vates,* esp. 100–114.
49. See Norden, on *Aen.* 6.255ff.; Williams, *Hymn to Apollo,* ad loc.
50. Cf. Booth, ad loc.

excidit ingenio Iuppiter ipse meo.
Iuppiter, ignoscas: nil me **tua tela** iuvabant;
  clausa tuo maius ianua **fulmen** habet.   20
blanditias elegosque leves, **mea tela,** resumpsi:
  mollierunt duras lenia verba fores.

[I had clouds in my hands and, along with Jupiter, a thunderbolt, which
he might easily send forth on behalf of his heaven. My girlfriend shut
the door; I lost his thunderbolt together with Jupiter; and Jupiter himself fell from my poetic thoughts. Jupiter, forgive me; your weapons
were no help to me; a closed door has a bolt greater than yours. I have
taken up again blandishments and light elegies, my weapons; gentle
words have made hard doors flexible.]

With the opening words *in manibus,* the poet makes life imitate art, portraying himself as quite literally manipulating his materials. He is about to
equip Jupiter for poetic battle, when the door slams and breaks the poet's
concentration. As it turns out, Jupiter's mighty thunderbolt is useless to
the poet in love; instead, gentle words and blandishments are the only sure
way to win the amatory struggle. The stylistic efficiency of these lines,
composed of short, staccato bits to underline the effect of this scene as
"aus dem Alltagsleben,"[51] is apparent. And several other features of this
passage draw special attention to themselves: the repetition of *cum Iove
fulmen* in the same metrical position in two successive hexameters, followed by the repetition of *tua tela/mea tela* in the same metrical position
in two successive hexameters, in turn enhanced by the fact that each of the
four hexameters ends in a trisyllabic verb, effects an explicit parallel
between Jupiter's cosmic struggle and the *militia amoris* of the lover-poet.
Each is armed for a battle of sorts; but even the omnipotence of Jupiter is
useless to the lover against a door that his *amica* has slammed. Unlike
Callimachus, whose βροντᾶν οὐκ ἐμόν, ἀλλὰ Διός (*Aet.* 1, fr. 1.20 Pf.) is
a pronouncement born of polemic, the poet's abandonment of Jupiter
and his lightning is ruefully apologetic. The ironic humor of the poet's
amatory predicament is underlined by artful repetition and structure: this
poet whose mastery of the materials of epic is so complete is undone, at
least temporarily, by a woman, the subject of his own embedded narrative.
For all his vatic bluster, the poet reveals that the truly outstanding strate-

---

51. The phrase is Reitzenstein's, in "Das neue Kunstwollen," 224 (= *Ovid,* 78); cf. D.
Korzeniewski, "Ovids elegisches Prooemium," *Hermes* 92 (1964): 189–91.

gist in this poem is not the poet composing it but the *amica* whose appearance is brief but decisive.[52]

As in several other cases we have already considered, the potential documentary interest of this poem has generally overshadowed other matters: did Ovid actually write, or contemplate writing, a gigantomachy?[53] Of more central relevance to our discussion, however, is the fact that the poet introduces the motif of gigantomachy into this elegy, much as he had introduced that of "epic themes" into 1.1; indeed, we might consider 2.1 to be in many senses a reprise of 1.1, with its would-be embracing of epic, abrupt intrusion by an entity who demands that the poet write love poetry, and recommitment to the genre for a second book by the poet. But the relationship between embedded and amatory narratives has changed somewhat: now the poet is already an elegist, already has a *puella,* and has already earned respect and admiration from his audience (*atque aliquis iuvenum quo nunc ego saucius arcu / agnoscat flammae conscia signa suae, / miratusque diu 'quo' dicat 'ab indice doctus / composuit casus iste poeta meos?,'* 7–10). Epic, meanwhile, appears to offer little in the way of personal advantage (***Quid mihi*** *profuit velox cantatus Achilles? /* ***quid pro me*** *Atrides alter et alter agent* . . . ?, 29–30). Love poetry, on the other hand, brings not only fame but also a flesh-and-blood *puella* (*at facie tenerae laudata saepe puellae, / ad vatem, pretium carminis, ipsa venit. /* ***magna datur merces***!, 33–35). Its advantages over epic would therefore seem to be immediately evident.

Thus, the poet need not search for an identity in 2.1; rather, from the very opening he can declare his name, his home, and the source of his fame (1–2):

> Hoc quoque composui Paelignis natus aquosis,
>   ille ego nequitiae Naso poeta meae.

> [I who was born in the Paelignian territory, rich in water, composed this, too; I am Naso, the famed poet of my own naughtiness.]

---

52. The shutting of the door may also be intended to recall, humorously, of course, a Callimachean epiphany of Apollo: in *h.* 2.3–7, Callimachus describes how Apollo knocks on the temple door with his foot and then orders the bolts and bars on the doors to fall away of their own accord. On the *Türöffnung* as a motif of epiphanies, see O. Weinreich, "Gebet und Sünder, II: Türöffnung in Wunder-, Prodigien- und Zauberglauben der Antike, des Judentums und Christentums," in *Genethliakon Wilhelm Schmid,* F. Folke et al. (Stuttgart, 1929), 200–452.

53. See Booth, on 2.1.11–16, for details of the question.

The identification of poet and lover made complete in book 1 is reaffirmed here, even as the poet indicates that love will continue to be his theme. The poet's struggle to find a poetic voice in amatory elegy has disappeared, and he has convincingly turned himself into Corinna's lover. The price of the poet's fame, however, is the loss of narrative tension and surprise; and as with 1.15 preceding it, we may well be inclined to wonder at the close of 2.1 how the poet intends to sustain his elegiac claim to fame. This poem itself is something *dejà vu.*

This thematic perplexity persists through much of book 2; we have already seen in this chapter how the poet's very success in becoming a lover translates into the ironic predicament of 2.6, on the death of the poetic *psittacus,* and we might look as well to the phenomenon of paired poems like 2.7 and 2.8 or 2.13 and 2.14, where the second poem in each pair consciously rewrites the theme of the first.[54] Even the two poems with which book 2 closes, 2.18 and 2.19, can be seen to reflect on the situation: in the first, the poet reports on his literary achievements to date and boasts of his success as amatory poet; in the second, meanwhile, the lover tells both a would-be rival (*stulte,* 2.19.1) and a desirable *puella* (*tu quoque, quae nostros rapuisti nuper ocellos,* 19)—or anyone else who will listen—to make the game of love a bit more of a challenge for him; as it becomes easier, it becomes less interesting (2.19.35–36):

> quidlibet eveniat, nocet indulgentia nobis:
> quod sequitur fugio; quod fugit ipse sequor.

> [Whatever may result, indulgence does me harm; I flee that which follows me; that which flees me, I myself follow.]

Scholars have conventionally been troubled by the relative positioning of 2.18 and 2.19, since it would be more usual to find a poem like the explicitly programmatic 2.18 at the end of the book;[55] and, again because of the documentary value of 2.18,[56] they have developed a number of explanations relating to the revised second edition of the *Amores.* If we read the

---

54. On paired poems, see n. 45 in this chapter; not all pairs, of course, work in the same way: Damon, "Poem Division," 280–85, discusses the paired relationship between 2.2 and 2.3, premised on a momentary dramatic pause.

55. See, e.g., Booth, ad loc.

56. See Cameron, "The First Edition of Ovid's *Amores,*" 331–33; Luck, *Die römische Liebeselegie,* 146; Jacobson, *Ovid's Heroides,* 300–318.

Amores as a double narrative, however, it is possible to see the first narrative as spoken by an overconfident poet, the second by the lover he has created as the focal character in the embedded amatory narrative. As the poet's success grows, the lover's future is at risk (2.19.25–26):

pinguis amor nimiumque patens in taedia nobis
  vertitur et, stomacho dulcis ut esca, nocet.

[A rich love that is too accessible turns tedious for me and harms me, as a sweet dish harms the stomach.]

Just as 2.6 had explored the tension between imitation and originality, so 2.18 and 2.19 cap the book with a literal division of the related problems of inspiration and generic constraints.[57] The *puella* continues to hold center stage for both poet and lover; but her continuing and insistent presence is itself a paradox. The vision captured in 2.1, of a *puella* most influential in her absence (*clausit amica fores,* 17), has become increasingly difficult for the poet to sustain.

With the opening of book 3, we again have an obviously programmatic statement, in a poem in which the poet indicates that the days are numbered for his dalliance with love elegy. As a whole, 3.1 is an effective means of marking the third book as the conclusion to the collection; instead of looking backward, as had the programmatic openings of books 1 and 2, this poem looks forward, to the literary career that awaits the poet after the completion of the *Amores*. At the same time, in moving beyond the formalities of the *recusatio,* as observed in 1.1 and 2.1, the poet replaces the conventional language and imagery of programmatic poetry with what I have called "realism." Only gradually, as the poet's vision unfolds, does the encounter of 3.1 take on a programmatic dimension.

The elegy opens with a generic ecphrasis for a numinous grove (1–4):[58]

---

57. D. Lateiner, "Ovid's Homage to Callimachus and Alexandrian Poetic Theory (*Am.* ii.19)," *Hermes* 106 (1978): 188–96, suggests that many of the images used in 2.19 can in fact be related to Callimachean programmatic diction, and so he believes that 2.19 is itself explicitly programmatic. My approach would make Lateiner's demonstration—some aspects of which are excessive—unnecessary; 2.19 need not be "explicitly" programmatic for it to reflect generally on the task the poet has set for himself in the course of the narrative, i.e., to become an accomplished love poet.

58. For evidence of the generic quality of the description, cf. Sen. *Epist.* 41.3: "si tibi occurrerit vetustis arboribus et solitam altitudinem egressis frequens lucus et conspectum caeli ramorum aliorum alios protegentium summovens obtentu, illa proceritas silvae et secretum loci et admiratio umbrae in aperto tam densae atque continuae fidem tibi numinis faciet. si

Stat vetus et multos incaedua silva per annos;
 credibile est illi numen inesse loco.
fons sacer in medio speluncaque pumice pendens,
 et latere ex omni dulce queruntur aves.

[There stands an ancient forest, uncut for many years; it is easy to
believe that there is something divine in that place. There is a sacred
spring in the middle and a cave suspended in the tufa stone, and on all
sides birds warble sweetly.]

An inspirited wood, a fountain, a cave, birds—this grove is a likely place, perhaps, for an encounter between the lover and his *puella*. But in the third couplet, we discover the poet here, apparently alone, pondering his next literary
move (5–6): *hic ego dum spatior tectus nemoralibus umbris— / quod mea,
quaerebam, Musa moveret opus*—(5–6). This grove is a poetic grove, then,
and Ovid's poet has come to it precisely in the hopes of receiving inspiration.

Am. 3.1 generally is interpreted as a creative reworking of the opening
to Propertius' third book, especially 3.1 and 3.3.[59] On a simple structural
level, the influence of Propertius is obvious: we are concerned in both cases
with the opening of the third book,[60] and we are confronted in both cases
with a poet in a sacred grove, pondering his next poetic step. In the course
of both narratives, two inspirational beings appear to each man and direct
his course: for Propertius' poet they are Apollo and Calliope, for Ovid's,
Elegy and Tragedy. But the differences between the two openings are
important as well, although less likely to be remarked: whereas Propertius'
Apollo and Calliope work in tandem, Elegy and Tragedy are on equal foot-
ing but diametrically opposed; and whereas Propertius' cave of inspiration
is distinctively elegiac and Alexandrian, the place depicted at the opening
of *Am.* 3.1 has as much in common with Virgil's description of Avernus
(*Aen.* 6.237–41) or the sacred grove on the Capitoline (*Aen.* 8.349–52) as it
does with Propertius's poetic grove.[61]

---

quis specus saxis penitus exesis montem suspenderit, non manu factus, sed naturalibus causis
in tantam laxitatem excavatus, animum tuum quadam religionis suspicione percutiet. magno-
rum fluminum veneramur. subita ex abdito vasti amnis eruptio aras habet; coluntur aquarum
calentium fontes, et stagna quaedam vel opacitas vel immensa altitudo sacravit. . . ."

59. See, e.g., Morgan, *Ovid's Art of Imitation,* 17–21; G. Luck, "The Cave and the Source,"
CQ 7 (1957): 175–79; Wimmel, *Kallimachos in Rom,* 296.

60. On the numbering of the books of Propertius, see the contrasting discussions of
Skutsch and Hutchinson in the articles cited in chap. 4 n. 31.

61. See Norden, on *Aen.* 6.237ff. (although of course birds are missing from Avernus: see
the interpolated line 242 transmitted only in MS R, *unde locum Grai dixerunt nomine Aor-
num*).

In fact, it is quite likely that, like Ovid's poet, this scene has more than one dimension, or source of inspiration: looking to Propertius again, for example, we might observe the bipolar structure of 4.1, in which two speakers, the poet and the astrologer Horus, define the thematic and stylistic parameters of book 4. Speaking first, the poet declares a newfound determination to leave aside his more conventional elegiac concerns, especially those embodied in Cynthia, and to embark instead on the sort of aetiological mission that would make him a *Romanus Callimachus.* Horus, however, exhorts the poet not to abandon his elegiac subject matter and declares that elegy is the poet's fate (*at tu finge elegos, fallax opus: haec tua castra!— / scribat ut exemplo cetera turba tuo,* 135–36). The opening of Propertius' fourth book offers us two voices, then, and two poetic alternatives; and the presence of these two voices helps to explain the fluctuation in the remainder of book 4 between typically Propertian material and novel aetiological poems. Again like Ovid in *Am.* 3.1, the poet Propertius does not fully reject either alternative. I am convinced, therefore, that the structural influence of Propertius 4.1 on *Am.* 3.1 is at least as great as that of the opening of Propertius' book 3.[62]

The most striking feature in this comparison is not, however, its suggestiveness regarding the contents of *Am.* 3; indeed, although some of the poems in this book do suggest aetiological experimentation in the Propertian vein—especially 3.10 and 3.13, on the festivals of Ceres and Faliscan Juno, respectively—we have already noted Ovid's tendency to avoid exclusive imitation of Propertius. We have also seen the irrelevance of generic constraints to Ovid's project in the *Amores.* Rather, Propertius 4.1 serves as a valuable predecessor because it taps directly into a philosophical tradition of broad scope, that of the Protagorean *Dissoi Logoi,* or the dispute between two entities, generally personifications, in diametrical opposition to each other. Aside from the parody of the *Dissoi Logoi* that appears in Aristophanes' *Clouds,* the allegory of their role in determining a man's course in life was most widely disseminated through the story of Hercules at the crossroads, attributed to the sophist Prodicus and summarized by Xenophon at *Mem.* 2.1.21–34.[63] The debate between Propertius' *poeta* and

---

62. On the "bipolar" program of Prop. 4.1, see M. Wyke, "The Elegiac Woman at Rome," *PCPhS* 33 (1987): 151–57.

63. For a recent discussion, see M. Kuntz, "The Prodikean 'Choice of Herakles': A Reshaping of Myth," *CJ* 89 (1993–94): 163–81; see also W.J. Froleyks, "Der ΑΓΩΝ ΛΟΓΩΝ in der antiken Literatur" (Diss. Bonn, 1973), esp. 133–43; J. Whitman, *Allegory: The Dynamics of an Ancient and Medieval Technique* (Cambridge, MA, 1987), 22–24. It is also worth noting the reference by Quintilian to a contest between Life and Death in Ennius' satire: *Mortem*

Horus, like that between Elegia and Tragoedia in *Am.* 3.1, develops the idea that the opening poem in a book is a crossroads of sorts for a poet, as the poet considers not only the future course of his or her work but also its ethical implications.

Let us consider the Prodicean narrative more fully, as summarized by Xenophon. On the threshhold of manhood, Hercules cannot decide which of two courses in life to take. He retires to a quiet spot to ponder his alternatives (ἐξελθόντα εἰς ἡσυχίαν, *Mem.* 2.1.21) and is there approached by two women, both lovely but in very different ways. The looks of one are characterized by σωφροσύνη (22), while the other's beauty is artificial, that of a coquette. The latter speaks first and offers him a life of pleasure if he will follow her; when asked, she identifies herself as Eudaimonia, nick-named Kakia by those who hate her (26). The former then offers a very different life, one filled with virtuous conduct and its rewards. This woman is of course Arete; and although Kakia attempts briefly once more to distract the hero, Arete clearly wins the day, promising Hercules that only by following her will he win the sort of εὐδαιμονία sanctioned by gods and humans alike (33). In other words, Prodicus' Hercules, like Ovid's *poeta,* wanders off into the wilderness and meets there two larger-than-life women, who plead their cases to him and struggle for his attention.

For much of this century, the similarity between the allegory of Hercules *in bivio* and Ovid's *poeta in nemore,* while not wholly unrecognized, has been downplayed.[64] In a recent article, however, Wyke argues that Elegia and Tragoedia, like the other, apparently more "real," women of elegy (especially Cynthia), are really personifications or embodiments of the poetics and politics of their creators.[65] In the course of her reading, she invokes the allegory of Hercules *in bivio* as a direct and highly influential model for *Am.* 3.1, rightly seeing in both scenes a detailed equivalence between the physical appearance of the personified women and their ethi-

---

ac Vitam, quas contendentes in satura tradit Ennius (*Inst.* 9.2.36; see Ennius *FLP* fr. 16 Court-ney), and a reference in Nonius (479) to a similar contest in an Atellan by Novius.

64. For an overview of the theme, see J. Alpers, "Hercules in bivio" (Diss. Göttingen, 1912); cf. Froleyks, "Der ΑΓΩΝ ΛΟΓΩΝ." Cf. also Reitzenstein, "Das neue Kunstwollen," 228–29 (= *Ovid,* 82), who noted the parallel between the Herculean allegory and the scene in *Am.* 3.1, but who limited his comments to a suggestion that a variation on the theme such as that later found in Lucian's *Somnium* may have been a more immediate model than the Prodicean fable in its original form.

65. M. Wyke, "Reading Female Flesh: *Amores* 3.1," in *History as Text: The Writing of Ancient History,* ed. A. Cameron (London, 1989), 111–43.

cal (and, in Ovid's case, poetic) value.[66] As I have already indicated, however, I differ from Wyke in believing that the influence of the Prodicean allegory is not unmediated: the complex allusiveness of Ovid's style ensures that the Propertian analogues (among others) are as important to this poem as is the philosophical tradition. When we compare the poet's description of his meeting with Elegia and Tragoedia with that of Hercules with Arete and Kakia, a number of similarities, primarily on the structural level, attest to the earlier tale's influence; but the structural parallels simultaneously emphasize those points where the poet diverges from the Prodicean narrative, and they show us what is most distinctive about this poet's silvan encounter.

Both narratives begin with the central character retiring to an isolated place for contemplation; but unlike Prodicus, who describes this setting only briefly, Ovid's poet uses the suspense of an ecphrastic opening to evoke a scene of epiphany. Both narratives then offer elaborate physical descriptions of the two women, and in both cases the one described second speaks first. But in Prodicus, the first speaker is the more seductive of the two, the one who would have Hercules follow an easier course, while in *Am.* 3.1 the first speaker is Tragoedia, the one who summons the poet to strive after a more lofty goal (*maius opus,* 24) than he had previously pursued. And so the debate proceeds in each case, but with a reversal of roles in the *Amores* version, as the seductive Elegia speaks second. This role-reversal serves two narrative functions within *Am.* 3.1. First, we are made to wonder which of the two women, Elegia or Tragoedia, is supposed to be the "right" choice, as Arete so clearly is in Prodicus' tale. Second, we must be struck by the compromise of the conclusion, in which the poet in effect chooses both (3.1.61–70):

desierat; coepi 'per vos utramque rogamus,
    in vacuas aures verba timentis eant.
altera me sceptro decoras altoque cothurno:

---

66. See Wyke, "Reading Female Flesh," 125: "The narrative strategy of positioning the conflict between Elegia and Tragoedia in a direct line of descent from that between Arete and Kakia discloses a structural function of female flesh as signifier of male political practices. For the recollection and comic debasement of the earlier moral allegory assigns the Ovidian narrator the role of a latter-day Roman Hercules deciding not just between writing-styles, but between life-styles, and it is through the shape, comportment and speech of the two female constructs that conflicting moral and political ideologies are articulated and appraised."

iam nunc contracto[67] magnus in ore sonus.
altera das nostro victurum nomen amori: 65
    ergo ades et longis versibus adde breves.
exiguum vati concede, Tragoedia, tempus:
    tu labor aeternus; quod petit illa, breve est.'
mota dedit veniam. teneri properentur Amores,
    dum vacat: a tergo grandius urget opus.   70

[She had stopped; I began, "I beseech both of you: may the words of one who fears you find your ears receptive. One of you equips me with scepter and cothurnus: the sound from my small mouth is now great. The other of you gives to our love a name that will live: be with me, then, and add short verses to long. Tragedy, grant a little time to your poet: you are an eternal project; what she asks for is of short duration." Moved by my words, Tragedy indulged me. Let the tender *Amores* hurry, while there is time; a greater work is coming after and presses on me.]

The poet's ambivalence here marks book 3 as the last in the collection; it also marks the poet's preference for compromise over polemic. After all, as critics are quick to observe, this poem is biographically valuable, because, like 2.18.13–18, it alludes to Ovid's foray into tragedy writing, contemporaneous perhaps with the *Amores*.[68] If we take Ovid's tragic enterprise as factual (and there is no reason not to), then the generic equivocation here leaves us with a *recusatio* that is no *recusatio* at all. In Hercules' case, after all, his choice matters; one option precludes the other. The poet, in contrast, effectively chooses both (here we may recall again the "double" agenda of Propertius 4.1); and thus he reminds us that his amatory narrative is a fiction he controls.

Nonetheless, in the course of book 3, Ovid moves increasingly further away from the amatory narrative of the *Amores*. In poems like 3.9 and 3.10, in which he locates himself in relation to his poetic heritage and demonstrates his ability to revive the form of the Callimachean hymn in Latin dress, respectively, and also in a poem like 3.7, in which his sexual

---

67. Or, less likely, *contacto:* I have printed the text as it appears in Kenney's second edition, as a result of the support for *contracto* provided by the Codex Hamilton 471: see F. Munari, *Il Codice Hamilton 471 di Ovidio,* Note e Discussioni Erudite 9 (Rome, 1965). See also R.F. Thomas, "Ovid's Attempt at Tragedy (*Am.* 3.1.63–64)," *AJP* 99 (1978): 447–50.

68. See Booth, on 2.18.13–14.

impotence as lover is expressed repeatedly in terms of past versus present, we can see Ovid distancing himself from his intimate involvement with the woman he has created for himself to love. The close of book 3 is appropriately brief: in only twenty lines, the poet bids farewell to his amatory narrative, indicates his intention to move on to tragedy, and looks to his future immortality, his place in the Roman tradition secured by the *Amores*. It is worth observing how elegantly, almost effortlessly, Ovid's poet is able, in the course of the short elegy 3.15, to look both back to his accomplishment in the *Amores* and forward to the continuation of his career in an *area maior* (18). The enterprise undertaken in *Am.* 1.1, to make himself into a lover and create a lover's narrative, has been completed; the poet thus no longer speaks as a lover, and instead completes the framing narrative, bringing to a successful conclusion his own poetic education.

I suggested earlier in this chapter that in 3.9, on the death of Tibullus, the poet uses the image of a literary genealogy to cast himself in the role of heir to a rich Roman poetic tradition. In the central lines of 3.15, he is more explicit in forecasting a place for himself in the literary tradition (7–14):

> Mantua Vergilio gaudet, Verona Catullo;
>   Paelignae dicar gloria gentis ero,
> quam sua libertas ad honesta coegerat arma,
>   cum timuit socias anxia Roma manus.   10
> atque aliquis spectans hospes Sulmonis aquosi
>   moenia, quae campi iugera pauca tenent,
> 'quae tantum' dicet 'potuistis ferre poetam,
>   quantulacumque estis, vos ego magna voco.'

[Mantua rejoices in Virgil, Verona in Catullus; I shall be called the glory of the Paelignian people, whom the cause of freedom compelled to take up honorable arms when Rome was in anxious fear of the forces of her *socii*. And some visitor will look on water-rich Sulmona's city walls, containing but a few acres of open country, and will say, "You who were able to bear so great a poet, however small you are, I call you great."]

For Ovid's poet, the rewards of originality have been won not simply among amatory elegists—although we have already seen that the poetic Elysium of 3.9 is an appropriately appealing prospect. Rather, he envisions himself as worthy to be ranked with Virgil and Catullus, poets whose universal appeal transcends the limited range of both genre and geography. We have already considered how the poet's Paelignian homeland has been transformed by the topography of literary tradition;[69] with the conclusion of the *Amores,* we are reminded how fertile this tradition's ground has been for narrative innovation.

And narrative innovation too receives a final nod, in the imagined words of *aliquis hospes* (11), like those of the *libelli* in the prefatory epigram. The words this anonymous visitor is to speak sound like an "oral epitaph":[70]

> 'quae tantum' dicet 'potuistis ferre poetam,
>   quantulacumque estis, vos ego magna voco.'

This epitaph helps us as well to go beyond the framing narrative and to look at Ovid's accomplishment in the *Amores* from the outside. Begun in dissonance and suspense, both narratives are now successfully concluded.

---

69. See my discussion of 2.16 earlier, in chap. 2.

70. This term is from I.J.F. deJong, "The Voice of Anonymity: *tis*-Speeches in the *Iliad,*" *Eranos* 85 (1987): 77, who also quotes the Homeric bT-scholion's comment on *Il.* 6.460–61: ἐπιγραμματικὸν ἔχει τύπον ὁ στίχος. Cf. R. Scodel, "Inscription, Absence, and Memory: Epic and Early Epitaph," *SIFC* 10 (1992): 57–76.

Chapter 6

Legisse Voluptas: Some Thoughts on the Future of Ovid's *Amores*

ars adeo latet arte sua
Ovid *Met.* 10.252

I began this book by asking how it has happened that Ovid's *Amores* have become increasingly isolated from the literary past with which these poems are in fact intimately connected. In subsequent chapters, I have attempted to open up the interpretative range of Ovid's readership, both present and past, by showing the extent to which Ovid's writing techniques automatically implicate him in the Augustan literary tradition, a tradition that almost by definition transcends generic boundaries. And in chapters 4 and 5, I have demonstrated how the double narrative of the *Amores* complements Ovid's technical achievement by making the dilemma of the would-be Augustan poet the "real" story of the *Amores,* a story that transcends the boundaries of conventional elegiac subject matter, much as Ovid's style so effortlessly transcends that conventionally found in elegy.

But what of the poetry that follows? The success of this collection demands a sequel, which we have in the other poems that Ovid wrote after the *Amores,* particularly those that date to the time before his exile. I want to conclude by looking briefly at how the *Amores* foreshadow Ovid's future and are all of a piece with the successful career that culminates in the *Metamorphoses.* In the introduction, I indicated my desire to locate the *Amores* in relation to their past; now I want to suggest how we might at least begin to see them as providing the program, as it were, for much of Ovid's subsequent poetic productivity. We shall look at several familiar scenes from Ovid's later poetry, that are already known to have a connection to scenes or episodes in the *Amores.* In looking at these later episodes and their prototypes, we can now also appreciate how the contrasts between the two result as much from the distinctive accomplishment of the *Amores* as they do from the acknowledged success of Ovid's later works.

Amores 3.2 has the form of a virtual monologue, in which Ovid's *amator* recalls a day spent at the Circus Maximus with a *puella* (perhaps not Corinna).[1] He was brought there not by his love of horses but by his love of her; and he proceeds to catalogue the ways in which his desire for her parallels her desire for the victories of her favorites in the races, as well as how his proximity to her causes him to desire even greater intimacy. The monologue moves seamlessly back and forth between what the *amator* must have said and the things he only thought, and so it evokes a minute-by-minute cataloguing of details that neatly parallels the excitement of a race. Only in the last couplet do we learn that this poem is reminiscence rather than reportage; the *puella* cuts off his monologue with a combination of reproach and promise (83–84):

> risit et argutis quiddam promisit ocellis:
>   'hoc satis est, alio cetera redde loco.'

> [She laughed, and with her sparkling eyes she promised a certain something: "This is enough; leave the rest for elsewhere."]

Much the same scene is transformed by Ovid the *praeceptor amoris* into a bit of shrewd advice in *AA* 1.135–62; here, of course, he addresses an audience of would-be playboys, and he uses the tight seating at the Circus as a convenient excuse for suggesting advances that in any other setting would be inappropriate (and to a great extent impossible). The similarities between the two passages are self-evident and have been catalogued by commentators;[2] and although the *Amores* scene is much longer than the *Ars* passage, the parallel structure of the two suggests that each is a sort of

---

1. See *novae . . . dominae,* 57. That the poem takes the form of a sort of dramatic monologue, however, may indicate that the speaker is looking back to some indeterminate past time when his affair with Corinna was just beginning. This possibility is suggested as well by the closing couplet's description of the *puella* as having *argutis . . . ocellis:* the next poem, 3.3, opens with the lover's bitter description of his *puella*'s unchanged beauty in the face of her newly discovered betrayal and concludes this description with mention of her eyes: *argutos habuit: radiant ut sidus* **ocelli,** / *per quos mentita est perfida saepe mihi* (9–10; on this passage, see also my discussion in chap. 1). These two instances are the only occasions on which the word *ocelli* is modified by the epithet *arguti* in the entire corpus of Ovid's works.

2. See Hollis, *Ars Amatoria I,* ad loc.; E. Thomas, "Ovid at the Races," in *Hommages à Marcel Renard,* ed. J. Bibauw, Collection Latomus 101 (Brussels, 1969), 1:710–24.

mirror image of the other. Indeed, when read side by side they are reminiscent of the about-face Ovid does in sets of paired poems in the *Amores:* *Am.* 2.7 and 2.8 are particularly good examples of how Ovid can play on both sides almost simultaneously.[3]

In his commentary on the *Ars* passage, however, Hollis expresses a decided preference for the *Amores* version of the scene: he calls the *Ars* version "a pallid reworking of the brilliant and delightful" scene in the earlier poem, adding that "in recasting the monologue as advice to another [Ovid] dissipates nearly all the wit."[4] Hollis' criticism is worth noting, I think, because inadvertently he has recognized that, as a participant in the internal narrative of the *Amores,* the *amator* can be an engaging character, of a sort that all but disappears in the *Ars.* The *praeceptor amoris* who dominates the *Ars* is by comparison a shallow and cynical character—but the more shallow and cynical he is, the less ironic, at least consciously so, is his advice.[5] Rather, it is as *poeta* of the *Amores* that Ovid can introduce irony into the scene at the Circus, by giving a personality as well to the lover who speaks in this poem.[6] I have already talked about poems, such as *Am.* 1.5, in which the voice of Ovid the poet gradually drowns out that of Ovid the lover;[7] *Am.* 3.2 offers us what is by comparison an almost uninterrupted audience with the lover, in this case aided and abetted by his poetic alter ego. When the *Amores* scene is viewed from this perspective, that in the *Ars* necessarily pales by comparison; and Ovid must surely have anticipated that his readers would have this double vision and so would all the better understand the relationship between the two passages.

Let us look at the really distinctive features of *Am.* 3.2 and at how the two versions of the Circus scene differ from each other. In the *Amores* version, the *amator* devotes the first half of the poem to setting the scene, explaining why he has come (not out of any interest in the races themselves, but because of her presence there, according to 1–6), and cataloguing obsessively the ways in which he, and he alone, can and should establish intimate contact with her as they watch the races. The seating

---

3. See chap. 5 n. 45.

4. Hollis, *Ars Amatoria I,* 58. He continues (59): "Happily, few other episodes are transferred from the *Amores* in so mechanical and lifeless a manner."

5. See my discussion of irony earlier, in chap. 4, as well as the essay by Conte, "Love without Elegy."

6. For a good overview of Ovid's use of irony in this poem, see J.T. Davis, "Dramatic and Comic Devices in Amores 3.2," *Hermes* 107 (1979): 51–69. Davis does not, however, distinguish the role of poet from that of lover in his discussion of irony.

7. See chap. 4.

arrangement in the Circus compels the spectators to sit close together (*cogit nos linea iungi,* 19); yet the *amator* wants neither the spectator on her other side nor the one behind her to touch her, even if only accidentally (21–24). Again, the *amator* does not want her *pallium* to be dirtied by trailing on the ground; rather, he will help her hold it up—and so gain a better view of her bare legs (25–28). In the *Ars,* the *praeceptor amoris* advises virtually the identical moves on the part of the would-be lover (1.153–58); but because of his perspective, the advice is businesslike and brief. There is nothing in the *Ars* passage, for example, like the apostrophe to the *puella's vestis* with which the lover interrupts his own catalogue and introduces his desire to uncover her legs: *invida vestis eras, quae tam bona crura tegebas; / quoque magis spectes—invida vestis eras* (27–28).

This apostrophe leads in turn to even greater flights of fancy, expressed through similes that are both evocative of Alexandrian influence and sexually suggestive (29–32):[8]

> talia Milanion Atalantes crura fugacis
>   optavit manibus sustinuisse suis;   30
> talia pinguntur succinctae crura Dianae,
>   cum sequitur fortes fortior ipsa feras.

[Such are the legs of swift Atalanta that Milanion hoped to lift with his hands; such are the legs of Diana when she is depicted with her skirt tucked up, bolder by far than the bold wild animals she pursues.]

Indeed, these similes are so much like exempla of the sort frequently used by the *praeceptor amoris* in the *Ars* that it is difficult to determine in this case whether these couplets are to be classified as similes or exempla; we can see quite clearly here how such passages are best served not by classification but by being located along the continuum of analogy I described in chapter 3. More important for our purposes here, however, is

---

8. On the Alexandrian pedigree of the Milanion exemplum, see Rosen and Farrell, "Acontius, Milanion, and Gallus"; for its sexual reading here, see Watson, "Mythological Exempla," 122 n. 27, 125–26; cf. Suet. *Tib.* 44.2. On the Alexandrian pedigree of Ovid's description of Diana, see Call. *h.*3.11–12; see also Virgil's description of Venus' appearance at *Aen.* 1.315–20, when she reveals herself to Aeneas disguised as a bare-legged huntress: *virginis os habitumque gerens et virginis arma / Spartanae, vel qualis equos Threissa fatigat / Harpalyce volucremque fuga praevertitur Hebrum. / . . . / nuda genu nodoque sinus collecta fluentis.* Aeneas responds to this apparition with amazement, recognizing that she must be divine and asking if she is in fact Diana (*an Phoebi soror?*, 329).

that in his advice regarding how best to get a look at the legs of one's chosen *puella,* the *praeceptor amoris* of the *Ars* does *not* launch into such comparisons. Ovid has given these images to the *amator,* rather than to the *praeceptor amoris.* He does so because his aim is not simply to instruct others on how to do this but to allow the *amator*—and the readers of *Am.* 3.2—to visualize the attractions of the *puella* who has inflamed his love. Watson argues that the sexually suggestive description of Milanion's lifting of Atalanta's legs reflects a scene that must have been well known in wall paintings;[9] thus, the visual function of these images is obvious. Likewise, the view of Diana's legs imagined here is expressed in emphatically visual terms, with *pinguntur* taking the place of a typical "Alexandrian footnote" like, for example, *dicuntur.*[10]

At the same time, in allowing these comparisons to be suggested by the *amator,* Ovid emphasizes the lesson long ago learned by the readers of these poems: as part of the embedded narrative of the *Amores,* the lover is a creation of the poet, a poet who, by book 3, is well on his way to becoming the *praeceptor amoris* of the *Ars.* This poet also has the ability to see beyond the *amor* of the lover and to focus, at least momentarily, on the explicit details of the lover's desire: again, there is an irony here as a result, which is conspicuously absent from the Circus scene in the *Ars.* This irony extends as well to the fact that both Atalanta and Diana happen to be not only heroines with lovely legs but racers; and this aspect of their characters is emphasized in the brief couplet devoted to each: *Atalantes . . . fugacis* (29); [*Diana*] *sequitur fortes fortior ipsa feras* (32). Will the lover win his beloved, as did Milanion? Or will he find instead that the *puella* he desires is as indefatigable as Diana? The poet invites us to choose.

In fact, these two couplets are not the first instances of mythological paradigms in *Am.* 3.2; Ovid had earlier used the story of Pelops' race to win Hippodamia to illuminate a number of aspects of the lover's situation (13–18):

> si mihi currenti fueris conspecta, morabor,
>
> > deque meis manibus lora remissa fluent.
>
> a, quam paene Pelops Pisaea concidit hasta,   15

---

9. Watson, "Mythological Exempla," 122 n. 27; cf. Ovid's use of the same image in a far more explicit catalogue of exempla at the close of *AA* 3, in a description of the various positions for sexual intercourse and how each is best suited to a particular female body type: *Milanion umeris Atalantes crura ferebat: / si bona sunt, hoc sunt accipienda modo* (3.775–76).

10. See Ross, *Backgrounds to Augustan Poetry,* 78; cf. my chap. 2 n. 53.

> dum spectat vultus, Hippodamia, tuos!
> nempe favore suae vicit tamen ille puellae:
>   vincamus dominae quisque favore suae.

[If you come into view while I am running, I shall slow down, and the reins will drop from my hands and slip down. Ah, how close Pelops came to falling when a spear was cast at him at Pisa, as he looked at your face, Hippodamia! Of course, he won nevertheless thanks to the goodwill of his girl: let us each win thanks to the goodwill of our own mistress.]

This exemplum works on a number of levels at once. First, its relevance to the setting of 3. 2 is clear—both involve races, as do the images of Atalanta and Diana. The next step in the creation of an analogy, however, is more complex: the lover identifies himself with Pelops, just as he has already imagined himself in the place of the *agitator equorum* (7), a man blessed because he has won the *puella*'s *favor*.[11] Parallel to this self-identification with a hero is the identification of the *puella* with Hippodamia, an identification suggested by the apostrophe to the heroine: she is addressed in the second person just as the *puella* herself has been since the opening of the poem. Having established these parallels, the *amator* proceeds to add another wrinkle to the comparison: just as he might drop the reins in midrace if he were to look up and see his beloved, so was Pelops almost caught off guard and felled by his foe. Thus, the respective victories of Pelops and our *amator* are the result not so much of their excellence as of the *favor* of the women they love. This exemplum is thus both clever and convoluted: its rhetorical logic reminds us that a poet controls this material, while its unusual interpretation of Pelops' victory in the race as a near miss evokes the emotional upheaval of an *amator* dangerously blinded by his own desire. Both dimensions are strikingly absent from the advice we find in the *Ars* scene.

At the midpoint of *Am.* 3.2, the *amator* describes the arrival of the grand procession of divinities that inaugurates the events in the Circus (43–58). In the *Ars,* the *praeceptor amoris* captures the entire parade in one quick couplet: *at cum pompa frequens caelestibus ibit eburnis, / tu Veneri dominae plaude favente manu* (1.147–48). Only one divinity, Venus, is mentioned by name; and the reason for this reference is so obvious that it

---

11. Davis, "Dramatic and Comic Devices," 57–58, summarizes earlier versions of this observation.

requires no further discussion. In the *Amores* scene, in contrast, the solemnity and pomp of the event receive detailed attention: *sed iam pompa venit: linguis animisque favete; / tempus adest plausus: aurea pompa venit* (43–44). A catalogue of divinities then follows: beginning with Victoria, the *amator* describes a procession including Neptune, Mars, Apollo, Diana, Minerva, Ceres, Bacchus, Castor, and Pollux, culminating in Venus. His poetic alter ego organizes this parade as a sort of *recusatio,* indicating with the mention of each god the group or type to whom each divinity is most appealing. Thus, the appearance of Venus at the end of the parade functions on two levels: it reflects the *poeta*'s choice of love and love elegy as his theme, in preference to other types of poetry and poetic themes; and it complements the mounting combination of desire and anticipation that the *amator* feels.[12]

In fact, even Venus is trumped, by the power of the *puella* herself to grant her lover victory or defeat as she chooses (55–62):

> nos tibi, blanda Venus, puerisque potentibus arcu   55
>   plaudimus: inceptis annue, diva, meis
> daque novae mentem dominae, patiatur amari;
>   annuit et motu signa secunda dedit.
> quod dea promisit, promittas ipsa, rogamus:
>   pace loquar Veneris, tu dea maior eris.   60
> per tibi tot iuro testes pompamque deorum
>   te dominam nobis tempus in omne peti.

[We applaud you, fair Venus, and the children who excel at the bow; goddess, show favor to my undertaking, and give my new mistress the idea that she should allow herself to be loved.

She nodded, and with the movement gave favorable signs. What the goddess has promised, I ask that you promise yourself; *pace* Venus, let me say that you will be a greater goddess. I swear to you by many witnesses and by this procession of the gods that you are sought as my mistress for all time.]

In thus personalizing the divine procession, the poet-lover of the *Amores* moves far from the course prescribed by the *praeceptor amoris* in the *Ars:*

---

12. On the sequence of the parade as known from other sources, cf. Suet. *Div. Iul.* 76; Cic. *ad Att.* 13.44.1; Tert. *Spect.* 7. Cf. also J.F. Miller, "Ovidius imitator sui: Fasti 4.179ff. and Amores 3.2.43ff.," *RhM* 132 (1989): 403–5.

where the latter's advice is fundamentally generic, the former's revision of the divine parade into the wishful triumph of love complements the vividness of this poem's narrative as a very private reading of a public event.

One other important feature separates this elegy from its didactic counterpart: the *amator* speaks of himself as a person in the grips of desire. His desire to let the *puella* know of his love is what has brought him to the Circus in the first place (4); and even as he thinks of offering her his *tabella* for use as a makeshift fan (37–38), he wonders whether the warmth he feels is the heat of the day or rather the burning he feels within, as his passion for her blazes in his heart (*an magis hic meus est animi, non aeris, aestus, / captaque femineus pectora torret amor?*, 39–40). He does not control this condition: rather, she, his *domina,* will decide his fate. From the opening of the poem, he has identified himself with the racer whom she favors; once the race actually begins, he conflates love and racing to such an extent that, when her favorite begins to go afoul, he exclaims with words that are virtually synonymous with the lover's lament, *me miserum*! (69). The *praeceptor amoris* of the *Ars,* by contrast, naturally has no business with any of this; the race, the racers, and even the Circus virtually disappear from his catalogue of tips once he has used them as a pretext for setting the scene.

The difference that Hollis observes between the two passages is, then, real: the intricate relationships, ironic humor, and emotive power of *Am.* 3.2 are replaced by the generic depersonalization of the scene in the *Ars.* Unlike Hollis, however, I am not inclined to attribute this difference to a presumed failure on the part of the poet of the *Ars* to replicate the same delightful effect he had achieved with this scenario in the *Amores.* Rather, I think it quite likely that this difference is just as Ovid intended it to be— indeed, that he wanted his reader to compare the two passages and learn something about each from the comparison.[13] For our purposes, the lesson is clear: the content of a given poem is only part of its meaning; much more telling are the ways in which this content is expressed and organized and the relationship of the narrator to his subject matter. The comparison of Ovid's two Circus scenes captures *ex parvo* both the differences between the two works in which they appear and the success of Ovid in both.

The worlds of the *Amores* and of the *Ars* are close to each other—it is

---

13. The possibility that the two were intended to be read side by side may well be complemented by the possibility that Ovid wrote them in close proximity to each other, although no one theory concerning the relative dating of the two editions of both the *Amores* and the *Ars* is more compelling than any other: see, e.g., Syme, *History in Ovid,* 13–15, 18–20; Hollis, *Ars Amatoria I,* xii–xiii; Murgia, "The Date of Ovid's *Ars Amatoria* 3," 82–86; idem, "Influence of Ovid's *Remedia amoris,*" 210.

the perspective from which they are viewed and interpreted that makes all the difference. A comparison of scenes in the *Amores* and *Fasti,* however, does not allow us to proceed from the same opening premise. After all, the *Amores* have as their ostensible subject love and the world of love poetry. The *Fasti,* in contrast, while elegiac, have left the world of love elegy far behind; the subject matter now is nothing less than the national religious tradition. This subject matter and the opportunities it provides to Ovid to adapt Callimachean aetiological elegy to Roman themes have been long noted and have particularly in recent years excited renewed interest in the *Fasti.*[14]

Yet the subject matter of *Fasti* and *Amores,* respectively, is not as mutually exclusive as we might at first expect it to be. We have just considered one instance of parallel episodes in which variation in expression, organization of material, and narrative point of view make a great difference to interpretation; I now want to turn to an instance of two episodes that should perhaps be called complementary rather than parallel, for they complete each other—each tells a different part of the same story, so to speak, and in so doing, illustrates Ovid's evident desire never to step into the same narrative stream twice. The two episodes to which I refer are the story of Ilia as reported in *Am.* 3.6 and that of Rhea Silvia as told at the opening of *Fasti* 3. It should be noted at the outset that even in his use of the two variant names traditionally given for the mother of Romulus and Remus, Ovid indicates his interest in the possibilities of difference—in the variant versions available for the narrative treatment of what is essentially the "same" myth.

Let us begin with the *Amores* version and with the frame into which Ovid's Ilia narrative is imbedded. The setting is an address to a river in spring flood. Its swell has overflowed the banks, and it prevents the lover, in a hurry though he is, from getting to his *puella's* side. The lover combines reproach, threat, and plea in a desperate attempt to get the river to subside; he even wishes that he might be Perseus or Triptolemus,[15] so that he could simply fly over the stream and thus achieve his heroic destiny (13–16).

---

14. For a sample of this activity, particularly fervid since the appearance of Hinds' *Metamorphosis of Persephone,* see my introduction n. 6.

15. The oblique reference to Triptolemus as missionary for Demeter suggests a source other than the *Homeric Hymn to Demeter:* see Richardson, *Homeric Hymn to Demeter,* on *h. Cer.* 153. Cf. also *Fasti* 4.550, where Ovid gives the name Triptolemus to the infant prince entrusted to Ceres for nursing: the latter version shows Ovid's close reading of the Homeric hymn, although Ovid has changed the baby's name to that which apparently became traditional sometime after the Homeric hymn was composed. Cf. Hinds, *Metamorphosis of Persephone,* 67.

It has recently been noted by several scholars that, in wishing for a small trickle of water rather than for a loud-rushing river, the lover here takes on the character of Callimachus' Apollo, who at the close of the hymn dedicated to him announces his preference for the water that trickles from a pure spring over that which the great Euphrates, full but filthy, carries in its wake (*h.* 2.108–12).[16] Yet this is not the only aspect of the poem's opening that might be called programmatic—that might, indeed, be attributed to the voice of Ovid the poet, rather than that of Ovid the lover. In fact, immediately after wishing for the flying abilities of a Greek hero, Ovid comments that such stories are after all just poets' lies (17–18):

> prodigiosa loquor, veterum mendacia vatum:
> nec tulit haec umquam nec feret ulla dies.

> [I tell of marvelous things, the lies of old poets; no day has ever seen these events or ever will.]

He thus rejects the sort of epic encounter that would allow him to transcend this watery obstacle, and he instead encourages the stream to adapt itself to his elegiac needs (19–22):

> tu potius, ripis effuse capacibus amnis,
> (sic aeternus eas) labere fine tuo.   20
> non eris invidiae, torrens, mihi crede, ferendae,
> si dicar per te forte retentus amans.

> [Instead, oh river, spilling over your generous banks, stay within your borders—so may you flow forever. Flood, believe me, you will not be able to endure my hatred, if I am said to have been a lover perchance kept back by you.]

In asking the river both to stay within its bounds and not to stand in the way of the *amator* and his poetic subject matter, Ovid continues to touch on motifs well known from the coda of Callimachus' hymn to Apollo. The

---

16. See my earlier discussion, in chap. 3, of Ovid's use of this important programmatic passage in *Am.* 1.7 also. For recent discussions of the equation between Ovid's flooding-river problem and the pronouncements of Callimachus' Apollo, see Suter, "Image to Narrative," 17–20; A. Barchiesi, "Voci e istanze narrative nelle Metamorfosi di Ovidio," *MD* 23 (1989): 57–64; C. Connors, "Ennius, Ovid, and Representations of Ilia," *MD* 32 (1994): 108–9.

reward Ovid extends to the river for going along with the poet's request can be read in literary terms, too: his parenthetical *sic aeternus eas* not only plays ironically on the seasonal nature of the stream's flooding but also recalls the claim to poetic immortality so common in programmatic verse (e.g., Catullus 1 and Ovid's own *Am.* 1.15).

The next stage in the poet-lover's attempt to make the swollen river subside entails the argument that rivers should, after all, be *praeceptores amoris,* for they know what love is (23–24). The universality of this knowledge on the part of rivers is illustrated by a catalogue of nine rivers and the mortal women they loved: Inachus and Melie, Xanthus and Neaera, Alpheus and Arethusa, Peneus and Creusa, Asopus and Thebe, Achelous and Deianeira, Nilus and Euanthe, Enipeus and Tyro, and Anio and Ilia. The catalogue is learned and obscurantist. As Courtney indicates, several of Ovid's versions of myths alluded to here are known from no other source; there are suggestions as well that Ovid has in some cases fused into one character or myth two previously distinct figures.[17] A likely source for such material is Callimachus' prose work on rivers, περὶ τῶν ἐν τῇ οἰκ- ουμένῃ ποταμῶν (frr. 457–59 Pf.).[18] Courtney also thinks it likely that Ovid has looked to the catalogue of localities that refused to receive Leto in Callimachus' hymn to Delos as a model for his own catalogue of rivers.[19] Thus, the poet follows his exhortation to the river to behave in an appropriately Callimachean manner with a demonstration of what such behavior would entail, expressed in a Callimachean format: Callimachean rivers, both programmatic and thematic types now merged into one, should make love, not floods.

Of course, Ovid's poet simultaneously outdoes Callimachus by concluding his list with a river and myth drawn from Roman territory and Latin lore: there could be nothing more Roman than a story concerning the mother of Romulus and Remus. Or could there be? The story of Ilia told here by Ovid recalls details of the Homeric story of Tyro's seduction by Poseidon: after having wandered along a river (Enipeus, whom she loved) and while resting beside it, Tyro is raped by Poseidon, who later tells her that she is to mother twins, future rulers (*Od.* 11.235–59).[20] Indeed, in

---

17. Courtney, "Some Literary Jokes," 20–22.

18. Courtney, "Some Literary Jokes," 22; Connors, "Ennius, Ovid, and Representations of Ilia," 109 n. 27.

19. Courtney, "Some Literary Jokes," 20–21.

20. See Skutsch, 194; Connors, "Ennius, Ovid, and Representations of Ilia," 102–4. Sophocles' *Tyro* may well have played an influential role in Roman reception of the tale, but our fragments are too little to help us fix the details: see frr. 648–69 Pearson. For the struc-

a clear attempt to demonstrate his awareness of the close relationship between the two stories, Ovid places his reference to the love of Tyro and Enipeus immediately before he launches into the tale of Ilia and Anio: the former tale serves as a sort of Alexandrian "footnote," as Connors suggests.[21] Ovid is not the first poet to make the connection between Tyro and Ilia, however: Ennius had it available to him and used it to shape his description of Ilia's dream.[22] Thus, the story of Anio and Ilia as Ovid tells it is the perfect sort of material for a poet who has already begun in the *Amores* to style himself an heir to a long literary tradition and who will in the *Fasti* make himself into the consummate *Romanus Callimachus*.

Let us consider more closely several details in the Ilia narrative of *Am.* 3.6 before we turn to the *Fasti*. We know from a comment in Porphyrio on Horace *Odes* 1.2.18 that Ennius told the story of Ilia's marriage to Anio subsequent to her rape by Mars and mothering of the twins: *Ilia auctore Ennio in amnem Tiberim iussu Amulii regis Albanorum praecipitata Antemnis* [Bücheler; *antea enim* codd.] *Anieni matrimonio iuncta est.*[23] Porphyrio makes this observation because the version of the story found in Ennius (and Ovid) differs from that found in Horace, who has Ilia marry Tiber. Thus, we know that in *Am.* 3.6, Ovid is following Ennius; and the alternative found in Horace tells us that Ovid had alternatives to choose from. Yet if we work from the assumption that Ovid is following Ennius closely here—and already we see that there is good reason to do so—we still must wonder at the aspects of Ennius' Ilia narrative that Ovid chooses to emphasize; likewise, we should observe what Ovid suppresses in his version.

First of all, there is the reason for Ilia's distress when we first hear her described (49–50):

---

tural similarities underlying these and other such tales, see also J. Bremmer, "Romulus, Remus, and the Foundation of Rome," in *Roman Myth and Mythography,* by J. Bremmer and N.M. Horsfall, BICS Suppl. 52 (London, 1987), 27–30.

21. Connors, "Ennius, Ovid, and Representations of Ilia," 103. Of course, even as he alludes to the tradition, Ovid replaces Poseidon with Enipeus; he is motivated at least in part by the requirements of his own theme, but this variation also allows him to vary the tradition. Cf. also Connors' observation that the description of the water's receding (*Am.* 3.6.43–44), while applied to Enipeus, most aptly describes what Poseidon did, according to Hom. *Od.* 11.243–44.

22. On the sources for the Tyro/Ilia connection, including Homer, Sophocles, Diocles of Peparethus (*PW* 47), and Fabius Pictor, see Skutsch, 194; Connors, "Ennius, Ovid, and Representations of Ilia," 101–6.

23. See Skutsch, on *Ann.* 1 fr. xxxix, and his quotation of Serv., on *Aen.* 1.273. Antemnae lies at the confluence of Anio and Tiber. See also Courtney, "Some Literary Jokes," 20.

illa gemens patruique nefas delictaque Martis
    errabat nudo per loca sola pede.

[Lamenting her uncle's crime and Mars' offense, she wandered barefoot
through abandoned regions.]

Ovid thus limits to one couplet a summary of all those aspects of her story
that we might expect to be of central importance in epic, history, or
tragedy, that is, her rape by Mars, the birth of the twins, their exposure by
Amulius, and her condemnation to drowning. Mars himself never appears
in the poem; the twins are never named, and their subsequent history is
never hinted at.[24] Instead, Ovid focuses all his attention on the postrape,
postpartum Ilia. In Livy's account of Romulus and Remus, Ilia simply and
literally disappears from the narrative after giving birth; the last we hear of
her is Livy's ominous report, *sacerdos vincta in custodiam datur* (*ab urbe
condita* 1.3.11–4.3). That Ovid's Ilia does have a past is evident from the
references both Anio and she make to her career as a vestal virgin: Anio
asks why she no longer wears the fillet in her hair that would symbolize her
vestal priesthood ('*quo cultus abiere tui? quid sola vagaris, / vitta nec evinc-
tas impedit alba comas?*,' 55–56); and she responds with rhetorical despair,
asking why she has thus been disgraced by her loss of credentials for the
priesthood ('*cur, modo Vestalis, taedas invitor ad ullas / turpis et Iliacis
infitianda focis?*,' 75–76). Since it seems likely that Ennius made Ilia a
vestal,[25] both characters may be seen to nod again to this source even as
Ovid refrains from narrating anything but the denouement of Ilia's
tragedy. His selection of events here, in fact, recalls a distinctive characteristic of much Hellenistic poetry, in which the expected narrative of a character's canonical heroic deeds is supplanted by a "nonevent" in the same
character's career, like, for example, Theseus' detour to the hut of
Hecale.[26] (I also suggest that we think of Ilia as someone much like the

---

24. Connors, "Ennius, Ovid, and Representations of Ilia," 111–12, notes that reference to
the twins is far more explicit in *Am.* 3.4, the poem that would immediately have preceded 3.6
in the second edition of the *Amores* before the intrusion of the spurious 3.5 into the manuscripts (on which, see Kenney, "On the *Somnium*"). The relevant verses are *rusticus est nimium, quem laedit adultera coniunx, / et notos mores non satis Urbis habet, / in qua Martigenae
non sunt sine crimine nati / Romulus Iliades Iliadesque Remus* (37–40). The difference in perspective between this indictment of Ilia and the sympathetic narrative of 3.6 is striking.

25. See Skutsch, 196.

26. See Hollis, *Hecale*, 5–10.

speakers of Ovid's *Heroides,* whom we encounter only after the "big" event that has changed their lives forever.)[27]

Again, let us consider the promise Anio makes to Ilia at the close of his speech, that is, that she will receive great gifts from him in return for becoming his bride (65–66): *'ne me sperne, precor, tantum, Troiana propago; / munera promissis uberiora feres.'* Ostensibly, Anio refers here to the honor that awaits her as queen among nymphs; yet his words look back as well to what Aeneas, father of Ennius' Ilia, says to her in her dream: *'o gnata, tibi sunt ante gerendae / aerumnae, post ex fluvio fortuna resistet'* (*Ann.* 1.xxix.44–45). Aeneas' "puzzling reference to the river" and "uncommon use of the word" *resistet* in his last clause[28] must be taken, despite their oracular opacity, as references to the fact that, although Ilia will drown, nevertheless her sons, and thus Rome, will rise anew, that is, be saved, from the river. When Ovid's Anio promises gifts to a pliant Ilia, we have *fortuna* of a very different order from what Aeneas intended when he alluded to something "arising from a river." It comes as no surprise, then, that Anio is successful in his suit (although here Ovid contrives a new doublet in the narrative tradition, for what Anio considers marriage, Ilia, Lucretia-like, clearly decides to treat as suicide: see 79–82).[29]

The Ilia story ends abruptly with her suicide-marriage, and the *poeta-amator* addresses the swollen river before him again. Apparently, the Alexandrian virtuosity displayed by his catalogue-poem on rivers has been to no avail—it has simply given the river time to grow even more swollen (85–86). After all, even before delivering this narrative, the *poeta-amator* had told us and the river that such stories are just poets' lies (*veterum mendacia vatum,* 17).[30] The poem concludes with a passage in which the poet-lover combines invective directed at the river with reproaches against himself for foolishly thinking that a narrative of rivers' loves (*fluminum amores,* 101) would help. As Barchiesi has suggested, the speaker of this poem has unthinkingly outwitted himself, for though his style has been, like that of the Alexandrian poets, arcane and learned, his theme has come from Ennian epic.[31] His request to the river to abate has not, therefore, been put in

---

27. See Barchiesi, "Future Reflexive."

28. The commentary is cited from Skutsch, 200.

29. The comparison of Ilia to Lucretia is made by Connors, "Ennius, Ovid, and Representations of Ilia," 110.

30. See Rosati, *Narciso e Pigmalione,* 87–93.

31. Barchiesi, "Voci e istanze narrative," 63, writes, "L'episodio . . . è in effetti un ospite inatteso in una poesia degli *Amores.*" My conclusions differ somewhat from Barchiesi's, however, since the equation he suggests between "Ennian" and "anti-Callimachean" subject mat-

unequivocally Callimachean terms; and so the river has chosen to take the epic course instead and easily overwhelms the concerns of the would-be elegiac lover. The placement of this poem in the third book of the *Amores* comes as no surprise—it is an apt harbinger of the *poeta*'s impending decision to put an end to his narrative about the *amator* and his *puella*.[32]

In *Fasti* 3, Ovid returns to the story of Ilia (9–48). It takes opening position in the stories of book 3 because this month is, of course, the month of Mars, whose importance as father of the founder of Rome is paramount in a poem on Roman holidays; and it leads naturally, and without any formal transition, into the story of the twins' salvation, their adolescence, and the eventual building of Romulus' wall. We can see immediately, therefore, that Ovid intends to do something quite different here from his treatment of Ilia and Anio among *fluminum amores* in *Am.* 3.6. Here we have what we might call the canonical narrative—the one that is the focus of, for example, Livy's history of the period and that Ovid had so clearly elided in *Am.* 3.6. As if to emphasize this change of emphasis, Ovid here calls his heroine not Ilia but Silvia (3.11 and 45). But it is also evident that he is still looking to Ennius' treatment of the story, just as he did in the earlier poem. Although the content of the two dreams is different, Silvia's prophetic dream is clearly modeled structurally on that of Ennius' Ilia; and like Ennius, Ovid gives direct speech to Silvia to describe this dream.[33]

Indeed, it is worthwhile to note in some detail how neatly the Silvia narrative of *Fasti* 3 dovetails with that of Ilia in *Am.* 3.6. Virtually nothing from one version is repeated in the other, not even the main character's variant names; rather, the two narratives "complete" each other, each providing details missing from the other. In the *Fasti,* the focus is on the circumstances of the rape (11–22) and on Silvia's resulting pregnancy and maternity (*somnus abit, iacet ipsa gravis: iam scilicet intra / viscera Romanae conditor urbis erat,* 23–24; *Silvia fit mater,* 45; *pariente ministra,* 47). Her dream has been adapted by Ovid, as Krevans shows, to the type of a classic pregnancy dream announcing the birth of kings.[34] Ovid carries

---

ter here is problematic. The story of Ilia and Anio is apparently just as Ennian as is her earlier history, yet it receives "Callimachean" treatment from Ovid. The river reacts so vehemently to the combination of the two. For *fluminum amores* as a type of Hellenistic catalogue poetry, see Courtney, "Some Literary Jokes," 23.

32. See Keith, *"Corpus Eroticum,"* 38–39.

33. See Connors, "Ennius, Ovid, and Representations of Ilia," 107–8, for further discussion of Ovid's references to Ennius here.

34. N. Krevans, "Ilia's Dream: Ennius, Virgil, and the Mythology of Seduction," *HSCP* 95 (1993): 266.

over only one detail from the *Amores* scene to that in the *Fasti,* the fillet that the vestal virgin wore in her hair as a sign of her priesthood. Silvia describes the slipping of the fillet from her hair as part of her dream (29–30):

> 'ignibus Iliacis aderam, cum lapsa capillis
>   decidit ante sacros lanea vitta focos.'

["I was an attendant to the fire brought from Troy, when my woolen fillet slipped from my tresses and fell before the sacred hearth."]

We already know from having heard Anio's speech in *Am.* 3.6 that this is no idle dream—the fillet really has fallen from Ilia's head. This detail thus both links the two versions of Ovid's Ilia/Silvia and points to the differences in them.

This comparison has, I hope, illustrated in some detail Ovid's determination never to repeat the same story twice—a determination that will be repeatedly challenged, and then affirmed, in the *Metamorphoses.* But it also tells us something about the difference as Ovid would have defined it between the elegy of the *Amores* and the elegy of the *Fasti.* The movement away from first-person, "subjective"-style narrative is one major difference, which in turn helps to explain differences in narrative focus. But there is also a change that is perhaps best defined not as a difference but as a consequence—namely, Ovid's increasing interest in redefining the world of epic in nonepic terms. I have given much attention in this book to Ovid's extrageneric breadth, and we have seen in the *Amores* his first significant attempt to change the horizons of elegy by broadening the genre's stylistic range. In the *Fasti,* however, Ovid's new style goes hand in hand with new subject matter, so that now even Mars, the quintessential divinity of epic, is stripped of his arms for his first major appearance in the work (*inermis,* 3.8 and 9).[35] No longer is Mars simply a part of the rhetorical ornamentation of Ovidian elegy, as he was in, for example, *Am.* 1.9.39–40; rather, he now *is* Ovidian elegy. We are no longer talking about extrageneric breadth; in the *Fasti,* we have a full-blown instance of what Hinds calls "generic complication": "The *Fasti* is an elegy. At times, however, it is a rather epic kind of elegy; and at times its choice of literary model can be argued to reflect this pull toward epic writing."[36] The preceding comparison of

---

35. See Hinds, "Arma in Ovid's *Fasti,*" part 1, 92.
36. Hinds, "Arma in Ovid's *Fasti,*" part 1, 108.

Ovid's Ilia and Silvia makes the distinction clear: the "same" story can be told either in a manner that is highly abstruse, arcane, and learned or in a way that reasserts and enhances its status as part of the national epic tradition. Ilia and Silvia are not different women; but what Ovid chooses to say about each in her respective poem tricks us for just a moment into thinking that they may be.

A further difference, and consequence, is that the *Fasti* take on the character of political poetry, a profile of far less importance to Ovid in the *Amores.* Partly a consequence and partly a cause of the fictive status of both narratives in the *Amores,* Ovid's ellipsis of almost all political subject matter except that which could be handled generically, like the triumph of *Am.* 1.2, perfectly suits the private world of erotic elegy. In the *Fasti,* however, Ovid constantly flirts with the political connotation, implication, and interpretation of the holidays and rituals he describes. The complicated publication and revision history of the *Fasti* has tantalized many scholars in their attempts to determine the degree of Ovid's Augustanism (or anti-Augustanism) evident in this poem; but at least there are extraliterary items of evidence with which scholars on both sides of the fence can attempt to bolster their arguments about the politics of the *Fasti.*[37] Perhaps this is the greatest difference of all between the *Amores* and Ovid's later poetry—and the best argument, therefore, for considering the role of narrative reversal in his earliest work.

Omnia mutantur, nihil interit. The double narratives of poet and lover that Ovid creates in the *Amores* appear again in the *Metamorphoses,* in an episode that many readers have considered emblematic of Ovid's own relationship to the poetry he creates, the tale of Pygmalion at *Met.* 10.243–98.[38] Sharrock has recently described in detail the ways in which Pygmalion's creation of his ivory woman parallels the creation of a *puella* by an elegiac poet;[39] I want to conclude by returning to a few aspects of the

---

37. Two articles that capture the essence of the debate are McKeown, "*Fabula proposito nulla tegenda meo,*" and Hinds, "Arma in Ovid's *Fasti,*" part 2. For a good overview of the political discourse of the *Fasti* and of critical debate surrounding the poem, see Herbert-Brown, *Ovid and the Fasti,* passim; see also Barchiesi, *Il poeta e il principe.*

38. For discussion of the self-reflexive nature of this episode, see, e.g., E.W. Leach, "Ekphrasis and the Theme of Artistic Failure in Ovid's Metamorphoses," *Ramus* 3 (1974): 123–25; D. Lateiner, "Mythic and Non-Mythic Artists in Ovid's Metamorphoses," *Ramus* 13 (1984): 18–19 and 28–29 n. 85; Rosati, *Narciso e Pigmalione,* 60–67; A. Sharrock, "Womanu-facture," *JRS* 81 (1991): 36–49; and J. Elsner and A. Sharrock, "Re-Viewing Pygmalion," *Ramus* 20 (1991): 149–82.

39. Sharrock, "Womanufacture"; she does not, however, draw a specific parallel between Pygmalion's ivory girl and Corinna but rather speaks of Pygmalion's creation in generic ele-

Pygmalion story that Sharrock does not discuss and by looking briefly at how the poet of the *Metamorphoses* draws on his earlier achievement in the *Amores* to achieve artistic perfection.

First, consider the structure of Ovid's Pygmalion narrative. It is an embedded narrative, framed by the tale of another creator who, like Pygmalion, has rejected all normal human women—Orpheus. The story of Pygmalion is among the long list of tales, otherwise unhappy, that Orpheus narrates in the course of *Met.* 10 after his loss of Eurydice. Thus, Orpheus' own tragedy and his subsequent recourse to nature and to *carmina* for the consolation he cannot find anywhere else become the subjects of the primary narrative. As in the *Amores,* we see here the embedding of one story into another; and as in the *Amores,* we can see the complementary nature of the two tales, one of a lover turned poet and the other of an artist turned lover. The two are distinct, yet their identities constantly overlap and begin to merge; in accordance with the relationship of the two narratives, that of the poet ultimately controls that of the lover, and Orpheus leaves Pygmalion behind, so to speak, once the latter has seen his creative desire fulfilled.

Like the lover into whom Ovid the poet transforms himself in the first three poems of the *Amores,* Pygmalion begins as a man without a woman: *sine coniuge caelebs / vivebat thalamique diu consorte carebat* (10.245–46). Meanwhile, he begins to sculpt in ivory; and as his work begins to take on shape (*forma,* 248), he falls in love with his own creation (*operisque sui concepit amorem,* 249). His transformation exactly parallels what we saw in *Am.* 1.1–3: the *poeta* moves from having no interest in love, to being compelled by Cupid to have his poetry take on a particular shape, and so to having his empty heart struck with love; and he finally emerges, by the conclusion of 1.3, as a full-fledged *amator.* All he needs now is a woman to love; and a flesh-and-blood woman finally enters his poetry, and becomes his love, in *Am.* 1.5.

Knox shows how Ovid reveals the affiliation of the Pygmalion story with elegy through his use of elegiac language in this passage, particularly the words *formosa* (266), "an adjective rigorously avoided by the epic poets," and *puella* (259, 280), likewise avoided in epic.[40] Other features of this narrative, however, link Pygmalion's love not just to the world of elegy

---

giac terms. She comes closer to my point in Elsner and Sharrock, "Re-Viewing Pygmalion," 169: "Like Ovid in *Amores* 1.2, Pygmalion is in love with love rather than with a love-object: he is in love with his own creative and erotic process." Sharrock does not pursue this analogy further, however. See also Knox, *Ovid's Metamorphoses,* 52–54.

40. Knox, *Ovid's Metamorphoses,* 53–54.

in general but to the *Amores* in particular. First of all, let us consider the fact that Pygmalion uses ivory to create his *puella*. Elsner focuses on the erotic and deceptive connotations of ivory to explain Pygmalion's choice of material,[41] but another association is equally important, namely, the use of ivory to craft chryselephantine statues of divinities. In the discussion of *Am.* 3.2 earlier in this chapter, I noted the emphasis Ovid gives to the procession of statues of divinities at the Circus by placing Venus at the end of the procession, as its culmination (55–58); this statue of Venus appears to come to life momentarily, to nod in assent to the lover's prayers (*annuit et motu signa secunda dedit,* 58). It is almost as if the statue created by Pygmalion in *Met.* 10 is a mirror image, a simulacrum, of the divine statue of Venus described in the earlier poem.[42] Indeed, whereas the *amator* of *Am.* 3.2 had proclaimed that his *puella* was a goddess greater than Venus (3.2.60), Pygmalion's divine sculpture becomes human thanks to Venus, in answer to Pygmalion's prayers at her festival (10.270–79).

Ovid's description of how the ivory girl gradually softens and becomes real under Pygmalion's hands again rewrites the *Amores* (*Met.* 10.283–89):

temptatum mollescit ebur positoque rigore
subsidit digitis ceditque, ut Hymettia sole
cera remollescit tractataque pollice multas   285
flectitur in facies ipsoque fit utilis usu.
dum stupet et medio gaudet fallique veretur,
rursus amans rursusque manu sua vota retractat;
corpus erat: saliunt temptatae pollice venae.

[The ivory grows soft at the touch, and, its stiffness gone, it yields to his fingers and gives way, like Hymettian wax, which softens in the sun, and is molded into many shapes by the fingers handling it, and becomes usable through use itself. While he marvels, and undecided both rejoices and fears a trick, again and again the lover touches the fulfillment of his prayers with his hand; it was flesh; when pressed by a finger, the veins throb.]

The transformation of the girl from ivory to flesh and blood in this scene recalls the metaphorical transformation of the *puella* in *Am.* 1.7.51–58: having been struck by her *amator,* she goes in the course of four couplets

---

41. Elsner and Sharrock, "Re-Viewing Pygmalion," 162–64.

42. For the use of ivory in the crafting of processional statues, see *AA* 1.147, *pompa frequens caelestibus ibit eburnis,* and Hollis, *Ars Amatoria I,* ad loc.

from being motionless and bloodless, like Parian marble, to melting into tears like the snows.[43] The terms of comparison used in the two poems are not the same but go through the same process and lead to the same conclusion. Most important, we see through comparison of the two scenes the maturation of the extended simile itself in Ovid's poetry. In the *Amores,* we remarked on the strikingly realistic and visual effectiveness of Ovid's similes; in the *Metamorphoses,* realism becomes reality, so that the girl Pygmalion wishes for, the girl *similis mea . . . eburnae* (276), is the living embodiment of what had begun its literary career as a rhetorical device. And as if with his signature, Ovid signs this transformation of simile into reality with another simile, that of melted wax, a material that, like similes themselves, can take new shape even as it carries the memory of its past.

As Pygmalion creates his love and as the *puella* raises her eyes to him, the creative power of his art is confirmed (*dataque oscula virgo / sensit et erubuit timidumque ad lumina lumen / attollens pariter cum caelo vidit amantem,* 292–94). Sharrock suggests that we compare Pygmalion's *puella* to Pandora as created by Hephaestus in Hesiod;[44] even more to the point, however, is Ovid's own description in the *Metamorphoses* of the creation of humanity by Prometheus and of the achievement of cosmic order: *os homini sublime dedit caelumque videre / iussit et erectos ad sidera tollere vultus* (1.85–86). An elegiac reflection of Prometheus, Pygmalion orders his own cosmos and creates the human being who will inhabit his love. His inspiration might be said to be Ovid himself, whose creative and ordering powers over poetry have been made manifest in the world of the *Amores.*

At the close of the *Metamorphoses,* Pythagoras offers a final commentary on the persistence of human nature and of life throughout multiple metamorphoses. The paradox of continuity and change that is at the core of his philosophy offers a fitting close too to this study of the nature and life of the *Amores* and of their afterlife in the rest of Ovid's oeuvre (*Met.* 15.165–72):

> Omnia mutantur, nihil interit: errat et illinc   165
> huc venit, hinc illuc et quoslibet occupat artus
> spiritus eque feris humana in corpora transit
> inque feras noster, nec tempore deperit ullo,

---

43. See chap. 3.
44. Sharrock in Elsner and Sharrock, "Re-Viewing Pygmalion," 173–76.

utque novis facilis signatur cera figuris
nec manet, ut fuerat, nec formas servat easdem, 170
sed tamen ipsa eadem est, animam sic semper eandem
esse sed in varias doceo migrare figuras.

[Everything changes, but nothing dies; our breath of life wanders, coming thence to here and hence to there, and takes up residence in any limbs it pleases, passing from beasts into human bodies and vice versa. It does not ever perish; and just as wax is easily imprinted with new shapes, and does not stay as it was, and does not keep the same shape though it is the same itself, thus I teach that the soul is always the same but passes into different bodies.]

Bibliography

Ahl, F. *Metaformations: Soundplay and Wordplay in Ovid and Other Classical Poets*. Ithaca and London, 1985.

Alewell, K. "Über das rhetorische ΠΑΡΑΔΕΙΓΜΑ." Diss. Leipzig, 1913.

Alfonsi, L. "Amores II,16,11–12." *Latomus* 18 (1959): 800–802.

Allen, A. "The Moon's Horses." *CQ* 25 (1975): 153–55.

Allen, A.W. "'Sincerity' and the Roman Elegists." *CP* 45 (1950): 145–60.

———. "Sunt qui Propertium Malint." In *Critical Essays on Roman Literature: Elegy and Lyric,* edited by J.P. Sullivan, 107–48. Cambridge, MA, 1962.

Alpers, J. "Hercules in bivio." Diss. Göttingen, 1912.

Alton, E.H., D.E.W. Wormell, and E. Courtney, eds. *Ovidius: Fasti*. Leipzig, 1978; 2d ed., 1985.

Anderson, R.J., P.J. Parsons, and R.G.M. Nisbet. "Elegiacs by Gallus from Qaṣr Ibrîm." *JRS* 69 (1979): 125–55.

Anderson, W.S., ed. *Ovidius: Metamorphoses*. Leipzig, 1977.

André, J.M. *L'otium dans la vie morale et intellectuelle romaine*. Paris, 1966.

Athanassaki, L. "The Triumph of Love and Elegy in Ovid's Amores 1,2." *MD* 28 (1992): 125–41.

Atti del convegno internazionale ovidiano. 2 vols. Rome, 1959.

Austin, R.G., ed. *Aeneidos liber secundus P. Vergili Maronis*. Oxford, 1964.

Axelson, B. *Unpoetische Wörter*. Lund, 1945.

Bailey, D.R. Shackleton. *Propertiana*. Cambridge, 1956.

Bal, M. "Notes on Narrative Embedding." *Poetics Today* 2 (1981): 41–59.

Barchiesi, A. "Voci e istanze narrative nelle Metamorfosi di Ovidio." *MD* 23 (1989): 55–97.

———. "Future Reflexive: Two Modes of Allusion and Ovid's *Heroides*." *HSCP* 95 (1993): 333–65.

———. *Il poeta e il principe: Ovidio e il discorso augusteo*. Rome and Bari, 1994.

———, ed. *P. Ovidii Nasonis Epistulae Heroidum 1–3*. Florence, 1992.

Bardon, H. *La littérature latine inconnue, I: L'époque républicaine*. Paris, 1952.

Barsby, J.A. *Ovid*. Greece and Rome New Surveys in the Classics 12. Oxford, 1978.

Becker, C. *Das Spätwerk des Horaz*. Göttingen, 1963.

Bednara, E. "De sermone dactylicorum Latinorum quaestiones." *ALL* 14 (1906): 317–60, 532–604.

Berman, K. "Some Propertian Imitations in Ovid's *Amores.*" *CP* 67 (1972): 170–77.

Bertini, F., trans. *Ovidio: Amori.* 2d ed. Milan, 1988.

Binder, G. *Aeneas und Augustus.* Meisenheim, 1971.

Bing, P. *The Well-Read Muse: Present and Past in Callimachus and the Hellenistic Poets.* Hypomnemata 90. Göttingen, 1988.

Bloom, H. *The Anxiety of Influence: A Theory of Poetry.* New York and London, 1973.

Blum, R. *Kallimachos: The Alexandrian Library and the Origins of Bibliography.* Translated by H. Wellisch. Madison and London, 1991. (= *Kallimachos und die Literaturverzeichnung bei den Griechen.* Frankfurt am Main, 1977.)

Bömer, F. "Ovid und die Sprache Vergils." *Gymnasium* 66 (1959): 268–87. (= *Ovid,* edited by M. von Albrecht and E. Zinn, 173–202. Wege der Forschung 92. Darmstadt, 1968.)

———. "Der Kampf der Stiere: Interpretationen zu einem poetischen Gleichnis bei Ovid (am. II 12,25f. met. IX 46ff.) und zur Frage der 'Erlebnisdichtung' der augusteischen Zeit." *Gymnasium* 81 (1974): 503–13.

Booth, J. "Aspects of Ovid's Language." *ANRW* 2.31.4 (1981): 2686–2700.

Booth, J., and A.C.F. Verity. "Critical Appreciations IV: Ovid, *Amores* 2.10." *G&R* 25 (1978): 125–40.

Bowie, E.L. "Theocritus' Seventh *Idyll,* Philetas, and Longus." *CQ* 35 (1985): 67–91.

Boyd, B. Weiden. "Tarpeia's Tomb: A Note on Propertius 4.4." *AJP* 105 (1984): 85–86.

———. "The Death of Corinna's Parrot Reconsidered: Poetry and Ovid's *Amores.*" *CJ* 82 (1987): 199–207.

———. "Propertius on the Banks of the Eurotas (A Note on 3.14.17–20)." *CQ* 37 (1987): 527–28.

Brandt, E. "Zum Aeneisprooemium." *Philologus* 83 (1927): 331–35.

Brandt, P., ed. *P. Ovidi Nasonis Amorum libri tres.* Leipzig, 1911.

Bremmer, J. "Romulus, Remus, and the Foundation of Rome." In *Roman Myth and Mythography,* by J. Bremmer and N.M. Horsfall, 25–48. *BICS* Suppl. 52. London, 1987.

Bright, D.F. *Haec mihi fingebam: Tibullus in his World.* Leiden, 1978.

Brunner, T.F. "The Function of the Simile in Ovid's *Metamorphoses.*" *CJ* 61 (1965–66): 354–63.

Buchan, M. "Ovidius Imperamator: Beginnings and Endings of Love Poems and Empire in the *Amores.*" *Arethusa* 28 (1995): 53–85.

Buchheit, V. *Vergil über die Sendung Roms.* Gymnasium Beiheft 3. Heidelberg, 1973.

Bulloch, A.W. "Hellenistic Poetry." In *The Cambridge History of Classical Literature,* vol. 1: *Greek Literature,* edited by P.E. Easterling and B.M.W. Knox, 541–621. Cambridge, 1985.

———, ed. *Callimachus: The Fifth Hymn.* Cambridge, 1985.

Bury, R.G., ed. *The Symposium of Plato.* Cambridge, 1932.

Cahoon, L. "Juno's Chaste Festival and Ovid's Wanton Loves: *Amores* 3.13." *CA* 2 (1983): 1–8.

———. "The Parrot and the Poet: The Function of Ovid's Funeral Elegies." *CJ* 80 (1984): 27–35.

———. "A Program for Betrayal: Ovidian *Nequitia* in *Amores* 1.1, 2.1, and 3.1." *Helios* 12 (1985): 29–39.

———. "The Bed as Battlefield: Erotic Conquest and Military Metaphor in Ovid's *Amores*." *TAPA* 118 (1988): 293–307.

Cairns, F. *Generic Composition in Greek and Roman Poetry.* Edinburgh, 1972.

———. *Tibullus: A Hellenistic Poet at Rome.* Cambridge, 1979.

———. "Imitation and Originality in Ovid *Amores* 1.3." *PLLS* 7 (1993): 101–22.

Cameron, A. "The First Edition of Ovid's *Amores*." *CQ* 62 (1968): 320–33.

———. "Genre and Style in Callimachus." *TAPA* 122 (1992): 305–12.

———. *Callimachus and His Critics.* Princeton, 1995.

Campbell, A.Y. "Sophocles' *Trachiniae:* Discussions of Some Textual Problems." *CQ* 8 (1958): 21–23.

Canter, H.V. "The Mythological Paradigm in Greek and Latin Poetry." *AJP* 33 (1954): 201–24.

Clausen, W. "Callimachus and Latin Poetry." *GRBS* 5 (1964): 181–96.

———. *Virgil's Aeneid and the Tradition of Hellenistic Poetry.* Berkeley and Los Angeles, 1987.

———, ed. *Virgil: Eclogues.* Oxford, 1994.

Clausing, A. "Kritik und Exegese der homerischen Gleichnisse im Altertum." Diss. Freiburg, 1913.

Coco, L., ed. *Callimaco: Epigrammi.* Manduria, Bari, and Rome, 1988.

Coffey, M. "The Function of the Homeric Simile." *AJP* 78 (1957): 113–32.

Commager, S. *The Odes of Horace.* New Haven and London, 1962.

Connors, C. "Ennius, Ovid, and Representations of Ilia." *MD* 32 (1994): 99–112.

Conrardy, C. "De Vergilio Apollonii Rhodii imitatore." Diss. Fribourg, 1904.

Conte, G.B. *The Rhetoric of Imitation: Genre and Poetic Memory in Virgil and Other Latin Poets.* Edited by C.P. Segal. Ithaca and London, 1986.

———. "Love without Elegy: The *Remedia amoris* and the Logic of a Genre." *Poetics Today* 10 (1989): 441–69.

———. *Latin Literature: A History.* Translated by J.B. Solodow. Revised by D. Fowler and G.W. Most. Baltimore and London, 1994.

Cornacchia, G.A. "Ovidio, *Am.* 3,9,58: Nota di lettura." In *Mnemosynum: Studi in onore di Alfredo Ghiselli,* 101–2. Bologna, 1989.

Corte, F. della. *La mappa dell' Eneide.* Florence, 1972.

———. "Gli 'Amores' di Ovidio Ripudiati." In *Kontinuität und Wandel: Lateinische Poesie von Naevius bis Baudelaire, Franco Munari zum 65. Geburtstag,* edited by U.J. Stache, W. Maaz, and F. Wagner, 70–78. Hildesheim, 1986.

Courtney, E. "Some Literary Jokes in Ovid's *Amores*." In *Vir bonus discendi peritus: Studies in Celebration of Otto Skutsch's Eightieth Birthday,* ed. N. Horsfall, 18–23. *BICS* Suppl. 51. London, 1988.

Croce, B. *The Aesthetic as the Science of Expression and of the Linguistic in General.* Translated by C. Lyas. Cambridge, 1992.

Curran, L.C. "Ovid *Amores* 1.10." *Phoenix* 18 (1964): 314–19.

———. "Rape and Rape Victims in the *Metamorphoses.*" In *Women in the Ancient World: The Arethusa Papers,* edited by J. Peradotto and J.P. Sullivan, 263–86. Albany, NY, 1984.

Damon, C. "Poem Division, Paired Poems, and *Amores* ii.9 and iii.11." *TAPA* 120 (1990): 269–90.

Davies, M., ed. *Sophocles: Trachiniae.* Oxford, 1991.

Davis, G. *The Death of Procris: 'Amor' and the Hunt in Ovid's Metamorphoses.* Rome, 1983.

Davis, J.T. *Dramatic Pairings in the Elegies of Propertius and Ovid.* Noctes Romanae 15. Bern and Stuttgart, 1977.

———. "Dramatic and Comic Devices in Amores 3.2." *Hermes* 107 (1979): 51–69.

———. "*Exempla* and Anti-*exempla* in the *Amores* of Ovid." *Latomus* 39 (1980): 412–17.

———. "*Risit Amor:* Aspects of Literary Burlesque in Ovid's 'Amores.' " *ANRW* 2.31.4 (1981): 2462–2506.

———. *Fictus Adulter: Poet as Actor in the Amores.* Amsterdam, 1989.

deJong, I.J.F. *Narrators and Focalizers: The Presentation of the Story in the Iliad.* Amsterdam, 1987.

———. "The Voice of Anonymity: *tis*-Speeches in the *Iliad.*" *Eranos* 85 (1987): 69–84.

Diggle, J. "Corinna's Bed (*Amores* 2.11.7)." *PCPhS* 209 (1983): 21–22.

Döpp, S. *Virgilischer Einfluss im Werk Ovids.* Munich, 1969.

Dowden, K. *Death and the Maiden: Girls' Initiation Rites in Greek Mythology.* London and New York, 1989.

Duclos, G. "*Nemora inter Cresia.*" *CJ* 66 (1971): 193–95.

Dunn, F. M. "The Lover Reflected in the *Exemplum:* A Study of Propertius 1.3 and 2.6." *ICS* 10 (1985): 233–59.

Du Quesnay, I.M.LeM. "The *Amores.*" In *Ovid,* edited by J.W. Binns, 1–48. London and Boston, 1973.

———. "Vergil's First *Eclogue.*" *PLLS* 3 (1981): 29–182.

Easterling, P.E., ed. *Sophocles: Trachiniae.* Cambridge, 1982.

Edwards, M.W. *The Iliad: A Commentary,* vol. 5, *Books 17–20.* Cambridge, 1991.

Elder, J.P. "*Non iniussa cano:* Virgil's Sixth Eclogue." *HSCP* 65 (1961): 109–25.

Elliott, R.C. *The Literary Persona.* Chicago and London, 1982.

Elsner, J., and A. Sharrock. "Re-Viewing Pygmalion." *Ramus* 20 (1991): 149–82.

Enk, P.J., ed. *Sex. Propertii Elegiarum Liber Secundus.* 2 vols. Leiden, 1962.

Evans, H.B. *Publica Carmina: Ovid's Books from Exile.* Lincoln, NE, and London, 1983.

Farrell, J. *Vergil's Georgics and the Traditions of Ancient Epic: The Art of Allusion in Literary History.* New York, 1991.

———. "Dialogue of Genres in Ovid's 'Lovesong of Polyphemus' (*Metamorphoses* 13.719–897)." *AJP* 113 (1992): 235–68.

Fedeli, P., ed. *Sexti Properti Elegiarum Libri IV.* Stuttgart, 1984.

Feeney, D. "'Shall I compare thee . . . ?': Catullus 68b and the Limits of Analogy."

In *Author and Audience in Latin Literature,* edited by T. Woodman and J. Powell, 33–44. Cambridge, 1992.

———. *"Si licet et fas est:* Ovid's *Fasti* and the Problem of Free Speech under the Principate." In *Roman Poetry and Propaganda in the Age of Augustus,* edited by A. Powell, 1–25. Bristol, 1992.

Ferguson, J. "Catullus and Ovid." *AJP* 81 (1960): 337–57.

Foley, H. "'Reverse Similes' and Sex Roles in the *Odyssey.*" In *Women in the Ancient World: The Arethusa Papers,* edited by J. Peradotto and J.P. Sullivan, 59–78. Albany, NY, 1984.

Forbes, W.T.M. "The Silkworm of Aristotle." *CP* 25 (1930): 22–26.

Fordyce, C.J., ed. *Catullus.* Oxford, 1961.

Fowler, D. "Virgil on Killing Virgins." In *Homo Viator: Classical Essays for John Bramble,* edited by M. Whitby, P. Hardie, and M. Whitby, 185–98. Bristol, 1987.

Fraenkel, E. *Horace.* Oxford, 1957.

Frank, R.I. "Catullus 51: *Otium* versus *Virtus.*" *TAPA* 99 (1968): 233–39.

Fränkel, H. *Die homerischen Gleichnisse.* Göttingen, 1921.

Frécaut, J.-M. *L'esprit et l'humour chez Ovide.* Grenoble, 1972.

Froleyks, W.J. "Der ΑΓΩΝ ΛΟΓΩΝ in der antiken Literatur." Diss. Rheinische Friedrich-Wilhelms-Universität, Bonn, 1973.

Gaisser, J.H. "Mythological *Exempla* in Propertius 1.2 and 1.15." *AJP* 98 (1977): 381–91.

Galinsky, G.K. "The Hercules-Cacus Episode in *Aeneid* VIII." *AJP* 87 (1966): 18–51.

———. "The Triumph Theme in the Augustan Elegy." *WS,* n.s., 3 (1969): 75–107.

———. *The Herakles Theme: The Adaptations of the Hero in Literature from Homer to the Twentieth Century.* Oxford, 1972.

———. *Ovid's Metamorphoses: An Introduction to the Basic Aspects.* Berkeley, 1975.

Genette, G. *Narrative Discourse: An Essay in Method.* Translated by J.E. Levin. Ithaca, 1980.

Giangrande, G. " 'Arte Allusiva' and Alexandrian Epic Poetry." *CQ* 17 (1967): 85–97.

Ginsberg, W. *The Cast of Character.* Toronto, 1983.

Goold, G.P. "*Amatoria Critica.*" *HSCP* 69 (1965): 1–107.

———. "Servius and the Helen Episode." *HSCP* 74 (1970): 101–68.

———. "The Cause of Ovid's Exile." *ICS* 8 (1983): 94–107.

Görler, W. "Ovids Propemptikon (*Amores* 2.11)." *Hermes* 93 (1965): 338–47.

Gössl, S. "Ovid, Amores I 7." *GB* 10 (1981): 165–80.

Gow, A.S.F., ed. *Theocritus.* 2d ed. 2 vols. Cambridge, 1952.

Gow, A.S.F., and D.L. Page, eds. *The Greek Anthology: Hellenistic Epigrams.* 2 vols. Cambridge, 1965.

———. *The Greek Anthology: The Garland of Philip.* 2 vols. Cambridge, 1968.

Gransden, K.W., ed. *Virgil: Aeneid Book VIII.* Cambridge, 1976.

Green, P. *Aspects of Antiquity.* London, 1960.

———, trans. *Ovid: The Erotic Poems.* London, 1982.

Griffin, J. *Latin Poets and Roman Life.* Chapel Hill, 1986.

Griffith, R.D. "Literary Allusion in Vergil, *Aeneid* 9.435ff." *Vergilius* 31 (1985): 40–44.

Gruen, E. *Culture and National Identity in Republican Rome.* Ithaca, 1992.

Hall, J.B., ed. *P. Ovidi Nasonis Tristia.* Stuttgart, 1995.

Hardie, P. *The Epic Successors of Virgil: A Study in the Dynamics of a Tradition.* Cambridge, 1993.

Harvey, F.D. "Cognati Caesaris: Ovid *Amores* 1.2.51/2." *WS,* n.s., 17 (1983): 89–90.

Henderson, A.A.R. "Tibullus, Elysium, and Tartarus." *Latomus* 28 (1969): 649–53.

Henry, J. *Aeneidea.* 5 vols. London and Dublin, 1873–92.

Herbert-Brown, G. *Ovid and the Fasti: A Historical Study.* Oxford, 1994.

Herescu, N.I., ed. *Ovidiana: Recherches sur Ovide publiées à l'occasion du bimillénaire de la naissance du poète.* Paris, 1958.

Heyworth, S.J. "Deceitful Crete: *Aeneid* 3.84 [*sic*] and the *Hymns* of Callimachus." *CQ* 43 (1993): 255–57.

Hinds, S. "Generalising about Ovid." *Ramus* 16 (1987): 4–31.

———. *The Metamorphosis of Persephone.* Cambridge, 1987.

———. "Arma in Ovid's *Fasti.*" Part 1, "Genre and Mannerism," and Part 2, "Genre, Romulean Rome, and Augustan Ideology." *Arethusa* 25 (1992): 81–112, 113–53.

Hollis, A.S., ed. *Ovid: Ars Amatoria Book I.* Oxford, 1977.

———, ed. *Callimachus: Hecale.* Oxford, 1990.

Hopkinson, N., ed. *Callimachus: Hymn to Demeter.* Cambridge, 1984.

———. *A Hellenistic Anthology.* Cambridge, 1988.

Horsfall, N.M. "Epic and Burlesque in Ovid, *Met.* viii.260ff." *CJ* 74 (1979): 319–32.

———. "Camilla, o i limiti dell' invenzione." *Athenaeum* 66 (1988): 31–51.

———. "Virgil and the Illusory Footnote." *PLLS* 6 (1990): 49–63.

———. *Virgilio: L'epopea in alambicco.* Naples, 1991.

———. "Virgil, Parthenius, and the Art of Mythological Reference." *Vergilius* 37 (1991): 31–36.

Hunter, R.L. "Bulls and Boxers in Apollonius and Vergil." *CQ* 39 (1989): 557–61.

———, ed. *Eubulus: The Fragments.* Cambridge, 1983.

Huntingford, N.P.C. "Ovid *Amores* 1.5." *AClass* 24 (1981): 107–17.

Hutchinson, G.O. "Propertius and the Unity of the Book." *JRS* 74 (1984): 99–106.

Jacobson, H. *Ovid's Heroides.* Princeton, 1974.

Jäger, K. "Zweigliedrige Gedichte und Gedichtpaare bei Properz und in Ovids Amores." Diss. Eberhard-Karls-Universität, Tübingen, 1967.

Jameson, M., trans. *Sophocles: The Women of Trachis.* In *Sophocles II,* edited by D. Grene and R. Lattimore, 63–119. Chicago, 1957.

Jauss, H.R. *Toward an Aesthetic of Reception.* Translated by T. Bahti. Minneapolis, 1982.

Jocelyn, H.D. "The Annotations of M. Valerius Probus." *CQ* 34 (1984): 464–72.

———. "The Annotations of M. Valerius Probus." Part 3, "Some Virgilian Scholia." *CQ* 35 (1985): 466–74.

Johnson, W.R. *Darkness Visible: A Study of Vergil's Aeneid.* Berkeley and Los Angeles, 1976.

———. "The Desolation of the *Fasti.*" *CJ* 74 (1978–79): 7–18.

———. "Ringing Down the Curtain on Love." *Helios* 12 (1985): 21–28.

Keith, A.M. "*Amores* 1.1: Propertius and the Ovidian Programme." In *Studies in Latin Literature and Roman History,* vol. 6, edited by C. Deroux, 327–44. Collection Latomus 217. Brussels, 1992.

———. *The Play of Fictions: Studies in Ovid's Metamorphoses Book 2.* Ann Arbor, 1992.

———. "*Corpus Eroticum:* Elegiac Poetics and Elegiac *Puellae* in Ovid's *Amores.*" *CW* 88 (1994): 27–40.

Kennedy, D. "The Epistolary Mode and the First of Ovid's *Heroides.*" *CQ* 34 (1984): 413–22.

———. "'Augustan' and 'Anti-Augustan': Reflections on Terms of Reference." In *Roman Poetry and Propaganda in the Age of Augustus,* edited by A. Powell, 26–58. Bristol, 1992.

Kenney, E.J. "Nequitiae Poeta." In *Ovidiana: Recherches sur Ovide publiées à l'occasion du bimillénaire de la naissance du poète,* edited by N.I. Herescu, 201–9. Paris, 1958.

———. "On the *Somnium* Attributed to Ovid." *Agon* 3 (1969): 1–14.

———. "The Style of the *Metamorphoses.*" In *Ovid,* edited by J.W. Binns, 116–53. London and Boston, 1973.

———. "Books and Readers in the Roman World." In *The Cambridge History of Classical Literature,* vol. 2, *Latin Literature,* edited by E.J. Kenney and W.V. Clausen, 3–32. Cambridge, 1982.

———. "Ovid." In *The Cambridge History of Classical Literature,* vol. 2, *Latin Literature,* edited by E.J. Kenney and W.V. Clausen, 420–57. Cambridge, 1982.

———, ed. *Ovid, Heroides: XVI–XXI.* Cambridge, 1996.

Kershaw, A. "Emendation and Usage: Two Readings of Propertius." *CP* 75 (1980): 71–72.

Khan, H.A. "*Ovidius Furens:* A Revaluation of *Amores* 1,7." *Latomus* 25 (1966): 880–94.

Knox, P.E. "The Epilogue to the *Aetia.*" *GRBS* 26 (1985): 59–65.

———. "The Old Gallus." *Hermes* 113 (1985): 497.

———. "Ovid's *Medea* and the Authenticity of *Heroides* 12." *HSCP* 90 (1986): 207–23.

———. *Ovid's Metamorphoses and the Traditions of Augustan Poetry.* Cambridge Philological Society Suppl. 11. Cambridge, 1986.

———. "The Poetry of Philetas." *PLLS* 7 (1993): 61–83.

———, ed. *Ovid. Heroides: Select Epistles.* Cambridge, 1995.

Kornhardt, H. *Exemplum: Eine bedeutungsgeschichtliche Studie.* Göttingen, 1936.

Korzeniewski, D. "Ovids elegisches Prooemium." *Hermes* 92 (1964): 182–213.

Kratins, O. "The Pretended Witch: A Reading of Ovid's *Amores,* I.viii." *PhQ* 42 (1963): 151–58.

Krevans, N. "Ilia's Dream: Ennius, Virgil, and the Mythology of Seduction." *HSCP* 95 (1993): 257–71.

Kroll, W. *Studien zum Verständnis der römischen Literatur.* Stuttgart, 1924.

———. "La lingua poetica latina." In *La lingua poetica latina,* edited by A. Lunelli,

2d ed., 1–66. Bologna, 1980. (= *Studien zum Verständnis der römischen Literatur,* 257–74. Stuttgart, 1924.)

———, ed. *C. Valerius Catullus.* 6th ed. Stuttgart, 1980.

Kuntz, M. "The Prodikean 'Choice of Herakles': A Reshaping of Myth." *CJ* 89 (1993–94): 163–81.

Lamacchia, R. "Ovidio interprete di Virgilio." *Maia* 12 (1960): 310–30.

Lateiner, D. "Ovid's Homage to Callimachus and Alexandrian Poetic Theory (*Am.* ii.19)." *Hermes* 106 (1978): 188–96.

———. "Mythic and Non-Mythic Artists in Ovid's Metamorphoses." *Ramus* 13 (1984): 1–30.

Leach, E.W. "Propertius 1.17: The Experimental Voyage." *YCS* 19 (1966): 209–32.

———. "Ekphrasis and the Theme of Artistic Failure in Ovid's Metamorphoses." *Ramus* 3 (1974): 102–42.

LeBonniec, H. *Le Culte de Cérès à Rome.* Paris, 1958.

Lee, A.G. "Tenerorum Lusor Amorum." In *Critical Essays on Roman Literature: Elegy and Lyric,* edited by J.P. Sullivan, 149–79. Cambridge, MA, 1962.

———, trans. *Ovid's Amores.* New York, 1968.

Leeman, A.D. *Orationis Ratio.* Amsterdam, 1963.

Lenz, F.W. "Ceresfest: Eine Studie zu Ovid Amores 3,10." *SIFC* 10 (1933): 299–313.

———. "Io ed il paese di Sulmona (Amores ii,16)." In *Atti del convegno internazionale ovidiano,* 2:59–68. Rome, 1959.

———. "Noch einmal 'Io ed il paese di Sulmona.' " *RCCM* 4 (1962): 150–53.

Leo, F. *Plautinische Forschungen.* 2d ed. Berlin, 1912.

Little, D. "Politics in Augustan Poetry." *ANRW* 2.30.1 (1982): 254–370.

Luck, G. "The Cave and the Source." *CQ* 7 (1957): 175–79.

———. *Die römische Liebeselegie.* Heidelberg, 1959.

———. *The Latin Love Elegy.* 2d ed. London, 1969.

———. "Love Elegy." In *The Cambridge History of Classical Literature,* vol. 2, *Latin Literature,* edited by E.J. Kenney and W.V. Clausen, 405–19. Cambridge, 1982.

Lyne, R.O.A.M. *The Latin Love Poets.* Oxford, 1980.

———. "Lavinia's Blush: Vergil, *Aeneid* 12.64–70." *G&R* 30 (1983): 55–64.

———. *Words and the Poet: Characteristic Techniques of Style in Vergil's Aeneid.* Oxford, 1989.

———. "Vergil's *Aeneid:* Subversion by Intertextuality, Catullus 66.39–40 and Other Examples." *G&R* 41 (1994): 187–204.

Mader, G. "The Apollo Similes at Propertius 4.6.31–36." *Hermes* 118 (1990): 325–34.

Maltby, R. *A Lexicon of Ancient Latin Etymologies.* Leeds, 1991.

———, ed. *Latin Love Elegy.* Bristol and Chicago, 1980.

Mayer, R., ed. *Horace: Epistles I.* Cambridge, 1994.

McCall, M. *Ancient Rhetorical Theories of Simile and Comparison.* Cambridge, MA, 1969.

McKeown, J.C. "*Fabula proposito nulla tegenda meo:* Ovid's *Fasti* and Augustan

Politics." In *Poetry and Politics in the Age of Augustus,* edited by T. Woodman and D. West, 169–87, 237–41 nn. Cambridge, 1984.

———. *"Militat omnis amans." CJ* 90 (1995): 295–304.

McLennan, G.R., ed. *Callimachus: Hymn to Zeus.* Rome, 1977.

Miles, G. *Virgil's Georgics: A New Interpretation.* Berkeley, Los Angeles, and London, 1980.

Miller, J.F. "Ovidius imitator sui: Fasti 4.179ff. and Amores 3.2.43ff." *RhM* 132 (1989): 403–5.

———. *Ovid's Elegiac Festivals: Studies in the "Fasti."* Studien zur klassischen Philologie 55. Frankfurt am Main, 1991.

———. "Ovidian Allusion and the Vocabulary of Memory." *MD* 30 (1993): 153–64.

———. "Reading Cupid's Triumph." *CJ* 90 (1995): 287–94.

Moles, J. "The Dramatic Coherence of Ovid, *Amores* 1.1 and 1.2." *CQ* 41 (1991): 551–54.

Moretti, G. "Trionfi d'amore: Due note esegetiche ad *Amores* 1,2." *Maia* 46 (1994): 47–52.

Morgan, K. *Ovid's Art of Imitation: Propertius in the Amores.* Mnemosyne Suppl. 47. Leiden, 1977.

Morrison, J. "Literary Reference and Generic Transgression in Ovid, *Amores* 1.7: Lover, Poet, and *Furor." Latomus* 51 (1992): 571–89.

Mossman, J. *Wild Justice: A Study of Euripides' Hecuba.* Oxford, 1995.

Munari, F. *Il Codice Hamilton 471 di Ovidio.* Note e Discussioni Erudite 9. Rome, 1965.

———, ed. *P. Ovidi Nasonis Amores,* 4th ed. Florence, 1964.

Murgatroyd, P. "Militia amoris and the Roman Elegists." *Latomus* 34 (1975): 59–79.

Murgia, C. "The Date of Ovid's *Ars Amatoria* 3." *AJP* 107 (1986): 74–94.

———. "Influence of Ovid's *Remedia amoris* on *Ars Amatoria* 3 and *Amores* 3." *CP* 81 (1986): 203–20.

Myers, K.S. "Ovid's *Tecta Ars: Amores* 2.6, Programmatics, and the Parrot." *EMC* 34 (1990): 367–74.

———. *Ovid's Causes: Cosmology and Aetiology in the Metamorphoses.* Ann Arbor, 1994.

Mynors, R.A.B., ed. *Virgil: Georgics.* Oxford, 1990.

Nagle, B.R. *The Poetics of Exile: Programme and Polemic in the Tristia and Epistulae ex Ponto of Ovid.* Collection Latomus 170. Brussels, 1980.

———. "Ovid, 'Facile' or 'Formulaic'? A Metrical Mannerism and Its Implications." *QUCC* 54 (1987): 73–90.

Némethy, G., ed. *P. Ovidii Nasonis Amores.* Budapest, 1907.

Neumann, R. "Qua ratione Ovidius in Amoribus scribendis Properti elegiis usus sit." Diss. Göttingen, 1919.

Newlands, C. "The Ending of Ovid's Fasti." In *Roman Literature and Ideology: Ramus Essays for J.P. Sullivan* (published as *Ramus* 23), edited by A.J. Boyle, 129–43. Victoria, 1994.

———. *Playing with Time: Ovid and the Fasti.* Ithaca and London, 1995.

Newman, J.K. *The Concept of Vates in Augustan Poetry.* Collection Latomus 89. Brussels, 1967.

Nicoll, W.S.M. "Ovid, Amores I 5." *Mnemosyne* 30 (1977): 40–48.

Nisbet, R.G.M. Review of *Latin Poets and Roman Life,* by J. Griffin. *JRS* 77 (1987): 165–73.

Ogilvie, R.M. *A Commentary on Livy Books 1–5.* Oxford, 1965.

O'Hara, J. "Etymological Wordplay in Apollonius of Rhodes, *Aeneid* 3, and *Georgics* 1." *Phoenix* 44 (1990): 370–76.

———. *True Names: Vergil and the Alexandrian Tradition of Etymological Wordplay.* Ann Arbor, 1996.

———. "Vergil's Best Reader? Ovidian Commentary on Vergilian Etymological Wordplay." *CJ* 91 (1996): 255–76.

Olstein, K. "*Amores* 1.3 and Duplicity as a Way of Love." *TAPA* 105 (1975): 241–57.

Otis, B. "Ovid and the Augustans." *TAPA* 69 (1938): 188–229.

Otto, A. *Die Sprichwörter und sprichwörtlichen Redensarten der Römer.* 2d ed. Leipzig, 1890. Reprint, Hildesheim and New York, 1971.

Owen, S.G. "Ovid's Use of the Simile." *CR* 45 (1931): 97–106.

Page, D.L. "Stesichorus: *The Geryoneis.*" *JHS* 93 (1973): 138–54.

———, ed. *Supplementum Lyricis Graecis.* Oxford, 1974.

Papanghelis, T.D. "About the Hour of Noon: Ovid, *Amores* 1,5." *Mnemosyne* 42 (1989): 54–61.

Parker, D. "The Ovidian Coda." *Arion* 8 (1969): 80–97.

Pasquali, G. "Arte allusiva." *Italia che scrive* 25 (1942): 185–87. (= *Stravaganze quarte e supreme,* 11–20. Venice, 1951.)

Pease, A.S., ed. *Virgil: Aeneid Book IV.* Cambridge, MA, 1935.

Perkell, C. *The Poet's Truth.* Berkeley, 1989.

Perkins, C.A. "Love's Arrows Lost: Tibullan Parody in *Amores* 3.9." *CW* 86 (1993): 459–66.

Pianezzola, E., ed. *L'arte di amare.* 2d ed. Milan, 1993.

Pichon, R. *De sermone amatorio apud Latinos elegiarum scriptores.* Paris, 1902.

Pillinger, H.E. "Some Callimachean Influences on Propertius, Book 4." *HSCP* 73 (1969): 171–99.

Platnauer, M. *Latin Elegiac Verse.* Cambridge, 1951. Reprint, Hamden, CT, 1971.

Platner, S.B., and T. Ashby. *A Topographical Dictionary of Ancient Rome.* Oxford, 1929.

Pohlenz, M. "De Ovidi carminibus amatoriis." Diss. Göttingen, 1913.

Poliakoff, M. "Clumsy and Clever Spiders on Hermann's Bridge: Catullus 68.49–50 and *Culex* 1–3." *Glotta* 63 (1985): 248–50.

Pöschl, V. "Ovid und Horaz." *RCCM* 1 (1959): 15–25.

———. *Die Dichtkunst Vergils: Bild und Symbol in der Äneis.* 3d ed. New York and Berlin, 1977.

Preston, K. *Studies in the Diction of the Sermo Amatorius in Roman Comedy.* Chicago, 1916.

Price, B. "Παράδειγμα and *Exemplum* in Ancient Rhetorical Theory." Ph.D. diss., University of California, Berkeley, 1975.

Putnam, M.C.J. *Virgil's Pastoral Art.* Princeton, 1970.

———. *Artifices of Eternity: Horace's Fourth Book of Odes.* Ithaca, 1986.

Quinn, K. *Latin Explorations.* London, 1963.

———. "The Poet and His Audience in the Augustan Age." *ANRW* 2.30.1 (1982): 75–180.

Reitzenstein, E. "Zur Stiltheorie des Kallimachos." In *Festschrift Richard Reitzenstein,* edited by E. Fraenkel, H. Fränkel, et al., 25–40. Berlin and Leipzig, 1931.

———. "Das neue Kunstwollen in den Amores Ovids." *RhM* 84 (1935): 67–73. (= *Ovid,* ed. M. von Albrecht and E. Zinn, 211–18. Wege der Forschung 92. Darmstadt, 1968.)

———. *Wirklichkeitsbild und Gefühlsentwicklung bei Properz.* Philologus Suppl. 29. Leipzig, 1936.

Renz, H. *Mythologische Beispiele in Ovids erotischer Elegie.* Würzburg, 1935.

Richardson, N.J. "Literary Criticism in the Exegetical Scholia to the *Iliad:* A Sketch." *CQ* 30 (1980): 265–87.

———, ed. *The Homeric Hymn to Demeter.* Oxford, 1974.

Richmond, J.A., ed. *P. Ovidi Nasonis Ex Ponto libri quattuor.* Leipzig, 1990.

Richter, G.M.A. "Silk in Greece." *AJA* 33 (1929): 27–33.

Richter, W. "Lunae labores." *WS,* n.s., 11 (1977): 96–105.

Rieks, R. "Die Gleichnisse Vergils." *ANRW* 2.31.2 (1981): 1011–1110.

Rissman, L. *Love as War: Homeric Allusion in the Poetry of Sappho.* Koenigstein/Ts., 1983.

Rosati, G. *Narciso e Pigmalione: Illusione e spettacolo nelle Metamorfosi di Ovidio.* Florence, 1983.

Rosen, R., and J. Farrell. "Acontius, Milanion, and Gallus: Vergil, *Ecl.* 10.52–61." *TAPA* 116 (1986): 241–54.

Ross, D.O. *Style and Tradition in Catullus.* Cambridge, MA, 1969.

———. *Backgrounds to Augustan Poetry: Gallus, Elegy, and Rome.* Cambridge, 1975.

———. *Virgil's Elements: Physics and Poetry in the Georgics.* Princeton, 1987.

Rothstein, M., ed. *Die Elegien des Sextus Propertius.* 2 vols. Berlin, 1920–24. Reprint, New York, 1979.

Sabot, A.-F. *Ovide poète de l'amour dans ses oeuvres de jeunesse: Amores, Héroïdes, Ars Amatoria, Remedia Amoris, De Medicamine Faciei Femineae.* Paris, 1976.

Salvatore, A. "Virgilio e Ovidio elegiaco." In *Virgilio e gli Augustei,* edited by M. Gigante, 179–202. Naples, 1990.

Schroeder, A. "De ethnographiae antiquae locis quibusdam communibus observationes." Diss. Halle, 1921.

Scodel, R. "Inscription, Absence, and Memory: Epic and Early Epitaph." *SIFC* 10 (1992): 57–76.

Segal, C. "Catullan *Otiosi:* The Lover and the Poet." *G&R* 17 (1970): 25–31.

———. "Archaic Choral Lyric." In *The Cambridge History of Classical Literature,* vol. 1, *Greek Literature,* edited by P.E. Easterling and B.M.W. Knox, 165–201. Cambridge, 1985.

Sharrock, A. "Womanufacture." *JRS* 81 (1991): 36–49.

———. *Seduction and Repetition in Ovid's Ars Amatoria II.* Oxford, 1994.

———. "The Drooping Rose: Elegiac Failure in Amores 3.7." *Ramus* 24 (1995): 152–80.

Skulsky, S. "The Sibyl's Rage and the Marpessan Rock." *AJP* 108 (1987): 56–80.

Skutsch, O. "Zu Vergils Eklogen." *RhM* 99 (1956): 193–201.

———. "The Second Book of Propertius." *HSCP* 79 (1975): 229–33.

Smith, K.F., ed. *The Elegies of Albius Tibullus.* New York and Cincinnati, 1913.

Snipes, K. "Literary Interpretation in the Homeric Scholia: The Similes of the *Iliad.*" *AJP* 109 (1988): 196–222.

Solmsen, F. "Propertius in His Literary Relations with Tibullus and Virgil." *Philologus* 105 (1961): 273–89.

Solodow, J.B. "*Raucae, tua cura, palumbes:* Study of a Poetic Word Order." *HSCP* 90 (1986): 129–53.

———. *The World of Ovid's Metamorphoses.* Chapel Hill and London, 1988.

Spies, A. "Militat omnis amans: Ein Beitrag zur Bildersprache der antiken Erotik." Diss. Tübingen, 1930.

Starr, R. "The Circulation of Literary Texts in the Roman World." *CQ* 37 (1987): 213–23.

Stewart, Z. "The Song of Silenus." *HSCP* 64 (1959): 179–205.

Stirrup, B.E. "Irony in Ovid Amores I 7." *Latomus* 32 (1973): 824–31.

———. "Structure and Separation: A Comparative Analysis of Ovid, Amores II.11 and II.16." *Eranos* 74 (1976): 32–52.

Stoessl, F. "Ovids Lebensentscheidung." In *Festschrift Karl Vretska,* edited by D. Ableitinger and H. Gugel, 250–75. Heidelberg, 1970.

Stroh, W. "Ovids Liebeskunst und die Ehegesetze des Augustus." *Gymnasium* 86 (1979): 323–52.

Sullivan, J.P. "Two Problems in Roman Love Elegy." *TAPA* 92 (1961): 522–36.

Suter, A. "Ovid, from Image to Narrative: *Amores* 1.8 and 3.6." *CW* 83 (1989): 15–20.

Syme, R. *History in Ovid.* Oxford, 1978.

Tabacco, R. "Le similitudini in Ovidio: Rassegna degli studi e prospettive di ricerca." *BStudLat* 25 (1995): 129–71.

Thibeault, J.C. *The Mystery of Ovid's Exile.* Berkeley and Los Angeles, 1964.

Thomas, E. "Variations on a Military Theme in Ovid's Amores." *G&R* 11 (1964): 151–65.

———. "A Comparative Analysis of Ovid, *Amores,* II,6 and III,9." *Latomus* 24 (1965): 599–609.

———. "Ovid at the Races." In *Hommages à Marcel Renard,* edited by J. Bibauw, 1:710–24. Collection Latomus 101. Brussels, 1969.

Thomas, R.F. "Ovid's Attempt at Tragedy (*Am.* 3.1.63–64)." *AJP* 99 (1978): 447–50.

———. "New Comedy, Callimachus, and Roman Poetry." *HSCP* 83 (1979): 179–206.

———. "Catullus and the Polemics of Poetic Reference (Poem 64.1–18)." *AJP* 103 (1982): 144–64.

———. "Gadflies (Virg. *Geo.* 3.146–148)." *HSCP* 86 (1982): 81–85.

———. *Lands and Peoples in Roman Poetry: The Ethnographical Tradition.* Cambridge Philological Society Suppl. 7. Cambridge, 1982.

———. "Callimachus, the *Victoria Berenices,* and Roman Poetry." *CQ* 33 (1983): 92–113.

———. "Virgil's *Georgics* and the Art of Reference." *HSCP* 90 (1986): 171–98.

———. "Prose into Poetry: Tradition and Meaning in Virgil's *Georgics.*" *HSCP* 91 (1987): 229–60.

———. "Turning Back the Clock." *CP* 83 (1988): 54–69.

———. "'Death,' Doxography, and the 'Termerian Evil' (Philodemus, *Epigr.* 27 Page = *A.P.* 11.30)." *CQ* 41 (1991): 130–37.

———. "The Old Man Revisited: Memory, Reference and Genre in Virg., Georg. 4,116–48." *MD* 29 (1992): 35–70.

———. "Sparrows, Hares, and Doves: A Catullan Metaphor and Its Tradition." *Helios* 20 (1993): 131–42.

Thompson, Sir D'A.W. *A Glossary of Greek Birds.* 2d ed. London, 1936.

Tränkle, H. *Die Sprachkunst des Properz und die Tradition der lateinischen Dichtersprache.* Hermes Einzelschrift 15. Wiesbaden, 1960.

Trüdinger, K. *Studien zur Geschichte der griechisch-römischen Ethnographie.* Basel, 1918.

Valk, M. van der, ed. *Eustathii Commentarii ad Homeri Iliadem Pertinentes.* 4 vols. Leiden, 1971.

Verducci, F. *Ovid's Toyshop of the Heart: Epistulae Heroidum.* Princeton, 1985.

Vessey, D.W.T. "Elegy Eternal: Ovid, *Amores,* I.15." *Latomus* 40 (1981): 607–17.

Veyne, P. *Roman Erotic Elegy: Love, Poetry, and the West.* Trans. D. Pellauer. Chicago and London, 1988. (= *L'élégie érotique romaine: L'amour, la poésie et l'Occident.* Paris, 1983.)

Wallace-Hadrill, A. "Propaganda and Dissent? Augustan Moral Legislation and the Love-Poets." *Klio* 67 (1985): 180–84.

———. "Time for Augustus: Ovid, Augustus and the *Fasti.*" In *Homo Viator: Classical Essays for John Bramble,* edited by M. Whitby, P. Hardie, and M. Whitby, 221–30. Bristol, 1987.

Washietl, J.A. "De similitudinibus imaginibusque Ovidianis." Diss. Vienna, 1883.

Watson, P. "Mythological Exempla in Ovid's *Ars Amatoria.*" *CP* 78 (1983): 117–26.

———. "Ovid Amores ii.7 and 8: The Disingenuous Defence." *WS,* n.s., 17 (1983): 91–103.

———. "Axelson Revisited: The Selection of Vocabulary in Latin Poetry." *CQ* 35 (1985): 430–48.

Weinreich, O. "Der Papagei und sein Caesar have." *Tübinger Beiträge zur Altertumswiss.* 4 (1928): 113–25.

———. "Gebet und Sünder, II: Türöffnung in Wunder-, Prodigien- und Zauberglauben der Antike, des Judentums und Christentums." In *Genethliakon Wilhelm Schmid,* edited by F. Folke et al., 200–452. Stuttgart, 1929.

West, D.A. "Multiple-Correspondence Similes in the *Aeneid.*" *JRS* 59 (1969): 40–49.

———. "Virgilian Multiple-Correspondence Similes and Their Antecedents." *Philologus* 114 (1970): 262–75.

Whitaker, R. *Myth and Personal Experience in Roman Love-Elegy: A Study in Poetic Technique.* Hypomnemata 76. Göttingen, 1983.

White, K.D. *Roman Farming.* Ithaca, 1970.

White, P. *Promised Verse: Poets in the Society of Augustan Rome.* Cambridge, MA and London, 1993.

Whitman, J. *Allegory: The Dynamics of an Ancient and Medieval Technique.* Cambridge, MA, 1987.

Wilamowitz-Moellendorff, U. von. *Hellenistische Dichtung in der Zeit des Kallimachos.* 2 vols. Berlin, 1924.

Wilkins, E.G. "A Classification of the Similes of Ovid." *CW* 25 (1932): 73–78, 81–86.

Wilkinson, L.P. *Ovid Recalled.* Cambridge, 1955.

———. "The Continuity of Propertius ii.13." *CR,* n.s., 16 (1966): 141–44.

Willetts, R.F. *Cretan Cults and Festivals.* London, 1962.

Williams, F. "A Theophany in Theocritus." *CQ* 21 (1971): 137–45.

———, ed. *Callimachus: Hymn to Apollo.* Oxford, 1978.

Williams, G. *Tradition and Originality in Roman Poetry.* Oxford, 1968.

———. *Change and Decline: Roman Literature in the Early Empire.* Berkeley, Los Angeles, and London, 1978.

———. *Figures of Thought in Roman Poetry.* New Haven and London, 1980.

Williams, G.D. *Banished Voices: Readings in Ovid's Exile Poetry.* Cambridge, 1994.

Wimmel, W. *Kallimachos in Rom.* Hermes Einzelschrift 16. Wiesbaden, 1960.

Winkler, M. *The Persona in Three Satires of Juvenal.* Hildesheim and New York, 1983.

Wyke, M. "The Elegiac Woman at Rome." *PCPhS* 33 (1987): 153–78.

———. "In Pursuit of Love, the Poetic Self, and a Process of Reading: Augustan Elegy in the 1980s." *JRS* 79 (1989): 165–73.

———. "Reading Female Flesh: *Amores* 3.1." In *History as Text: The Writing of Ancient History,* edited by A. Cameron, 111–43. London, 1989.

Zanker, G. *Realism in Alexandrian Poetry.* London and Sydney, 1987.

Zetzel, J.E.G. "Gallus, Elegy, and Ross." *CP* 72 (1977): 249–60.

———. "Recreating the Canon: Augustan Poetry and the Alexandrian Past." *Critical Inquiry* 10 (1983): 83–105.

Zingerle, A. *Ovidius und sein Verhältnis zu den Vorgängern und gleichzeitigen römischen Dichtern.* 3 vols. Innsbruck, 1869–71.

Index Locorum

Apollonius of Rhodes
Argon.
  1.790–91: 116n.58
  2.88–89: 84
  3.297–98: 116
  3.876–86: 101n.23
Aratus
Phaen. 803: 114n.51

Brevis Expositio Georgicorum
  on *Geo.* 1.27: 145–46
Callimachus
Aet. 1, fr. 1.20 Pf.: 192
  3, fr. 80.10–11 Pf.: 116n.58
Epigr. 25 Pf.: 41–42
fr. gram.
  fr. 465 Pf.: 145
fr. incert. sed.
  fr. 612 Pf.: 78
Hec.
  SH 285.10–12: 120, 121n.75
Hymns
  1.4–9: 71
  2.2: 191
  2.22: 126
  2.24: 126
  2.108–9: 129
  3.190–91: 72n.42
  5.23–26: 107
  6.17: 71
Calvus
FPL 85 Morel: 70n.34

Catullus
  1.1–2: 144n.29
  3.1–18: 171
  3.10: 173
  3.11–14: 174
  46.1: 24
  50.7–17: 150
  64.48: 115n.53
  64.58–59: 44
  64.61: 126
  64.89: 107
  64.100: 127n.90
  65.24: 116n.58
  68.70: 155
  70.3–4: 44
Cicero
de Orat. 3.205: 96n.15
[Cicero]
ad Her. 4.49.62: 95–96
Ctesias
FGrHist 688 F 45 (*Indica*):
  172

Ennius
Ann. 1.xxix.44–45: 216
  fr. 16 *FLP* Courtney: 197n.63

Festus
  p. 235 Lindsay: 173n.13

Gallus
FPL 99 Morel: 39

239

Aulus Gellius
  NA 9.9.12–14: 99–100
Hesiod
  Th. 969–71: 69
Homer
  Il.
    4.141–42: 113
    14.394–401: 94
  Od.
    5.125–28: 69
    5.295–96: 25
    5.306: 25
    6.102–8: 99
    18.196: 115
    19.204–8: 125
Homeric scholia
  on *Il.* 6.460–61: 202n.70
  on *Od.* 5.125: 72n.40
Horace
  Odes
    1.19.5–6: 127
    1.31.6: 115n.53
    2.8.1–8: 45
  Epist. 1.16.1–16: 57–58
  Epod. 7.15: 127n.92

Isidore
  Orig. 9.7.9: 88n.76

Leonidas of Tarentum
  AP 7.198: 176
Livy
  1.4.3: 215
Lucretius
  5.14–15: 74n.45
  5.95: 169

Musaeus
  160–61: 116n.58

Ovid
  Am.
    epig. 1–4: 142
    1.1.1: 142
    1.1.1–2: 148
    1.1.4: 148 and n.41
    1.1.7–12: 97
    1.1.9: 78
    1.1.9–10: 98
    1.1.17–18: 148
    1.1.19–20: 148
    1.1.24: 148

1.1.25–26: 148
1.2.1–6: 149
1.2.5: 149
1.2.7–8: 149–50
1.2.9–10: 150
1.2.11–16: 98
1.2.29: 151
1.2.51: 151
1.3.3–4: 152
1.3.11–12: 152
1.3.19–20: 152
1.3.21–24: 152
1.3.25–26: 152
1.5.1: 154
1.5.9–12: 154
1.5.10: 155
1.5.13: 155 and n.54, 156
1.5.15–16: 155
1.5.19: 156
1.5.23: 156
1.5.25–26: 156
1.5.26: 162
1.6.51–54: 37
1.6.57–58: 43n.45
1.7.3–4: 123, 157
1.7.11: 123, 157
1.7.13: 124
1.7.13–18: 123
1.7.17: 124
1.7.27: 123
1.7.33: 157
1.7.43–48: 128, 158
1.7.43: 129
1.7.49–50: 129, 158
1.7.51: 127, 129, 159
1.7.51–58: 124
1.7.52: 127
1.7.53: 126, 159
1.7.57: 126, 159
1.7.60: 159
1.7.67–68: 159
1.9.1–2: 160
1.9.29–30: 161
1.9.31–32: 162
1.9.37–38: 124n.81
1.9.41–44: 162
1.9.46: 163
1.10.1: 107
1.10.1–7: 104
1.10.7: 107
1.10.15–16: 106
1.13.47–48: 113

1.14.1–12: 117
1.14.1: 121n.75
1.14.5: 118
1.14.6: 119, 121
1.14.11–12: 120–21
1.14.13: 118
1.14.23: 119
1.14.25–26: 43n.45
1.15.7–14: 166–67
1.15.15–22: 167
1.15.23–30: 168
1.15.24: 169
2.1.1–2: 191, 193
2.1.3: 191
2.1.7–10: 193
2.1.15–22: 191–92
2.1.17: 191, 195
2.1.29–30: 193
2.1.33–34: 191
2.1.33–35: 193
2.1.37–38: 191
2.5.33–42: 110–11
2.5.34: 116
2.5.35: 113
2.5.36: 113
2.5.39–40: 114–15
2.5.38: 114n.50
2.5.42: 116n.60
2.5.43–44: 116
2.6.1: 171
2.6.3: 173, 174
2.6.18: 172
2.6.19: 170, 177n.24
2.6.26: 172
2.6.29: 172
2.6.37: 172
2.6.38: 170
2.6.48: 173, 175
2.6.49–58: 173–74
2.6.51–52: 174
2.6.58: 174
2.6.59: 176
2.6.59–62: 175
2.6.61: 176
2.6.61–62: 177–78
2.6.62: 172
2.9.17–18: 40n.41
2.10.1–2: 39
2.11.1–56: 20–22
2.11.7: 24
2.11.9–10: 25
2.11.17: 26

2.11.25: 25
2.11.30: 25
2.11.33–34: 24
2.11.34: 23, 27, 28
2.12.1–4: 81
2.12.5–6: 89
2.12.13–14: 81
2.12.17–26: 81–82
2.12.25: 87, 93
2.12.27: 89
2.16.1–10: 54
2.16.2: 59
2.16.9–10: 59
2.16.11–12: 53, 54–55, 60
2.16.14: 44
2.16.32: 61n.22
2.16.33–40: 55
2.16.41–42: 61
2.16.43–46: 44, 65
2.16.44: 44
2.16.51–52: 65
2.18.19: 143n.27
2.19.1: 194
2.19.19: 194
2.19.25–26: 195
2.19.35–36: 194
3.1.1–4: 196
3.1.5–6: 196
3.1.24: 199
3.1.61–70: 199–200
3.2.7: 208
3.2.13–18: 207–8
3.2.19: 206
3.2.27–28: 206
3.2.29: 207
3.2.29–32: 206
3.2.31: 207
3.2.32: 207
3.2.39–40: 210
3.2.43–44: 209
3.2.55–62: 209
3.2.57: 204n.1
3.2.58: 221
3.2.69: 210
3.2.83–84: 204 and n.1
3.3.1–14: 41
3.3.9: 44
3.3.9–10: 204n.1
3.3.13–14: 44
3.3.23–24: 46
3.3.25–26: 46
3.3.42: 46

Ovid *(continued)*
   3.3.47–48: 46
   3.4.37–40: 215n.24
   3.6.17–18: 212, 216
   3.6.19–22: 212
   3.6.20: 213
   3.6.49–50: 215
   3.6.55–56: 215
   3.6.65–66: 216
   3.6.75–76: 215
   3.6.101: 216
   3.9.1–6: 180
   3.9.4: 181
   3.9.13–14: 182
   3.9.14: 51
   3.9.17–18: 183, 188
   3.9.21: 183
   3.9.23–24: 183
   3.9.27–28: 183
   3.9.29–30: 183
   3.9.35–36: 183
   3.9.49–52: 184
   3.9.53–58: 185
   3.9.58: 184n.39
   3.9.59–60: 183
   3.9.59–66: 185–86
   3.9.66: 187
   3.10.1–6: 68
   3.10.7–14: 73
   3.10.17–18: 69
   3.10.19–20: 71
   3.10.20: 72
   3.10.24: 75, 78
   3.10.25–26: 72
   3.10.25–28: 75
   3.10.27: 77n.48
   3.10.43–48: 68
   3.13.13–14: 44
   3.13.31–34: 51–52
   3.13.33–34: 52
   3.13.36: 52
   3.15.7–14: 201
   3.15.11: 202
   3.15.13–14: 202
   3.15.18: 201
  AA
   1.147–48: 208, 221n.42
   3.775–76: 207n.9
  Fasti
   3.8–9: 218
   3.23–24: 217

   3.29–30: 218
   3.45: 217
   3.47: 217
  Medic. 10: 115n.53
  Met.
   1.85–86: 222
   1.530: 124n.82
   9.46–49: 85n.66
   10.245–46: 220
   10.248: 220
   10.249: 220
   10.259: 220
   10.266: 220
   10.276: 222
   10.280: 220
   10.283–89: 221
   10.292–94: 222
   15.165–72: 222–23
  Pont. 2.3.75–78: 134n.4

Plato
  Symp. 183b: 41
Pliny
  NH
   6.54: 119n.63
   10.117: 175
Porphyrio
  on *Odes* 1.2.18: 214
Prodicus
  apud Xen. *Mem.*
   2.1.21–22: 198
   2.1.33: 198
Propertius
  1.1.1–6: 137
  1.1.2: 148n.41
  1.1.7: 137
  1.1.9–16: 76
  1.1.10: 72n.41
  1.1.25–28: 43n.45
  1.2.7–8: 106
  1.2.19–20: 106
  1.3.1–8: 105
  1.8a.17–18: 23
  1.15.33–38: 42
  1.20.31: 38
  2.3.14: 44
  2.3.43–44: 169
  2.5.11: 37n.33
  2.16.19–20: 40n.41
  2.33.1–2: 68
  2.34.52: 114n.50

3.7.11–14: 37
3.13.15–16: 113n.49
3.14.17: 107
3.22.18: 59n.20
4.1.135–36: 197

Seneca
  Epist. 41.3: 195n.58
Servius
  on *Geo.*
    1.96: 75n.45
    2.465: 115n.53
    2.121: 120
    3.82: 127
Sophocles
  Tr.
    507–9: 85
    517–19: 85
    521 (and schol. ad loc.): 85n.64
    530: 85

Theophrastus
  HP 3.11.4: 121
Tibullus
  1.3.57–58: 186
  1.3.59–66: 186

Virgil
  Aen.
    1.1: 169
    1.2–5: 51
    1.3–5: 52
    1.85–86: 26
    1.94–96: 25
    1.315–20: 206n.8
    1.329: 206n.8
    1.498–502: 99
    1.503: 107
    2.403–6: 124
    3.15: 24
    3.126: 127n.93
    3.168: 72n.40
    4.66–73: 77
    4.648: 24
    [6.242]: 196n.61
    6.258: 191
    6.470–71: 127
    7.45–46: 82

7.723: 52
7.723–24: 51
9.433–37: 109
12.64–69: 111, 116
12.715–23: 84
12.716–17: 85
12.718: 87n.71
12.721: 85
12.721–22: 89
  Ecl.
    1.1: 169
    2.1: 62
    2.3: 62
    2.4–5: 62
    2.8–13: 62
    2.27–31: 63
    2.67–68: 62
    10.42–43: 63
    10.52–57: 63
    10.55–61: 76
    10.64–69: 64
  Geo.
    1.1: 169
    1.7–8: 74
    1.27: 145
    1.57: 115n.53
    1.125–28: 73
    1.147–49: 73–74
    1.430–31: 114
    2.16: 74
    2.67: 74n.43
    2.109: 59
    2.115: 121n.76
    2.120–21: 119 and
      n.65
    2.140–44: 59n.20
    2.177: 59
    2.465: 115n.53
    3.215–23: 83
    3.221: 89
    3.244: 60, 89
    3.260: 61n.22
    4.260–63: 95n.12
[Virgil]
  Ciris 440: 115n.53
  Culex
    62: 115n.53
    134–36: 74n.44

General Index

Accius, 168
Achelous, 85, 85n.66, 88, 213
Achilles, 162
acorns and oracle, 73
Adonis, 182
adynaton, 78
aemulatio, 34
Aeneas, 24, 86, 88, 181–82, 216
Aeneid (Virgil), 5, 25–26, 32, 38n.35, 51, 83,
    83n.61, 89, 182, 182n.36
   comic elements in, 86
Aeschylus, 87
Aetia (Callimachus), 33, 145, 145n.33
aetiological poetry, 15
Agamemnon, 51, 162
agricultural analogy, in erotic poetry, 61
Ajax, 123, 124, 129, 157
Alcestis (Euripides), 5
Alexandrian poetry, 34, 38, 52, 72, 78, 107,
    116, 120, 123, 128, 136, 176n.18, 177,
    178, 206, 207, 216
   "footnotes" in, 78, 78n.53, 207, 214
allusion, 27, 117, 178
   multiple, 67, 89
   See also memorability test
amatory narratives, 142. *See also* autobiog-
    raphy, amatory
Amores (Gallus), 66
Amores (Ovid), 4, 138
   prefatory epigram, 142–47, 202
   1.1: 137, 147–49
     exempla in, 97–98
   1.2: 149–51
     exempla in, 98–99

1.3: Ovid's program in, 151–53
1.5: Corinna introduced in, 154–56
1.6: use of formula in, 36–38
1.7:
   exempla and similes in, 123–30
   furor as fiction in, 157–60
1.9: *militia amoris* as cliché in, 160–63
1.10: similes in, 104–9
1.14: similes in, 117–22
1.15:
   catalogue of poets in, 165, 166–70,
     170n.6, 188n.42
   response to Livor in, 166, 167
2.1: narrative realism of, 191–94
2.5: similes in, 110–16
2.6: dead parrot in, 165, 170–79,
    170nn.7–8, 187
2.10: reference to Gallus in, 39–40
2.11: multiple allusion in, 20–30
2.12:
   exempla in, 81–89
   women compared to cow(s) in, 87–89
2.16:
   Sulmo described in, 53–66
   swearing by the eyes in, 44
2.18–2.19: as double narrative, 194–95
3.1:
   allegory of Hercules *in bivio* and,
     198–200
   debate between Elegy and Tragedy in,
     195–201
3.2:
   catalogue of divinities in (procession),
     209

Amores (Ovid) *(continued)*
    compared to scene in *Ars Amatoria* 1, 204–5, 210–11
    day at the races in, 204–10, 221
    3.3: multiple allusion in, 41–46
    3.6:
        catalogue of rivers and their lovers in, 213
        compared to scene in *Fasti* 3, 211, 217–18
        Ilia episode in, 211–19
    3.9: death of Tibullus in, 165–66, 179–89, 201
    3.10: multiple allusion in, 67–79
    3.13: Halaesus as anti-Aeneas in, 51–53
    3.15: and narrative frame, 201–2
    in critical vacuum, 9
    dating of, 179, 188n.42
    as elegy, 7, 8–9, 132–33
    extended similes in, 103–31
    generic range of, 13
    humor in, 15, 16, 17–18, 178. *See also* irony
    imitation in, 19–48
    narrator in, 16
    poet vs. lover in, 139–42, 139n.17, 141, 142, 146, 148n.41, 149–61 passim, 165, 179, 191–92, 219
    and the progressive fallacy, 5–8
    publication history of, 143n.27, 144–45, 146, 194
    sequential ordering within, 190–91
    structure of, 136, 136n.10
    Virgilian precedents for, 50–53, 61–64, 79–89, 191
Amymone, 104
Andromache, 162
Andromeda, 105
Anio, 213, 214, 215, 216
anthropomorphism
    in the *Amores,* 173
    in the *Georgics,* 87–88, 88n.74
Apollo, 97, 98, 193n.52, 196
    worship of, in Crete, 77
Apollonius, 38n.35, 84–85, 85n.64, 87, 93, 101, 112n.42, 116, 116n.58
apparent reference, 52
apposition, inserted, 74n.44, 181n.34
Apuleius, 134
Aquilo, 37, 37n.33. *See also* Boreas

Aratus, 114n.51, 167
Arete, personified, 198, 199
Argonautica (Apollonius), 38n.35, 101, 112n.42
Argonautica (Varro of Atax), 24
Ariadne, 124, 157
Ars Amatoria (Ovid), 4, 15–16, 17, 83n.62, 146n.39, 204–10
Atalanta, 76, 77, 123, 157, 206, 207
Athena, 107n.33. *See also* Minerva
Atticus (addressee of *Am.* 1.9), 134, 161
auctor, 145
audience limitation, fallacy of, 30n.20
Augustus, 170n.6
    in the *Amores,* 151
    moral legislation under, 16
Aulus Gellius, 99–102
Aurora, 112, 113
authorial intention, 30n.20
autobiography, amatory, 135–37, 142
    in the *Amores,* 137, 138, 153–63
autopsy, 93, 126. See also *vidi ego*
avis/ave pun, 178

Bacchae (Euripides), 5
Bacchylides, 119
blurring of view, in extended similes, 108–9, 130
blushing
    in the *Amores,* 110–16, 116–17nn.59–60
    in Virgil, 112n.42
Boreas, 25–26, 37–38. *See also* Aquilo
Briseis, 162
bulls, fighting over heifer, 82–89
burlesque, 86

Callimachus, 12, 28n.16, 32, 33, 34, 41–42, 45, 69, 70, 116, 116n.58 164, 170n.6, 176n.18, 177, 193n.52
    Aetia, 145, 145n.33
    in the *Amores,* 167
    fifth hymn (*Bath of Pallas*), 107, 107n.33
    Hecale, 119, 120
    hymn to Apollo, 126, 212
    hymn to Artemis, 72, 72n.42
    hymn to Zeus, 71–72
    influence on Ovid, 130
Calliope, 196
Calvus, 70n.34, 80, 87, 187

Cassandra, 124, 157, 162
Catullus, 10, 12, 24, 28, 29n.17, 34, 35, 41,
    44, 45, 80, 122, 136, 144n.29, 187
  in the *Amores,* 201
  on Ariadne, 124, 126
  on death of sparrow, 171–72, 172n.11
  Lesbia's epiphany in, 155
  ludus poeticus, 150–51
  on poetic immortality, 213
  on spiders, 119
cedar, 120
Ceres, 97, 98
  festival of, 197
  as literary character, 67–79
  See also Demeter
Ceres (Calvus), 70n.34
Cinna, 28n.16
Circus Maximus, 204, 205–6
Clouds (Aristophanes), 197
color, symbolism of, in Virgil, 75n.45
competitive polemic, 73
conflation, in Virgil, 26n.8
coniunx, 88, 88n.76
Corinna, 134, 134n.2
  entrance in the *Amores,* 154–56
  as prize won in love's war, 81
  struck by poet-lover, 122, 158–59
  and triumph of love, 93
  as worshipper of Ceres, 67
Corydon, 62–64
cow(s), women compared to, in the *Amores,*
    87–89
Crete, 69, 70
  as home of liars, 71
  worship of Apollo on, 77
Crinagoras, 174, 175–76n.16, 174
Cupid
  grieving, 181–82
  and meter, 147–49
  in triumph, 151

dating of Ovid's work, 7n.13, 179, 188n.42
Deianeira, 85, 85n.66, 213
Delia, 184, 184n.39, 185
Demeter, 211n.15. *See also* Ceres
Demeter (Philetas), 70n.34, 70n.36
Diana, 97, 98, 101, 206, 207
didactic poetry, 15, 16, 99, 105
Dido, 24, 77–78, 101, 127
Diomedes, 123, 124, 129, 157

Dissoi Logoi, 197
double narrative, *Amores* as, 195, 219. See
    also *Amores* (Ovid): poet vs. lover in

Eclogues (Virgil), 5, 6, 13, 25, 61–64, 65, 66,
    75–76, 83n.62, 168, 169, 181
egelidus, 24
Elegia, personified, in *Amores,* 180–81, 182,
    196, 198, 199
elegy, 3, 15, 16, 32, 33, 91
  aetiological, 68, 79
  amatory narrative in, 189
  code of, 137
  didactic, 105
  domina in, 177
  and embedded narrative, 163
  vs. epic, 130
  extended simile in, 104
  as genre of dissent, 7
  and landscape, 55–56
  mimesis in, 157
  as parrot's choice, 175
  realism in, 133n.1
  redefined by Ovid, 132–33
  techniques adapted to epic, in *Metamor-
    phoses,* 14
Elysium
  for birds, 174
  for poets, 185–87
embedded narrative, 140n.23, 142, 163,
    190
enargeia, 128
Enipeus, 213, 214n.21
enjambment, emotive, 166
Ennius, 8, 24, 214, 215
  in the *Amores,* 168
entropy, generic, 132–33
epic
  elegiac techniques applied to, in *Meta-
    morphoses,* 14
  vs. elegy, 130
  hero's fate in, 25
  similes in, 91
  themes of, 193
epicedion, 37, 174, 175, 188
Epimenides of Crete, 72
epiphanies, 155, 193n.52
Epistulae (Horace), 7n.13, 57–59, 59n.20
epitaphs
  human, 176n.18

epitaphs *(continued)*
  literary, Ovid's, 202
  pet, 176, 177
Epodes (Horace), 13
Erysichthon, 70
ethnography, 56–58, 121, 121n.76
Eudaimonia/Kakia, 198, 199
Euripides, 5, 24, 126
Europa, 152–53
Euryalus, 109–10
exempla, 89, 93, 94, 95, 130
  of beautiful women, 104–5
  of bulls fighting over heifer, 82–89
  cataloguing of, 122
  contrasting, in the *Amores,* 98
  didactic function of, 96
  of *furor,* 157
  of heroines, 123
  of mythological warrior-lovers, 162
  oxymoronic, 97
  as proof, 96–97
  in Propertius, 105
  quasi-heroic, 123
  of racing women, 206–7
  and sexual imagery, in *Ars Amatoria,*
    207n.9
  vs. similes, 92, 93, 95–96
  of women as causes of battles, 81–82,
    83n.61
extended similes
  Aulus Gellius on, 99–102
  blurring of view in, 108–9
  in elegy, 104
  Homer's, 94
  Ovid's, 90, 91, 93–94, 103–31
  Propertius', 105–6
  Virgil's, 107
eyes, 44–45, 46, 47

faithlessness, 64. *See also* lying
Fasti (Ovid), 17, 50, 67, 79
  and *Amores* compared, 16–17, 211,
    217–19
femina, 88
forgeries, Ovidian, 6n.13
"formula," 29, 30, 38, 43, 43n.45, 49, 53, 99,
    114n.50
furor
  in bulls, 83–84
  exempla, in the *Amores,* 157

in Propertius, 137
  lover's, 63–64, 87, 88, 116, 116n.59, 123,
    158

Galatea, 23, 24, 26–27n.11, 26–29
Galatea (Philoxenus of Cythera), 26n.11
Galatea (Callimachus), 26n.11
Gallus, 10, 12, 14, 25, 32, 33, 39–40, 64n.26,
    168, 169, 187
  Amores, 66
  interest in landscape, 65
  style, 39
  Virgil's and Propertius' homage to, 38
  in Virgil's *Eclogues,* 63–64, 65, 75–76, 181
Gellius, Aulus, 99–102
generic complication, 218
generic entropy, 132–33
generic fallacy, 10–15, 32
generic propriety, 90, 93, 112, 131
genre criticism, 9–10
Georgics (Virgil), 33, 56, 59, 59n.20, 60,
    61n.22, 73–74, 83–84, 83n.61, 86, 87,
    87nn.71–72, 88, 88n.74, 89, 119, 120,
    168, 169
  Ovid's familiarity with, 83n.62
gigantomachy, 191, 193
Graecinus (addressee of *Am.* 2.10), 39,
    39n.39, 134
groves, sacred, 195, 196

Halaesus, 51, 52, 81, 103
Hecale (Callimachus), 119, 120, 215
Hector, 162
heifers, 83–84, 85n.66. *See also* cow(s)
Helen, 82, 83n.61, 93, 104, 106, 107n.33
Helvius Cinna, C. *See* Cinna
Hercules/Heracles, 85, 85n.66, 86, 88
  at the crossroads, 197, 198–99
Hero and Leander, 60, 61n.22, 87n.72
Heroides (Ovid), 2–3, 15, 216
Hesiod, 27n.11, 34, 72, 78, 221
  in the *Amores,* 167
  Virgil's *Georgics* imitative of, 33
Hippodamia, 82, 83n.61, 106, 207–8
Homer, 32
  on Ajax and Diomedes, 129
  in the *Amores,* 167
  Callimachus' imitation of, 34
  death and immortality of, 183
  on Demeter and Iasion, 69

extended similes in, 94
on Galatea, 27n.11
imitated by Virgil, 19, 20, 95n.12
ivory similes in, 112n.42, 113, 115
names of winds in, 25
on Odysseus' tears, 103
on Penelope, 125, 127
similes in, 91
on spiders, 119
versification strategy, 29
Homeric Hymn to Demeter, 70, 70n.36, 78,
    211n.15
Horace, 42, 188n.42
    climactic and emotional balance in, 56
    commentary by Porphyrio on, 214
    Epistulae, 7n.13, 57–58, 59n.20
    Epodes, 13
    on lovers' oaths, 45
    Odes, 6, 6n.12, 13, 127, 136, 146, 214
Horus, in Propertius, 197
humor
    in the *Aeneid,* 86
    in the *Amores,* 15, 16, 17–18, 178
    in the *Ars Amatoria* and *Fasti,* 17
    Ovidian, 37
    vs. parody, 18
hymns, literary, 67. *See also* Callimachus

Iasius/Iasion, 67, 70n.34, 72, 72nn.40–41,
    76, 77, 78–79
Ilia, 211, 213, 214, 215, 216
    and Rhea Silvia, 217–19
imitation, 90, 106, 178
    in the *Amores,* 19–48
    Ovid's, pedigree of, 102
    stylistic vs. generic, 33
    Virgil's, 102
immortality, poetic, 165–202, 213
inserted apposition, 74n.44, 181n.34
intention, authorial, 30n.20
Io, 152–53
irony, 4, 12, 18, 89, 118, 121, 124, 134n.1,
    141, 147, 157, 166, 205
Isis worship, 67
Iulus, 182
ivory, 111, 112–13, 112n.42, 114–15,
    115n.53, 115n.56, 221–22

Juno, Faliscan festival of, 51, 52, 52n.7, 197
Jupiter, 192

lovers of, 152–53, 155
oracle of, at Dodona, 74

Kakia/Eudaimonia, 198, 199

Lais, 154
landscapes, literary
    in Gallus, 65
    Horace's, 56, 57–58, 59n.20
    Sulmo, in *Amores,* 53–55, 57, 58–61, 65,
        66
    in Virgil's *Eclogues,* 61–64, 65
Lapiths, 82, 83n.61
Latinus, 82
Lavinia, 82, 83n.61, 93, 111, 112n.42, 114
Leander. *See* Hero and Leander
Leda, 104, 152–53
Leonidas of Tarentum, 176n.18
lilies and roses, 112–13n.45
Linus, 183
Livor, Ovid's response to, in *Amores,* 166,
    167
Livy, 215, 217
love
    irresistibility of, 98
    poetry of, personal, 42
    triumph of, 81, 93
    as war. *See militia amoris;* triumph of
        love
lovers' oaths, 41, 45, 46
Lucian, 198n.64
Lucretius, 168, 169
Lygdamus, 42
lying. *See also* faithlessness
    by Cretans, 71
    by poets, 212, 216
lyric poetry, Greek, 160

Macer (addressee of *Am.* 2.18), 134
Macrobius, 175
Maecenas, 144n.31, 146
Maeonia, 115
marble, Parian, 127
Mars, 97, 98, 161, 162, 218
Medea, 112n.42, 126
Medea (Euripides), 24, 126
Medicamina Faciei Femineae (Ovid), 4, 15
memorability test, 27, 28, 36, 39, 43, 52, 73,
    79. *See also* poetic memory
Menander, 167

Metamorphoses (Ovid), 1–2, 6, 14, 38n.35, 50, 67, 85n.66, 129, 218, 219–23
meter, 4, 29n.17, 38, 38nn.35–36, 39, 147–49, 160
Milanion, 76, 77, 206, 207
militia amoris, 81–82, 151, 156, 159, 160–63
mimesis, 135, 147
 elegiac, 157
Minerva, 97, 98
Monobiblos (Propertius), 6, 55–56, 137, 144n.31
moon, blushing, 114, 114n.51
multiple allusion, 67, 89
multiple correspondence, 122

narrative embedding, *see* embedded narrative
narrative reversal, 138
 in the *Amores,* 219
 See also *Amores* (Ovid), poet vs. lover in
narrative technique, in *Metamorphoses,* 1–3
narratological theory, 140, 140n.23
negative simile, 109, 130
Nemesis, in Tibullus, 184, 184n.39, 185
Niobe, 126, 127
Nisus, 110
Notus, 173

oaths, lovers,' 41, 45, 46. *See also* faithlessness
Octavian, 175. *See also* Augustus
Odes (Horace), 13, 127, 136, 146, 214
Odysseus, 103
oppositio in imitando, 32, 52, 107
Orestes, 123, 124, 157
Origines (M. Porcius Cato Censorius), 52n.7
Orithyia, 37–38, 38n.35
Orpheus, 174, 183, 220
Ovid, 9
 Amores. See *Amores*
 Ars Amatoria, 15–16, 17, 83n.62, 146n.39, 204–10
 as *auctor,* 145
 dating of work, 3n.8, 6–7, 7n.13, 179, 188n.42
 Epistulae ex Ponto, 2, 6
 in exile, 16, 16n.46, 31, 134n.4
 Fasti, 2, 3, 17, 50, 67, 79
 forgeries of, 7n.13
 Heroides, 2–3, 15, 216

 humor in, 15, 16, 17–18, 37, 178
 imitation in, 102
 irony in. *See* irony
 literary genealogy of, 201–2. See also *Amores* (Ovid): catalogue of poets in
 Medicamina Faciei Femineae, 4, 15
 Metamorphoses, 1–2, 6, 14, 38n.35, 47, 50, 67, 85n.66, 129, 218
 on own future, in the *Amores,* 167. *See also* immortality, poetic
 own view of *Amores,* 31–32
 Remedia Amoris, 4, 15
 self-reference by, 47
 Somnium (attr.), 7n.13
 Tristia, 2, 6, 32
oxymoron, in exempla, 97
paired poems, in the *Amores,* 194, 205
paraclausithyron, 37, 153
parallels, 30
Parian marble, 127
Paris, 106
parody, 10
 vs. humor, 18
 vs. irony, 12
parrot, dead, in *Am.* 2.6, 165, 170–79, 170n.8, 187
patronage, 134n.4, 146
Pelops, 106, 207–8
Penelope, 125, 127
persona theory, 139–40
petrifaction, 126
Phaeacia, in Tibullus, 184
pictorialism, literary, 128
Pindar, 13, 34
Plinius Secundus, C. *See* Pliny the Elder
Pliny the Elder, 112n.45, 121, 175
poet
 immortality of, 165–202
 as liar, 212, 216
 as parrot, 170–79, 170n.8, 187
poetic memory, 30, 36, 48, 49, 79, 107, 128, 163, 166, 178. *See also* memorability test
poetry
 Alexandrian, 34, 38, 52, 72, 107, 116, 120, 123, 128, 136, 176n.18, 177, 178, 206, 207, 216
 realism in, 128
 didactic, 15, 16, 99, 105
 love, personal, 42

Theophrastus, 120–21
Theseus, 157, 215
Tibullus, 9, 10, 12, 14, 25, 32, 42, 55, 75n.45,
    168, 169
    amatory narrative in, 142
    in *Am.* 3.9, 179–89
    climactic and emotional balance in, 56
    funerary fantasy, 177, 179, 184, 184n.39
    Phaeacia in, 184
    poet-lover distinction in, 185–87
Trachiniae (Sophocles), 85, 93
Tragoedia, personified, 196, 198, 199
travesty, 11
Triptolemus, 211, 211n.15
Tristia (Ovid), 32
triumph of love, 81, 93
Trojan War, 191
Turnus, 88
Tyro, 213–14
Tyro (Sophocles), 213n.20

Valerius Messalla Corvinus, M., 134n.4
Valerius Probus, M., 100–101, 102
variety, in the *Metamorphoses,* 1–2
Varro of Atax, 24, 168
Venus, 97, 98, 161, 162, 182, 208, 221
vestal virgins, 215, 218
vidi ego, 87, 93, 98
Virgil
    aemulatio in, 34
    Aeneid, 5, 6, 25–26, 32, 38n.35, 51, 83,
        83n.61, 86, 89
    allusions to, in *Amores,* 108, 191
    and Aratus' acrostic, 114n.51
    on Avernus, 196

on Cassandra, 124
on Ceres, 70n.34
climactic and emotional balance in, 56
conflation in, 26n.8
context and simile in, 122
as critical ideal, 8
on Dido, 77–78, 127
Eclogues, 5, 6, 13, 25, 61–64, 65, 66,
    75–76, 83n.62, 168, 169, 181
extended similes in, 107, 109–10
Georgics, 33, 56, 59, 59n.20, 60, 61n.22,
    73–74, 83–84, 83n.61, 86, 87,
    87nn.71–72, 88, 88n.74, 89, 119, 120,
    168, 169
imitation of Homer, 19, 20, 95n.12
influence on Ovid, 1, 130
on Iulus, 182, 182n.36
laudes Galli, 38
on Lavinia's blush, 111, 112n.42
on lilies and roses, 112–13
naming of, in *Am.* 3.15, 201
as precedent for Ovid's *Amores,* 50–53,
    79–89
prefatory epigram, 144n.28
self-reference in, 87n.71
similes in, 93, 100–101, 102
vowel length, 178n.26

"window" reference, 85, 115n.54
witness, claim to. *See* autopsy
women, as causes of battles, 81–82, 83n.61
wordplay, 178n.26

Xanthus, 213
Xenophon, 197

lyric, Greek, 160
polemic, competitive, 73
politics, 15
  of the *Amores,* 16–17, 56–57, 66, 219
  of the *Fasti,* 17, 219
Porcius Latro, M., 99n.20
Porphyrio, 214
Poseidon, 213, 214n.21
praeceptor amoris, 16, 161, 204, 205, 206,
    207, 209, 210
Probus. *See* Valerius Probus, M.
programmatic narrative, 141
progressive fallacy, 5–7
Prometheus, 221
propemptikon
  in the *Amores,* 20–24, 27, 29, 36
  origins of, 28n.16
  in Propertius, 23, 27
  in Tibullus, 25
Propertius, 4, 6, 9, 10, 11, 14, 20, 30, 31, 32,
    40n.41, 42, 44, 70n.34, 108, 188n.42
  amatory autobiography in, 135
  amatory narrative in, 135, 142
  Apollo and Calliope as inspiration in,
    196, 197
  on Cynthia as Muse, 136–37
  on the death of Paetus, 37, 37n.33
  extended similes in, 105–6
  fond of exempla, 92
  funerary fantasy, 176, 177, 179
  homage to Gallus, 38
  on Horus, 197
  imitativeness of, 35
  on Isis worship, 67, 68
  landscape in, 55–56
  on Milanion and Atalanta, 76
  Monobiblos, 6, 55–56, 137, 144n.31
  propemptikon, 23
  on spiders, 119
  on Tarpeia, 79
  on women as causes of battles, 82, 83n.61
propriety, generic, 90, 93, 112, 131
Proserpina/Persephone, 67, 71
Pygmalion, 219–22
Pythagoras, 221

realism, 130, 191
  of Augustan elegy, 133n.1
  in Hellenistic poetry, 128
  Ovid's, 133–35, 155, 163

visual, 108
recusatio, 26, 135, 148, 195, 200, 209
reference, 30–31
  apparent, 52
  illusion of, 117
  multiple, in Ovid, 35, 36
  to own work, 47, 87n.71, 89
  vs. poetic memory, 49
  "window," 85, 115n.54
Remedia Amoris (Ovid), 4, 15
Rhea Silvia, 211, 217
rivers and their loves, in *Am.* 3.6, 213
Rome, early, moral superiority of, 40n.41
Romulus and Remus, 215
roses and lilies, 112–13n.45

Sabine women, 82
Scylla and Charybdis, 60
self-reference
  in Ovid, 89
  in Virgil, 87n.71
Semiramis, 154
"sepulchral" epigrams, Greek, 144n.29
Servius, 113, 120, 127
silk, 118–19
similes
  distancing effect of, 155
  epic, 91
  vs. exempla, 92, 93, 95–96
  extended. *See* extended similes
  Homeric, 101
  transformed into reality, 221
  visual effectiveness of, 96
sincerity, 90
  illusion of, 9
Somnium (attr. to Ovid), 7n.13
Somnium (Lucian), 198n.64
Sophocles, 85n.66, 93, 213n.20
  in the *Amores,* 167
sphragis, 135, 145n.33, 166
spider, 119–20, 120n.68
spondaic hexameter, 38
storms at sea, 25–26
Suetonius, on Horace, 6n.12
Sulmo, 53–55, 56–61

Tarpeia, 79
taste, bad, 90
Theocritus, 107n.33
Theogony (Hesiod), 27n.11, 221